Effortless App Development with Oracle Visual Builder

Boost productivity by building web and mobile applications efficiently using the drag-and-drop approach

Ankur Jain

BIRMINGHAM—MUMBAI

Effortless App Development with Oracle Visual Builder

Copyright © 2021 Packt Publishing

Group Product Manager: Aaron Lazar
Publishing Product Manager: Shweta Bairoliya
Senior Editor: Rohit Singh
Content Development Editor: Rosal Colaco
Technical Editor: Gaurav Gala
Copy Editor: Safis Editing
Project Coordinator: Deeksha Thakkar
Proofreader: Safis Editing
Indexer: Tejal Daruwale Soni
Production Designer: Nilesh Mohite

First published: March 2021
Production reference: 2310321

Published by Packt Publishing Ltd.
Livery Place
35 Livery Street
Birmingham
B3 2PB, UK.

ISBN 978-1-80056-980-5

www.packt.com

A special thank you to my mother, Mrs. Sunita Jain, and my father, Mr. Surendra Kumar Jain. Without you, I would not be the person I am today. To my wife, Nancy, thank you for your love and support, and to my little daughter, Aarohi, my lucky charm.

– Ankur Jain

Foreword

"Even a journey of a thousand miles begins with a single step"

– Laozi

Congratulations! You are about to start your journey of learning a new development platform. This is one of the fun things you get to do as a software developer who likes to keep up with new technologies. Picking up Visual Builder as your next development platform is a smart move - it's the same decision Oracle took for our new Oracle Cloud Applications. With Visual Builder and the information in this book, you'll be able to create cutting-edge web and mobile apps in no time.

Visual Builder, the platform that this book is about, is the latest development platform offered by Oracle. As a cloud-native platform, VB's goal is to help developers be more productive when working with the combination of JavaScript, HTML5, and REST services. Over the past 5 years, VB has evolved to become a complete, advanced platform that is used by thousands of companies as well as by Oracle's own development teams to build enterprise apps faster.

From the get-go, we designed VB to simplify the complex task of building apps by focusing the development on a more visual and declarative approach. Leveraging visual page editors, diagrams for defining business logic flows, and declarative aspects to defining connectivity to data delivered a productive way to create apps.

VB started as a tool for the citizen developer, allowing everyone to create apps without the need for any code. In fact, you can still build such basic apps without the need to code in VB today. But as demands for more complex capabilities kept coming, we added more and more features that allowed professional developers to leverage programming techniques to add advanced functionality. The result is a powerful tool that combines easy development with endless capabilities to extend the platform.

It's great to have this book as your guide to adopt the Visual Builder platform. Ankur Jain has been a very active member of the Oracle community and an early adaptor of the tool. He has shared his knowledge through blogs, videos, and other publications. In this book, he will take your hand and guide you through the various features offered by Visual Builder. You will learn everything you need to get going – from provisioning the environment, through connecting to various data sources, creating advanced web and mobile UIs, and all the way to collaborating with other developers and implementing best practices. This book will take you beyond the wizard and into the inner working of VB and the architecture it uses.

The world of Oracle development tools is always an evolving one, and we - at the Oracle Cloud Development Tools team - are adding many new features into Visual Builder in each new release. With the knowledge you get from this book, adopting these new features will be easier as you continue on your learning journey in the ever-evolving tech world.

Hope you enjoy the learning journey!

Shay Shmeltzer
Director of Product Management and Strategy
Oracle Cloud Development Tools (March 2021)

Contributors

About the author

Ankur Jain is passionate about learning new technologies and exploring new things on his own. He has worked on a number of different technology stacks, including Oracle OIC, VB, API PCS, Oracle SOA, OSB, WebCenter Content, and Java. He has implemented various projects on Oracle Integration and the Visual Builder.

He has earned various prestigious awards and recognition from different groups and communities, including Oracle's elite Oracle ACE program. He has become a spotlight member of the Oracle Cloud community: UKOUG has published an article in PTK issue number 73, the tech edition; he is OIC certified, and has been selected as a speaker to present a paper at the Groundbreakers Yatra, organized by AIOUG.

He is a prolific blogger and YouTuber, helping thousands of users to learn.

I wish to thank the people who have been close to me and supported me, especially my wife Nancy, my parents, and my friends.

About the reviewer

Prasad Puttachar is a senior IT professional with more than 20 years of experience in various industry-leading CRM applications, including Oracle CX (sales and service, CPQ, and commerce) and Siebel CRM industry applications (call center, Telco, automobile, and financial services). He has worked on solution designs for a variety of software package products, as well as in development, architecture, implementation, and presales, possessing a broad set of skills applicable across different industries and roles.

His core competencies are Oracle SaaS applications (sales and service, CPQ, and commerce), Oracle IaaS, and Oracle PaaS (Integration Cloud, Process Cloud, and Visual Builder Cloud).

Table of Contents

5

Creating and Managing Service Connections

6

Building Web Applications Using Real-World Examples

7

Working with Life Cycle Events, Validations, and UI Logic

Section 3: Building Web and Mobile Apps Using Various VB Components

8

Exploring Other Visual Components and Their Advanced Functionalities

9

Extending Oracle and Non-Oracle SaaS Applications

10
Working with Business Processes

11
Building a Mobile Application with Live Examples

Section 4: Security, Recommendations, Best Practices, and Troubleshooting

12
Securing VB Applications

13
Understanding and Managing Various Stages of a VB App

14
Best Practices and Recommendations for VB Applications

15
Troubleshooting and Debugging VB Applications

16
Managing VB Apps Using Visual Builder Studio

Assessments

Other Books You May Enjoy

Index

Preface

Oracle Visual Builder (**VB**) is a modern, cloud-based **Platform as a Service** (**PaaS**) and hosted environment that allows you to develop robust web and mobile applications using a drag-and-drop approach. With the simplicity of the platform, you can develop and deploy web and mobile applications quickly, without the need for any extra software on your local machine.

This book will help you to learn the whole platform, end to end, with a wide variety of examples, using which you can adopt the platform quickly. The applications you develop in VB can run on both desktop and mobile devices.

The book starts with a detailed description of the platform that helps you to understand the need for the platform and how the platform addresses your business challenges. The first few chapters help you to understand the platform, set up your VB environment, and get to grips with the navigation aspect. They also cover detailed descriptions of all the building blocks of VB, including Business Objects, Service Connections, Action Chains, and variables, as well as their scopes.

In the next couple of chapters, you'll start building web applications and executing a lot of real-world, step-by-step use cases using various UI components such as tables, lists, input text, input dates, text areas, checkboxes, headings, buttons, visual components, and much more. The book covers various real-world scenarios that will help you to jump into your own projects and work independently.

The book includes two different use cases covering how to extend Oracle and non-Oracle applications. You will learn how to develop mobile applications for Android and iOS. You will also learn how to enable a mobile application to run as a **Progressive Web App** (**PWA**). We have created a separate web application to show you how to interact with a workflow developed in **Processes**, using a unified platform to initiate and manage process instances.

One chapter is dedicated to showcasing how to enable security for your applications with a working example. In VB, you can apply both role-based and data based security to develop a secure application and protect the application from unauthorized access. We will explain how to manage VB applications and talk about the various stages of an application.

In order to make your software successful and robust, you need to follow the best practices and recommendations. In one of the chapters, we explain various best practices and recommendations that you need to adopt right from the start if you want to develop highly scalable applications. We cover various techniques to debug and troubleshoot VB applications. In the last chapter, you will learn how to use **Visual Builder Studio (VBS)** to manage the life cycle of your application code.

By the end of this book, you will be proficient in Oracle VB and will be able to work independently on your live projects.

I wish you all the best in your learning and taking your first step here. I hope you enjoy reading this book; thank you for buying it.

Who this book is for

This book is for IT professionals working with UI technologies to develop web and mobile applications for various industries. Developers and UI designers who want to understand how to use VB, develop scalable web and mobile applications using drag and drop features, and design applications in a better way with the help of real-world use cases and code examples will find this book helpful. Prior experience in any UI technology, JavaScript, and REST APIs would be useful.

What this book covers

Chapter 1, *What, Why, and How (WWH) of Visual Builder*, helps you to become familiar with the basics of VB to get you started with the platform. In order to use VB, you should know about all the tools and skills that are required for doing so, and this chapter focuses on all these basic concepts. It explains the VB architecture and describes how different components communicate with each other.

Chapter 2, *Provisioning and Understanding the Visual Builder Instance*, covers VB instance creation using the Oracle Cloud portal and what you should have before you create an instance. This is really important in terms of knowing how much you need to pay to use VB; this chapter focuses on the cost of using VB. We'll also look at how to log in to VB and the purpose of various navigation under VB.

Chapter 3, *Exploring Visual Builder Ingredients*, introduces the basic building blocks of VB, which are Business Objects, Service Connections, JET components, web applications, mobile applications, Action Chains, variables and their scopes, flows, sub-flows, pages, shells, and more, so that you can become familiar with all these basic building blocks to start your journey with VB.

Chapter 4, Creating and Managing Business Objects, focuses on Business Objects and how to manage them. Using examples, we'll demonstrate how to create a Business Object, modify it, and import and export data with it, with the help of `.csv` and `.xlsx` files. When you create Business Objects, different REST APIs are created automatically along with them, so we will explain how to use them. We will talk about how to switch VB embedded database to use a different Oracle database.

Chapter 5, Creating and Managing Service Connections, focuses on different options for Service Connection to connect to external REST APIs, Oracle Cloud APIs, and non-Oracle APIs. You will learn how to use a built-in catalog to create Service Connections with Oracle Cloud and Integration Cloud.

Chapter 6, Building a Web Application Using Real-World Examples, explains how to create web applications and connect with Business Objects and external REST APIs to pull and push data on VB Pages. We'll also see how to create different pages and how to connect them and pass data from one page to another. We will start using JavaScript to create different business logic whenever required and perform client-side validation for different UI components.

Chapter 7, Working with Life Cycle Events, Validations, and UI Logic, focuses on events, Action Chains, and various actions on an Action Chain that are used to create complex business logic, UI validations, enable logout features, and more. We will explore the different life cycle methods of VB to initialize and clean up tasks. We will create an example here to show you how to load data before page load and render that data on the page.

Chapter 8, Exploring Other Visual Components and Their Advanced Functionalities, discusses how to start using different Oracle JET (JET) components and explores the features of these components, such as searching, sorting, and pagination. You will learn how to enable inline editing in a table. You will work with dialogs, checkboxes, and list components. You will learn how to use different visualization components and load data.

Chapter 9, Extending Oracle and Non-Oracle SaaS Applications, demonstrates how to extend Oracle and non-Oracle applications using VB. The main intent of VB is to help you create SaaS extensions, and the details of this are described in this chapter. This chapter will cover enabling your VB application to render in different languages to accommodate a wide variety of audiences in different countries.

Chapter 10, Working with Business Processes, helps you to learn how to establish a connection with Processes and how to use business processes in VB to initiate, approve, and reject tasks from VB applications directly. Here you will start using various UI components to kick off processes.

Chapter 11, Building a Mobile Application with Live Examples, discusses how VB can be used to develop mobile applications for different devices. In this chapter, you will learn how to create PWAs using VB. You will create different pages, connect them with each other, and pass data between those pages. You will learn how to enable mobile applications to support both landscape and portrait mode. You will learn how to create builds for Android and iOS devices.

Chapter 12, Securing VB Applications, discusses how to secure your VB pages and data. VB applications can be used by anonymous users without login. You will learn how to enable role-based and data security in VB to secure your applications. You will also learn how to enable basic authentication for mobile applications.

Chapter 13, Understanding and Managing the Various Stages of a VB App, helps you to migrate your code from one instance to another. You will learn what does and does not get migrated. VB applications have different phases that we are going to talk about in this chapter.

Chapter 14, Best Practices and Recommendations for VB Applications, discusses the various best practices for developing an application that will enhance the performance of your applications. Following best practices while you create Business Objects and Service Connections will reduce your development and migration efforts too.

Chapter 15, Troubleshooting and Debugging VB Applications, discusses how to handle exceptions and enable logging so that debugging can be made easier at runtime. We will show you how to troubleshoot your development and production issues to make your life easier.

Chapter 16, Managing VB Apps Using Visual Builder Studio, demonstrates how to manage the VB code life cycle using Git repositories. In this chapter, we'll describe Oracle Visual Builder Studio and the benefits it offers. We'll demonstrate how to provision Oracle VB using the **Oracle Cloud Infrastructure** (**OCI**) dashboard, which will help you manage DevOps for your VB code. We'll demonstrate how to create a project in Visual Builder Studio and create the empty Git repositories needed to manage a VB application.

Assessments contains the answers to the questions from all the chapters.

To get the most out of this book

All the examples and demos are captured using **VB version 21.04**, *which is the latest version of VB at the time of writing this book. However, the code will also be compatible with future releases of VB.*

Software/Hardware covered in the book	OS Requirements
Oracle VBCS	None
Oracle Visual Builder Studio	None
Google Chrome browser	None
Oracle Integration Cloud	None
Oracle Cloud application instance	None
Salesforce developer instance	None
Android and iOS devices to test mobile apps	None

If you are using the digital version of this book, we advise you to type the code yourself or access the code via the GitHub repository (link available in the next section). Doing so will help you avoid any potential errors related to the copying and pasting of code.

After completing this whole book, you will be able to work on live VB projects independently and guide your team members on them too.

Download the example code files

You can download the example code files for this book from GitHub at https://github.com/PacktPublishing/Effortless-App-Development-with-Oracle-Visual-Builder. In case there's an update to the code, it will be updated on the existing GitHub repository.

We also have other code bundles from our rich catalog of books and videos available at https://github.com/PacktPublishing/. Check them out!

Download the color images

We also provide a PDF file that has color images of the screenshots/diagrams used in this book. You can download it here: https://static.packt-cdn.com/downloads/9781800569805_ColorImages.pdf.

Conventions used

There are a number of text conventions used throughout this book.

`Code in text`: Indicates code words in text, database table names, folder names, filenames, file extensions, pathnames, dummy URLs, user input, and Twitter handles. Here is an example: "To define the JavaScript function, the `prototype` function is used within the module."

A block of code is set as follows:

```
PageModule.prototype.calculate = function(number1,number2,op){
    if(op=="add"){
        return number1+number2;
    }
    else if(op=="sub"){
        return number1-number2;
    }
    else if(op=="mul"){
        return number1*number2;
    }
    else if(op=="div"){
        return number1/number2;
    }
}
```

When we wish to draw your attention to a particular part of a code block, the relevant lines or items are set in bold:

```
AppModule.prototype.functionName = function (param1,param2){
    // write your logic here
    return "xyz";
}
```

Any command-line input or output is written as follows:

```
{
    "id": "0062v00001R0hMgAAJ",
    "success": true,
    "errors": []
}
```

Bold: Indicates a new term, an important word, or words that you see onscreen. For example, words in menus or dialog boxes appear in the text like this. Here is an example: "Select the **French** radio button and see that the table columns will be rendered in French."

> **Tips or Important Notes:**
> Appear like this.

Get in touch

Feedback from our readers is always welcome.

General feedback: If you have questions about any aspect of this book, mention the book title in the subject of your message and email us at customercare@packtpub.com.

Errata: Although we have taken every care to ensure the accuracy of our content, mistakes do happen. If you have found a mistake in this book, we would be grateful if you would report this to us. Please visit www.packtpub.com/support/errata, selecting your book, clicking on the Errata Submission Form link, and entering the details.

Piracy: If you come across any illegal copies of our works in any form on the Internet, we would be grateful if you would provide us with the location address or website name. Please contact us at copyright@packt.com with a link to the material.

If you are interested in becoming an author: If there is a topic that you have expertise in and you are interested in either writing or contributing to a book, please visit authors.packtpub.com.

Reviews

Please leave a review. Once you have read and used this book, why not leave a review on the site that you purchased it from? Potential readers can then see and use your unbiased opinion to make purchase decisions, we at Packt can understand what you think about our products, and our authors can see your feedback on their book. Thank you!

For more information about Packt, please visit packt.com.

Section 1: Exploring the Building Blocks of VB

In this section, we'll start with the Visual Builder (VB) basics. This part will help you to understand VB, its benefits, and its features. You will become familiar with all the tools that are required to start VB, what technologies are used in VB, and what you should know in advance.

This section explains the VB architecture, which helps to understand different components of VB and how they communicate with each other in order to build web and mobile applications. In further chapters, you will learn about the creation of a VB instance, how to log in to it, and the directory structure of the web application. The purposes of different navigations are also explained. We will explain various building blocks of VB with examples.

This section comprises the following chapters:

- *Chapter 1, What, Why, and How (WWH) of Visual Builder*
- *Chapter 2, Provisioning and Understanding the Visual Builder Instance*
- *Chapter 3, Exploring Visual Builder Ingredients*

1

What, Why, and How (WWH) of Visual Builder

The first chapter of every book is one of the most important chapters as it mainly focuses on the introduction of the technology covered in the book. So, the first chapter of this book will help you to know more about **Visual Builder** (**VB**), why you need to use it, and how to use it.

At a high level, the VB is the cloud offering by **Oracle** that helps you to build engaging web and mobile applications by dragging and dropping the UI components. VB is a declarative approach for building cross-platform applications.

In this chapter, we will cover the following topics:

- Introducing VB
- Reviewing the features and benefits of VB
- Knowing the tools required to use VB
- Knowing the technologies used in VB
- Understanding the VB architecture

After completing this chapter, you will be familiar with **Visual Builder**, its features, and the benefits of using VB. In this chapter, we have explained what tools are required to start the VB, and what technologies you should know or you should learn. Along with this, we have drawn out the VB architecture, which explains how different VB components work together in order to develop web or mobile applications.

Technical requirements

You don't require any software or hardware to follow this chapter.

Introducing VB

VB is an Oracle Cloud **Platform as a Service (PaaS)** offering that enables us to build web and mobile applications declaratively by dragging and dropping a wide variety of built-in **User Interface (UI)** components. VB helps you to build enterprise-grade applications that can be developed and deployed quickly and can be accessed from anywhere at any time. You don't need to install any additional software on the local machine to use VB. The complete development life cycle is managed by the browser interface. From development to testing to deployment, everything is managed by a single unified tool called **Visual Builder**.

VB allows developers to access the source code of visual development, which makes it easy to write custom code (**HTML**, **JavaScript**, **JSON**) to enhance the functionality of applications. You don't require any programming experience to develop applications using Visual Builder. The VB uses the open source Oracle technology called **Oracle JavaScript Extension Toolkit (JET)** for visual development. All the visual UI components belong to the JET family; however, you have the option to use HTML tags and/or the code editor when required.

VB provides a way to store and manage data into the embedded database and a mechanism to call any type of external REST API to interact with a wide variety of external applications. VB provides a declarative way to call any REST API without any coding. VB allows us to call REST-based integrations developed in the integration cloud seamlessly. A VB application interacts with an embedded database or external REST APIs to interact with data.

Having understood what VB really is, next we will have a look at its features and advantages.

Reviewing the features and benefits of VB

It is worthwhile knowing the benefits **VB** offers. In this fast-growing world, organizations are looking for a development tool that can help to deliver responsive web and mobile applications quickly and efficiently. VB allows quick development, requires no additional software cost, is a drag and drop tool, has a user-friendly interface to develop UIs, and more. It's a browser-based tool that helps to deliver engaging web and mobile applications.

VB is best suited for situations when you need to extend Oracle and non-Oracle SaaS applications quickly. Using the inbuilt catalog of the Oracle SaaS application, you can extend the Oracle SaaS application very easily.

Let's try to understand with an example. Let's say there is a set of external users who want to access the Oracle SaaS procurement module in order to create **Purchase Orders** (**POs**), approve POs, list POs, and so on, but the organization is not willing to accord access to the Oracle SaaS application to the external users.

If the organization has VB, then as a solution, the organization can plan to build a web or mobile application in VB and create different flows and pages. Developers can use the built-in catalog of Oracle SaaS to communicate with the Oracle SaaS application in VB and create/approve/list POs and so on in real time from the VB application directly instead of logging into the Oracle SaaS application.

Once the VB application is developed, you can deploy it with a single click and provide access to the external users so that external users can use SaaS application functionality using the VB application as required.

The features that VB offers are as follows:

- **Embedded database**: Oracle VB comes with an embedded database that helps you to manage transactional data. Using the data manager of the embedded database, you can import and export bulk data quickly from .csv or .xlsx files. This database has a set of features that makes it easy to maintain the data in the database.

> Important Note:
> An embedded database has a limit of 5 GB storage space.

- **Connect to different database**: Oracle VB is provisioned with a local database automatically, but VB gives you the option to switch the local database to another Oracle database such as **Database as a Service** (**DBaaS**) or **Autonomous Transaction Processing** (**ATP**). Once you connect to a different database, all the data can be managed by the corresponding database.

- **Connect to external REST APIs**: Oracle VB allows you to communicate with external REST APIs using a declarative approach without a single line of code. You can connect to any type of REST API and interact with external applications in real time.

- **Integration with Oracle SaaS application**: VB allows out-of-the-box connectivity with Oracle SaaS that helps to extend Oracle SaaS application functionality. With the help of an built-in catalog, VB streamlines the process of communicating with Oracle SaaS applications in real time without any extra effort.

- **Connect to Processes**: VB allows you to interact with the **Processes Cloud Service (PCS)**, which helps you to fetch lists of tasks and take necessary action (approve or reject) from the VB application directly.

- **Web application development**: VB allows you to deploy responsive web applications that run on the VB server engine without the need for any additional servers. However, VB web applications can be deployed on any external server but the VB features will be limited.

The following screenshot shows one of the pages of a VB web application:

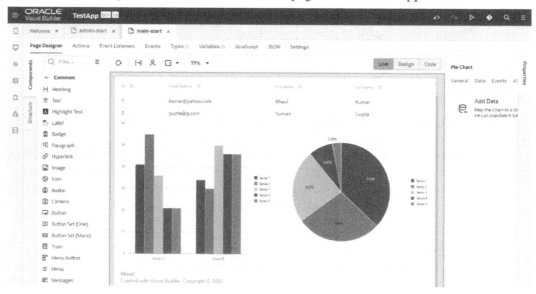

Figure 1.1 – Web application

- **Mobile application development**: VB also allows you to develop a mobile application and build it for **Android** and **iOS**. You can build **Progressive Web Apps (PWAs)** from mobile applications too with just a single click.

The following screenshot shows one of the pages of a mobile application:

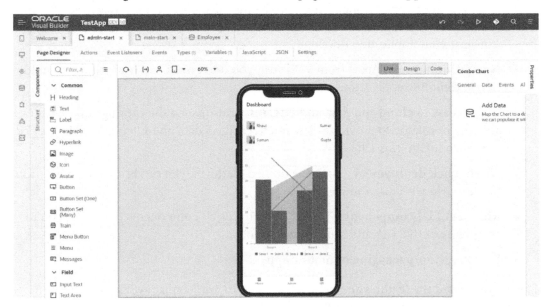

Figure 1.2 – Mobile application

- **Custom code**: In addition to dragging and dropping out-of-the-box components, you have the choice to extend your VB app's functionality using **HTML5** and **JavaScript**.

- **Inbuilt security framework**: Security is one of the top priorities of web and mobile applications, especially when the application is exposed over the internet. VB comes with an embedded security framework that allows you to secure data as well as applications. Application security alone is not enough as anyone can spoof requests in between, change roles, and steal data. So, along with application security, data security is also required.

With the previously listed features, VB is one of the strongest cloud platforms and allows you to build cross-platform applications and solve all the organization's problems.

The benefits of VB are as follows:

- **Unified platform**: The complete life cycle of application development is managed by a single unified platform. Every stage of the application is managed by a single browser-based tool.

- **Quick development**: Web and mobile applications can be developed and deployed in a single day using VB as the entire development is just drag and drop. VB provides a user-friendly wizard and other browser-based tools that allow fast development.

- **No additional software**: To develop and deploy web and mobile applications, you don't require any additional software to be installed on your local machine. You just require a browser, good internet connectivity, and a VB subscription, and then you can start your application development.

- **No additional cost**: Apart from VB's cost, you don't need to pay anything to build web and mobile applications.

- **Easy access to cloud app data and OIC integrations via the catalog**: VB provides an built-in catalog to provide access to Oracle SaaS data and integrations developed in Oracle Integration Cloud.

- **Single-click deployment**: Using the unified platform, you can bring the application to the world with just a single click.

- **Rich set of UI components**: There is a big list of UI components that allow you to create interactive web and mobile applications.

- **Easy creation/packaging of mobile apps**

Having discussed the features and benefits of VB, next we'll explain what tools are required to start development on VB.

Knowing the tools required to use VB

Oracle VB is a pure browser-based development tool that makes it easy for developers to manage the complete life cycle of the development process. To start development in VB, you should be equipped with the following tools:

- **Oracle VB subscription**: First and foremost, you must have a VB subscription. A VB instance can be created separately from Oracle Cloud, but VB is also a part of **Oracle Integration Cloud (OIC)**. If you already have an OIC instance, you can leverage the VB feature of OIC without creating a separate VB instance.

- **Browser**: Since VB development and deployment is purely browser based, you only need to install a browser to start development. Having a browser-based tool simplifies the development process. You can view the list of supported browsers in the Oracle official documentation at `https://docs.oracle.com/en/cloud/paas/app-builder-cloud/abcrn/supported-browsers.html`.

- **Good quality internet**: Since VB is a cloud-based tool, you should have good quality internet to speed up your application development process.

Having discussed the tools required to develop with VB, next we'll explain what technologies you should know about before you start developing.

Knowing the technologies used in VB

You don't require any programming skills to work with on VB as it provides a drag and drop feature with which you can build an enterprise-grade application. But it's really worth knowing what technologies are used in VB development:

- **JET**: JET stands for **Java Extension Toolkit**, which is Oracle open source technology that is used to build interactive UIs. VB uses JET to design UIs using a rich set of UI components for web and mobile applications. To find out more about JET, you can visit `http://oraclejet.org`. You can also refer to the JET cookbook for working with UI components at `https://www.oracle.com/webfolder/technetwork/jet/jetCookbook.html`.

  The following screenshot shows various JET components in the VB component palette:

Figure 1.3 – JET components

- **HTML5**: HTML stands for **Hypertext Markup Language**, which is used to build responsive web user interfaces. In combination with JET, VB allows us to use HTML5 to extend your UI's functionality in order to make interactive web and mobile applications. To learn more about HTML5, refer to `https://www.w3schools.com/html/`.

- **JavaScript**: **JavaScript** is a web scripting language that's used to develop and control dynamic content. It is also used for client-side validation of web pages. In VB, JavaScript can be used extensively to extend web page functionalities such as client-side validation, filtering records at the client side, and so on. To learn more about JavaScript, refer to `https://www.javascript.com/`.

- **CSS**: CSS stands for **Cascading Style Sheets**, and is used in web applications to make UIs interactive. With the help of CSS, you can completely change the design of web applications. VB also allows you to write custom CSS to make your web and mobile application interactive. To learn more about CSS, refer to `https://www.javatpoint.com/css-tutorial`.

Having understood what technologies you should know for VB, next we'll explain the VB architecture.

Understanding the VB architecture

It's important to understand how different VB components are placed and communicate with each other in order to develop web or mobile applications. You also need to understand that VB is not just a development platform, but it also allows you to host the applications, so you don't require a separate hosting environment to run applications developed in VB.

The following screenshot shows how different components communicate with each other:

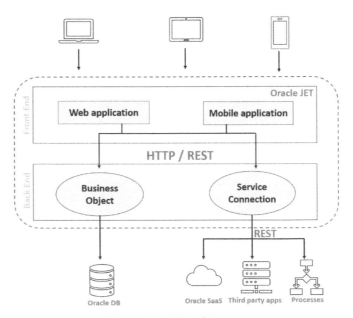

Figure 1.4 – VB architecture

VB uses industry standards such as **Oracle JET**, **HTML5**, **CSS**, and **REST**. VB uses REST technology for data communication when the UI needs to push/pull data from an embedded database or external applications.

Let's take a look at the different VB components:

- **Oracle JavaScript Extension Toolkit** (**JET**): JET is the open source technology used to develop web and mobile interfaces in VB. A rich set of components is available in the VB component list that help us to develop a user-friendly UI.

- **HTTP/REST**: The communication between the frontend and backend happens via HTTPS or REST calls.

- **Frondend**: VB mainly uses Oracle JET to develop the UI using drag and drop features. However, in order to extend the VB application, you have the option to use HTML and JavaScript. Mobile applications that you build in VB use **Apache Cordova** to access device features such as the camera or location.

- **Backend**: The backend of VB web or mobile applications is the embedded or external database (Oracle SaaS, non-Oracle SaaS, third-party integrations, Processes, and so on). All the communication between the frontend and backend happens using REST APIs. This is the only mechanism available to communicate with the data in VB. However, you also have the option to use **SOAP** APIs, but this is not straightforward and you have to use JavaScript to communicate with SOAP APIs. Whenever you create objects (**Business Objects**) in an embedded database, VB exposes the REST APIs for those objects and interactions happen using only those APIs.

Instead of using an embedded database, you can switch to use other Oracle database services, such as **DBaaS** or **ATP**. After you switch database, all the database objects (Business Objects) that you create in the database will be created in the destination database. In this case, the communication will also happen via REST APIs.

In order to communicate with external applications, you have to build a connection (**Service Connection**) in VB and consume the REST interfaces of those applications. The VB Service Connection can also be used to interact with Oracle SaaS, Processes, and OIC seamlessly.

Now you know how the different components fit in VB, which will make it easier for you to develop applications in VB.

Summary

In this chapter, we took a look at a lot of topics that will help you start your journey with VB. With this chapter, you learned about Visual Builder, how it works, and its features and benefits. This will help you adopt VB quickly and easily.

We also covered various tools that are required to start development on VB. This will prepare you for the next chapters. You have also learned what technologies will be used in VB, and we have provided a few references that help you to learn all of them easily. Although you are not required to know them all in detail, having an understanding of all those technologies will help to adopt VB quickly.

You have seen how different VB components communicate with each other with a good architecture image. We have explained all the components in detail to aid your understanding.

In the next chapter, you will learn how to provision a VB instance, create users, and assign roles to the application. We will also explain the various ways to navigate around VB.

Questions

1. If someone doesn't know JET, can they use VB?
2. Can the 5 GB of space in the embedded database be increased on request?

2
Provisioning and Understanding the Visual Builder Instance

In the previous chapter, you learned what VB is and its benefits and features. That gave you a good start in knowing about Visual Builder.

In this chapter, you will get started with VB instance creation using the **Oracle Cloud** portal and learn what you should have before you create an instance. This is really important to know how much you need to pay to use VB, and in this chapter, we will focus on the cost derivation of using VB. Once an instance is created, you will learn how you can access the VB instance.

We will also go through the various navigations provided by **Visual Builder**.

In this chapter, we will cover the following topics:

- Provisioning a VB instance

- Creating users and assigning roles

- Deriving the cost of using VB

- Accessing the VB instance

- Exploring various navigations of VB

The main objective of this chapter is to give you an understanding of how to create and manage a Visual Builder instance along with how to access Visual Builder. With that, you will be able to manage your Visual Builder instance independently.

Technical requirements

To complete this chapter, you should have the following:

- A valid email address

- A valid phone number

- A valid credit card

Provisioning a VB instance

In order to get started with VB, a VB instance needs to be provisioned that will be used to develop and deploy web and mobile applications. In order to create a VB instance, you must have an Oracle Cloud account in place. Don't worry if you don't have one; you can create one to practice for 30 days.

To create an Oracle Cloud account, you must have a credit card; Oracle will hold the nominal amount for verification purposes, which will be reversed immediately.

Copy and paste the link `https://signup.oraclecloud.com/` into a browser to sign up for an Oracle Cloud account. Skip this step if you already have an Oracle Cloud account.

> **Important Note:**
> VB is also part of the **Oracle Integration Cloud** (OIC) service, so if you already have an OIC instance, then you don't need to create a VB instance separately.

Once the free Oracle Cloud account is created successfully, you will get the following:

- A 30-day free trial

- US $300 in free credit

- A few services that are always free and can be used forever

Refer to `https://www.oracle.com/cloud/free/` to find out what services are free forever.

> **Important Note:**
> Oracle will not charge anything unless you choose to upgrade the account.

The 30-day free services will be terminated after 30 days but the Oracle Cloud account will remain active as you can use other free services forever.

> **Important Note:**
> To set up a VB instance, you must have admin privileges. If you don't have admin privileges, ask your Oracle Cloud administrator to create a VB instance for you.

There are two ways to create an Oracle VB instance:

- Quick Start

- Custom instance

Once the Oracle Cloud account is created successfully and all Oracle cloud services are available, then you can create the VB instance using either approach.

> **Important Note:**
> Sometimes, the Oracle Cloud account takes time to bring up all the Oracle Cloud services. So, you might not see all the services under the Cloud dashboard for the first few hours.

In the next sections, we will discuss each approach in detail.

Creating an instance using Quick Start

This option uses default settings while creating a VB instance. To create the VB instance, you must log in to the Oracle Cloud dashboard with admin privileges. The **Quick Start** option creates the instance with the following features:

- An Oracle-managed Visual Builder instance
- A cluster with two nodes
- An embedded database

To create a new VB instance, perform the following steps:

1. Log in to the Oracle Cloud dashboard using your **unique cloud account** name and enter the credentials on the login page. Upon successful login, you will land on the **Oracle Cloud Infrastructure** (**OCI**) dashboard.

2. From the dashboard, click on the hamburger menu at the top left of the screen. Expand **Platform Services** and click on **Visual Builder**.

> **Important Note:**
> Don't select **Visual Builder Classic** (if you see this as one of the options) as this is for old customers who are using old VB versions.

The following screenshot shows us these menu selections:

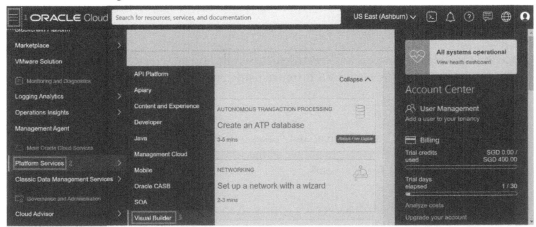

Figure 2.1 – Visual Builder

This action will take you to a new tab and will open the **Visual Builder instance** management page.

3. Click on **QuickStarts** near the **Welcome** link. This will open the **Create Instance** page. The Quick Start option only allows you to enter the instance name.

4. Enter the information for *__Instance Name__. This is a unique name across all the VB instances and will be used to identify the instance. The name must start with a letter, must contain only letters and numbers, and can contain up to 24 characters. Enter vbcs01 for the time being and click on the **Create** button.

   The following screenshot shows the **QuickStarts** page under **Create Instance**:

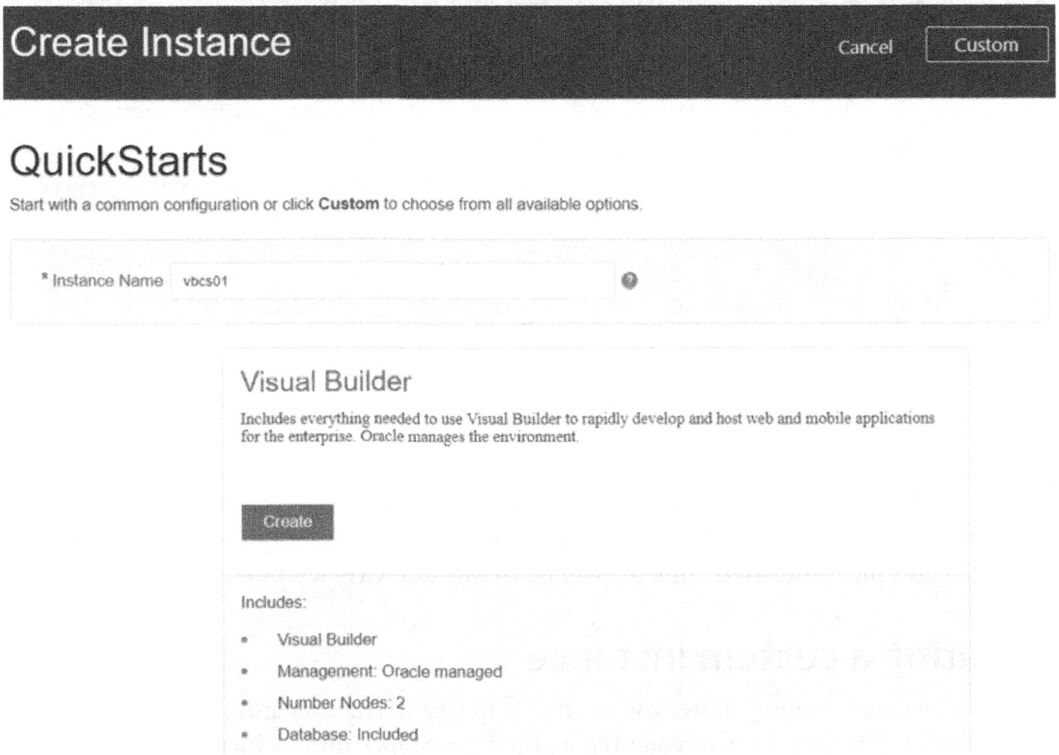

Create Instance

Cancel   Custom

QuickStarts

Start with a common configuration or click **Custom** to choose from all available options.

* Instance Name   vbcs01   ❷

Visual Builder

Includes everything needed to use Visual Builder to rapidly develop and host web and mobile applications for the enterprise. Oracle manages the environment.

Create

Includes:

- Visual Builder
- Management: Oracle managed
- Number Nodes: 2
- Database: Included

Figure 2.2 – Quick Start option to create a Visual Builder instance

5. The instance creation process will start once you click on the **Create** button. The instance creation will take 2–5 minutes and even longer, sometimes.

6. You will be returned back to the **Visual Builder** page where you will see **Status** as **Creating service…** and the **Submitted On** label, as shown in the following screenshot:

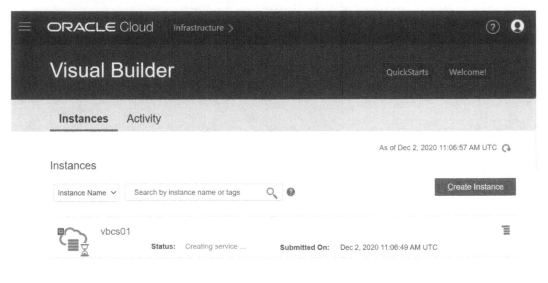

Figure 2.3 – Visual Builder instance creation status

While the instance is in the creation state, you cannot take any actions (stop, start, or delete) on the VB instance. Once the instance is created successfully, the status will be removed and the **Submitted On** label will be changed to **Created On**.

Creating a custom instance

Custom instance creation allows you to choose more information and is the recommended approach when you prepare the VB instance for production. Perform the following steps to create a VB instance:

1. Log in to the Oracle Cloud dashboard.
2. Click on the hamburger menu at the top left of the screen, expand **Platform Services**, and click on **Visual Builder**.
3. Click on the **Create Instance** button, which will open the instance creation page.
4. Specify the following details and click on the **Next** button:

Label	Value	Description
*Instance Name	vbcs02	This is a unique name across all the VB instances and will be used to identify the instance name. The name must start with a letter, must contain only letters and numbers, and can contain up to 24 characters.
Description	This is a custom VBCS instance.	
Notification Email	ankur.jain1@techsupper.com	By default, it will take the login email address, but you can change it. This is used to send the instance Provisioning status.
*Region	No Preference	Region where the instance will be installed.
Tags		It is used to search and categorize the instances.
Optional: Select only if you received a special tag from Oracle for creating this instance		It's only used if Oracle has given the special tag to create the VB instance. Once selected, it will allow you to enter the Special Tag value.

Table 2.1 – Details for the instance creation page to create a VB instance

5.   Enter the preceding instance creation details, as shown in the following screenshot:

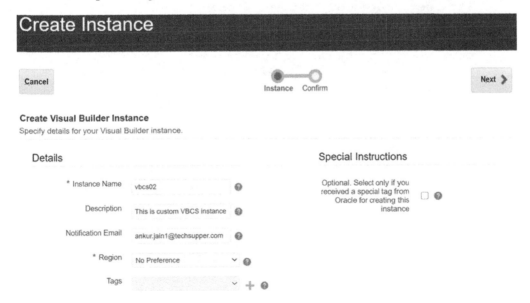

Figure 2.4 – Custom instance option to create a Visual Builder instance

6. Click on the download icon on the next page, which will download the **JSON** file, as shown:

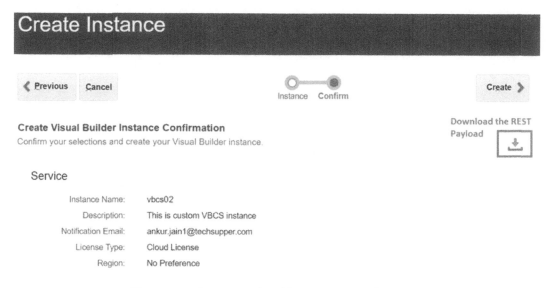

Figure 2.5 – Create Visual Builder Instance Confirmation

This JSON file contains a payload that will allow you to provision a VB instance using the REST API. A snippet of the JSON file is as follows:

```
{"serviceVersion":"1.0","specialInstructions"
:"false","managedSystemType":"oracle","
edition":"SUITE","enableNotification":"
true","serviceDescription":"This is
custom VBCS instance ","serviceName":
"vbcs02","serviceLevel":"PAAS","
subscriptionId":"1145011","
notificationEmail":"ankur.jain1@techsupper.
com","isBYOL":"false"}
```

7. Click on the **Create** button. This will initiate the instance creation process. Once the instance is created successfully, you can use it to start development.

The following screenshot shows the VB instances:

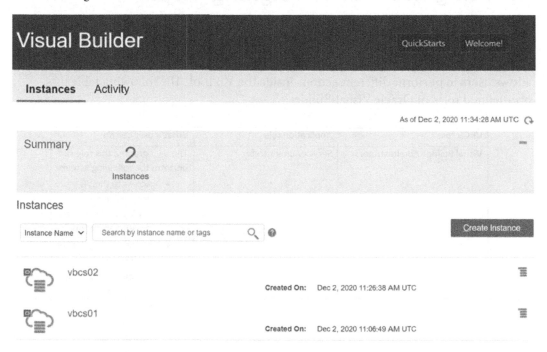

Figure 2.6 – Visual Builder instance page

Once a VB instance is created successfully, you can perform the following actions from the VB instance name. Click on the action icon (on the right side) of the VB instance name to view the available actions, which are as follows:

- **Start**: This action will allow you to start the VB instance if already stopped.

- **Stop**: This action will allow you to stop the VB instance. Once the VB instance is shut down, the billing will be stopped for the duration that the instance is stopped.

- **Manage Tags**: The action will allow you to manage the tags for this instance.

- **Delete**: This action will allow you to delete the instance permanently. Please think twice before taking this action as once the instance is deleted, it cannot be recovered.

> Tip:
> It is always good to stop a VB instance if not in use to save costs.

After provisioning a VB instance, next we'll have a look at how to create users and assign roles.

Creating users and assigning roles

Every application (OIC, VB, **API PCS**, and so on) in Oracle Cloud has pre-defined roles but only a few of the roles are mapped to the pre-defined role of VB.

Each and every VB instance has pre-defined roles with certain responsibilities. A role allows users to perform different actions inside the VB tool. The following table lists pre-defined roles of Oracle Visual Builder:

VBCS role	Application role	What a user can do
Visual Builder Administrator	ServiceAdministrator	The user granted this role can perform the following actions: • Access to the VB designer to develop, deploy, and manage the VB application • Modify the application ownership • Security configuration of the application • Specify the error message for access denied pages
Visual Builder Developer	ServiceDeveloper	The user granted this role can perform the following action: Access to the VB designer to develop, deploy and manage the VB application
Visual Builder User	ServiceUser	The user granted this role can perform the following action: Can access only stage and publish application

Table 2.2 – Pre-defined roles of Oracle Visual Builder

In the following sections, we will learn how to create a user.

Adding a user to IDCS

In order to assign roles to a user, a user must exist in Oracle **Identity Cloud Service** (**IDCS**). The following are the steps to create a user in IDCS:

1. Log in to IDCS using the following URL: `https://<unique_idcs_identifer>.oraclecloud.com/ui/v1/adminconsole`.

2. Click on **Users** from the dashboard.

3. Click on the + **Add** button.

4. Enter the details as follows and click on the **Finish** button:

Label	Value	Description
*First Name	Ankit	The user's first name.
*Last Name	Jain	The user's last name.
*User Name / Email	ankurjain.jain26@gmail.com	Enter the user's email address.
Use the email address as the username	Checked	If this is checked, the email address entered will become the username too. If unchecked, you will be allowed to enter both separately.

Table 2.3 – Details for creating a user in IDCS

The following screenshot shows the **Add User Details** dialog box:

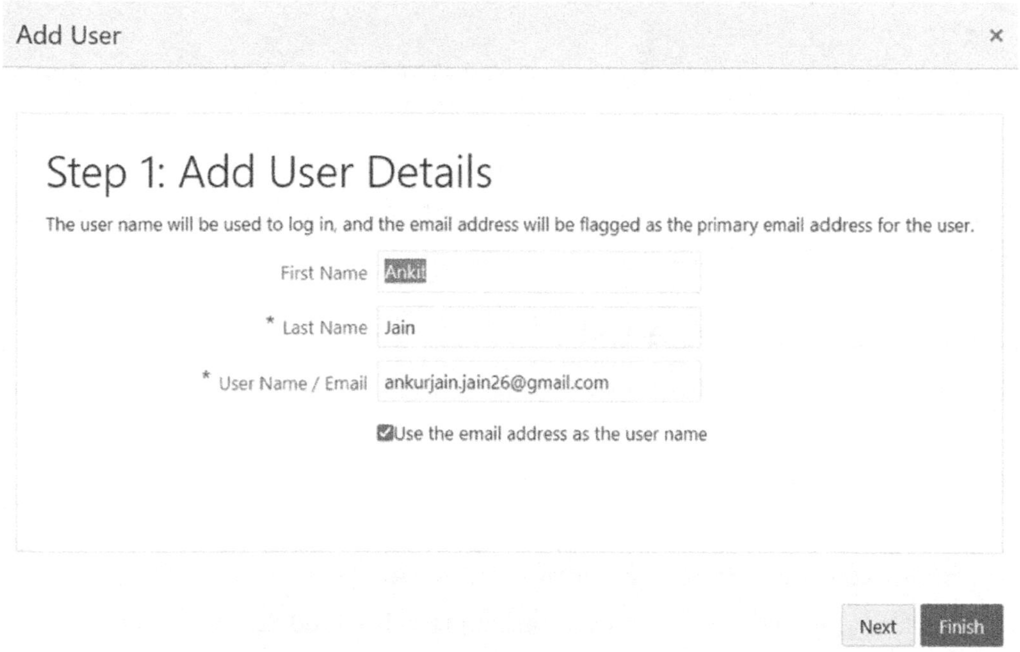

Figure 2.7 – Add User Details dialog box

The user will get an email notification at the specified email address upon user creation with the account activation link, using which the user can set the password in order to log in to their Oracle Cloud account.

The following screenshot shows the user information page:

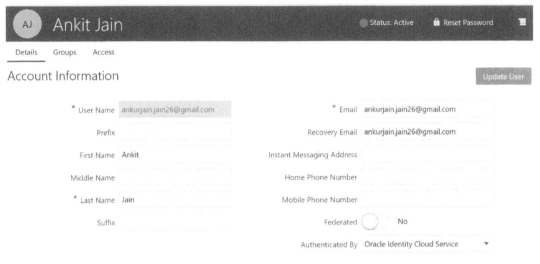

Figure 2.8 – User information page

You can use the user details page to add or modify the user details. Once modified, click on the **Update User** button.

Assigning a role to a user

Assigning a role to a user is done to specify what tasks a user can perform. Only the Identity Domain administrator can assign roles to a user.

The following are the steps to assign a role to a user:

1. Log in to IDCS using the IDCS link: `https://<unique_idcs_identifer>.oraclecloud.com/ui/v1/adminconsole`.

2. Click on the hamburger menu and click on **Oracle Cloud Services**.

3. Search for your VB instance with the name, for example, `VBINST`. This will show all the VB instances that you have previously created.

The following screenshot shows the **Oracle Cloud Services** page:

Figure 2.9 – List of the Visual Builder instances

4. Click on any of the instances to which you want to assign roles to a user. Here we will click on **VBINST_vbcs01**.

5. Click on the **Application Roles** tab, which will show all the roles specific to the application. Select the action icon (on the right side) next to the role and select **Assign Users** to assign the role.

6. Search the user, select the checkbox next to the name of the user, and click on **OK**.

The following screenshot shows how to assign a role to users:

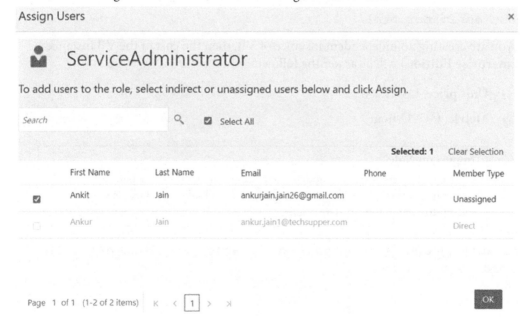

Figure 2.10 – Assigning a role to a user

Now the **ServiceAdminstrator** role is assigned to the user.

Now that we have looked at user creation and role assignment, next we'll look at how to derive the VB cost.

Deriving the cost of using VB

Cost plays a vital role whenever you buy any product and it helps you to make the correct decision. Cost is an important aspect to evaluate any product and helps to onboard the product in an organization. The correct decision to onboard a new product can help an organization to save huge costs. The cost derivation of any product should be easy and clear.

The Oracle Cloud pricing model is based on the unit cost structure. There are two pricing models that Oracle offers:

- **Simple unit pricing**: This model allows you to quickly provision a service and only pay for what you use. You have an option to switch off the service when not in use to save costs.

- **Bring Your Own License (BYOL)**: This model allows existing on-premise customers to use their existing on-premise licenses.

The cost of VB can be derived using the **Oracle Cost Estimator** tool, which is easy to access and understand. This tool is accessible at `https://www.oracle.com/cloud/cost-estimator.html`.

If you are creating an independent instance of VB, then the cost of the VB instance (**Enterprise Edition**) will be as per the following:

- **Unit price**: US $1.2365
- **Metric**: OCPU/hour

> **Important Note:**
> Oracle is fully authorized to update the price list at any time. So, before you commit anything to a customer, always have a look at the **Oracle Cost Estimator** tool for up-to-date pricing.

You can view the price list at `https://www.oracle.com/cloud/price-list.html#visual-builder`.

If you are using Visual Builder as part of the OIC instance, then the cost will be different than for an independent instance. The cost model of OIC is different than VB. OIC licenses are based on messages/hour, as follows:

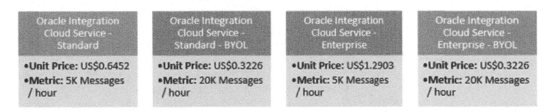

Figure 2.11 – Cost model of OIC

View the up-to-date price for OIC at `https://www.oracle.com/cloud/price-list.html#integration`.

If you are using the VB feature of OIC, then **100 messages** will be consumed per concurrent user/hour. If there are two concurrent users, 200 messages will be consumed from the OIC messages pack.

Refer to `http://www.oracle.com/us/corporate/contracts/paas-iaas-universal-credits-3940775.pdf` to see the Oracle PaaS and IaaS universal credits service descriptions.

We have seen how to work out the VB cost, so in the next section, we'll look at how to access the VB instance.

Accessing the VB instance

There are two ways to access the VB instance. You can use the VB instance management page or directly use the VB link to access Visual Builder. We will discuss each in the next sections.

Accessing VB via the Visual Builder instance page

For this, you need to perform the following steps:

1. Log in to the Oracle Cloud dashboard.

2. Click on the hamburger menu, expand **Platform Services**, and click on **Visual Builder**.

3. Click on the action menu to the right of the Visual Builder instance name and click on **Open Visual Builder Home Page**, as shown:

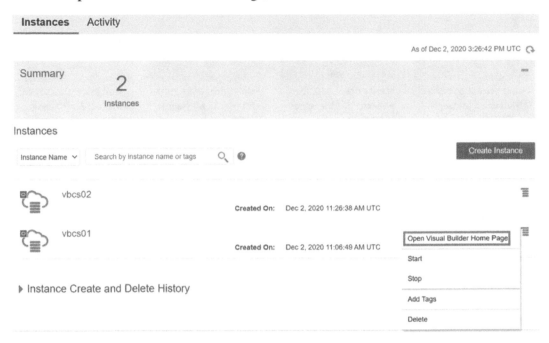

Figure 2.12 – Open to log in to Visual Builder

This action will take you to the Visual Builder home page.

Accessing VB using a direct URL

If you already know the Visual Builder URL, you can directly paste the URL into the browser and enter the login details. This is how a VB URL is structured: `https://<vbcs_instane_name>-<cloud_account_name>.builder.ocp. oraclecloud.com/ic/builder`.

Replace `vbcs_instance_name` and `cloud_account_name` with the actual values, for example, `https://vbcs01-ankurjain1.builder.ocp.oraclecloud. com/ic/builder/`.

You can bookmark the VB direct URL for easy login. The login page will appear if you enter the direct URL into the browser and if you are not already logged in in the same browser.

> **Tip:**
> Every application in Oracle Cloud is secured via the **Oracle Identity Cloud**. Hence, the login page is common for each application.

The following screenshot shows the login page:

Figure 2.13 – Login page

Upon successful login, you will land on the Visual Builder home page.

Next, we'll explore different navigations of Visual Builder.

Exploring various navigations of VB

Once you log in to Visual Builder, you will see three main navigations under the home page. It's really important to be familiar with each and every navigation before you start development as it will help you to choose the right navigation to do the right things.

The three main navigations of Visual Builder are as follows:

- **All Applications**
- **Settings**
- **Certificates**

The following screenshot shows these three main navigations:

Figure 2.14 – Visual Builder's all navigations

Let's discuss each option in the next sections.

All Applications

Once you click on the **All Applications** navigation, you will be landed on the all applications page. It shows all the Visual Builder applications created earlier, if any, else the page shows only two buttons: **+ New Application** and **+ Import Application**.

The following screenshot shows the all applications page when no application exists:

Figure 2.15 – All applications page

The **+ New Application** button will allow you to create a new application; however, the **+ Import Application** button will allow you to import an existing application.

If you have at least one application in Visual Builder, the all applications page looks as follows:

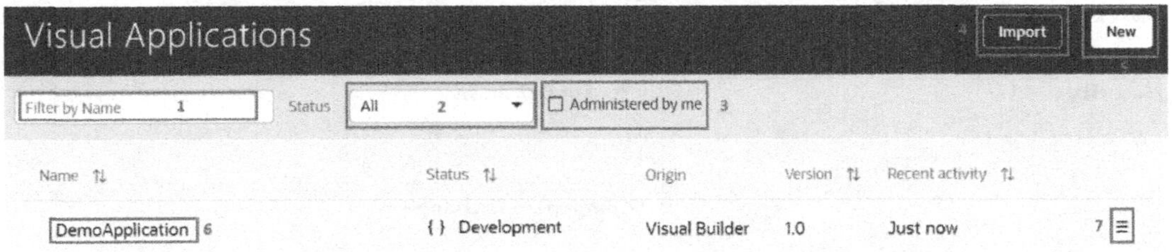

Figure 2.16 – All applications page with various options

The following list explains each and every action marked in the previous screenshot:

1. **Filter by Name**: Allows you to search the application using the application name.

2. **Status**: Allows you to filter the application status-wise. There are different statuses of an application.

3. **Administered by me**: Developers can view and manage applications on the application page. If the logged-in user is the administrator of the Visual Builder instance, then only this checkbox is visible. If checked, it will list all the applications, even if the admin is not a team member in the application.

4. **Import**: Allows you to import the existing application.

5. **New**: Allows you to create a new application.

6. **Name**: Represents the name of the application.

7. **Action**: Shows different actions of an application. This menu differs as per the application status (**Development**, **Stage**, or **Live**).

Settings

Only **service administrators** are allowed to view the settings navigation. This is used to manage the global-level settings of the VB instance. There are different security settings that can be managed using this page. We'll discuss all of them in detail in this section.

There are two tabs on the settings page:

- **General**
- **Services**

The following screenshot shows the page when you are on the **General** tab:

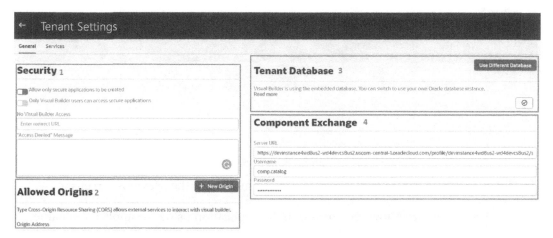

Figure 2.17 – Tenant Settings page – the General tab

Let's have a quick look at each section.

Security

This section is used to manage the security of all applications in the VB instance. When **Allow only secure applications to be created** is checked, then all the published and staged applications will require user login. Without user login, the application can't be accessed. When this checkbox is checked, then only **Only Visual Builder users can access secure applications** will be enabled.

So, if you want only authenticated users to access all your VB applications, then check the **Allow only secure applications to be created** option.

Message for access denied errors

Authenticated users can see the default access denied message and page when they attempt to access the page or application for which they don't have proper roles. VB allows an administrator to override the default access denied message and page. Specify the redirect URL and **"Access Denied" Message** options, shown in the following screenshot:

Figure 2.18 – Access denied options

This setting is applicable for all the applications in a VB instance.

Allowed Origins

In general terms, **Cross-Origin Resource Sharing (CORS)** is a mechanism that allows restricted resources to be accessed from another domain. By default, incoming requests from outside domains are blocked. For example, if any SaaS application wants to embed the VB application and try to access it, then the request will be rejected and the client can see the CORS error in the browser console.

In order to enable an outside domain to access the VB application, you have to add the origin by clicking on the **+ New Origin** button under the **Allowed Region** section, as shown in the following screenshot:

Type Cross-Origin Resource Sharing (CORS) allows external services to interact with visual builder.

Origin Address

| Enter allowed origin URL | ✕ | ✓ |

Figure 2.19 – CORS origin settings

Once you click on the button, it will allow you to enter the allowed origin URL. Click on the right icon to save the settings.

Tenant Database

As I mentioned earlier, the VB instance is provisioned with an embedded database but this database has a limitation in terms of space. The embedded database comes with 5 GB of space across applications in a VB instance. If you think this limit is insufficient for all your applications, then you have an option to switch your embedded database with another Oracle database, as follows:

- Oracle **Database as a Service (DBaaS)**
- Oracle **Autonomous Transaction Processing (ATP)**

In order to switch the database, click on the **Use Different Database** button under the **Tenant Database** section. Once you click on the button, it will open a wizard that gives you the option to select either **Oracle Database Connection with JDBC** or **Oracle Autonomous Transaction Processing Cloud Wallet**. To use a different database, you need the database admin user.

If you are willing to use Oracle DBaaS, assign privileges to the user as per the following script:

```
GRANT CONNECT, RESOURCE, DBA TO [adminuser];
GRANT SELECT ON SYS.DBA_PROFILES TO [adminuser] WITH GRANT
OPTION;
GRANT SELECT ON SYS.DBA_USERS TO [adminuser] WITH GRANT OPTION;
GRANT SELECT ON SYS.DBA_DATA_FILES TO [adminuser] WITH GRANT
OPTION;
GRANT SELECT ON SYS.DBA_SEGMENTS TO [adminuser] WITH GRANT
OPTION;
```

In the case of ATP, the following privileges are required for the database user:

```
GRANT CREATE USER, ALTER USER, DROP USER, CREATE PROFILE TO
[adminuser]
WITH ADMIN OPTION;
GRANT CONNECT TO [adminuser] WITH ADMIN OPTION;
GRANT RESOURCE TO [adminuser] WITH ADMIN OPTION;
GRANT CREATE SEQUENCE, CREATE OPERATOR, CREATE SESSION,ALTER
SESSION,
CREATE PROCEDURE, CREATE VIEW, CREATE JOB,CREATE
DIMENSION,CREATE
INDEXTYPE,CREATE TYPE,CREATE TRIGGER,CREATE TABLE,CREATE
PROFILE TO
[adminuser] WITH ADMIN OPTION;
GRANT UNLIMITED TABLESPACE TO [adminuser] WITH ADMIN OPTION;
GRANT SELECT ON SYS.DBA_PROFILES TO [adminuser] WITH GRANT
OPTION;
GRANT SELECT ON SYS.DBA_USERS TO [adminuser] WITH GRANT OPTION;
GRANT SELECT ON SYS.DBA_DATA_FILES TO [adminuser] WITH GRANT
OPTION;
GRANT SELECT ON SYS.DBA_SEGMENTS TO [adminuser] WITH GRANT
OPTION;
```

In the next section, we'll look at the component exchange repository.

Component Exchange

Component exchange is a repository of custom components available in **Visual Builder Studio** (**VBS**). All these components can be used on the web or on mobile applications.

Navigate to the **Services** tab from the **Tenant Settings** page in order to enable connections with backend services, as follows:

- **Oracle Cloud Application Instance**: This will allow you to configure a connection with the Oracle SaaS application. Once the connection is established, you can use the **extend the Oracle SaaS application** functionality in the VB application.

- **Integrations**: This will allow you to set up the connection with Integration. By default, the Integration connection is configured. But you have an option to update the connection details and point them to other Integration instances.

- **Process**: This will allow you to connect to **Processes**. If VB is part of an OIC instance, then this will also be configured by default. If not added, you can simply add the process connection.

- **Custom**: This allows you to create your own backend that will point to a custom server other than the inbuilt backends such as Integration, Process, and Oracle Cloud applications.

- **Custom ADF Describe**: This will allow you to add a custom ADF describe file as a backend.

Click on the + button in order to configure the backend services, as shown:

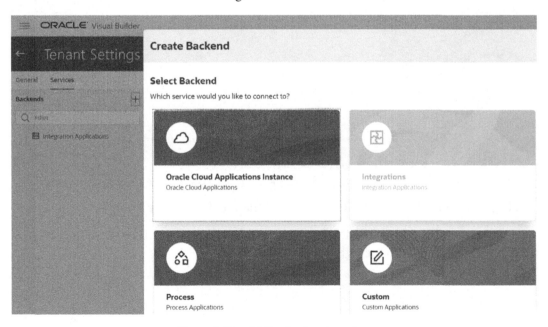

Figure 2.20 – Adding backend services

Once the backends are added, you have an option to update the connection properties. In order to update the connection properties, select the backend, go to the **Servers** tab, and click on the pencil icon to the right of the backend name.

Certificates

The page allows administrators to upload and manage the self-signed certificates used by this VB instance. The certificates allow inbound and outbound SSL communications to the REST APIs.

This page lists all the certificates that have been added already. You can delete an existing certificate using the delete icon next to the certificate name.

In order to upload a new certificate, click on the **Upload** button in the top-right corner of the page and upload or drag the certificate file. The following screenshot shows how to upload a certificate:

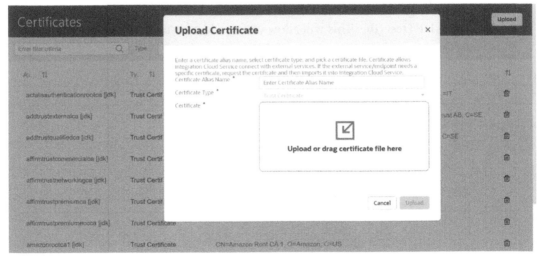

Figure 2.21 – Upload Certificate

Click on the **Upload** button in order to upload the certificate successfully.

In this section, we have explored various navigations of VB that will help you to choose the right navigation to do the right things.

Summary

In this chapter, we learned about two ways to provision a VB instance and saw the different actions that you can perform once a VB instance is created successfully. We explained various pre-defined roles of applications and VB, which will help you to provide a suitable role to users as per the requirements. We went through all the steps to provision a user via IDCS and how to assign pre-defined roles to a user.

We also discussed the VB costing, learned how you can get the VB cost, and looked at various links to derive the cost. You learned about two ways to access the VB instance to start your development. We also saw various navigations of VB with a detailed explanation that will help you to choose the right navigation to do the right thing.

This chapter helped you to learn various important things to kick off the VB journey. In the next chapter, we'll talk about various building blocks of Visual Builder that will be used throughout the book. So, don't skip the next chapter, and read it carefully to understand each and every building block.

Questions

1. Why is a credit card required during account creation?
2. Will Oracle charge after the 30-day free subscription period is over?
3. Does VB come under the free service program?
4. How can I practice once the VB service is terminated after 30 days?
5. Can the embedded database size be increased somehow?

3
Exploring Visual Builder Ingredients

Undoubtedly, ingredients or terminology play a vital role in the understanding of any technology in the world. It's a given fact that without understanding the basics of any technology, you cannot work upon it. If the basic building blocks of a technology are clear, then it makes life easier when working upon it quickly and efficiently.

So, in this chapter, we'll discuss different basic building blocks of **Visual Builder** (**VB**) that will help you to work in VB quickly. This chapter will give you a deep understanding of Business Objects, Service Connections, and variables, along with their types and scope. You will learn about events and Action Chains. You will also get an understanding of the web application structure and the various editors available to create and modify artifacts inside applications.

This is one of the important chapters of the book, so don't skip it, and read it carefully. Although this is a theoretical chapter, it covers a lot of important aspects of VB. To avoid confusion while working in VB, it's very important for you to understand all these basic building blocks in detail. The terminology we'll explain in this chapter will be used throughout the book.

In this chapter, you will learn about various building blocks of Visual Builder that will help you to work on web or mobile applications easily.

In this chapter, we will cover the following topics:

- Creating a VB application
- Understanding Business Objects
- Exploring Service Connections
- Understanding variables, their types, and their scope
- Understanding implicit objects of VB
- Exploring events and Action Chains
- Understanding the application's structure
- Understanding the various editors and the application designer

Technical requirements

To complete this chapter, you should have the following:

- A VB instance
- VB login credentials

Creating a VB application

A VB application is the starting point of web and mobile applications. It is a superset of multiple web and mobile applications. A visual application can have multiple web and mobile applications.

In order to create a new VB application, navigate to the **All Application** tab from the Visual Builder home page and click on the **New** button. Once you click on the **New** button, the **Create Application** dialog box will open.

Enter the details as follows, and then click on the **Finish** button:

- **Application Name**: Enter a unique application name.
- **Application ID**: The application ID represents the context path of the application. This will be populated automatically based on **Application Name**; however, you can modify it. It should be unique across all VB applications.
- **Description**: Enter a description of the application optionally.
- **Application Template**: By default, this uses the **Empty Application** template; however, you can choose other templates (**Oracle SaaS R13 Light Theme** for **VBCS** or **Oracle Visual Builder Cookbook**) as well using the **Change Template** link.

The following screenshot shows the **Create Application** dialog box (* represents a mandatory field):

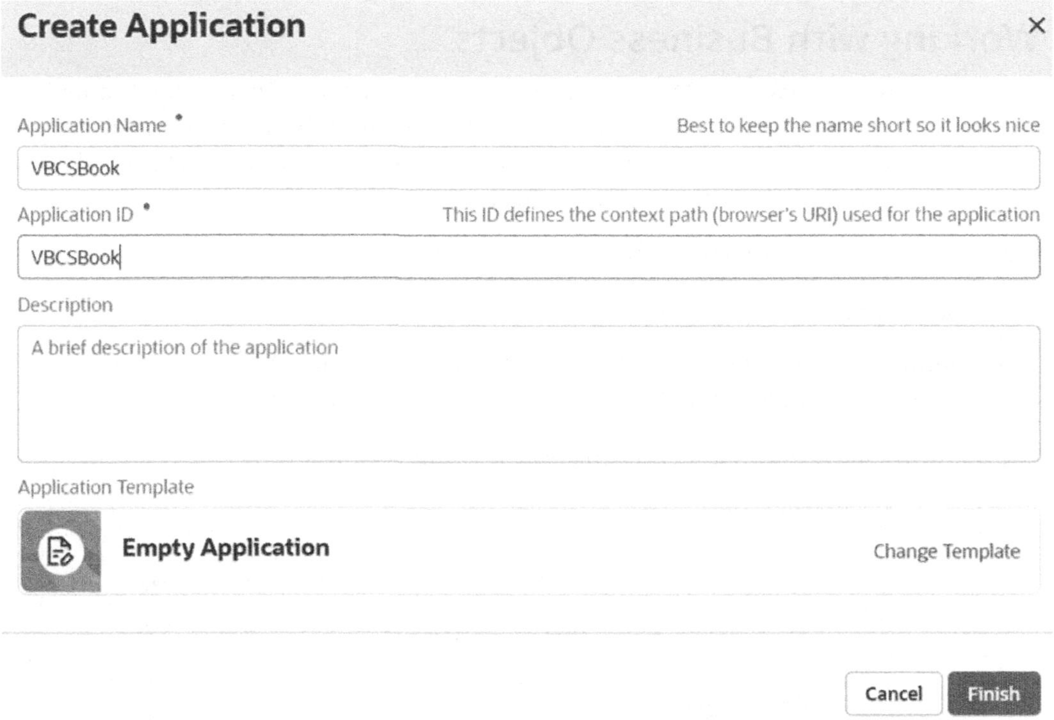

Create Application   ✕

Application Name *   Best to keep the name short so it looks nice

VBCSBook

Application ID *   This ID defines the context path (browser's URI) used for the application

VBCSBook

Description

A brief description of the application

Application Template

Empty Application   Change Template

Cancel   Finish

Figure 3.1 – Create Application dialog box

Once an application is created, it will take you to the visual application welcome page.

After creating our VB application, next we'll understand Business Objects.

Understanding Business Objects

A **Business Object** represents an object such as an employee, address, contact details, and so on. You can consider a Business Object like a table in a database having a different set of fields. Like a table, a Business Object contains a set of fields with structured data used for Visual Builder applications. Business Objects are stored in the database.

When you create a Business Object in Visual Builder, its structure and data are accessed via REST endpoints as Business Objects create the endpoints automatically. Business Objects are reusable components and once created, they can be used in multiple web or mobile applications simultaneously.

When a Visual Builder application is created, then only Business Objects can be created under that application.

Working with Business Objects

In order to create a Business Object, a VB application must exist. Once an application is created, open it, and click on the **Business Objects** pane from the application navigator. The **Business Objects** section will open, which will show all the Business Objects already created. Click on the + button and select + **Business Object**.

Enter the following information and click on the **Create** button:

- **Label**: This is a user-friendly name.

- **Name**: This is the unique name of the Business Object. It will be populated automatically based on **Label**; however, you can modify it also.

The following screenshot shows how to create a Business Object:

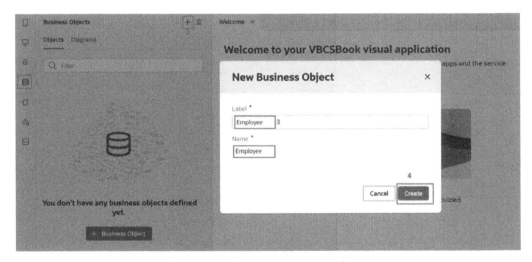

Figure 3.2 – Creating a Business Object

Once a new Business Object is created, you will see different tabs. We have explained each and every tab as follows:

- **Overview**: This shows the ID of the Business Object and allows you to add a **Plural Label** value also. The **Contains Application Setup Data** option signifies that the Business Object contains foundational data and that this is always required for the application to work functionally. If this is checked, then this Business Object data will always be part of the application during migration. From the **Overview** tab, you can create a relationship between different Business Objects.

The following screenshot shows the **Overview** tab of a Business Object:

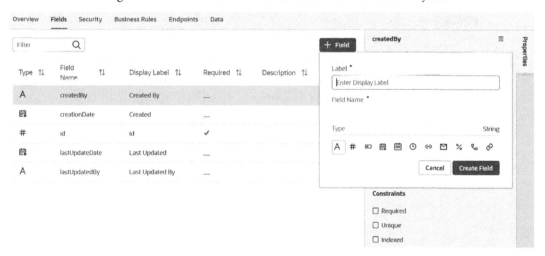

Figure 3.3 – Business Object Overview tab

- **Fields**: Allows you to create a different set of fields to hold the data. Five fields are created by default and one of the fields (**id**) is the primary key. You can create a new field using the **+ Field** button.

The following screenshot shows the **Fields** tab of the Business Object:

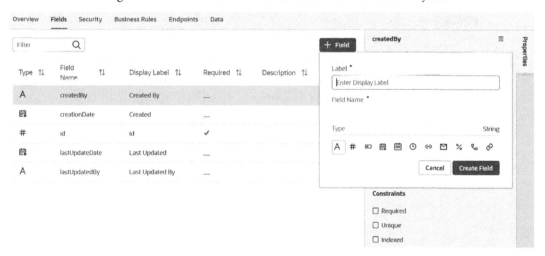

Figure 3.4 – Business Object Fields tab

- **Security**: The **Security** tab allows you to enable role-based security for a Business Object. Once enabled, you can control who can do what (view, create, update, delete) to data.

- **Business Rules**: Allows you to specify the business rules for the Business Object. You can create Object Triggers, Field Triggers, Object Validators, Field Validators, and Object Functions.

- **Endpoints**: As mentioned earlier, VB creates various REST endpoints for each and every Business Object. This tab displays all the REST endpoints that are exposed automatically. There are other endpoints available to access the Business Object metadata and data.

The following screenshot shows the **Endpoints** tab of a Business Object:

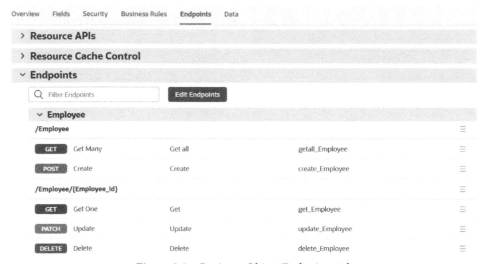

Figure 3.5 – Business Object Endpoints tab

- **Data**: This tab shows the data inside the Business Object. You can add rows to the Business Object by clicking on the **+ Row** button. The **Data** tab offers you the option to export or import data using a `.csv` file.

The following screenshot shows the **Data** tab of a Business Object:

Figure 3.6 – Business Object Data tab

After getting an understanding of Business Objects, we'll focus on the next building block of VB in the following section.

Exploring Service Connections

Whenever you have a requirement to call external REST APIs, Service Connections play an important role in helping you to build a connection with those REST APIs. The **Service Connection** is one of the main components of VB that helps you to communicate with external applications using REST APIs.

A Service Connection specifies the connection to a REST service, including the service URLs, authentication details, and the payload.

Like Business Objects, Service Connections are also reusable components and once created can be used in multiple web or mobile applications simultaneously. These are not specific to any application.

The following subsections help you to understand various options to create a Service Connection.

Various options to create a Service Connection

In order to create a Service Connection, a VB application must exist. Once an application is created, click on the **Services** pane from the application navigator. The **Service Connection** section will open up, which will show you all the Service Connections created earlier.

Go to the **Service Connections** tab, click on the + button, and then click on the **Service Connection** option to create a new Service Connection. The previous action will open a dialog box that will allow you to choose one of the options to create a Service Connection.

The following screenshot shows the various options to create a Service Connection:

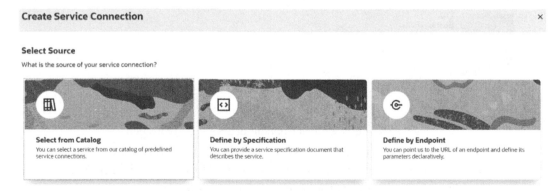

Figure 3.7 – Options to create a Service Connection

Let's discuss each option in detail:

- **Select from Catalog**: This option allows you to create a Service Connection using the defined backend, such as Oracle cloud applications, Oracle Integration, or a custom backend. At least one backend must be added to use this option. The backends are added in the **Tenant Settings** section under the **Services** tab. Refer to the *Settings* section under *Exploring various navigations of VB* in the previous chapter to revisit how to add backends.

  The following screenshot shows the different options to create a Service Connection using **Service Catalog**:

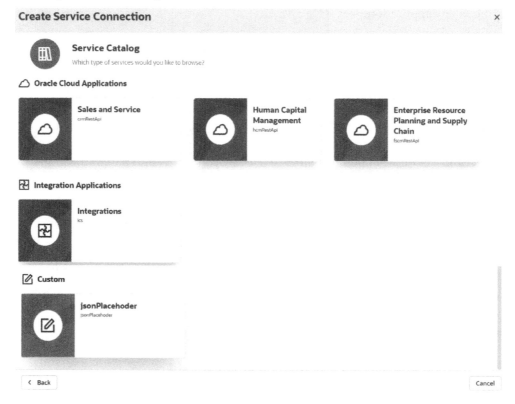

Figure 3.8 – Service Catalog options of a Service Connection

  You can choose either of the options to create the Service Connection. The catalog populates all the services and endpoints automatically associated with Oracle cloud applications, Integration, or other backend server instances.

- **Define by Specification**: This option allows you to create a connection when you already know the URL of the **OpenAPI / Swagger** or **ADF** file that describes the service. You can upload the description file from your system too.

The following screenshot shows the options to create a Service Connection when you choose this option:

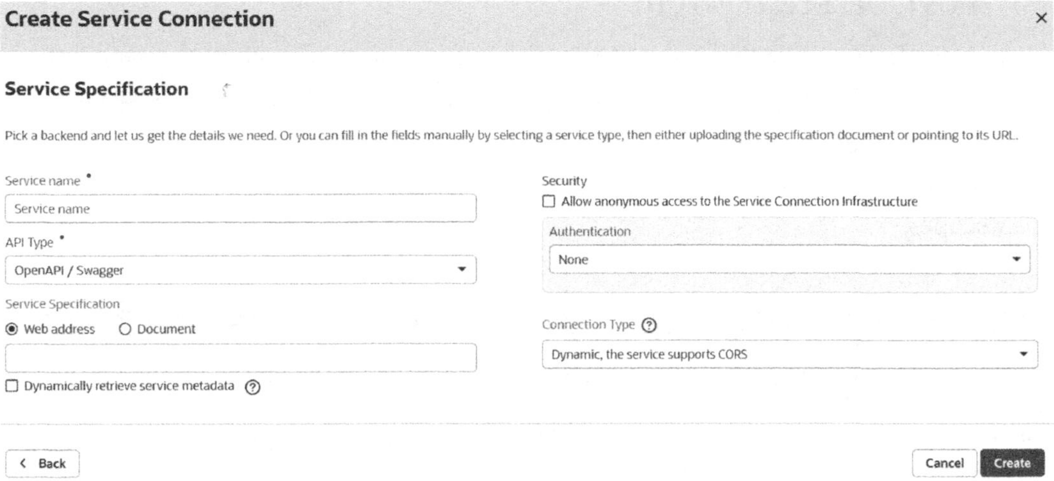

Create Service Connection   ×

Service Specification

Pick a backend and let us get the details we need. Or you can fill in the fields manually by selecting a service type, then either uploading the specification document or pointing to its URL.

Service name *   Security
[Service name]   ☐ Allow anonymous access to the Service Connection Infrastructure

API Type *   Authentication
[OpenAPI / Swagger   ▼]   [None   ▼]

Service Specification
◉ Web address   ○ Document   Connection Type ⓘ
[   ]   [Dynamic, the service supports CORS   ▼]

☐ Dynamically retrieve service metadata ⓘ

[‹ Back]   [Cancel] [Create]

Figure 3.9 – Define by Specification options of a Service Connection

- **Define by Endpoint**: This option allows you to create the connection with a REST API base URI. You have to provide the necessary details in order to create a successful connection.

The following screenshot shows the options to create a Service Connection when you choose the **Define by Endpoint** option:

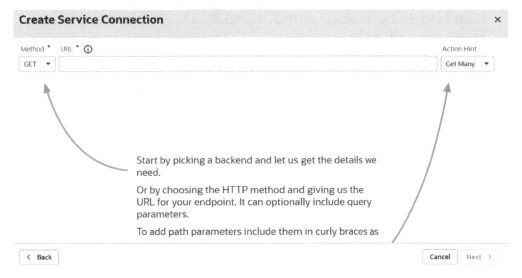

Figure 3.10 – Define by Endpoint options of a Service Connection

We see the following fields in this screenshot:

a. **Method**: This dropdown allows you to select the REST endpoint verb (**GET**, **POST**, **DELETE**, or **PATCH**).

b. **URL**: You can either choose to use the existing backend or enter the endpoint.

c. **Action Hint**: This option allows you to specify the result (**Get One**, **Get Many**, **Create**, **Update**, **Delete**, or **Custom**) of the entered REST URL.

Post exploring the Service Connection, next we will discuss variables, types, and their scopes.

Understanding variables, their types, and their scopes

Variables in any programming language play a vital role and they are used to store any type of information, such as names, contact numbers, ages, and so on. Similarly, VB variables are also used to store information that can be referred to at any place in the application depending upon the scope of the variable.

Different types of variables that can be created are as follows:

- **Primitive**: These are simple variables such as String, Number, or Boolean.
- **Complex variables**: These are complex variables used to store data structures, such as Employee or Address.
- **Built-in variable**: These are variables that are used to get the metadata of the application, such as logged-in user information, page information, application information, and so on.

You can set the default value of a variable using the `defaultVariable` property of the variable.

Types are complex variables that define the data type and structure of a variable. When you create a variable, it's mandatory to assign the type. The type can be custom or based on the endpoint.

All the variables and types are created within the scope. The scope defines the life cycle of the variables and indicates where the variables can be seen or used within the application. There are different scopes for variables in VB:

- **Application**: The variables and types created under the application scope have visibility in every flow and page of the application.

- **Flow**: The visibility of the variables and types is within the flow only. The variables and types created under the flow scope can be referred to in all the pages within the flow only.

- **Page**: The visibility of the variables and types is limited only to the page in which they are defined. The variables and types created inside a page can only be referred to within the same page.

- **Action Chain**: The visibility of Action Chain variables is limited to the Action Chain only.

The values of the variables can be used to pass between different pages. In order to pass the variable value, you have to enable the **Input Parameter** property of a variable.

The following screenshot shows how to make a variable an input parameter to make it sharable:

Figure 3.11 – Variables page

You can also make it required to enforce the caller to always pass the value in the parameter. As is visible in *Figure 3.11*, click on the **Required** property to make it mandatory.

Each variable you create in Visual Builder has a few properties, as follows:

- **type**: The type property signifies the type of the variable, such as String, Number, Boolean, and so on.

- **input**: The input property indicates the variable will become the input variable when the page is called by some other page.

- **required**: The required property makes it mandatory for the variable to be set when you call the page from another.

- **defaultValue**: You can define the default value of the variable. It can be either an expression or a static value.

- **persisted**: You can make the lifespan of the variable longer than the scope using this property. You can set the value of the `persisted` property to either a session, a device, or none.

We have understood variables and types, so next we'll look at implicit objects of VB.

Understanding implicit objects of VB

Implicit objects are those objects that are defined inside Visual Builder and can be used to extract the values of variables. These are treated as keywords in VB. Implicit objects are prefixed with the $ sign. VB implicit objects are as follows:

- `$application`: The application implicit object is used to get the value of the variable that is defined at the application scope. For example, if you have defined a variable called `firstName` at the application level, the expression `$application. variables.firstName` will be used to get the value of this variable.

- `$flow`: The flow implicit object is used to get the value of the variables that are defined at the flow scope. For example, if you have defined a variable called `firstName` at the flow level, the expression `$flow.variables.firstName` will be used to get the value of the variable.

- `$page`: The page implicit object is used to get the variable values that are defined at the page scope. For example, if you have defined a variable called `firstName` at the page level, the expression `$page.variables.firstName` will be used to get the value of this variable.

- `$variables`: This is a shortcut to get the variable values in the current scope. For example, the variable (`firstName`) defined inside the page can also be extracted using the expression `$variables.firstName` instead of `$page.variables. firstName`.

- `$chains`: This is used to refer to the variables inside chains.

- `$chain`: The chain implicit object refers to those variables that are defined inside the chain.

- `$parameters`: The existence of this object is in `beforeEvent` only and is used to refer to the page input parameters.

- `$listeners`: This object is used to refer to the event listeners of a flow or page.

- $event: This object is used to refer to the event listeners of a flow or page, for example, the onValueChange listener on a variable. Event implicit object can be used to get the values of variables such as name, oldValue, value, or diff.

After exploring the implicit object, next we will discuss events and Action Chains.

Exploring events and Action Chains

Events play an important role when you work on the web or a mobile application with any technology and help you to make the application interactive. Events are fired on any actions that happen inside the application. Events may occur on page load, application load, button click, value change of the components, and so forth. After an event occurs, a few actions can take place, such as calling another page, doing some clean-up work, refreshing the variables, calling an external API, and so forth.

Similarly, in VB, events and actions also play an important role and make the application interactive. So, it becomes important to understand events and Action Chains as they are both the basic building blocks of VB.

Events

Visual Builder offers various events to which the application can react in order to execute a series of actions to perform various tasks. These tasks can include calling another event, calling an external REST API, changing the behavior of a variable, and so on. These actions can run one by one or in parallel as per the requirements.

The application reacts to events through event listeners. There are the following various events that can be fired during the runtime:

- **Page and flow events**: These events are life cycle events defined by the system. The event listeners are defined in a page or flow. The page events have a vb prefix. When the page event is fired, the framework calls the defined page event listener.

- **Declared events**: These events are explicitly defined in the application model. These events can be declared at the application, flow, or page level.

- **Component events**: These events are also referred to as a **Document Object Model (DOM)** and they are fired by components such as a button, link, focus in, focus out, and so on. The event listener can be declared by any name but must be bound to a component event.

- **Custom events**: These events are user-defined events and are similar to the page events. The event listeners of custom events can be declared at the application, flow, or page level.

- **onValueChanged event**: This event is specific to a variable and it is raised when a variable value changes. You can get the old and new values using the implicit event object as follows:

  a. $event.oldValue: This provides you with the variable's old value.

  b. $event.newValue: This provides you with the variable's new value.

  c. $event.diff: This is used for complex type variables and provides the difference between two stages, old and new.

Action Chains

An **Action Chain** is a series of actions that will be executed after an event is fired by any component on the page. The series of actions you define in an Action Chain can be executed in parallel or sequentially. Every Action Chain must be attached to at least one listener in order to execute it.

Action Chains are executed by events such as a click, onValueChange, and so on. Each and every Action Chain you define can be in the application, flow, or page scope. The Action Chain defined under the application scope can be executed from a flow or page, but the Action Chain defined under a page can't be called from the application or flow.

The following screenshot depicts a diagram of an Action Chain:

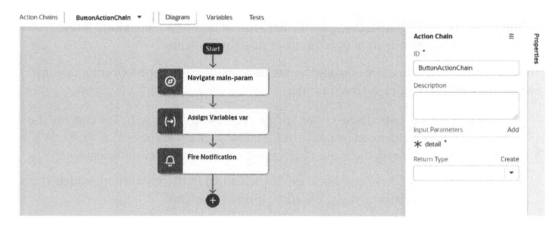

Figure 3.12 – Action Chain diagram

The **JSON** code is generated for every action, which is configured on the Action Chain. You can see this in the **JSON** file of the page. Click on the action menu near **Action Chain**, as shown in *Figure 3.12*, and click on **Go to Code**, which will show the JSON code.

You can define the variables in the Action Chain. For every Action Chain, a few variables are created automatically depending on the event with which the Action Chain is associated. You can also create custom variables within the Action Chain and the scope of these variables will be an **action**. These variables can only be accessed inside the Action Chain. Click on the **Variables** tab near the **Diagram** tab to create or view the Action Chain variables.

The following screenshot depicts the **Variables** tab. Click on the **+ Variable** button in order to create a new variable:

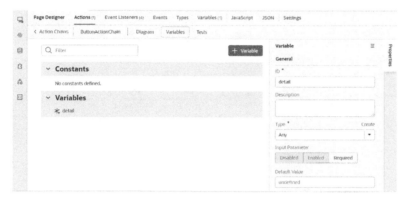

Figure 3.13 – Creating a variable in an Action Chain

Once your Action Chain is defined, you can plan to test it independently. In order to test the flow of the Action Chain, click on the **Tests** tab near the **Variables** tab.

The following screenshot depicts the **Tests** tab of an Action Chain:

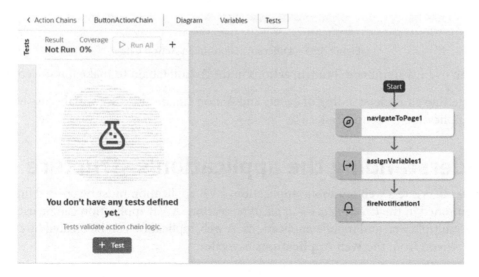

Figure 3.14 – Testing the Action Chain

Actions inside an Action Chain

An Action Chain provides a rich set of built-in actions that we can drag and drop on the Action Chain canvas in order to define the logic of the Action Chain. Once an action is dropped on the canvas, the **Properties** palette of that action will be visible, which allows us to define certain properties of that action. The properties differ from action to action.

The following screenshot depicts the different actions available in an Action Chain:

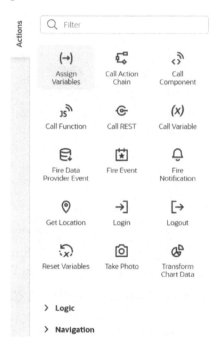

Figure 3.15 – Different actions in an Action Chain

You can use any number of built-in actions in the Action Chain to make it more complex.

After getting an understanding of events and Action Chains, next we will discuss what your application structure looks like.

Understanding the application's structure

In order to create a web or mobile application, a VB application must be created first, as mentioned in the *Creating a VB application* section. A VB application can be used to create multiple web and mobile applications. A web application can be created by clicking on the + icon from the **Web Applications** navigator.

The following screenshot depicts how to create a web application:

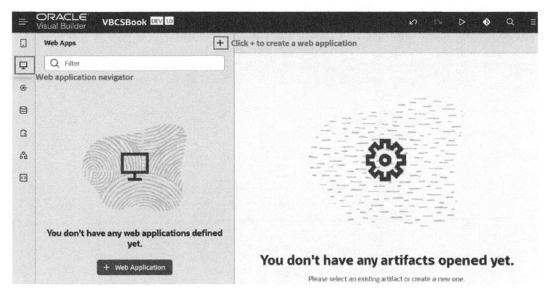

Figure 3.16 – Creating a web application

Similarly, a mobile application can be created by clicking on the + icon from the **Mobile Applications** navigator.

The following screenshot depicts how to create a mobile application:

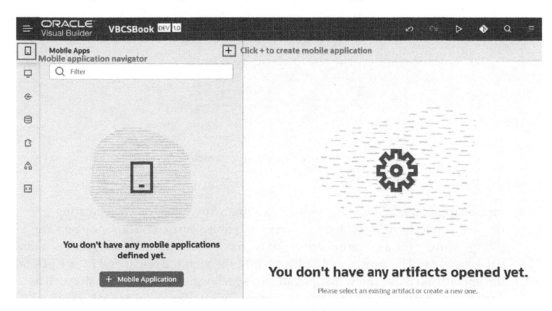

Figure 3.17 – Creating a mobile application

When a web or mobile application is created, a default structure of an application will be created with the necessary folders and files.

The following screenshot depicts the web application structure:

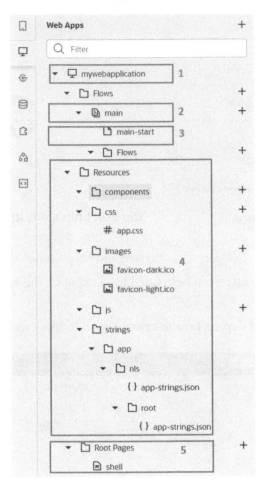

Figure 3.18 – Web application structure

Let's talk about each section shown:

- **mywebapplication**: This is the web application name you gave when creating the web application. This is the top-level node, and all artifacts (flow or page) are grouped under the application node. For each new web or mobile application, a new parent node will be created and, subsequently, the required folder and files. Click on the application name (**mywebapplication**), which will show different tabs such as **Page Flow**, **Actions**, **Event Listeners**, **Events**, **Types**, **Variables**, **HTML**, **JavaScript**, **JSON**, and **Settings**.

The artifacts created under the application are application-scoped and can be used in each and every flow and page of the same application. When you create the web application, the top-level files, `app-flow.json`, `app-flow.js`, and `index.html`, are generated, which show the description and metadata of the application. Click on the **Source View** pane from the application navigator, and see all those files, as shown in the following screenshot:

Figure 3.19 – Application-related files

- **Flows:** All the application pages are grouped under a flow. A flow is nothing more than a group of related pages. For example, if your application has different modules such as HR, Admin, Finance, and so on, then create different flows and keep all the related pages under the subsequent flow.

Depending on the template of the application, one or more flows are created. As shown in *Figure 3.18*, a flow with the name **main** is created by default. You can delete or rename it if required. Right-click on the flow name and select the necessary action.

In order to create a new flow, click on the + button next to **Flows**, as shown in *Figure 3.18*. Similar to the application, if you click on the flow (**main**), you will see different tabs. The artifacts created under the flow are **flow-scoped** and can be used on every page under that flow.

The `<flowname>-flow.json` and `<flowname>-flow.js` source files are created for each and every flow and contain a description of the file. Jump to the **Source View** to view both the files under the application name.

You can create a sub-flow under a flow if required. Click on the + button to the right of **Flows** under the flow.

- **Pages**: The pages are grouped under the flow. A single flow can have multiple pages. You use a page to drag and drop various UI components. By default, a page is created under a flow. For example, for the `main` flow, a page is created with the name `main-start`. You can duplicate, delete, or rename a page if required. Right-click on the page name and select the necessary action.

  In order to create a new page, click on the + button next to the flow name (**main**) as shown in *Figure 3.18*. Similar to the application or flow, if you click on the page name (**main-start**), you will see different tabs. The artifacts created under a page are **page-scoped** and can be used within that page only.

  For every page, three different files are created with the names `<page-name>-page.html`, `<page-name>-page.js`, and `<page-name>-page.json`, which contain a description of the page artifacts. Jump to the **Source View** to view all the under-application names.

> **Important Note:**
> The nomenclature of the page name looks as follows: `<flowname>-nameofthepage`. It is better to follow the same nomenclature when you create a new page.

- **Resources**: This folder contains the static resources used in the application. The default structure of the **Resources** folder is created automatically upon the web or mobile application creation. The following folders are created by default under **Resources**:

  a. `components`: This folder is used to keep custom components.

  b. `css`: This folder is used to keep all stylesheet files. VB automatically generates the `app.css` file, which you can use to extend as per your requirements.

    c. `images`: This folder contains two images that are by default used for a favicon. You can use this folder to store the custom images and use these images on the UI component.

    d. `js`: This folder is used to keep external **JavaScript** files.

    e. `strings`: This folder is used to keep translation bundles for the application.

- **Root Pages**: This folder contains a template that is applied on different pages. This template contains a header, footer, and content section that can be modified as per the requirements.

    For a web application, a template is created with the name `shell` but for mobile applications, the template name is `app`. These are basically called the shell of the application.

    You can create more shells as per the requirements. Click on the + button next to **Root Pages** to create a new shell, as shown in *Figure 3.18*.

In this section, we understood the application structure. Let's move on to the next section, where we will discuss various editors and the application designer.

Understanding the various editors and the application designer

As you create different artifacts in web or mobile applications, you will see different options and editors that will help you to view and modify the artifacts and pages. So, it is really important to understand each and every option and the editors that VB provides.

The designer is used to design the application flows, pages, variables, types, Action Chains, JavaScript, and so on. For each and every artifact, you will deal with different editors and options. For example, in order to create a new variable, you have to switch to the variable editor and have to deal with different options. You have access to the source code of artifacts in order to modify them using the code editor.

You can simply switch between different editors by clicking on the different available tabs.

See the following screenshot, which shows different options and editors of the page:

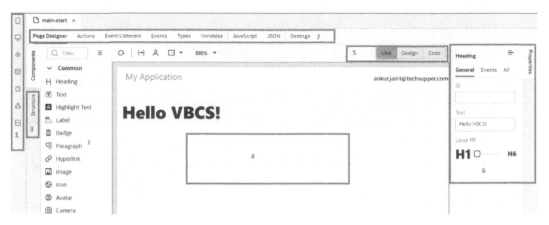

Figure 3.20 – Editors and designers

Now, let's discuss each section:

- **Navigator**: This is used to switch between different Visual Builder building blocks, such as web applications, mobile applications, Business Objects, services, source view, and so on.

- **Components palette**: The **Components** palette is available in the page designer and is fully loaded with a lot of JET components. You use the **Components** palette to drag and drop components onto the page to make it interactive.

- **Structure**: Click on **Structure** to open the structure of the page. This panel opens the page structure, which shows all the components dropped on the page. You can simply drag and drop components from one place to another in order to restructure the page.

- **Page designer**: The page designer canvas is used to drag and drop different components. This is used to compose the layout of the page.

- **Page view**: The page view allows you to switch your pages into **Live**, **Design**, or **Code** view:

  a. The **Design** view shows the design of the page.

  b. The **Code** view will take you to the source code of the page, which you can use to modify the UI components directly, and you can put your logic in here too.

  c. The **Live** view shows the page in live mode in exactly the same way as it will be visible to end users once the application is live. Along with this, you can interact with the page as on how it behaves during runtime, for example, opening popups, clicking on buttons, and so on.

- **Properties palette**: The **Properties** palette will be visible only once you select a component from the page designer view. The properties are different for each and every component. The **Properties** palette is used to set different properties of UI components, such as **ID**, **Text**, **CSS**, and so on.

- **Editors**: There are different editors available that allow us to create or modify different artifacts, as follows:

  a. **Page Designer**: Once open, this will show the designer of the page, which allows you to compose the layout of the page.

  b. **Actions**: This is used to list the available Action Chain, and you can also create a new Action Chain using the actions editor.

  c. **Event Listeners**: This editor is used to list all the life cycle events that are already defined for the selected artifact. You can use this editor to create new events as well.

  d. **Events**: The event editor shows all the custom events that have been created for the selected artifacts, the type of event, and the Action Chain that is kicked off by the event. You can also use this editor to create a new custom event.

  e. **Types**: The type editor lists all the data types previously created for the artifact. This can also be used to create and modify the types.

  f. **Variables**: The variables editor allows us to view all the variables defined in the artifacts. You can use this editor to create a new variable, as well as modifying existing variables.

  g. **JavaScript**: The JavaScript editor allows us to define the JavaScript functions that can be used to call by the Action Chain as well as from UI components. By default, application artifacts use a file named `app-flow.js`, flow artifacts use a file named `<flowname>-flow.js`, and page artifacts use a file named `<pagename>-page.js`.

  h. **JSON**: The JSON editor shows the JSON files where artifact metadata is defined. You can use this editor to modify it manually as per the requirements. By default, application artifacts use a file named `app-flow.json`, flow artifacts use a file named `<flowname>-flow.json`, and page artifacts use a file named `<pagename>-page.json`.

i. **Settings**: The settings section contains various tabs, **General**, **Imports**, and **Translations**, which can be used to change the settings of the page, as shown:

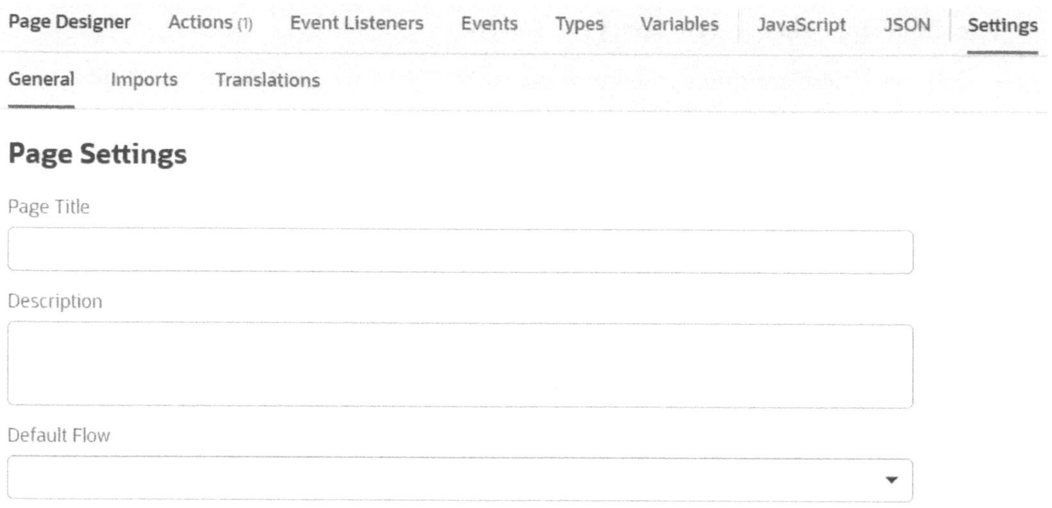

| Page Designer | Actions (1) | Event Listeners | Events | Types | Variables | JavaScript | JSON | Settings |

| General | Imports | Translations |

Page Settings

Page Title

Description

Default Flow

Figure 3.21 – Page settings

You can set various properties of the page, such as **Page Title**, **Description**, and **Default Flow**.

By completing this section, you have learned about different editors and options of the VB application.

Summary

In this chapter, you learned about various building blocks of Visual Builder that will help you to start your journey in Visual Builder. We focused on Business Objects and various options that will allow you to create a Business Object quickly. You learned about Service Connections and the different ways to create a Service Connection. You will now be able to pick the right option when you create a Service Connection.

You learned about variables, types, and their different scopes with a good explanation that will help you to create variables at the right scope. Along with this, you learned about various implicit objects of VB. You also learned about various events, Action Chains, and out-of-the-box actions inside the Action Chain.

At the end, you learned about the default application structure and various folders and files inside the application structure. We explained various editors that will allow you to create different artifacts inside applications. These topics have helped you to learn the basic building blocks of VB and now you are ready to take the next step.

In the next chapter, we will learn how to create Business Objects, how to create business rules, various ways to export and import data into a Business Object, how to explore Business Object REST APIs, and how to switch to a different database.

Questions

1. Can we call Business Object REST APIs from outside Visual Builder?

2. Can we add or modify the Business Object REST APIs?

3. What are the various options available to import bulk data into a Business Object?

4. Are Business Objects and Service Connections reusable components?

5. Can we call the SOAP API using a Service Connection?

6. How can we send email notifications from an Action Chain?

Section 2: Working with Data and Services

The main focus of all the chapters in this section is to explain how to work with data and REST APIs. Without knowing how data is stored in VB and how to communicate with external applications, you cannot build an application because data is the basis of each and every application that exists.

In the first few chapters, you will learn how to manage data within VB and import and export bulk data. We will work with different external REST APIs to communicate with external applications, and then we will start building the web application in the later chapters of this section.

This section comprises the following chapters:

- *Chapter 4, Creating and Managing Business Objects*
- *Chapter 5, Creating and Managing Service Connections*
- *Chapter 6, Building Web Applications Using Real World Examples*
- *Chapter 7, Working with Life Cycle Events, Validations, and UI Logic*

4
Creating and Managing Business Objects

In the previous chapter, we learned about various VB building blocks such as **Business Objects**, **Service Connections**, **Events**, **Action Chains**, and so on. This chapter is dedicated to exploring the functionality of Business Objects, how to create them, how to establish a relationship between Business Objects, various business rules, and Business Object **REST APIs**.

Once you understand how to create a Business Object and how different options that make up the Business Object work together, one of the useful components for a web or mobile application, then you will be able to easily use them. Business Objects are reusable components and once created, they can be used in multiple web or mobile applications.

In this chapter, we will cover the following topics:

- Creating and modifying a Business Object
- Creating business rules in a Business Object
- Managing Business Object data

- Exploring Business Object REST APIs
- Switching to a different database

After completing this chapter, you will be familiar with creating Business Objects, know how to establish a relationship between different Business Objects, know about business rules, know how to create business rules, know various ways to import and export Business Object data, know how the Business Objects REST APIs work, and how to switch an embedded database to point out a different **Oracle database**.

Technical requirements

To complete this chapter, you should have the following:

- A **Visual Builder** cloud instance
- **VB** login credentials
- An **Oracle Autonomous Transaction Processing** database

Creating and modifying a Business Object

Business Objects are used to store transactional data of your application and interactions with Business Objects happen via REST APIs. You cannot use SQL to access the BO; however, you can use the **q** parameter to query the data that is exposed by BO GET REST APIs.

The following sections will help you to create new Business Objects, add custom fields into them, add a formula field, and show you how to create relationships between Business Objects.

Creating a Business Object

In order to create a new Business Object, a VB application must exist. Refer to *Chapter3, Exploring Visual Builder Ingredients*, under the *Creating a VB application* section to learn how to create a VB application. We'll use the same application to create a new Business Object.

The following are the steps to create a new Business Object:

1. Click on the **Business Object** icon from the left-side navigator of the application.
2. Click on the **+** button and select **Business Object** as shown in the following screenshot:

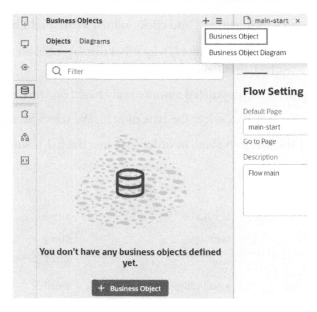

Figure 4.1 – Open the Business Object palette

3. Then, enter `Employee` in the **Label** field and click on the **Create** button. This step will create a Business Object with the name **Employee** in the VB embedded database. When a new Business Object is created, five fields (`id`, `creationDate`, `lastUpdateDate`, `createdBy`, and `lastUpdatedBy`) will be created automatically. You cannot delete or modify the unique names of these fields.

4. After that, switch to the **Fields** tab and click on the **+ Field** button in order to add a new field. A dialog box will be opened as shown in the following screenshot:

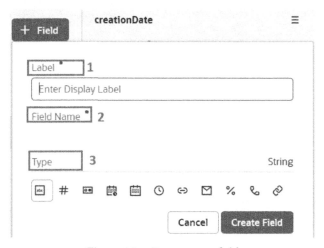

Figure 4.2 – Create a new field

5. Then, enter the following details and click on the **Create Field** button:

a. **Label**: Enter the name of the field, which is a display label for the field. Enter First Name in the **Label** field.

b. **Field Name**: It will be populated automatically based on the **Label** being **firstName**.

c. **Type**: This allows you to select the type of field. We select **String** for **First Name**.

We will repeat the previous steps in order to create the fields shown in the following table:

Label	Field Name	Type
First Name	firstName	String
Last Name	lastName	String
Age	Age	Number
Email Address	emailAddress	Email
Qualification	qualification	String
Contact Number	contactNumber	String
Full Name	fullName	String

Table 4.1 – Employee Business Object fields

6. Once the Business Object is created, it will look as shown in the following screenshot:

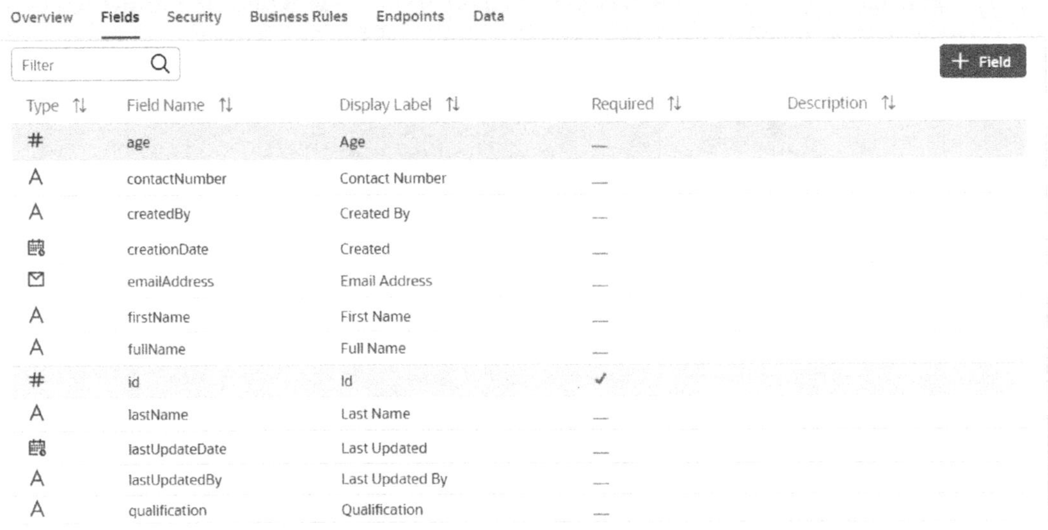

Overview	**Fields**	Security	Business Rules	Endpoints	Data

Type ↑↓	Field Name ↑↓	Display Label ↑↓	Required ↑↓	Description ↑↓
#	age	Age	—	
A	contactNumber	Contact Number	—	
A	createdBy	Created By	—	
🗓	creationDate	Created	—	
✉	emailAddress	Email Address	—	
A	firstName	First Name	—	
A	fullName	Full Name	—	
#	id	Id	✓	
A	lastName	Last Name	—	
🗓	lastUpdateDate	Last Updated	—	
A	lastUpdatedBy	Last Updated By	—	
A	qualification	Qualification	—	

Figure 4.3 – A Business Object

As you can see, the previous screenshot shows you the Business Object in tabular format with the type of the field, the name of the field, the display label, the required field, and a description of the field. Similarly, you can create more and more Business Objects.

Modifying a Business Object

Once a Business Object is created, you can delete and update the field properties also. Click on the field whose properties you want to update. A field properties palette will be visible on the right side, which will allow you to update the selected field property.

The following screenshot shows the property palette of the selected field:

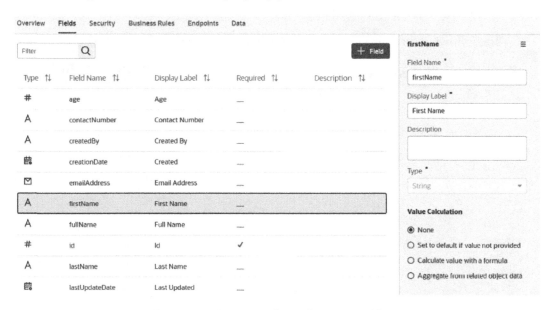

Figure 4.4 – Property palette of a Business Object

The properties available in the property palette depend on the data type of the selected field. You cannot update the data type of a field once created.

Adding a formula to a field

You can modify a field of a Business Object to add a formula.

For example, in order to save the full name of an employee in the **Full Name** field, you can create a formula in the **Full Name** field to store values such as `first name+' '+last name`. Similarly, you can create a formula to calculate a salary based on experience.

The following are the steps to create a formula in a field. Here, we are creating a formula in the **Full Name** field:

1. Go to the **Fields** tab of the Employee Business Object.

2. Click on the **Full Name** field to open the property palette.

3. Click on the **Calculate value with a formula** radio button under the **Value Calculation** section. This action will open the **Field Formula** dialog box.

4. You can drag and drop fields from the left panel to the designer page to create an expression. Add the following expression and click on the **OK** button:

```
firstName+' '+lastName
```

The following screenshot shows the expression to create the formula field:

Figure 4.5 – Creating a formula field

By doing so, the **Full Name** field will be populated automatically with *first name + last name* separated by a single space when a new row is added to a Business Object.

Creating a relationship between Business Objects

A relationship shows the **primary** and **foreign** key relationship between two or more Business Objects. In order to create a relationship, at least two Business Objects must exist in the same VB application.

When you create a new field, you can refer to a Business Object in order to create a new relationship using the `Reference` data type.

I have created a new Business Object called **Address** with the following fields to show the relationship between two Business Objects:

Label	Field Name	Type
Address1	address1	String
Address2	address2	String
City	city	String
State	state	String
Country	country	String
Zip Code	zipCode	Number
Employee Id	employeeId	Reference

Table 4.2 – Address Business Object fields

The following screenshot shows how to refer to another Business Object while creating the new field. Click the Reference data type, select the Business Object from the **Referenced Business Object** dropdown, and select **Id** from the **Display Field** dropdown:

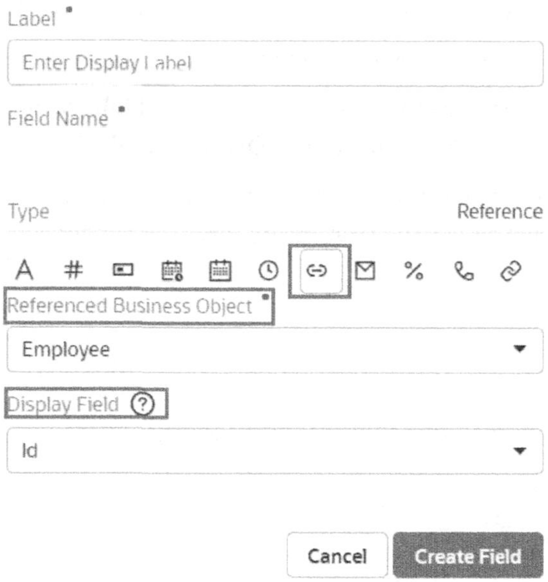

Figure 4.6 – Creating a new field to refer to a Business Object

Once a field is created having the reference of a Business Object, by default a *many-to-one* relationship will be created. This relationship shows that an employee can have many addresses. The relationship can be seen in the **Overview** tab of the Business Object under the **Relationships** section, as shown in the following screenshot:

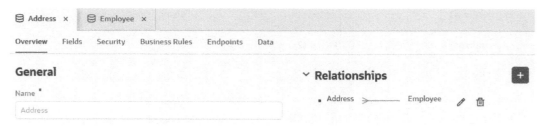

Figure 4.7 – Relationship between two Business Objects

The following are the steps in order to create an additional relationship:

1. Click on the + icon under the **Relationships** section. It will open the **Create Relationship** dialog box.

2. Select the cardinality (**Many** or **One**) for each object.

3. From the opened dialog box, you can perform the following actions but for the time being keep everything as it is:

    a. Reverse the relationship between one-to-many and many-to-one. Use **Reverse Relationship** to reverse the relationship.

    b. Create one-to-one and many-to-many cardinality.

4. Update the properties of the relationship such as **Field Name**, **Display Label**, the **Required** checkbox, **Delete Rule**, and **Display Field**.

5. Then, click on the **Create Relationship** button, as shown in the following screenshot, which shows the relationship properties between two Business Objects:

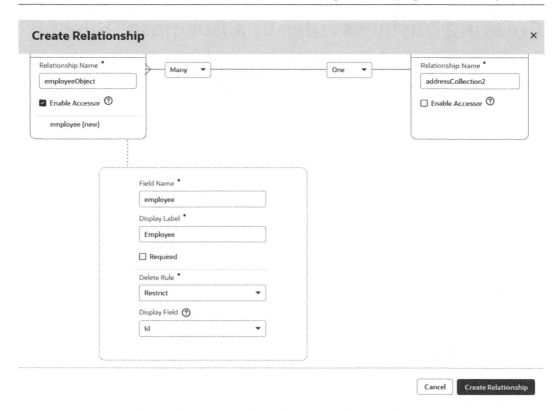

Figure 4.8 – Create a relationship between Business Objects

Once a new relationship is defined, it will be visible under the **Relationships** section showing all the Business Objects taken to define a new relationship. You can edit or delete a relationship if required.

In this section, we learned about creating and modifying a Business Object as well as adding a formula to a field. We also learned about creating a relationship between Business Objects.

After creating and modifying Business Objects, we will look at how to create business rules in a Business Object.

Creating business rules in a Business Object

Business rules are like constraints that can be defined on Business Objects declaratively. These business rules are similar to the triggers, constraints, and validations that are created on database tables. Similarly, we can define all those business rules on Business Objects too. Click on the **Business Rules** tab of a Business Object to view or create a new business rule.

The following types of business rules can be created on a Business Object:

- **Object Triggers**
- **Field Triggers**
- **Object Validators**
- **Field Validators**
- **Object Functions**

We will look at all the preceding types of business rules in the following sections.

Creating Object Triggers

An Object Trigger is like a database trigger. For example, you want to send an email notification to an employee once a new entry is made on the Employee Business Object.

To meet this requirement, you can create an **Object Trigger** on the Employee Business Object; this will always execute, and send an email to the employee's email addresses.

These are the steps to create an Object Trigger:

1. Open the **Employee** Business Object, click the **Business Rules** tab, and click on the **Object Triggers** icon in the left panel.
2. Then, click on **+ New Object Trigger** as shown in the following screenshot:

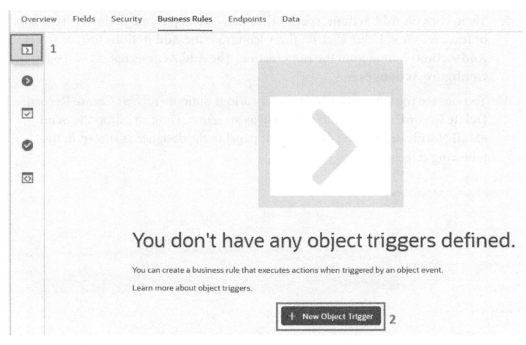

Figure 4.9 – Create a new Object Trigger

3.   After clicking on the **+ New Object Trigger** button, the **Create Object Trigger** dialog box will open. Enter the following information in the opened dialog box, and click on the **Create Object Trigger** button:

a. In the **Trigger Name** field, enter `SendEmail`.

b. In the **Description** field, enter `An email notification will be sent once an employee is created`.

c. In the **Start Event** field, you have a choice to select one of **Before Insert**, **Before Update**, or **Before Delete**. For this case, select **Before Insert** as we want to send an email before inserting the record into the Business Object.

4.   On the **Trigger Designer** page, click the + icon to define a new criterion. Once you have chosen the + icon, you may select one of the following (choose **Always Execute** for this case, as we always want to send an email to an employee):

a. **Execute Conditionally**: Using this criterion, you can set a condition basis on which a defined action will be executed.

b. **Always Execute**: If you select this, the defined action will always be executed.

c. **Custom Code**: This allows you to create the Groovy script to execute.

5. Then, click on **Add Actions**, specify the **Action Group Name** in the right section or leave it as it is. Either click on the + icon from the **Add Actions** box, or select the **Add Actions** button from the right section. The **Add Actions** option will open the **Configure Actions** page.

6. You can see the left panel, which shows various options (such as **Create Record**, **Delete Record**, and so on) to add them as an action. Drag and drop the **Send eMail Notification** action from the left panel to the designer as shown in the following screenshot:

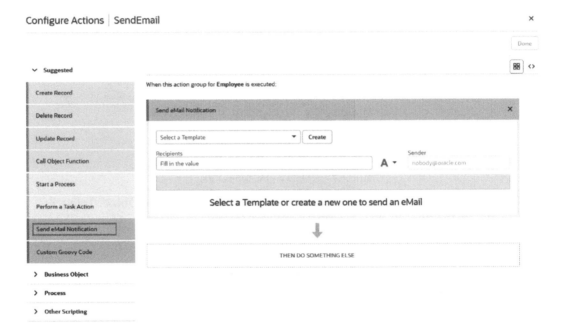

Figure 4.10 – Define the action

7. Click on the **Create** button aligned with **Select a Template**. This option allows you to create a template of email notifications. You can choose either **Save as new Template** to save this template to use for future purposes, or **Save for this Action only**. Choose **Save for this Action only** in this case.

8. Enter Employee Created Successfully as the **Subject and Body** input text and the other body information. Then, click on the **Insert Parameter** icon to set any value dynamically. Click on the **Save** button as shown in the following screenshot:

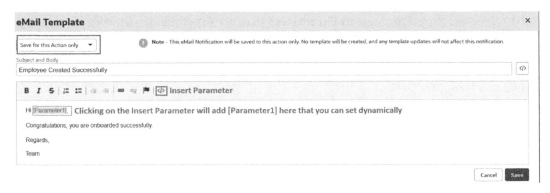

Figure 4.11 – Define the email template

As you can see in the preceding screenshot, here is the body we entered in the body section of the email template:

```
Hi [Parameter1],
Congratulations, you are onboarded successfully.
Regards,
Team
```

9. Now, expand the dropdown right to **Recipients** and select **Expression**. From the left panel, drag and drop **Email Address** as shown in the following screenshot and click on the **OK** button:

Figure 4.12 – Define the recipients

10. Click the dropdown next to **Parameter1** in order to set the dynamic value of **Parameter1**, and select **First Name** as shown in the following screenshot. Click the **Done** button to close the **Configure Actions** designer:

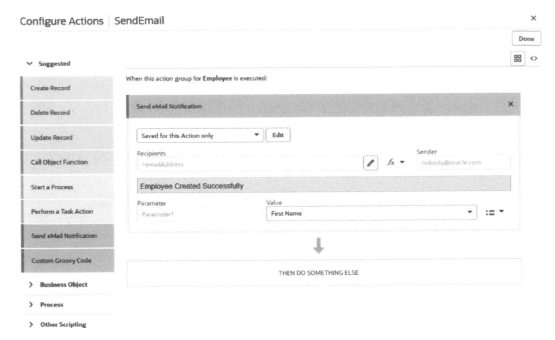

Figure 4.13 – Define the value of Parameter1

11. Click on **Object Triggers** to return to the main page. By default, the trigger will be activated. Uncheck the **Active** checkbox to disable the trigger. Select the **Action** icon to **Edit**, **Copy**, **Delete**, or **Deactivate** the trigger as shown here:

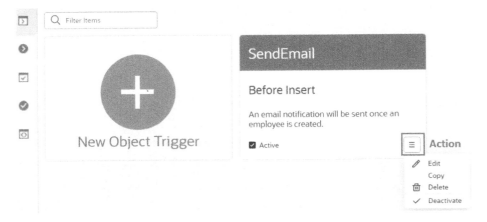

Figure 4.14 – Object Trigger

12. Lastly, click on **New Object Trigger** to create a new Object Trigger.

In order to test the Object Trigger, switch to the **Data** tab, add a new row, and check your email address entered in the **Email Address** field. You should get an email notification.

Creating Field Triggers

Similar to an Object Trigger, you can create a field-level trigger. This is used to define field-level conditions that apply whenever the field changes the value in the Business Object.

We have created another Business Object, **Expense**, in order to show how to create a Field Trigger. The following are the fields created in the **Expense** Business Object:

Label	Field Name	Type
Amount	amount	Number
Subject	subject	String
Description	description	String
Employee Id	employeeId	Reference (refer to the Employee Object object)
Approved	approved	Boolean

Table 4.3 – Expense Business Object fields

We'll create the field trigger on the **Amount** field of the Expense Business Object. We'll add two conditions on the field trigger as follows:

1. If **Amount** is less than 100, then update the **Approved** field value to `true`.

2. If **Amount** is greater than or equal to 100, then update the **Approved** field value to `false`.

The following are the steps to create a **Field Trigger**:

1. Open the **Expense** Business Object and click on the **Business Rules** tab.

2. Click on the **Field Triggers** icon in the left panel.

3. Click on the **+ New Field Trigger** button.

4. From the **Created Field Trigger** dialog box, enter the following information and click on the **Create Field Trigger** button:

    a. In the **Trigger Name*** field, enter `Approval Trigger`.

    b. In the **Field*** field, select **Amount**.

5. On the **Trigger Designer** page, click the + icon to define a new criterion. Choose **Execute Conditionally**.

6. Select **Execute Conditionally**, change **Criteria Name** to `Amount is less than 100`, and click on the **Add Conditions** button as shown here:

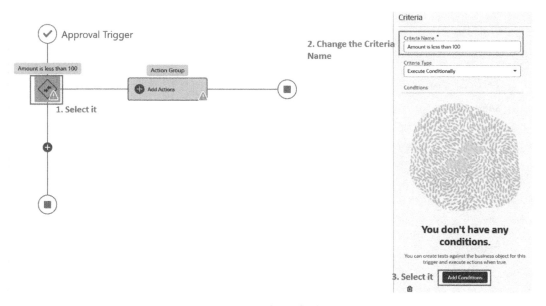

Figure 4.15 – Define a field trigger

7. The **Add Condition** button action will open the **Build Conditions** page. Configure the following information and click on the **Done** button:

    a. Select **Amount** as a field.

    b. Select **less than** as an operator.

    c. Enter `100` as a value.

The following screenshot shows the configuration of the **Build Conditions** page:

Build Conditions | Approval Trigger   ×

Done

Match All   Match Any

IF   Amount ▼   less than ▼   100   A ▼   🗑

Add Condition   Add Group

Figure 4.16 – Build condition of the field trigger

8. Then, click on **Add Actions**, specify **Action Group Name** in the right section or leave it as it is. Either click on the + icon from the **Add Actions** box or select the **Add Actions** button from the right section. This option will open the **Configure Actions** page.

9. Drag and drop **Update Record** from the left panel to the designer. Select the **Expense** Business Object from the **Data to Update** dropdown, select the **Approved** field from the **Value Updates** field, select **true** as a value, and click the **Done** button. We can see this configuration on the **Configure Actions** designer page, shown here:

Configure Actions | Approval Trigger   >

5. Click Done button   Done

∨ Suggested

Create Record

Delete Record

Update Record   1. Drag and drop it on
                 designer

Call Object Function

Start a Process

Perform a Task Action

Send eMail Notification

Custom Groovy Code

> **Business Object**

When this action group for **Expenses** is executed:

Update Record   ×

Data to Update
Expenses   2. Select the Expense Business object

Value Updates
Approved ▼   true 4. Select the true value ▼   A ▼   ×
3. Select the Approved field
Add Value Update

⬇

THEN DO SOMETHING ELSE

Figure 4.17 – Configure action of the field trigger

10. Repeat the previous five steps, from *step 5* to *step 9*, to add one more action, **Amount is greater than or equals to 100**, then update the **Approved** field with the **false** value. The following screenshot shows the Field Trigger designer page after the final configuration:

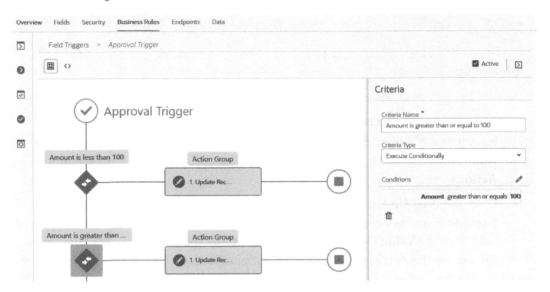

Figure 4.18 – Configure action of the Field Trigger

In order to test the Field Trigger, switch to the **Data** tab, add rows, and see that the **Approved** field values should be updated automatically based on the **Amount** you enter.

Creating Object Validators

Object Validators specify validation on the object level. The specified validations are enforced when we try to add data to an object.

The conditions that are specified must return a true value that will indicate the object is valid. You can specify more than one condition on an object, and if all validation evaluates to true then only data will be saved in an object, otherwise, the specified error message will be returned.

We'll add an Object Validator on the **Expense** Business Object, which will force you to enter an amount between 1 and 500 only. The following are the steps to create **Object Validators**:

1. Open the **Business Rules** tab of the **Expense** Business Object, select the **Object Validators** icon from the left panel, and click on the + **New Object Validator** button.

2. From the **Create Object Validator** dialog box, enter the following information and click on the **Create Object Validator** button:

a. Enter `Amount validator` in the **Validator Name** field.

b. Enter `The amount must be between 1 to 500` in the **Error Message** field.

3. From the designer, drag and drop **amount** from the left panel and make or write the condition `amount > 0 && amount <= 500` as shown in the following screenshot:

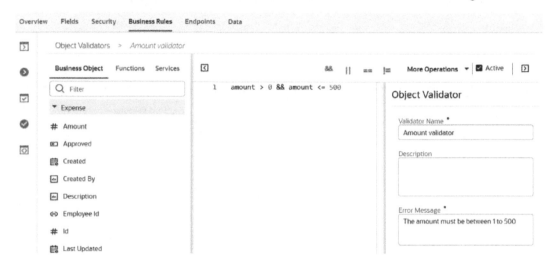

Figure 4.19 – Configure a condition for the object validator

4. Click on **Object Validators** to return to the **Object Validators** page.

In order to test the Object Validator, switch to the **Data** tab and add rows. Enter an amount beyond the limit and you'll see that you will not be allowed to save the object. You will see an error message in the **Add row** dialog box.

Creating Field Validators

Similar to Object Validators, Field Validators are used to specify validation on custom fields of an object. The conditions that are specified must return a true value.

We'll create a Field Validator on the **Age** field of the **Employee** Business Object to check if *age >= 18*. If it is, then we'll only create a record. We take the following steps to create **Field Validators**:

1. Open the **Business Rules** tab of the **Employee** Business Object, select the **Field Validators** icon from the left panel, and click on the + **New Field Validator** button.

2. From the **Create Field Validator** dialog box, enter the following information, and click on the **Create Field Validator** button:

    a. We enter `Age Validator` in the **Validator Name** field.

    b. Select **Age** from the **Field** field.

    c. Enter `Age must be greater or equal to 18` in the **Error Message** field.

3. From the designer, drag and drop **newValue** from the left panel, and create the condition `newValue>=18` as shown in the following screenshot:

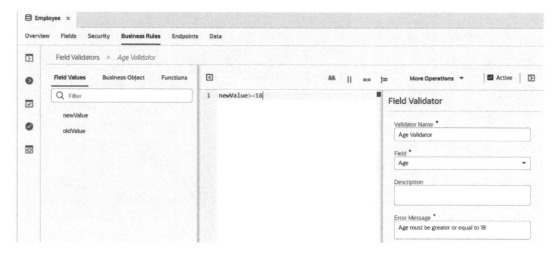

Figure 4.20 – Configure a condition for a trigger validator

4. Click on **Field Validators** to return to the **Field Validators** page.

In order to test the Field Validator, switch to the **Data** tab, and add a row. Try to enter an amount of less than 18 and notice an error in the **Add row** dialog box itself.

Creating Object Functions

An Object Function is used to write custom logic for a specific Business Object. The Object Function we defined inside the Business Object can be used by other object functions related to the Business Object.

Once an object function is created, it can be called by an external system if the **Callable by External System** property is enabled for an Object Function. This property exposes the function as a REST endpoint. If this property is not enabled, then the REST endpoint will not be exposed and the function can be called with the function name by another script.

For the demonstration purposes, we'll create an Object Function on the **Employee** Business Object that will return a count of users based on their first name. We follow these steps in order to create an Object Function:

1. Open the **Business Rules** tab of the **Employee** Business Object, select the **Object Functions** icon from the left panel, and click on the **+ New Object Function** button.

2. Enter the function name as `TotalUsers` and click on the **Create Object Function** button. You will land on the **Object Function** designer page.

3. You can choose the function return type of the Object Function from the available list. Select the **Long** data type from the **Function Return Type** dropdown in the right panel.

4. Select the **Callable by External System** property checkbox from the right panel as per the following screenshot:

Figure 4.21 – Configure the Object Function

5. Click on **PARAMETERS** in order to create input parameters. Click on the **Add Parameter** button and add one parameter called `name` of the `String` type. The parameters need to pass in the JSON payload while testing the Object Function.

6. Enter the following Groovy script to get the total users:

```
def vo = newView('Employee');
vo.appendViewCriteria("firstName ='"+name+"'");
vo.executeQuery();
    def totalUsers = 0
    while (vo.hasNext()) {
        vo.next()
        totalUsers = totalUsers + 1
    }
    return totalUsers;
```

In the preceding script, the first line creates a variable (vo) that holds the reference of the **Employee** Business Object. In the second line, a new view criterion is added that will work as a **where** clause. The third line executes the view object query. The next few lines hold the logic to count the total users.

In order to test the function, switch to the **Endpoints** tab and you should see a new endpoint visible under the **Endpoint** section. Whenever you create an Object Function, it will be exposed as **POST** and you need to pass a primary ID as the path parameter.

The following screenshot shows the endpoint of the Object Function:

Figure 4.22 – Object Function endpoint

Click on the **Endpoint**, switch to the **Test** tab, and in the **Body** section, enter the following JSON and pass any valid primary ID in the path `Employee_Id` parameter under the **URL Parameter** tab:

```
{
    "name":"Ankur"
}
```

The following screenshot shows the test case of the Object Function endpoint:

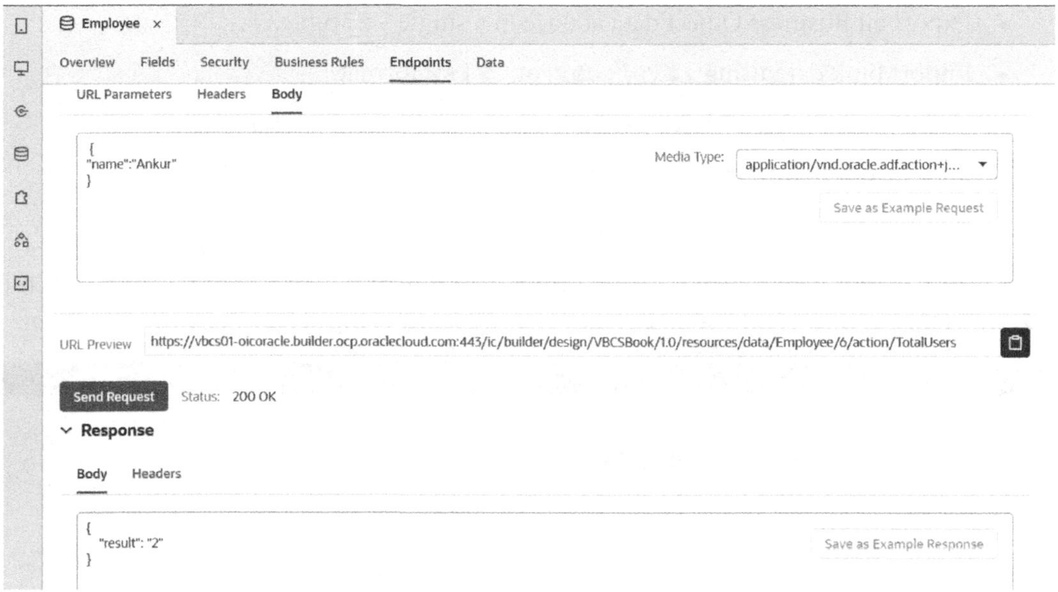

Figure 4.23 – Test the object function

Refer to the documentation to learn more about Groovy script: `https://docs.oracle.com/en/cloud/paas/app-builder-cloud/visual-builder-groovy/groovy-tips-and-techniques.html`.

In this section, we learned about the creation of Object Triggers, Field Triggers, Object Validators, Field Validators, and Object Functions.

After creating the different business rules in a Business Object, next, we'll look at various tools to manage Business Object data.

Managing Business Object data

Data management is one of the crucial parts of each and every application as we may need to export or import data in bulk using a file mechanism or sometimes between different schemas or databases.

Visual Builder provides a rich tool out of the box called **Data Manager**, which helps us to manage Business Object data. Every VB application has three different phases (**development**, **staging**, and **live**) and each phase has an independent database. You may need to manage data between three phases, such as importing data from live to staging, live to development, or importing bulk data into a Business Object, and so on. You can use the Data Manager to manage data in all phases.

The capabilities of the Data Manager are as follows:

- Export all Business Object data at once in a single `.zip` file.

- Import bulk data using `.zip`, `.csv`, or `.xlsx` format.

- Create new Business Objects using `.zip`, `.csv`, or `.xlsx` format.

- Replace development data with live data.

- Replace development data with staging data or vice versa.

To access the Data Manager, click on the **Business Objects** icon in the left panel, select the **Options** menu, and select **Data Manager** as per the following screenshot:

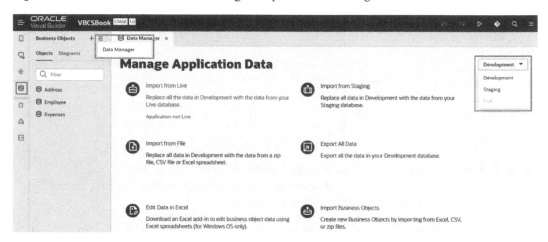

Figure 4.24 – Open the Data Manager

Once you click on **Data Manager**, it will show all the tools of the Data Manager. As you can see from the preceding screenshot, there's a dropdown in the top-right corner. This dropdown contains the VB application phase values: **Development**, **Staging**, and **Live**.

The option values are enabled depending on the current phase of the application. For example, if the current phase of the application is **Staging**, then only current and previous phase option values will be enabled, and you will be able to manage the data of those phases.

The next section will describe all the available tools of the Data Manager.

Exporting bulk data

To export bulk data of a Business Object, you can use the **Export All Data** tool of the Data Manager. **Export All Data** allows us to export the data of all Business Objects in a single `.zip` file. It creates a separate `.csv` file of each Business Object and zips all of them.

In order to export all data, execute the following steps:

1. Open **Data Manager**.

2. Select the application phase value from the dropdown for which data needs to be exported.

> **Important Note:**
>
> If you want to export the data of an individual Business Object, go to the **Data** tab of the Business Object, and use the export icon to export the data of the particular Business Object.

3. Click on the **Export All Data** option. Once clicked, it will download a .zip file having a separate CSV file of each Business Object.

Importing bulk data

The **Import from File** tool of the Data Manager allows you to replace the data of one or multiple Business Objects at once. You can either upload a .zip (containing single or multiple CSVs or spreadsheet files), .csv, or .xlsx file to upload the data into the Business Objects.

If you are using a .csv file to upload the data, make sure the name of the .csv file is the same as the Business Object name.

An Excel spreadsheet can also be used to import data into multiple Business Objects. An Excel spreadsheet can contain multiple sheets and the name of each sheet must match with the Business Object name.

> **Important Note:**
>
> When you import bulk data via the Data Manager, it replaces the existing data with the data being imported. So, import data safely.

In order to import bulk data, execute the following steps:

1. Open **Data Manager**.

2. Select the application phase in which data needs to be imported.

3. Click the **Import from File** option.

4. Upload or drag a .zip, .csv, or an Excel file from the opened dialog box.

5. Once a file is selected, click on the **Import** button.

6. Once the data is imported, it will show a successful message, as per the following screenshot:

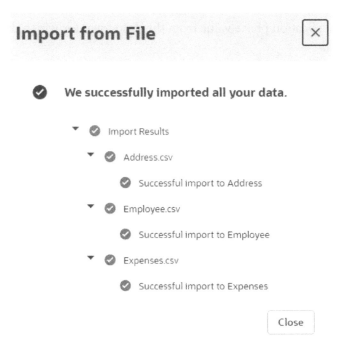

Figure 4.25 – Data imported successfully

This is how you can import more and more data into Business Objects. You can also invoke the import/export functionality from outside VB using REST commands. Follow the Oracle document to see how to import/export from outside VB: `https://docs.oracle.com/en/cloud/paas/app-builder-cloud/visual-builder-developer/manage-application-data.html#GUID-7A613AE1-C747-4BA5-824F-F196F6C60D89`.

Importing data from a different database

The Data Manager allows you to import data between different database schemas. You can replace development data from staging or vice versa. You can also replace live data from the development database or vice versa.

In order to replace development data from live data, perform the steps that follow:

1. Open **Data Manager**.

2. Considering we have selected the development phase from the dropdown and the application is in the live phase, select **Import from Live**.

3. Select the **Import** button in order to replace data.

4. Once the data is imported successfully, you will get a confirmation dialog box.

This is how we import data from different databases.

Importing a Business Object

The Data Manager allows you to create Business Objects using a .csv file or an Excel spreadsheet. The **Import Business Object** tool of Data Manager allows you to create Business Objects.

When you use a .csv file to create a Business Object, the Business Object is created with the same name as the .csv file, and fields mentioned in the file will also be created. Even if there is any data in the .csv file, then data will also be imported.

When you use a spreadsheet to create Business Objects, the number of Business Objects created depends on the number of worksheets in the spreadsheet. If there are two worksheets, then two Business Objects will be created with the same name as the worksheet name along with fields.

You can also upload a .zip file in order to import multiple Business Objects.

Considering there is an Excel file with the name Inventory Details, the details are shown as follows:

Name	Quantity	Emloyee Id	Description
Laptop	1	1	One Dell Laptop
Mouse	2	1	One wired and one wireless
Keyboard	1	2	Wired Keyboard
Headphone	1	2	One dell headset issued

Table 4.4 – Sample data in the Inventory Details file

The following are the steps to import a Business Object:

1. Click on **Import Business Objects** from the Data Manager.

2. Select or drop the `Inventory Details` file. Once selected, the dialog box will show that the Business Object is imported successfully along with the number of records, as shown in the following screenshot. Then, click on the **Next** button:

Figure 4.26 – Import the Business Object

3. The next screen will show you a list of the Business Objects that have been created. You can change the object name or deselect the filename that you don't want to use to create the Business Object. Then, click on the **Next** button to move ahead.

4. The next screen will allow you to modify **Field Name**, **Display Label**, **Type**, and **Required**. As per the following screenshot, I have modified the type of **Employee Id** as **Reference** and pointed to the **Employee** object:

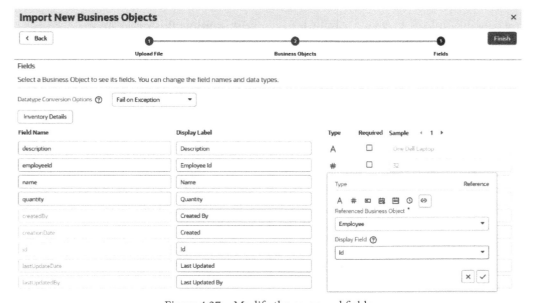

Figure 4.27 – Modify the name and fields

5. Click on the **Finish** button to import the Business Object. Once imported successfully, it will show you a successful message.

In this section, we learned about the business object Data Manager and its capabilities. We learned how to use the Data Manager to import and export bulk data via the Data Manager. Along with this, we learned about importing data from one database to another and how to import Business Objects from files.

We also learned about the various tools to manage Business Object data. Next, we'll explore Business Object REST APIs.

Exploring Business Object REST APIs

The best part of **Oracle VB** is that, apart from creating the UI, it also creates the backend of applications. For every Business Object we create, VB generates REST endpoints automatically. The communication between the UI and Business Objects happens via REST endpoints only. These REST endpoints are not limited to internal use for VB applications; the exposed REST APIs can be used by external systems too. So, if any external system wants to push data into a Business Object, then this can be easily achieved with the help of REST APIs.

> **Important Note:**
> All Business Object REST APIs are secured via **Basic Authentication** by default.

In order to view all the Business Object REST endpoints, switch to the **Endpoints** tab of the Business Object.

The following screenshot shows the REST endpoints of the **Employee** Business Object:

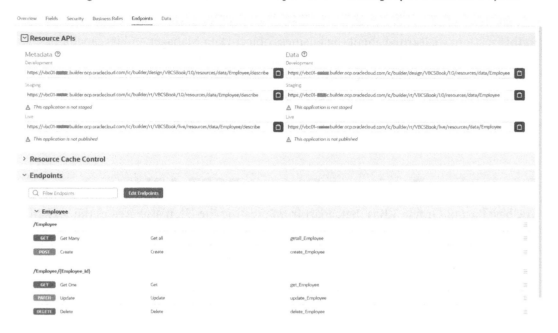

Figure 4.28 – Endpoints of the Business Object

The Business Object also exposes the endpoints to extract metadata as well as the data of the Business Object.

In the following sections, we'll see an explanation of the sections of the **Endpoints** tab, which are listed as follows:

- **Resource APIs**
- **Resource Cache Control**
- **Endpoints**

We'll begin by looking at the Resource APIs section.

Resource APIs

The Resource APIs of Business Objects allow us to retrieve Business Object metadata and data. REST endpoints are different for each phase of the VB application.

In order to test the metadata URL, copy the development metadata URLs from the **Resource APIs** section and hit it using the **POSTMAN** tool. Refer to https://www.postman.com/ to read about Postman.

The following screenshot shows the response of the metadata API:

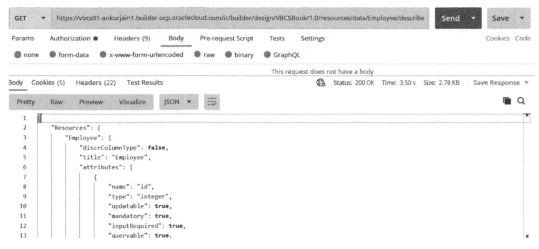

Figure 4.29 – Test the metadata URL

Similarly, you can use **Data** APIs to retrieve the data of a Business Object.

Resource Cache Control

The Resource Cache Control allows us to cache Business Object data into the browser cache to enhance the performance of the application. By default, the cache is disabled for each and every Business Object for security purposes.

Endpoints

The **Endpoints** section lists all the available endpoints of a Business Object. By default, every Business Object has the following endpoints:

- **Get Many**: This is the **GET** endpoint and it's used to retrieve the data from a Business Object.

- **Create**: This is the **POST** endpoint and it's used to create a record in a Business Object.

- **Get One**: This is the **GET** endpoint and it's used to retrieve a single record basis on the primary ID.

- **Update**: This is the **PATCH** endpoint and it's used to update the record basis on the primary ID.

- **Delete**: This is the **DELETE** endpoint and it's used to delete a single record basis on the primary ID.

If a Business Object refers to other Business Objects, you can view other endpoints that allow you to retrieve, create, delete, and update those Business Objects' data.

The following screenshot shows the endpoints available for the **Address** Business Object, which is referring to the **Employee** Business Object:

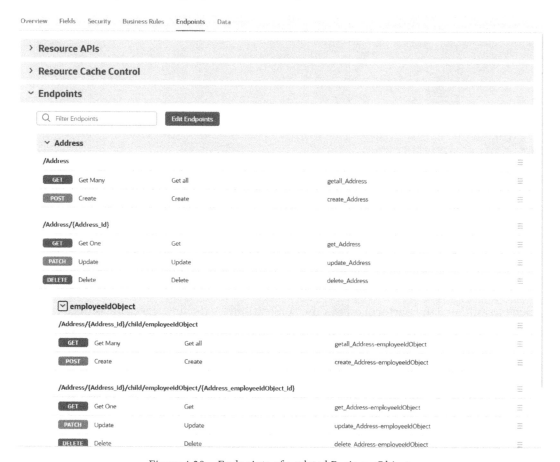

Figure 4.30 – Endpoints of a related Business Object

You can click on an endpoint to view the details of the endpoint, such as settings, request, response, header details, and so on, but in read-only mode. You can click on **Test** in order to test an endpoint.

> **Important Note:**
> The **GET** endpoints of a Business Object support the **query** parameter, which can be used to filter records.

In this section, we explored the Business Object resources API and REST APIs. We tested the metadata API using Postman to get the business object metadata.

Next, we'll look at how to switch from an embedded database to a different database. While working with the BO REST endpoints, you can explore the Oracle document that gives information on possible parameters, content-type setting, and more: `https://docs.oracle.com/en/cloud/paas/app-builder-cloud/consume-rest/index.html`

Switching to a different database

As mentioned in *Chapter 2, Provisioning and Understanding the Visual Builder Instance*, in the *Tenant Database* section, VB comes with an embedded database that can be used to manage the data in your VB application. VB allows us to switch the embedded database with other Oracle databases.

The following are the steps to switch the embedded database with **Oracle ATP** database:

1. Go to the **VB Settings** page and open the **General** tab.

2. Click on **Use Different Database** button under the **Tenant Database** section.

3. Configure the following options and click on the **Next** button:

Label	Value	Description
Connection Type	Oracle Autonomous Transaction Processing Cloud Wallet	
Upload Wallet	Wallet_atpdb.zip	Upload or drag the wallet
Wallet Password	Enterpassword	Enter the wallet password
TNS Name	atpdb_low	TNS name will be populated automatically from the wallet. Select either one.
DBA User name	admin	Enter a user who has dba privileges
Password	Enterpassword	Enter user password

Table 4.5 – Information entered for the ATP database

The following screenshot shows the preceding database information we entered:

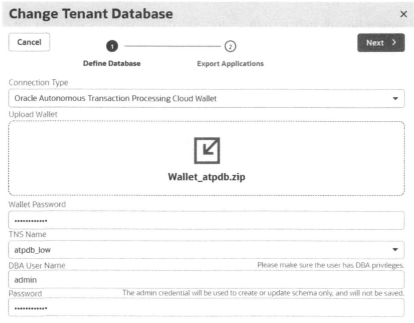

Figure. 4.31 – Switch to a different database

4.   If the connection is verified, the wizard allows you to move to the next screen:

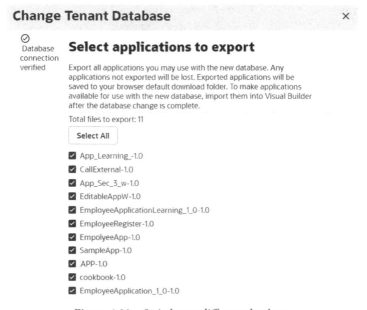

Figure 4.32 – Switch to a different database

When you switch the database, it will allow you to select the applications to export. Any application that is not exported will be lost. Once you click on the **Finish** button, all the selected applications will be exported and will be saved on your local drive. All the applications will be exported into an individual .zip file.

Once the database is switched successfully, you will see a confirmation dialog box as per the following screenshot:

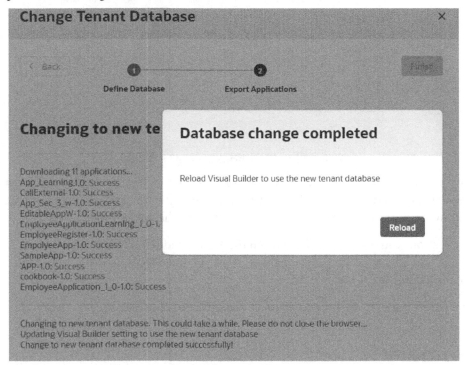

Figure 4.33 – Database change completed

5. After the database is switched, all the applications will be deleted from VB and you will have to import all exported applications one by one from your local drive.

In the target database, you will see a separate schema for individual applications with the prefix VB_ followed by a random string. You have to find out which schema is used for which application. For example, if you have two applications in VB, two separate schemas will be created in the target database.

> **Important Note:**
> The separate schemas will be created for each phase (dev, stage, and live) of an application.

The following screenshot shows the schema `VB_VB_RC8LIRHRSEJ` created for one of the VB applications:

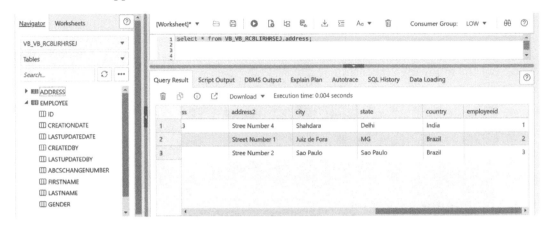

Figure 4.34 – The schema in the ATP database

Every time you create a new version of the application, a new schema will be re-created for the dev and test instances. For the live application, the schema can be as it is when you specify not to replace data while changing the stage of the application.

In this section, you learned how to switch the VB embedded database with the ATP database, and after switching the database, what you need to do in order to use the destination database.

We have now understood how to connect to a different database.

Summary

In this chapter, you learned about all the functionalities of Business Objects in detail with concrete examples. Now you will be able to create different Business Objects and modify them as per your application requirement. You will also be able to create a relationship between different Business Objects as required.

You also learned about business rules in detail and how to create various business rules such as Object Triggers, Field Triggers, Object Validators, Field Validators, and Object Functions with a good explanation and examples.

You learned about using the Data Manager tool to manage Business Object data. Now you will be able to import and export bulk data into Business Objects using `.csv` files and spreadsheets. You now have the skills to replace data between different database schemas.

You also saw the different REST endpoints of a Business Object such as the metadata and data APIs. You learned about the REST endpoints available for each Business Object. You now have the skills to switch the embedded database with the ATP database.

In the next chapter, you will learn how to create a service connection using an endpoint, define by specification, and catalog options. You will also learn how to add backend servers and manage different application profiles pointed to by different backend servers.

Questions

1. Can we change the data type of the Business Object field after it is added?

2. Can we delete Business Object fields that are created automatically?

3. Can we change the primary key of a Business Object?

4. Can we add custom endpoints in a Business Object?

5. Can we add or delete endpoints?

6. Are Business Objects accessible outside the VB application?

7. Once the embedded database is switched to point to a different database, can we revert the changes?

5

Creating and Managing Service Connections

In the previous chapter, you learned about Business Objects, how to create and modify Business Objects, add formula fields, add relationships between Business Objects, create different business rules, and manage Business Object data. You explored various Business Object endpoints, how to use them, and how to switch embedded VB databases to point to the ATP database.

This chapter will focus on Service Connections, which is one of the main components that help us to call external REST APIs. Refer to *Chapter 3*, *Exploring Visual Builder Ingredients*, under the *Exploring Service Connections* section, to learn about Service Connections where we have explained this in detail. In this chapter, you will learn how to create Service Connections, manage Service Connections, and how to consume different types of REST API.

In this chapter, we will cover the following topics:

- Managing backends in visual applications
- Creating application profiles
- Creating a Service Connection from a REST endpoint

- Creating a Service Connection from a service specification
- Creating a Service Connection using an inbuilt catalog
- Managing Service Connections

After completing this chapter, you will be familiar with how to create a Service Connection with external REST APIs, how to establish a Service Connection with Oracle SaaS, and how to create a Service Connection with Integration Cloud, as well as how to manage backend servers, create application profiles, and configure authentication for Service Connections. All aspects of Service Connections are covered in this chapter.

Technical requirements

To complete this chapter, you will require the following:

- A **Visual Builder** instance
- **VB** login credentials
- Public REST APIs
- **Oracle Cloud Application** credentials
- **Integration Cloud Application** credentials

Managing backends in visual applications

A backend is a collection of servers that we use to access backend REST APIs from visual applications. These backends are **Integration Applications**, **Oracle Cloud Applications**, **Processes**, and **Custom backends**. You can refer to *Chapter 2, Provisioning and Understanding the Visual Builder Instance*, in the *Exploring various navigations of VB:* section, under the *Settings* section, to see how to add backends.

Let's understand the different terminology that is used to describe backends:

- **Backends**: Backends represent the applications, such as Integration Applications, Oracle Cloud Applications, Processes, and Custom backends. Backends can be added at the tenant level from the **Settings** menu of the VB and under the VB applications.
- **Servers**: The servers (backend servers) serve requests from the backend applications and there may be different servers on which the backend applications are deployed, including development, UAT, and production.

- **Application profiles**: Application profiles are used by the VB application to refer to the appropriate backend server with the appropriate environment.

- **Environments**: The environments are referred to as backend instances, such as development, UAT, and production.

The following diagram shows the relationship between backends, servers, application profiles, and environments:

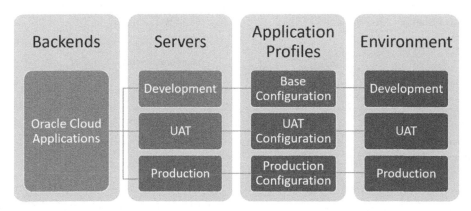

Figure 5.1 – Relationship between backends, servers, application profiles, and environments

You can use a single application profile on multiple servers. For example, the Base Configuration application profile can be used by Development and UAT servers.

The following screenshot shows the backend details that are added at the tenant (instance) level:

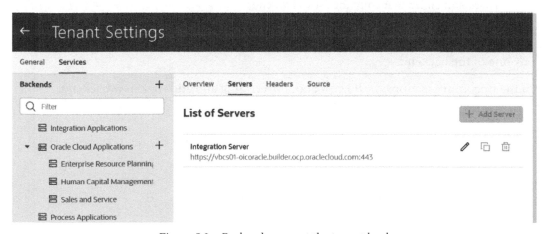

Figure 5.2 – Backend server at the tenant level

Click on the pencil icon to modify the configuration if required. Whenever you add or modify a new backend at the tenant level, you will only see three authentication options – **None**, **Propagate Current User Identity**, and **Oracle Cloud Account**, as per the following screenshot. You can override these properties at the VB application level, as described in the next section:

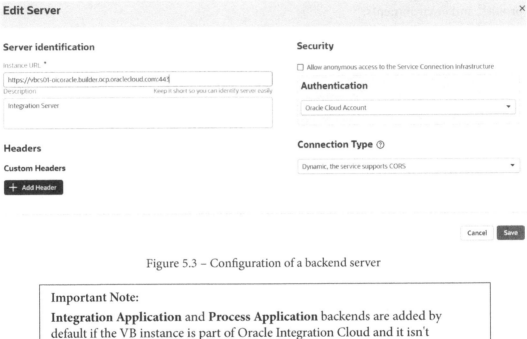

Figure 5.3 – Configuration of a backend server

> **Important Note:**
>
> **Integration Application** and **Process Application** backends are added by default if the VB instance is part of Oracle Integration Cloud and it isn't recommended to modify these two backends.

Whenever you create the Service Connection's **Select from Catalog** option, you choose any one of the backends.

In the upcoming sections, we'll learn about overriding and adding a new backend.

Overriding the backends

The backends can be seen and managed from the visual application under the **Backends** tab of the **Services** navigator. You can add or override existing backends at the application level, too. The backend you add or override at the application level will only be affected for that application.

The following are the steps to override the backend:

1. Open any of the applications, let's say, the VBCSBook application.
2. Go to the **Services** tab from the application navigator and move to the **Backends** tab.
3. Select the backend that you want to override.
4. Click **Override Backend** to override the settings and go to the **Servers** tab.
5. Under the **Servers** tab, click on the pencil icon to override the backend properties.

The following screenshot shows backends for overriding the settings:

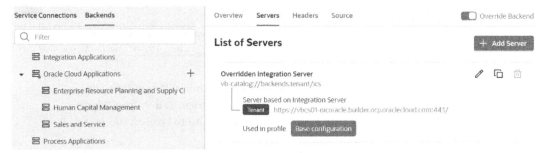

Figure 5.4 – Overriding the backends

You can only override the backends if the **Override Backend** option is enabled. This option is designed to override the tenant-level settings.

When you click on the pencil icon to the right of the server, the **Edit Server** dialog box will be opened, which will allow the server properties to be overridden. Click on the detach icon under the **Instance URL** textbox to update the instance URL, update the **Authentication** type as required, and enter any other details as required. Click on the **Save** button to update the changes.

The following screenshot shows the **Edit Server** dialog box for overriding the server properties:

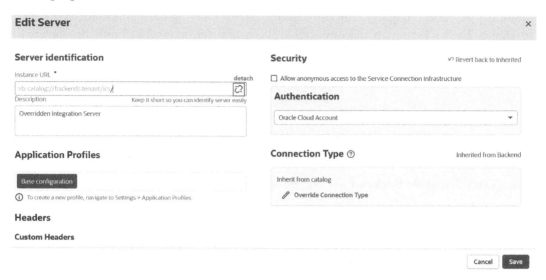

Figure 5.5 – Editing the Server dialog box to override server properties

> **Important Note:**
> Since my VB and Integration Cloud instances are both in different tenancies,
> I have updated the Instance URL and updated the authentication from None
> to Basic. Enter the backend's username and password to create a successful
> connection.

Adding a new backend

If the backend is not added at the tenant level, you can add backends such as **Integration Applications**, **Oracle Cloud Applications**, **Process Applications**, or **Custom**. Only one instance of each backend can be created, except in the case of the custom option.

The following are the steps to add a new backend to any of the **Integration Applications**, **Oracle Cloud Applications**, or **Process Applications** catalogs:

1. Open any of the applications, let's say, the VBCSBook application.

2. Go to the **Services** tab from the application navigator and move to the **Backends** tab.

3. Click on + and **Backend**.

4. From the opened **Create Backend** dialog box, click on **Integrations** to register the integration backend, click on the **Oracle Cloud Applications** instance to register the Oracle Cloud backend, and then click on **Process** to register the Process backend as per the following screenshot:

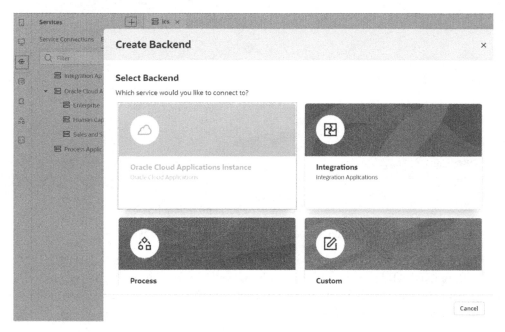

Figure 5.6 – Adding backend dialog box

5. Click on the **Integrations** backend for the purposes of this demonstration. Configure the following options from the opened **Create Backend** dialog box and then click on the **Create** button:

a. **Instance URL**: Enter the Instance URL of the new backend.

b. **Description**: Enter a description (optional).

c. **Application Profiles**: Leave this field as it is as all the available profiles will be selected when the backend is added.

d. **Headers**: Add custom or secure headers if required.

e. **Authentication**: Select the type of authentication from the list. In this instance, select **Basic** and then enter the username and password by clicking on the pencil icon for this demonstration.

f. **Connection Type**: Select the value depending on the backend. Leave the default setting as is for the purpose of this demonstration.

The following screenshot shows the **Create Backend** dialog box:

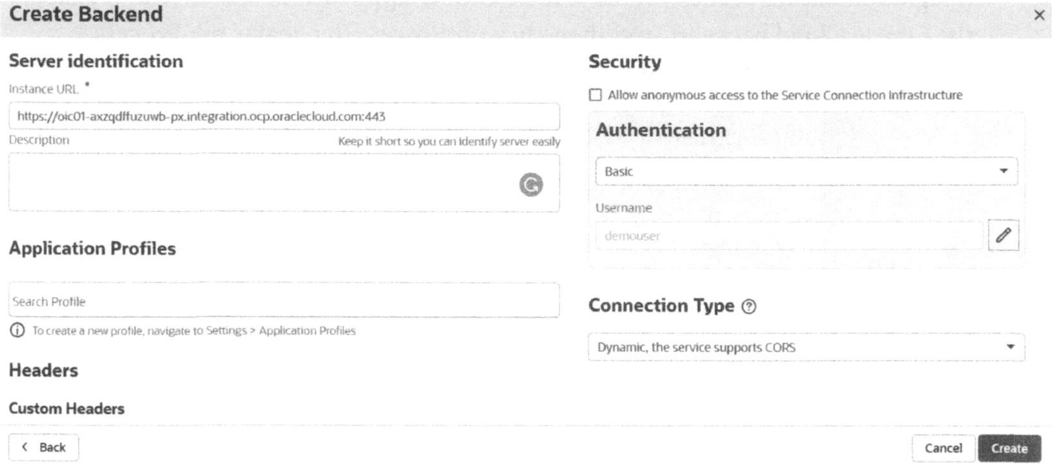

Figure 5.7 – Creating a backend dialog box

This is how you can create other backends, too, at application level.

In this section, you have learned about backends and understood the different terminology used while managing backends, as well as the relationship between them. Along with this, you learned how to override existing backends. Also, we learned how to add a backend at application level.

Having got to grips with backends, next we will look at application profiles and how to create them.

Creating application profiles

Application profiles make life easy when you switch the phases (Development to Stage, and Stage to Live) of your web or mobile application. If you use different application profiles specific to each instance, then you don't need to change the Service Connection credentials when you switch the phases of the VB application.

Application profiles are the reusable components and denote the instances (development, UAT, production, and so on) of the backend REST APIs. You can create different application profiles that are specific to the instance and use them while adding the backend servers, as shown in the previous section.

By default, an application profile is created with the name **Base configuration**. In order to access the application profiles, open any one of the VB applications, go to the **Action** menu from the top-right corner, click **Settings**, and then move to the **Application Profiles** tab.

The following screenshot shows the application profiles:

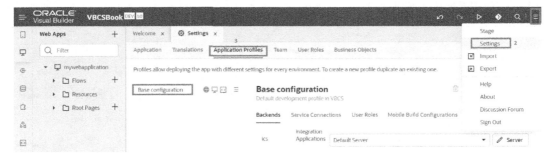

Figure 5.8 – Application profiles of the VB application

By default, the **Base configuration** profile is for each phase of the application.

In order to create a new profile, click on the **Duplicate** button. This action will open the **Duplicate Application Profile** dialog box. Enter the following information and then click on the **Duplicate** button:

1. **Name***: Enter the unique name of the profile as Test Configuration.

2. **ID***: The ID will be populated automatically on the basis of the name, but you can update it.

3. **Description**: You can enter a description (optional).

   The following screenshot shows the configuration of the new application profile:

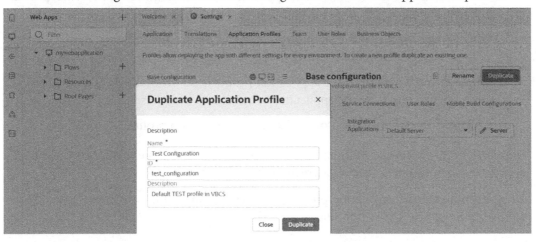

Figure 5.9 – Adding a new application profile

Once a new profile is added, it will be visible under the **Application Profiles** tab, as per the following screenshot:

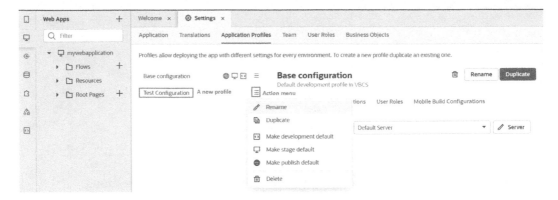

Figure 5.10 – Actions of the application profile

You can perform the following actions on an application profile using the action menu aligned to the profile name, as shown in the preceding screenshot:

- **Rename**: This option allows you to rename the application profile. Once renamed, the new application profile name will be updated in the backend servers, too, where applicable.

- **Duplicate**: This option allows you to create a new application profile.

- **Make development default**: If the application profile is set for **Make development default**, then it will be used for the application when it is in development phase.

- **Make stage default**: If the application profile is set for **Make stage default**, then it will be used for the application when it is in stage phase.

- **Make publish default**: If the application profile is set for **Make publish default**, then it will be used for the application when it is in live phase.

- **Delete**: This option allows you to delete the application profile.

In this section, we learned about application profiles, how to create them, and various actions that can be performed after creating the application profile.

Having learned about application profiles, next, we will look at how to create a Service Connection using a REST endpoint.

Creating a Service Connection from a REST endpoint

While creating a Service Connection, you will see various options for establishing communications with third-party REST APIs, Oracle APIs, and so on. In this section, we will see how to create a Service Connection with third-party REST APIs using an endpoint.

To complete this section, you must have the public external REST endpoint details along with the authentication details. If you don't have any of the REST APIs handy, you can use any from the following list. These are free and accessible over the internet:

- JSON Placeholder APIs: `https://jsonplaceholder.typicode.com/`.
- REST Countries APIs: `http://restcountries.eu/`.
- No code API: `https://nocodeapi.com/`.

You can find more on **Google** and use it.

For the purposes of this demonstration, we will use the **No code API**. In order to use the No code API, you have to create an account, which is absolutely free.

Creating a No code API account

The following are the steps to create an account for the No code API:

1. Go to the No code API sign-up URL on the browser: `https://app.nocodeapi.com/signup`.

2. Enter **Email address** and **Password** on the sign-up page and then click on the **Signup** button.

3. The next screen will allow you to enter the unique username for your No code API account. Enter your username of choice as per the following screenshot. Click on the **Setup Account** button once a username has been entered:

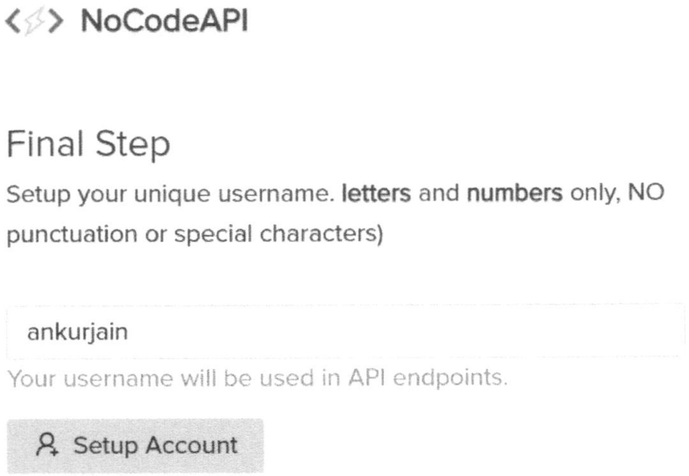

Final Step

Setup your unique username. **letters** and **numbers** only, NO punctuation or special characters)

ankurjain

Your username will be used in API endpoints.

A Setup Account

Figure 5.11 – Setting up the No code API account

4. You will land on the dashboard page following the preceding action.

5. Go to the **Marketplace** navigation from the left-hand side menu and then activate the API of your choosing. For the purposes of this demonstration, I have activated the **Currency Exchange** API. Click on the **Activate** button to activate it.

6. Switch to the **Applications** tab and click on the **+ Make Currency Exchange API** button, enter a name, Exchange API, and then click on the **Create** button.

7. Click on the **View Documentation** link, which will show you all the endpoints of the **Currency Exchange** API. There are three endpoints of the **Currency Exchange** API. Expand the endpoints node to view the endpoint information and query parameters if any.

8. The following screenshot shows all the **Currency Exchange** APIs:

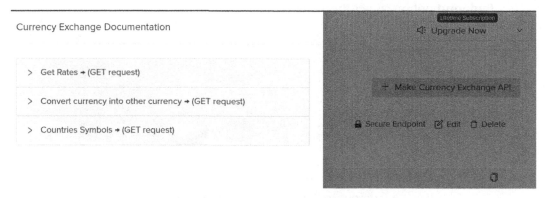

Figure 5.12 – Currency Exchange REST APIs

The REST common endpoint (`https://v1.nocodeapi.com/ankurjain/cx/NmPBrfRfmiPJ`), which is built from all three APIs, as shown in the previous screenshot, is explained as follows:

a. `https://v1.nocodeapi.com` is the base URI of the REST endpoint.

b. `ankurjain` is the unique username of the No code API account.

c. `cx` represents the currency exchange API.

d. `NmPBrfRfmiPJ` is the unique key for the currency exchange API.

The following section will guide you in how to create a Service Connection with the **Get Rates** API.

Creating a Service Connection from an endpoint

If you know the base URI of the REST endpoint, then the **Define by Endpoint** option is used to create a Service Connection. When you use this option, you can configure the endpoint URL, the verb, authentication details, and the request and response details.

The following are the steps to create a Service Connection with the currency exchange API that we configured in the previous section:

1. Open the existing VB application, let's say, `VBCSBook`, click on the **Services** tab from the application navigator, go to the **Service Connections** tab, and then click on + **Service Connection**, or the + icon and **Service Connection**.

2. From the opened **Create Service Connection** dialog box, choose the **Define by Endpoint** option, as per the following screenshot:

Define by Endpoint

You can point us to the URL of an endpoint and define its parameters declaratively.

Figure 5.13 – Define by Endpoint option to create a Service Connection

3. Select the HTTP method from the **Method** dropdown, choose either the existing backend or enter the **URL** of your REST endpoint, and then select **Action Hint** if you know what the entered endpoint is going to do. Then, click on the **Next** button. For this demonstration, we entered the URL as `https://v1.nocodeapi.com/ankurjain1/cx/{key}`.

4. The following screenshot shows the configured URL on the Service Connection page:

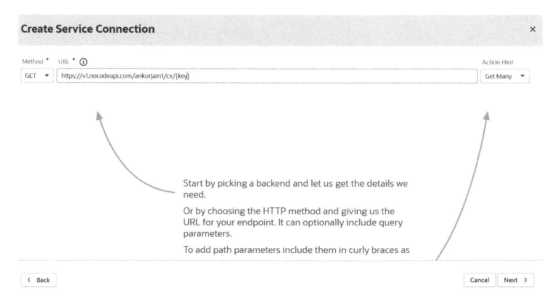

Figure 5.14 – Creating a Service Connection using an endpoint

We have added the path parameter as **key** so that the API key can be passed dynamically.

5. On the next screen, suffix the /rates relative resource URL in the URL input box.

6. On the same screen, you will see various tabs. On the **Overview** tab, you can update the values of **Service name**, **Title**, **Version**, and **Description**. We have updated **Service name** and **Title** as nocodeapi.

7. Switch to the **Server** tab. The following are explanations of the options available on this tab:

    a. **Instance URL**: This represents the URL of the endpoint you entered on the first screen of the Service Connection.

    b. **Description**: This is the description of your endpoint.

    c. **Application Profiles**: The application profile stores the credentials for the server (https://v1.nocodeapi.com). You can create different application profiles for each of the application phases (Development, Staging, and Live).

    d. **Headers**: You can add **Custom** and **Secure headers** fields, to be used when the Service Connection connects to the REST service using this server.

    e. **Security**: The **Allow anonymous access to the Service Connection Infrastructure** checkbox allows anonymous users to access data from this service if this is enabled. By default, this option is disabled.

    f. **Authentication**: This dropdown contains a list of the REST API authentication mechanisms. Choose as per the REST API authentication. Choose **None** for the No code API as this only requires authentication credentials in the path parameter (key).

    g. **Connection Type**: This dropdown holds the values related to the CORS policy. The CORS setting here refers to the setting on another server and whether they allow access from the VB app/server. Choose the appropriate option as per the external REST API. Leave the default option as is for the time being.

8. The **Operation** tab only shows the endpoint name that is added. You can change it if required.

9. Switch to the **Request** tab. You can configure the **Parameters**, **Headers**, and **Body** fields of the REST API. The body section is only enabled for REST verbs such as **POST**, **PUT**, or **PATCH**. You can add a **Static** or **Dynamic** header under the **Headers** section. Similarly, you can add **Dynamic** and **Static Query Parameters** under the **Parameters** section. On the **Parameters** tab, you can view **Path Parameters**, which are added as per the following screenshot:

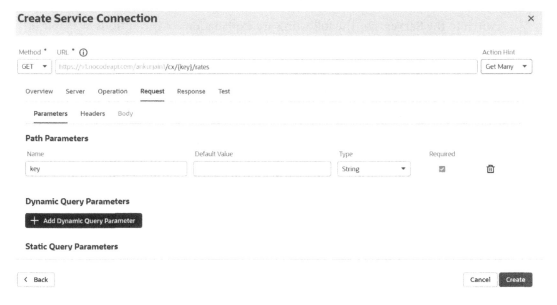

Figure 5.15 – Parameters tab of the Service Connection

10. Switch to the **Response** tab to configure the sample response.

11. Switch to the **Test** tab to test the API. Pass the values to the required parameters and body if applicable and then click on the **Send Request** button. Once you click on the **Send Request** button, you will see the response as per the following screenshot. Click on **Save as Example Response** to save the response in order to create the sample schema:

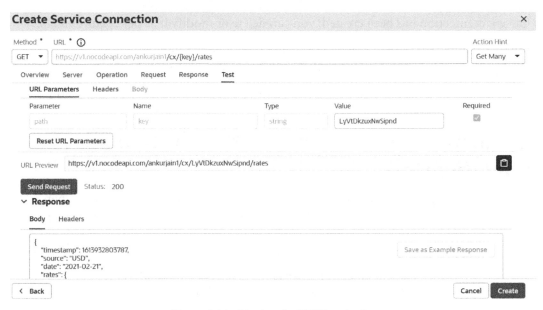

Figure 5.16 – Testing the REST endpoint

12. Click on the **Create** button in order to successfully create the Service Connection.

> **Important Note:**
> You need to enter the request and response body in the respective text area
> under the **Request** and **Response** tabs in order to create the sample schema
> wherever applicable.

13. Once a connection has been created successfully, you can view the same in the
Services panel, as per the following screenshot:

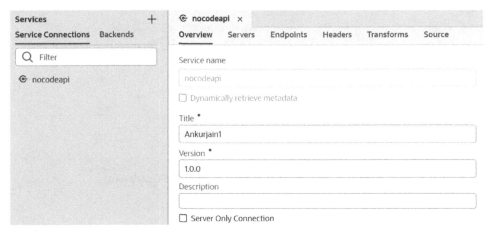

Figure 5.17 – Service Connection

Once a connection has been created, you can delete or modify it as per requirements.

In this section, you learned how to create a No code API account as well as create a Service Connection using the No code currency exchange API.

Next, we'll look at how to create a Service Connection using the service specification.

Creating a Service Connection from a service specification

The **Define by Specification** option allows you to create a Service Connection when you already know the URL of the **OpenAPI/Swagger** or **ADF** file that describes the service.

> **Important Note:**
> If you don't have the OpenAPI/Swagger URL, you can create a REST API in Integration Cloud. Click the endpoint, which will give you the OpenAPI/Swagger URL separately.

The following screenshot shows one of the integration REST endpoint descriptions, along with the OpenAPI/Swagger URL:

Endpoint Description

Endpoint URL

https://oic01-axzqdffuzuwb-px.integration.ocp.oraclecloud.com:443/ic/api/integration/v1/flows/rest/GETSPECIFICROW/1.0/get?firstName={firstName-value}&lastName={lastName-value}

Swagger

https://oic01-axzqdffuzuwb-px.integration.ocp.oraclecloud.com:443/ic/api/integration/v1/flows/rest/GETSPECIFICROW/1.0/metadata/swagger

Open API

https://oic01-axzqdffuzuwb-px.integration.ocp.oraclecloud.com:443/ic/api/integration/v1/flows/rest/GETSPECIFICROW/1.0/metadata/openapi

How to Run

http://www.oracle.com/pls/topic/lookup?ctx=oic_en&id=ICSUG-GUID-205B916C-1075-4603-A9E2-72A6C8C4AB3C

Resource /get

Method GET

Query Parameters

- firstName
- lastName

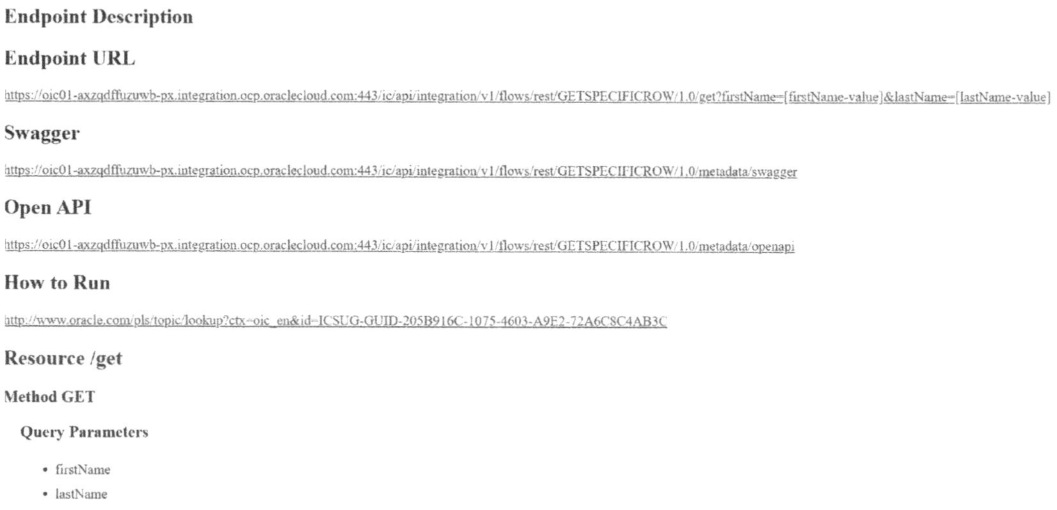

Figure 5.18 – Swagger endpoint of the REST endpoint

The following are the steps to create a Service Connection using the Swagger URL:

1. Open the existing VB application, let's say, VBCSBook, click on **Services** from the application navigator, go to the **Service Connections** tab, and then click on **+ Service Connection**, or the **+** icon and **Service Connection**.

2. From the opened **Create Service Connection** dialog box, choose the **Define by Specification** option as per the following screenshot:

Figure 5.19 – Define by Specification option to create a Service Connection

3. From the **API Type** dropdown, either choose **OpenAPI / Swagger** or **ADF Describe** options. Here, we will choose the first option, **OpenAPI / Swagger**, as we have the Swagger URL.

4. You can either enter the URL or upload the descriptor document from **Service Specification**. Choose the **Web address** option.

5. The service name will be populated automatically based on the URL entered; however, you can modify it.

6. From the **Authentication** dropdown, choose one of the options depending on the type of service authentication. Select **Basic** for the configured API.

7.   Click on the pencil icon to configure the username and password:

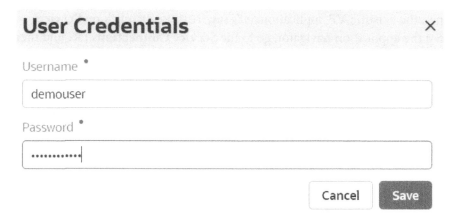

Figure 5.20 – Dialog box to enter a username and password

8.   Select **Connection Type** as per the configured API. Leave the default option as is for the time being.

9.   Then, click on the **Create** button to create the Service Connection successfully:

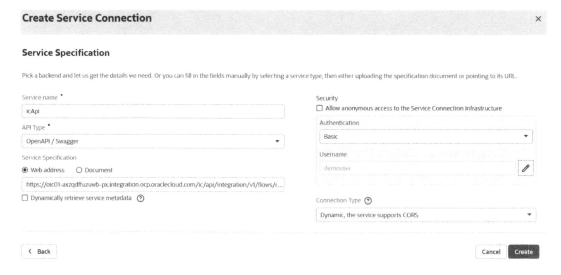

Figure 5.21 – Defining the Swagger URL

Once a connection has been created, you can view it in the **Services** panel and modify it as per your requirements.

In this section, you learned how to create a Service Connection using the Swagger URL. Next, we will look at how to create a Service Connection using the catalog option.

Creating a Service Connection using an inbuilt catalog

Creating a Service Connection using the **Catalog** option allows you to choose the available APIs from **Oracle Cloud Applications**, **Oracle Integration**, or **Custom backend**.

Before you use any of these options, the backends must be added at tenant or application level.

The catalog option saves you time when it comes to creating a Service Connection as the common properties are already added in the backend and it's a one-time activity. Once the backends are added, you can use any one of the available APIs from the backends (Oracle Cloud Applications, Oracle Integration, or custom).

Creating a Service Connection with Integration Cloud

In order to create a Service Connection using Integration Cloud, make sure that the **Integration Applications** backend is added under the **Settings** section of the VB.

The following are the steps to create a Service Connection with Integration Cloud:

1. Open the existing VB application, let's say, VBCSBook, then click on the **Services** tab from the application navigator, go to the **Service Connections** tab, and then click on + **Service Connection**, or the + icon and **Service Connection**.

2. From the opened **Create Service Connection** dialog box, choose the **Select from Catalog** option as per the following screenshot:

Figure 5.22 – Selecting from a catalog option to create Service Connections

3. From the next screen, select **Integrations**. This action will take you to the next screen and will populate all the custom REST integrations under the configured Oracle Integration instance. Select one or more as required.

The following screenshot shows all the REST integrations under the Oracle Integration instance:

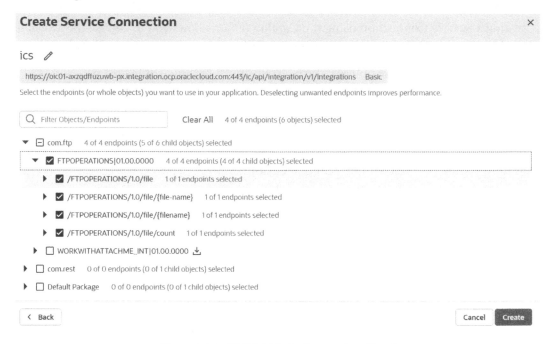

Figure 5.23 – REST APIs for Integration Cloud

4. Click on the **Create** button. This action will add a Service Connection with the name `ics` in the **Services** navigator.

5. You can add more services later if required.

Creating a Service Connection with Oracle Cloud Applications

In the same way as we have added a Service Connection with Integration Cloud, you can create a Service Connection with Oracle Cloud Applications, too.

> **Important Note:**
> Before you create the Service Connection with **Oracle Cloud Applications**, make sure that you have overridden the Oracle Cloud application properties as mentioned in the *Overriding the backends* section of the same chapter. You can use **Basic Authentication** as of now to connect to Oracle Cloud Applications.

The following are the steps to create a Service Connection with Oracle Cloud Applications:

1. Open the existing VB application, let's say VBCSBook, click on the **Services** tab from the application navigator, go to the **Service Connections** tab, and then click on **+ Service Connection**, or the + icon and **Service Connection**.

2. From the opened **Create Service Connection** dialog box, choose **Select from Catalog** option.

3. From the next screen, select one of the available applications as **Sales and Service(crmRestApi)**, **Enterprise Resource Planning and Supply Chain(fscmRestApi)**, and **Human Capital Management(hcmRestApi)** under the **Oracle Cloud Applications** section as per the following:

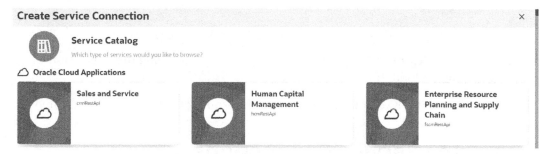

Figure 5.24 – List of Oracle Cloud applications

4. Select **Sales and Service(crmRestApi)** for this configuration. This will populate all the REST APIs under the CRM application, as shown in the following screenshot. Select the required API and click on the **Create** button. I have selected the **sales order** API as per the following screenshot:

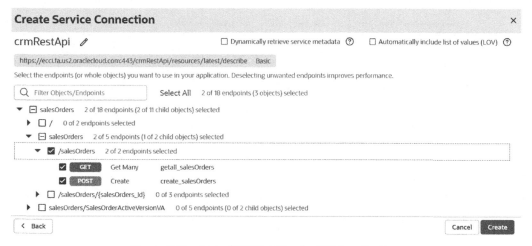

Figure 5.25 – List of REST APIs of a CRM application

You will be returned to the Service Connection after adding the REST API where you can see all the endpoints you selected.

The following screenshot shows all the endpoints you selected from the CRM applications:

Figure 5.26 – Service connection from the Oracle Cloud application

In this section, we learned how to create a Service Connection using the Integration Cloud and Oracle Cloud Applications catalog and added a few services.

Next, we will look at how to manage Service Connections once they have been created.

Managing Service Connections

Once the Service Connections have been created, you can manage them in terms of adding or modifying endpoints, adding more REST API servers, updating server properties, and so on.

The following screenshot shows the various tabs of the Service Connection that will be used to manage the Service Connections:

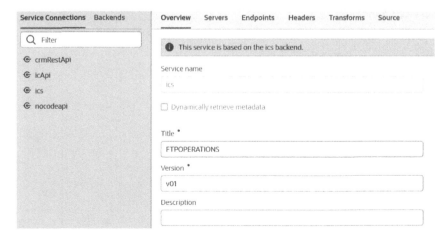

Figure 5.27 – Various Service Connection options

- **Overview**: The overview tab shows general information pertaining to the Service Connection, including **Service name**, **Title**, **Version**, and **Description**. You can modify them if required.

- **Servers**: The servers tab is used to manage the servers of backend REST APIs. You can add a new server to point to a different instance, for example, UAT or Production, modify the existing server, or copy the server details. A single entry of the server contains the base URL, headers, security, and network configuration attributes that are required to connect to the REST API.

- **Endpoints**: The endpoint tab shows the REST endpoint that you have already added. This is used to add or modify existing endpoints.

- **Headers**: The headers tab shows all the custom or secure headers that you have added already to the REST endpoints. This is used to add or modify the existing headers.

- **Transforms**: The transforms tab facilitates filtering, sorting, and pagination on the REST endpoints. Once the **Enable filtering, sorting, and pagination transforms** checkbox is enabled, this shows the default JavaScript function, which you can extend to filter, sort, and paginate your service data.

- **Source**: The source code shows the **OpenAPI 3** description of the configuration of the REST APIs.

Adding a server to the Service Connection

Once a Service Connection has been added, you can add servers that point to the other instance of the same API. This will help you to manage the different phases of your application. For example, if you are using an external REST API that is hosted on the development and production instances; a development instance of REST API you want to point to for dev and stage VB applications; and a production instance of REST API you want to point to for live VB application.

To meet this requirement, you can add two servers; one will point to the development instance, and the second will point to the production instance. Then, the application profile will decide which server will be used for dev, stage, and live applications.

The following are the steps to add a new server to the Service Connection:

1. Open any of the applications, let's say, VBCSBook.

2. Go to the **Services** tab in the navigator and move to the **Service Connections** tab.

3. Open the Service Connection where you want to add a server.

4. Go to the **Servers** tab and click on the **+ Add Server** button as per the following screenshot:

Figure 5.28 – Adding a server under the Service Connection

5. Enter the details and then click on the **Create** button:

    a. **Instance URL***: Enter the Instance URL that will point to the new server.

    b. **Description**: Enter a description of the server (optional).

    c. **Application Profiles**: Choose the existing application profiles from the list.

    d. **Headers**: Add custom or secure headers if needed, otherwise leave as is.

    e. **Authentication**: Select the type of authentication from the available list. Select **Basic**. Click on the pencil icon and then add a username and password from the opened dialog box.

    f. **Connection Type**: Choose the value depending on the CORS of the backend service.

    The following screenshot shows the information entered to add a new server:

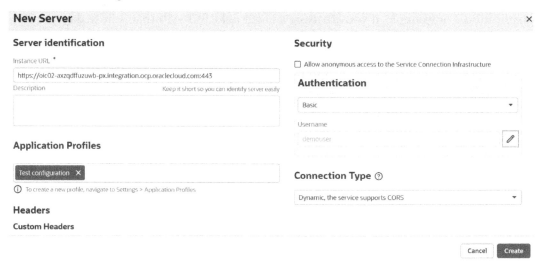

Figure 5.29 – Adding a new server dialog box

Once a new server has been added, it will be visible under the list of servers. You can edit, copy, and delete the server using the respective icon next to the server.

The following screenshot shows a list of servers added to the Service Connection:

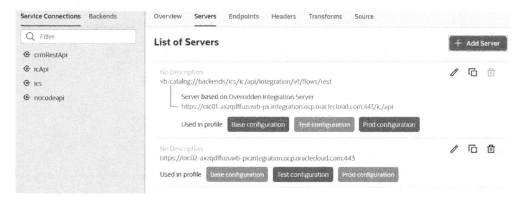

Figure 5.30 – List of servers

You can add more servers and select the different application profiles to manage the different stages of your application.

Adding more endpoints to the Service Connection

Once a Service Connection has been added, you can add more endpoints from the same source or you can add custom endpoints.

The following are the steps to add more endpoints to the Service Connection:

1. Open the Service Connection where you want to add more endpoints.

2. Go to the **Endpoints** tab and click on **+ Endpoint**. If the Service Connection has been created from the catalog, you will see two options – **Custom** or **From service_ name**. Select **From service_name** in this instance, as per the following screenshot:

Figure 5.31 – Adding a new endpoint to the existing Service Connection

3. The previous action will open the **Add Endpoint** dialog box. Add the endpoint as per requirements and then click on the **Add** button as per the following screenshot:

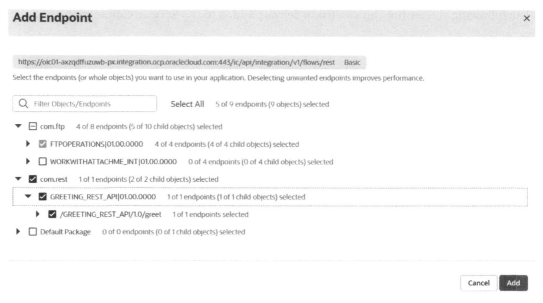

Figure 5.32 – Adding a new endpoint

Once the endpoints have been added, they will be visible under the **Endpoints** tab, as per the following screenshot:

Figure 5.33 – List of endpoints of a Service Connection

This is how you can add more and more REST endpoints to a Service Connection. If you want to delete any one of the endpoints, click on the action menu right next to the endpoint and choose the delete option.

In this section, you learned how to manage connections and the different options available for a Service Connection. You also learned how to add new backend server and how to add more endpoints to a Service Connection.

Summary

In this chapter, you have learned about creating and managing Service Connections that will help you to interact with the external world while developing web or mobile applications. You learned about backends, how to add and override backends, and the relationship between backends, servers, application profiles, and the environment, with its solid architecture. You learned about application profiles and how to create a new application profile.

You became proficient in creating a Service Connection using the different options available, including how to create a Service Connection with REST endpoints, how to use the Swagger URL to create a Service Connection, how to create a Service Connection with Integration Cloud, and how to create a Service Connection with Oracle Cloud Applications. With this, you can use any type of REST API to extend your Oracle and non-Oracle applications.

Lastly, you learned how to manage a Service Connection post-creation. You learned step by step how to add or modify the existing backend servers of a Service Connection, and how to add or modify endpoints to a Service Connection.

Armed with all of this knowledge, you became an expert in how to create and modify Service Connections in the VB.

The next chapter is going to be very interesting. We will start to develop a web application, perform various operations using a Business Object, render the data on pages from external REST APIs, pass the data between two different pages, work with JavaScript, and perform client-side validation on the UI components.

Questions

1. Do we need to modify the backends for Integration Cloud and Process Applications?

2. Can we create a Service Connection with an external REST endpoint that is **OAuth 2.0** enabled?

3. How do we connect REST APIs that are behind a firewall?

4. Can single application profiles be used in different servers?

5. Is it mandatory to save sample request and response bodies while creating a Service Connection using REST endpoints?

6

Building Web Applications Using Real-World Examples

In the previous two chapters, you learned about creating and managing Business Objects, as well as creating and managing Service Connections. These two chapters are very important as regards this particular chapter as we are going to use both Business Objects and Service Connections throughout this chapter and in those that remain. So, it is really important to read the previous two chapters in detail.

In this chapter, we'll execute various use cases that are taken from real-world examples. We'll start by creating a web application and different web pages, where we will communicate with Business Objects to pull and push data. We'll be creating a few other web pages where I will demonstrate how to fetch data from external REST APIs using a Service Connection. We'll create variables that will be used to pass data between two different pages. We will work with JavaScript in the web application and show how to call it on the component actions.

In this chapter, we will cover the following topics:

- Building a web application and connecting it to the Business Object
- Connecting a web application with external REST APIs
- Changing the default flow and the default page of a flow
- Navigating between pages, flows, and passing parameters between pages
- Working with JavaScript

After completing this chapter, you will be familiar with creating a web application, communicating with Business Objects, and communicating with external REST APIs. You will be able to pass data between different pages as and when required. Along with this, you will be able to create JavaScript and call it on different UI components as per your requirements.

Technical requirements

To complete this chapter, you will require the following:

- A **Visual Builder** instance
- **VB** login credentials
- A Business Object
- A Service Connection

You can find the full source code used in this chapter here: `https://github.com/PacktPublishing/Effortless-App-Development-with-Oracle-Visual-Builder/tree/main/Chapter06`.

Building a web application and connecting it to the Business Object

In order to create a web application, we must have a VB application in the Visual Builder instance. We have already created a VB application with the name **VBCSBook**. Refer to *Chapter 3, Exploring Visual Builder Ingredients*, the *Creating a VB application* section, to learn how to create a VB application. A VB application is a collection of multiple web or mobile applications. We have already created a web application with the name **mywebapplication**. Refer to *Chapter 3, Exploring Visual Builder Ingredients*, the *Understanding the application's structure* section, to learn how to create a web application. Throughout this chapter, we'll use the same web application to render the data from the Business Object and Service Connection.

In this section, we'll execute the **CRUD** (Create, Read, Update, Delete) use case as follows:

- Create a web page to read all employees from the **Employee** Business Object.
- Create a web page to onboard a new employee and push details into the **Employee** Business Object.
- Create a web page to update existing employee details.
- A button for deleting the selected employee.

Creating a web page to read all employees

When we create a new web application, a flow and a page will be created by default. So, we'll use the default page (**main-start**) to read all employees from a Business Object.

After completing this use case, your page will look like the following screenshot:

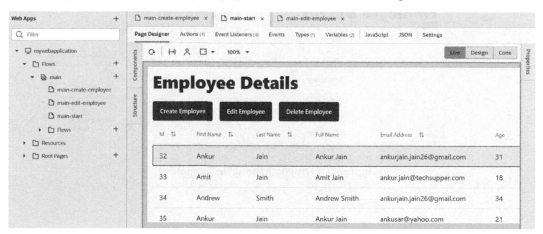

Figure 6.1 – A web application

The following are the steps to read all employees:

1. Click the **main-start** page under the main flow to open the web page. From the component palette, drag and drop the **Heading** component on the page as per the following screenshot:

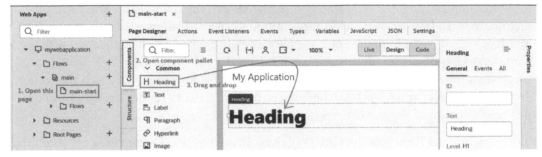

Figure 6.2 – Dropping the Heading component

2. From the **Properties** palette of the **Heading** component, change the **Text** field to `Employee Details`. You can change the level of heading as required, but leave it like this for now.

3. From the component palette, find the **Table** component and drag and drop it just below the **Heading** component, as per the following screenshot:

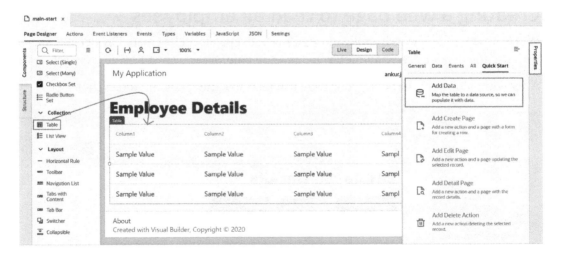

Figure 6.3 – Dropping the Table component

4. As per the previous screenshot, click on **Add Data** from the **Properties** palette. This action will open an **Add Data** dialog box. This dialog box will allow you to select the data source to populate data on the web page. Now, select the **Employee** Business Object and click on the **Next** button, as per the following screenshot:

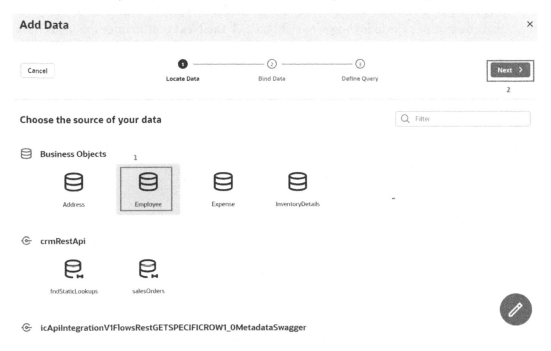

Figure 6.4 – Selecting the Employee Business Object

5. The following screen will populate all the fields from the selected data source (**Employee**). Choose the fields that you want to show on the web page from the left panel. By default, all the selected fields are regarded as text fields. In order to change the data type, select the dropdown next to the field name and then change the data type as per requirements. For this, change the data type of the **age** field to #Input Number as per the following screenshot. Click the **Next** button once the fields have been selected:

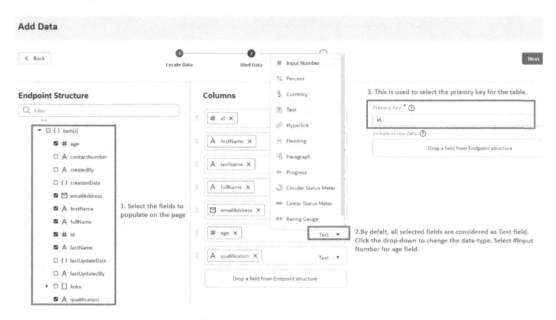

Figure 6.5 – Selecting the fields

6. The next screen allows you to add the filter to the Business Object. For example, if you want to limit the number of rows to be fetched initially, you can use the **getall_Employee/uriParameters/limit** field to hardcode the number. For the time being, leave all the options as they are and click on the **Finish** button.

7. Once the **Add Data** dialog box is finished, you will be returned to the web page where it will show all the selected fields, along with the Business Object data.

> **Tip:**
> All the actions are autosaved. You don't need to save your application manually.

The following screenshot shows the page after completing this section:

My Application   ankur.jain1@techsupper.com ▼

Employee Details

Id ⇅	First Name ⇅	Last Name ⇅	Full Name	Email Address ⇅	Age	Qualification ⇅
32	Ankur	Jain	Ankur Jain	ankurjain.jain26@gmail.com	31	MCA
33	Amit	Jain	Amit Jain	ankur.jain@techsupper.com	18	BTech
34	Andrew	Smith	Andrew Smith	ankurjain.jain26@gmail.com	34	BBA
35	Ankur	Jain	Ankur Jain	ankusar@yahoo.com	21	MTech
36	Gyial	Hasan	Gyial Hasan	gyial@test_test.com	54	BBA

Figure 6.6 – The employee details page

This declarative approach will create a type and variable with the **getallEmployeeResponse** and **employeeListSDP** IDs, respectively. You can view it in the **Types** and **Variables** tab of the page.

Once a table is created, you can use the **Properties** palette of the table to set the different properties.

Switch to the **Data** tab from the property palette to add or update the fields. The following screenshot shows various page options:

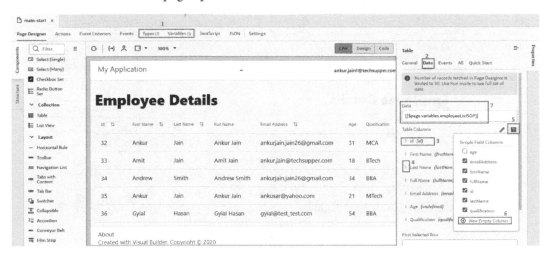

Figure 6.7 – Updating the table's properties

The following are the explanations of the marked properties:

1. The **Types** and **Variables** tabs show the types and variables that are created. You can update **Types** to add more fields from the Business Object or custom fields.

2. This represents the **Data** tab of the table properties.

3. Double-click on the field to rename the display label.

4. Re-order the fields by using the drag and drop feature.

5. Click on this table icon to add more fields to the table, either from a Business Object or a new empty column. If you add new fields from **Types**, these newly added fields will be visible here.

6. Click on + **New Empty Column** to add a new field.

7. This represents the fact that the table data is populating the **employeeListSDP** variable, which is created by default.

Creating a web page to onboard a new employee

We will not manually create a new page to onboard a new employee. However, the approach that is followed is the declarative approach, and a new page will be created automatically.

The following are the steps to onboard a new employee:

1. On the **main-start** page, select the table that we created in the previous step. From the **Table Properties** palette, move to the **Quick Start** tab and then select the **Add Create Page** action, as per the following screenshot:

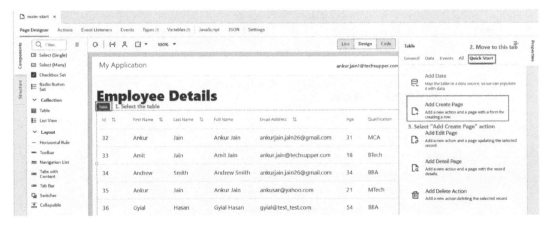

Figure 6.8 – Add Create Page action

2. The previous action will open the **Add Create Page** dialog box, which will allow you to select the data source. Select the `Employee` Business Object from this screen and click the **Next** button.

3. The next screen will allow you to choose the fields that you want to use to onboard a new employee. Select **firstName**, **lastName**, **emailAddress**, **age**, and **qualification** from the left-hand panel. Once you select these fields, they will be shown under the **Fields** section. The right-hand section allows you to change **Button label**, **Page title**, and **Page name**. If you wish to change these, you may do so, otherwise leave them as is. For the time being, leave everything as per the following screenshot and click on the **Finish** button:

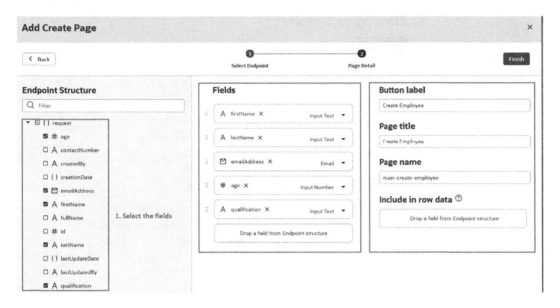

Figure 6.9 – Selecting the fields

Once the previous action is completed, this creates a new page with the name **main-create-employee** and a button, **Create Employee**, on the **main-start** page, as per the following screenshot. So, this was the declarative approach that we followed in order to create a new page to insert data into a Business Object or Service Connection. Obviously, there are a few other artifacts (events, Action Chains, variables, and so on) that will be created automatically with this declarative approach:

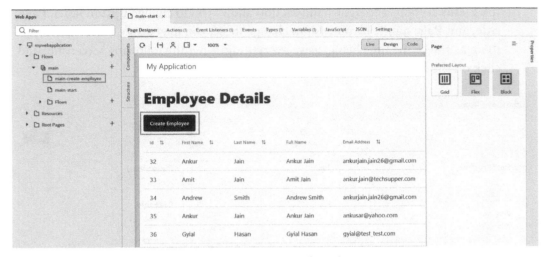

Figure 6.10 – Create Employee button

Once we click on the **Create Employee** button, this will redirect us to the **main-create-employee** page and allow us to create a new employee as per the following screenshot:

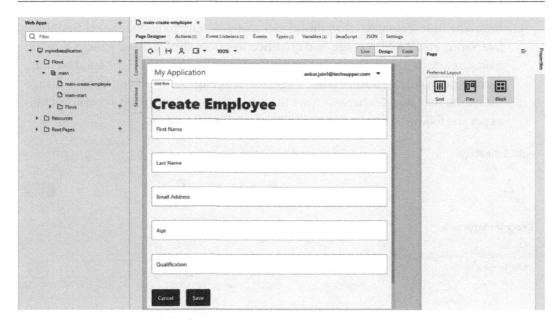

Figure 6.11 – Create Employee page

We'll test the whole use case once it has been developed fully.

Creating a web page to update existing employee details

Similar to the onboard new employee functionality, we'll follow the same declarative approach to create another web page that will allow us to update the employee details.

The following are the steps to execute the update employee detail functionality:

1. On the **main-start** page, select the table that we created in the previous step. From the **Table Properties** palette, move to the **Quick Start** tab and select the **Add Edit Page** action.

2. The previous action will open the **Add Edit Page** dialog box, which will allow you to select the data source. Select the **Employee** Business Object from this screen and click the **Next** button.

3. From the next screen, select the **Employee** Business Object and then click the **Next** button.

4. From the next screen, select all those fields that you want to update. Select **firstName**, **lastName**, **emailAddress**, **age**, and **qualification** from the left-hand panel. Once the fields are selected, it will be shown under the **Fields** section. The right-hand section allows you to change **Button label**, **Page title**, and **Page name**. If you wish to change these, you may do so, otherwise leave them as is. For the time being, leave everything as per the following screenshot and click on the **Finish** button:

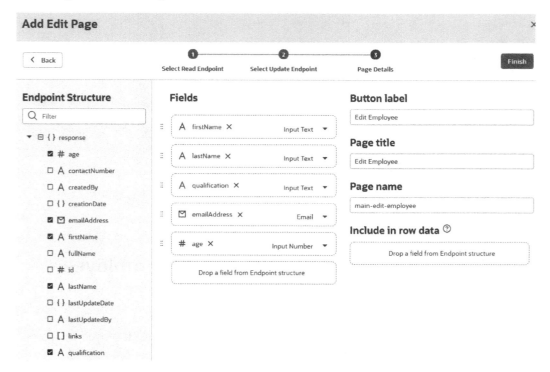

Figure 6.12 – Selecting the fields

Once the previous action is completed, this creates a new page with the name **main-edit-employee** and a button, **Edit Employee**, on the **main-start** page. Initially, this button will be disabled, but it will be enabled only once a row is selected from the table and then, once the button is clicked, you will be redirected to the **main-edit-employee** page, where the selected employee information will be populated as per the following screenshot:

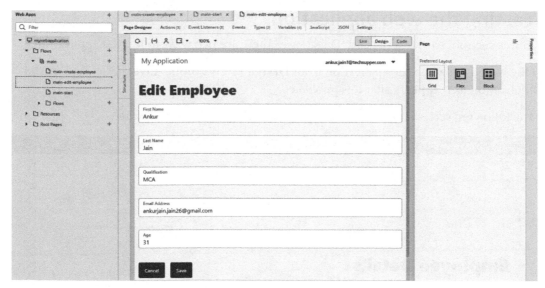

Figure 6.13 – Edit Employee page

We will test the functionality once the whole use case is complete.

A button for deleting the selected employee

Similar to the previous functionalities, we'll choose the declarative approach to provide the delete functionality. Once this is completed, a button is created that will allow you to delete the selected employee from the table.

The following are the steps in order to achieve the delete functionality:

1. On the **main-start** page, select the table that we created in the previous step. From the **Table Properties** palette, move to the **Quick Start** tab and then select the **Add Delete Action** option.

2. The previous action will open the **Add Delete Action** dialog box, which will allow you to select the data source. Select the **Employee** Business Object from this screen and click the **Finish** button.

Once the previous action is completed, this adds a **Delete Employee** button to the **main-start** page. Initially, this button is disabled, but it will be enabled once a row is selected from the table and the action of this button will delete the selected employee.

Now, the CRUD use case is completed and it's time to test the application.

Testing the web application

In this section, we'll test the CRUD use case. There are two ways to test the application.

One way is to switch the application from **Design** to **Live** mode. **Live** mode displays the application as it appears after it is published.

The following screenshot shows the application when it is in **Live** mode:

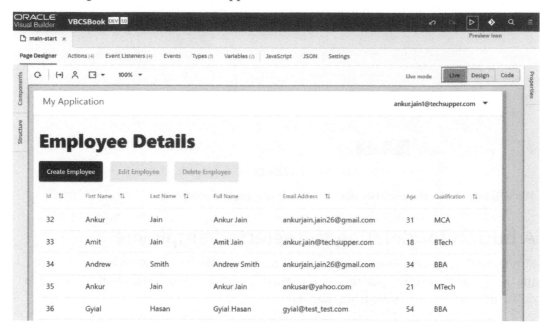

Figure 6.14 – Live mode of the application

Another way to test the web application is by using a different browser tab by running the application using the **preview** icon from the top-right corner of the page, as shown in the previous screenshot. Click on the **preview** icon, which will open the web application in a new tab.

The default page of the web application is **main-start**. As per the functionality, it will list all the employees, as per the following screenshot:

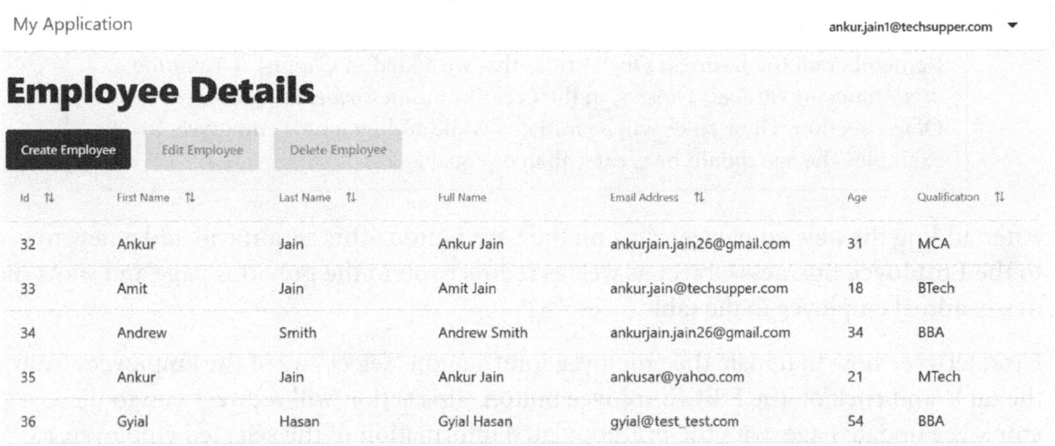

My Application   ankur.jain1@techsupper.com ▼

Employee Details

| Create Employee | Edit Employee | Delete Employee |

Id ↑↓	First Name ↑↓	Last Name ↑↓	Full Name	Email Address ↑↓	Age	Qualification ↑↓
32	Ankur	Jain	Ankur Jain	ankurjain.jain26@gmail.com	31	MCA
33	Amit	Jain	Amit Jain	ankur.jain@techsupper.com	18	BTech
34	Andrew	Smith	Andrew Smith	ankurjain.jain26@gmail.com	34	BBA
35	Ankur	Jain	Ankur Jain	ankusar@yahoo.com	21	MTech
36	Gyial	Hasan	Gyial Hasan	gyial@test_test.com	54	BBA

Figure 6.15 – Listing employee details

Now, click on the **Create Employee** button to onboard a new employee. This will take you to the new page, which will allow you to enter employee information as per the following screenshot:

My Application   ankur.jain1@techsupper.com ▼

Create Employee

First Name
Nish

Last Name
Kumar

Email Address
nish@techsupper.com

Age
22

Qualification
MCA

| Cancel | Save |

Figure 6.16 – Creating a new employee

The **Cancel** button will take you to the previous page, and the **Save** button will save the information to the **Employee** Business Object.

> **Important Note:**
>
> Remember all the Business Object rules that we added in *Chapter 4, Creating and Managing Business Objects*, in the *Creating business rules in a Business Object* section. These rules will be initiated while adding a new employee, for example: The age should be greater than or equal to 18.

After adding the new employee, click on the **Save** button. This action will add a new row to the **Employee** Business Object as well as redirect you to the previous page and show the newly added employee in the table.

Now, let's see how to update the employee information. Select any of the employees from the table and click on the **Edit Employee** button. This action will redirect you to the employee update page, with the pre-populated information of the selected employee, as per the following screenshot:

Figure 6.17 – Updating the existing employee information

Update the information and click on the **Save** button. This button action will save the updated information to the **Employee** Business Object and redirect you to the previous page, where you will see the updated employee information.

To test the delete employee functionality, select the employee and click on the **Delete Employee** button. This action will delete the employee from the **Employee** Business Object as well as refresh the table.

In this section, we learned how to connect to the Business Object and perform various actions (Create, Update, Read, and Delete) on the Business Object. Next, we'll look at how to connect a web application with external REST APIs.

Connecting a web application with external REST APIs

In the previous section, we learned how to communicate with Business Objects to pull and push data. In this section, we'll see how to communicate with external REST APIs in the VB.

Here, we'll execute another use case that will connect to the external REST API and will list all the data on the web page.

In this section, we'll execute the **communication with external REST API** use case as follows:

- Creating a Service Connection with an external API
- Creating a new web page
- Listing the data from the external API

In the upcoming sections, we'll look at the preceding use case points in detail.

Creating a Service Connection with an external API

We have seen how to create a Service Connection in *Chapter 5, Creating and Managing Service Connections*, in the *Creating Service Connections from a REST endpoint* and *Creating a Service Connection from an endpoint* sections, so we'll follow a similar approach to create a new Service Connection using a different external REST API that is publicly accessible on the endpoint: `https://jsonplaceholder.typicode.com/users/`.

The following are the steps to create a Service Connection:

1. Click on the **Services** tab from the application navigator, and then click on the + button and the Service Connection.
2. Select **Define by Endpoint** from the opened dialog box.

3. Enter the `https://jsonplaceholder.typicode.com/users/` URL as per the following screenshot and then click on the **Next** button:

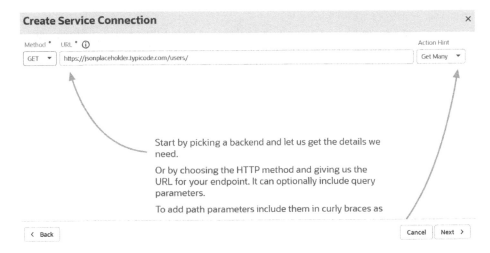

Figure 6.18 – Adding a new Service Connection

4. Switch to the **Test** tab and then click on the **Send Request** button. When you click on the **Send Request** button, it will show the REST API response in the response body section. Then, click on the **Save as Example Response** button to create the sample schema.

The following screenshot shows how to test and save the response:

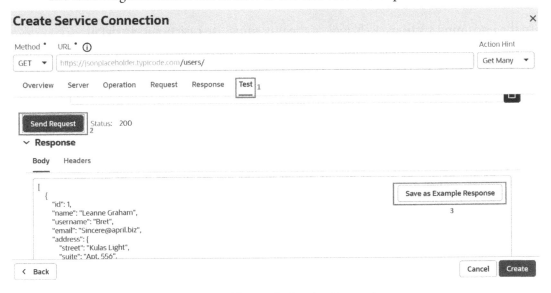

Figure 6.19 – Testing the Service Connection

5. Click on the **Create** button to create the Service Connection successfully.

The Service Connection can be seen in the Service Connection list.

Creating a new web page

We'll create a new web page in the same web application, **mywebapplication**, that we used in the previous section.

The following are the steps to create a new web page:

1. Open **mywebapplication** and then click on the + button to align to the flow name (**main**) as per the following screenshot:

Figure 6.20 – Creating a new page

2. On the opened dialog box, enter the page ID as main-external-data and then click on the **Create** button.

A new page with the name **main-external-data** will be created under the **main** flow.

Listing the data from the external API

Now, we'll use the Service Connection to pull the data from the external API.

The following are the steps to list the data from the external API:

1. Open the new page, **main-external-data**, and drop the **Table** component on to the page designer.

2. Select the table, click the **Quick Start** tab from the **Table Properties** palette, and then click on the **Add Data** action.

3. The previous action will open the **Add Data** dialog box. Scroll down the dialog box, expand the endpoint under **jsonplaceholderTypicodeCom**, and then select the /users/ endpoint as per the following screenshot. Click the **Next** button:

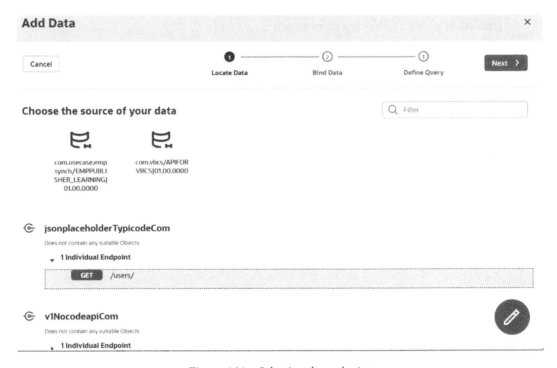

Figure 6.21 – Selecting the endpoint

4. The next screen will show all the REST service response fields in the left panel. Select id, name, username, email, phone, and website from the left-hand panel and click on the **Next** button. From the next screen, click on the **Finish** button to complete the configuration.

Once the previous action is completed, all users will be fetched from the external API and will be listed on the web page. If you preview the web application, the **main-start** default page will be opened. So, in order to change the default page, follow the *Change the default flow and default page of a flow* section.

Preview the application and you will see that the page should be rendered with a list of users as per the following screenshot:

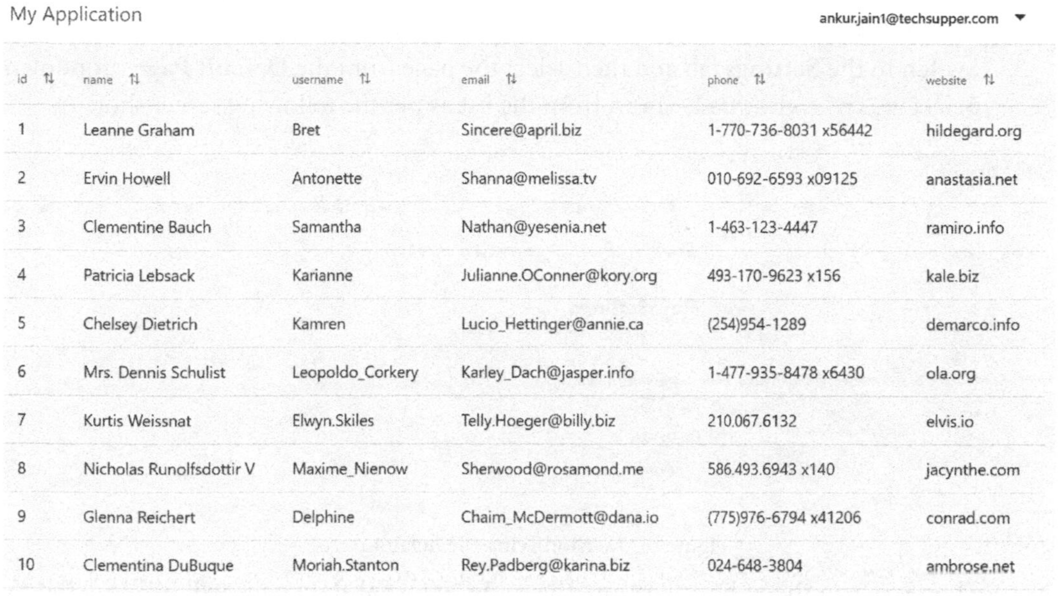

id ⇅	name ⇅	username ⇅	email ⇅	phone ⇅	website ⇅
1	Leanne Graham	Bret	Sincere@april.biz	1-770-736-8031 x56442	hildegard.org
2	Ervin Howell	Antonette	Shanna@melissa.tv	010-692-6593 x09125	anastasia.net
3	Clementine Bauch	Samantha	Nathan@yesenia.net	1-463-123-4447	ramiro.info
4	Patricia Lebsack	Karianne	Julianne.OConner@kory.org	493-170-9623 x156	kale.biz
5	Chelsey Dietrich	Kamren	Lucio_Hettinger@annie.ca	(254)954-1289	demarco.info
6	Mrs. Dennis Schulist	Leopoldo_Corkery	Karley_Dach@jasper.info	1-477-935-8478 x6430	ola.org
7	Kurtis Weissnat	Elwyn.Skiles	Telly.Hoeger@billy.biz	210.067.6132	elvis.io
8	Nicholas Runolfsdottir V	Maxime_Nienow	Sherwood@rosamond.me	586.493.6943 x140	jacynthe.com
9	Glenna Reichert	Delphine	Chaim_McDermott@dana.io	(775)976-6794 x41206	conrad.com
10	Clementina DuBuque	Moriah.Stanton	Rey.Padberg@karina.biz	024-648-3804	ambrose.net

My Application   ankur.jain1@techsupper.com ▼

Figure 6.22 – User details page

This is how you can call any type of external REST APIs and get the data. In this section, you learned how to create a Service Connection, create a new web page, and populate the data from the external REST API. Next, we'll look at how to change the default flow and the default page of a flow.

Changing the default flow and the default page of a flow

Each web application can have multiple flows, and each flow can have multiple pages. Each web application has a default flow and each flow has a default page. When you run the web application, the default page of the default flow is rendered.

If you want to change the default behavior, you can do that. The following are the steps to change the default flow:

1. From the web application, expand **Root Pages** and click on **shell**.

2. Go to the **Settings** tab and select the flow name from the **Default Flow** dropdown to make it the default.

The following are the steps to change the default page of a flow:

1. Select the flow whose default page you want to change. Select the **main** flow for the time being.

2. Switch to the **Settings** tab and then select the page from the **Default Page** dropdown. Select main-external-data from the list as per the following screenshot:

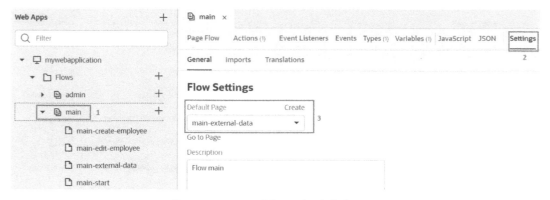

Figure 6.23 – Modifying the default page

Now, when you run the web application, the **main-external-data** page will be rendered by default on the main flow. In this section, we learned how to change the default behavior of the web application. Next, we'll look at how to navigate between pages, flows, and passing parameters between pages.

Navigating between pages, flows, and passing parameters between pages

Whenever you create different pages and flows, then you may need to jump from one page to another or from one flow to another. Similarly, you may need to pass parameters between pages.

In this section, we'll look at how to navigate from one page to another and flows.

Navigating between pages

In this section, we'll create a new page to show the user details from the external API, https://jsonplaceholder.typicode.com/users/1. The new page will be opened when we click on a row from the **main-external-data** page.

After completing the use case, the new page will look like the following screenshot:

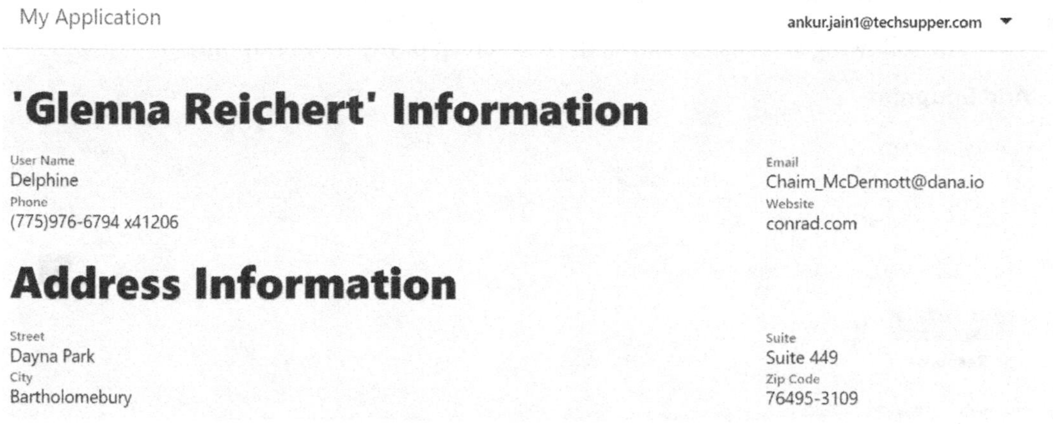

My Application   ankur.jain1@techsupper.com ▼

'Glenna Reichert' Information

User Name
Delphine

Email
Chaim_McDermott@dana.io

Phone
(775)976-6794 x41206

Website
conrad.com

Address Information

Street
Dayna Park

Suite
Suite 449

City
Bartholomebury

Zip Code
76495-3109

Figure 6.24 – The user information page

The following are the steps to complete the use case:

1. Add a new endpoint, `https://jsonplaceholder.typicode.com/users/1`, to the existing Service Connection, **jsonplaceholderTypicodeCom**.

2. Create a new type and variable.

3. Create a new page to show the user details.

4. Register an event on the row selection on the **main-external-data** page.

5. Create logic in the Action Chain to call the external API and perform a redirection to the new page.

Adding a new endpoint

The following are the steps to add a new endpoint:

1. To add a new endpoint, go to **Services** from the application navigator and click on **jsonplaceholderTypicodeCom**.

2. Switch to the **Endpoints** tab and then click on the + **Endpoint** button.

3. From the opened dialog box, enter `/users/{userid}` in the **Path** field. Since this endpoint will only return single pieces of data at a time, select **Get One** from the **Action Hint** dropdown and then switch to the **Test** tab.

4. On the **Test** tab, move to the **URL Parameters** tab under the **Request** section, enter the user ID (for example, `1`), and then click on the **Send Request** button.

5. Click on the **Save as Example Response** button to create the sample schema. Then, click on the **Add** button to add the endpoint.

The following screenshot shows the test screen of the new endpoint:

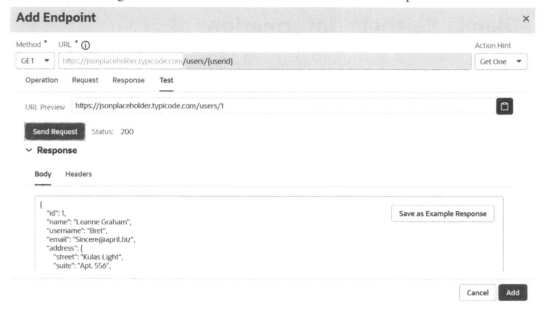

Figure 6.25 – Testing the Service Connection

This new endpoint will be used to fetch a single user detail.

Creating a new type and variable

The type and variable will be used to hold the user information. The following are the steps to create the type and variable:

1. Move to the web application tab, select the **main** flow, and then move to the **Types** tab.

2. Click on the **+ Type** and select From Endpoint.

3. The previous action will open the **Create Type From Endpoint** dialog box. Expand **Services | jsonplaceholderTypicodeCom**, select **GET /users/{userid}**, and then click on the **Next** button.

4. The type name **getUsersUserid** will be taken as a basis regarding the selected endpoint. If you wish to modify it, you can modify it.

5. Select the checkbox right next to the **Response** element, which will select all subsequent checkboxes and will be visible on the right-hand section. This means that all the fields will be added to the **getUsersUserid** type. Then, click on the **Finish** button to create the type, as per the following screenshot:

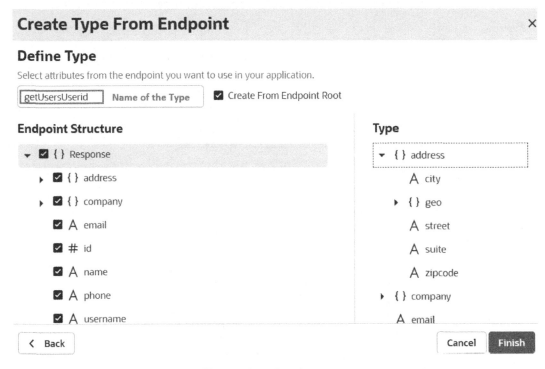

Figure 6.26 – Creating a type

A type will be created with the name getUsersUserid. This will be visible under the **Types** tab.

Next, we'll create a variable of the **getUsersUserid** type. The following are the steps to create the variable:

1. Switch to the **Variables** tab in the same **main** flow and click on the + **Variable** button.

2. Select the **Variable** radio box, enter the ID as `UserInformation`, select **getUsersUserid** as the type, and then click on the **Create** button as per the following screenshot:

Figure 6.27 – Creating a variable

This will create a variable of the **getUsersUserid** type.

> **Important Note:**
> Types and variables are created under the **main** flow so that they can be used in any pages inside the main flow.

Creating a new page

Now we'll create a new page that will be used to show the user information. The following are the steps to create a new page:

1. Click on the + button next to the **main** flow, enter the page ID as `main-user-information`, and then click on the **Create** button.

2. On the **main-user-information** page, drag and drop the **Heading** component on to the page.

3. Drag and drop the four **Input Text** components just below the **Heading** component.

4. Drag and drop another **Heading** component below **Input Text**.

5. Drag and drop another four **Input Text** components just below another **Heading** component.

    After dropping all the components, the page will appear as per the following screenshot:

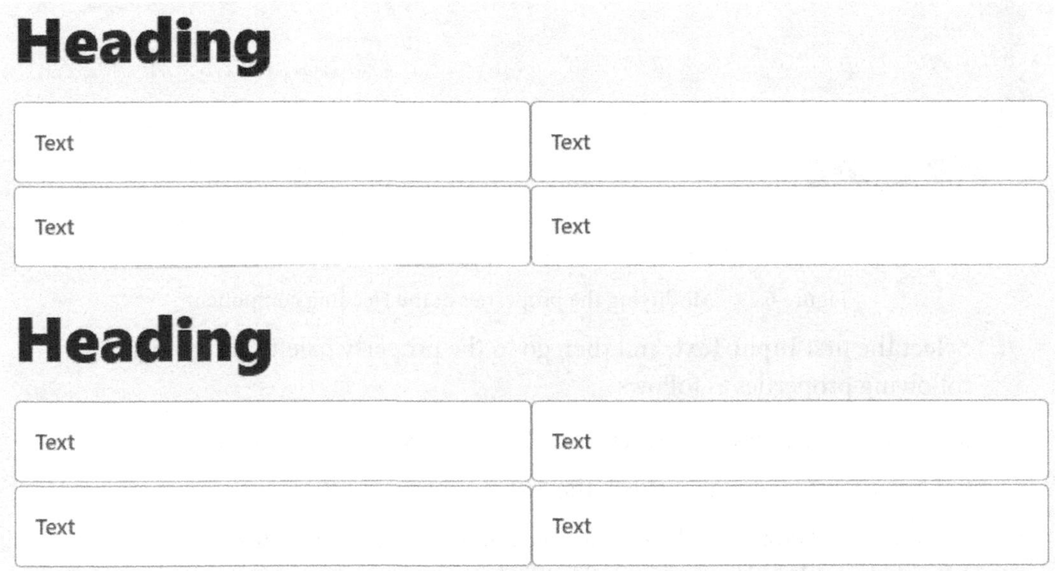

Heading

Text	Text
Text	Text

Heading

Text	Text
Text	Text

Figure 6.28 – The user information page

6. Select the first **Heading** component, go to the property palette on the right, under the **General** tab, and click on **Select Variable**, expand **Flow | Variables | UserInformation**, and then select **name** as per the following screenshot. This will add an expression in the **Text** property as `[[ $flow.variables. UserInformation.name ]]`. Modify this expression slightly to append `Information` with the name and enclose the name within single quotes. Therefore, modify the expression as `[[ "' "+$flow.variables. UserInformation.name + "' Information"]]`:

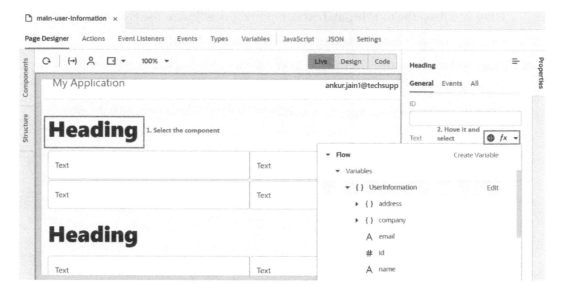

Figure 6.29 – Modifying the properties of the Heading component

7. Select the first **Input Text**, and then go to the property palette and change the following properties as follows:

    a. Under the **General** tab, enter `Label Hint` as the User Name.

    b. Under the **General** tab, check the `Readonly` property.

    c. Under the **Data** tab, select a variable and then select **username** from the **Flow | Variables | UserInformation** node.

8. Repeat *step 7* and update the properties for the remainder of the **Input Text** components as per the following table. Apply the changes from left to right and keep all input text read only:

Label Hint	Value
Email	{{ $flow.variables.UserInformation.email }}
Phone	{{ $flow.variables. UserInformation.phone }}
Website	{{ $flow.variables. UserInformation.website }}
Street	{{ $flow.variables. UserInformation.address.street }}
Suite	{{ $flow.variables. UserInformation.address.suite }}
City	{{ $flow.variables. UserInformation.address.city }}
Zip code	{{ $flow.variables. UserInformation.address.zipcode }}

Table 6.1 – Properties of the UI component

9. Change the text for the second **Heading** component to Address Information.

Now the page is ready and it will appear as per the following screenshot:

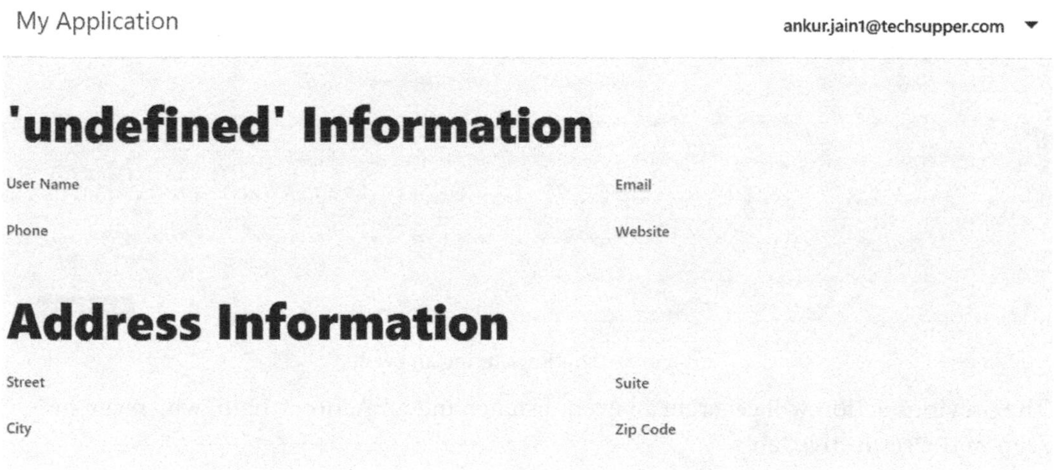

Figure 6.30 – The user information page

Next, we'll register an event on the **Table** component.

> **Tip:**
> You can also use the **Quick Start** (**Add Details** page) approach to show the user details as you have seen while listing the employee's information from BO in the *Building web-application and connecting to the Business Object* section. Here, we have used the manual approach to help you understand the components that make up a page.

Registering an event on the row selection

We'll register an event on the row selection that will be fired when a row is selected from the **Table** component. The following are the steps to register for an event:

1. Open the **main-external-data** page and then select the **Table** component.

2. From the **Table** property palette, move to the **Events** tab.

3. Click on the **+ New Event** button and select the **Quick Start: 'first-selected-row'** event as per the following screenshot:

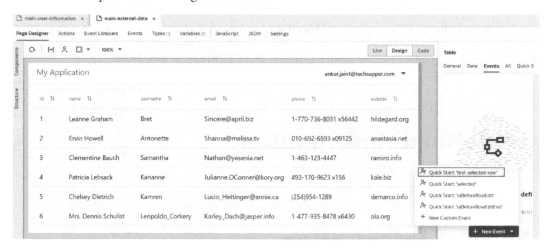

Figure 6.31 – Registering an event

The previous action will generate an event listener and an Action Chain, which can be seen in the respective tab.

You will land on the Action Chain designer to write the logic.

Creating logic in the Action Chain

The Action Chain is full of various actions that will be used to write the logic of an event and will be executed once an event is fired.

In this Action Chain, we'll call the external REST API and assign the REST API response to the **UserInformation** variable created in the previous section.

The following are the steps to write the logic in the Action Chain:

1. Drag and drop the **Call Rest** action (used to call any REST endpoint) from the **Actions** panel just below the **Start** action.

2. Select the **Call Rest** activity, modify the ID property to `callRestEndpointUserInformation`, and then click on **Select** from the right-hand properties palette.

> **Tip:**
> It's always good to change the ID of each action you drop on the Action Chain. To do so, select the action and then change the **ID** property of the selected action from the properties panel.

3. The previous action will open the **Select Endpoint** dialog box. Expand **Services | jsonplaceholderTypiCodeCom**, select **GET /users/{userid}** as per the following screenshot, and then click the **Select** button:

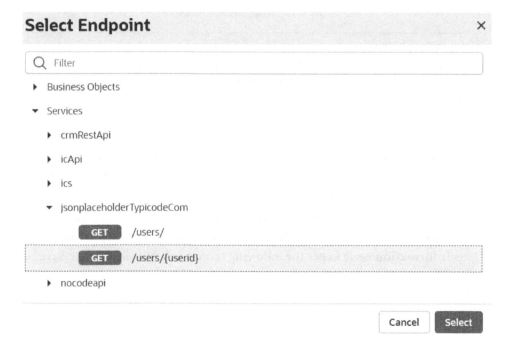

Figure 6.32 – Selecting the endpoint

4. Since the selected REST API requires **userid** as the input parameter, we have to map
    it with a user ID of the selected row. Select the **Call Rest** activity again and, from
    the properties palette, and click on **Assign** right next to **Input Parameters**. This
    action will open the **Assign Input Parameters** dialog box. Drag and drop **rowKey**
    to **userid** as per the following screenshot and then click on the **Save** button:

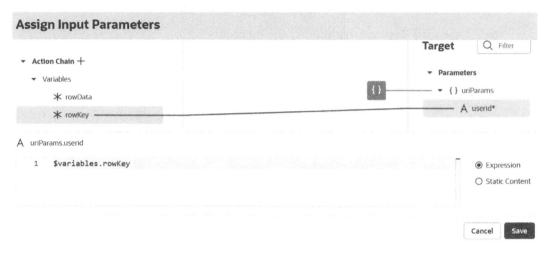

Figure 6.33 – Mapping the variables

> **Important Note:**
> The **rowKey** element contains the primary key of the table. This variable is
> created automatically with the Action Chain, and the scope of this variable is
> limited to just that Action Chain.

5. On the success path, drop the **Assign Variables** activity (used to assign
    values to the variables) from the **Actions** palette, modify the **ID** property to
    `assignVariablesRestResponse`, and then click on **Assign** from the
    right-hand properties palette.

6. The previous action will open the **Assign Variables** dialog box. Expand the
    callRestEndpointUserDetail node, and then drag and drop **body** to the
    UserInformation node as per the following screenshot and click on the **Save** button:

Figure 6.34 – Mapping the variables

7. Drag and drop the **Navigate** action (used to navigate from one page to another, and from one flow to another) from the **Actions** palette just below the **Assign Variables** action. Change the **ID** property to `navigateToPageUserInformation`. Set the **Target** property as `main-user information` from the **Properties** palette.

The following screenshot shows the Action Chain after implementing the whole logic:

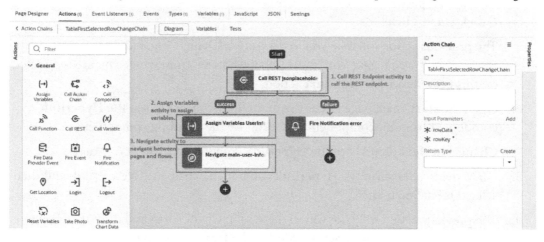

Figure 6.35 – Action Chain

The use case is complete and ready to test now. If you want to preview the web application, change the default page to **main-external-data**.

Preview the application and select any of the rows from the table. You will be directed to the new page with the user information as expected.

Navigating between flows

In the previous section, we saw how to navigate from one page to another in the same flow. Now, let's suppose you have different flows, and wish to navigate between pages of different flows. How can this be achieved? This is not straightforward compared to navigating between two pages of the same flow. In this section, you will become familiar with how to fulfill this requirement.

To complete this use case, we should have at least two flows in the same web application. So, let's create another flow first.

The following are the steps to execute this use case:

1. Open the web application and click on the + button right next to **Flows**. Enter `main-admin` as the flow ID and then click on the **Create** button. This action will create a new flow with a default page named **admin-start**.

2. Open the **admin-start** page, drag and drop the **Heading** component from the component palette and change the **Text** property in the **Heading** component to `Hey, I'm in admin flow now!`.

3. Drag and drop the **Hyperlink** component below the **Heading** component and change the **Text** property value to `<- Back`.

4. Click on **Hyperlink**, move to the **Events** tab, click on + **New Event**, and then select **Quick Start: 'click'**.

5. The previous action will take you to the Action Chain. Drag and drop the **Navigate Back** action (used to take you to the previous screen from where you are redirected on this page) just below the **Start** action.

6. Open the **start-main** page under the **main** flow. Drag and drop the **Hyperlink** component from the component palette above the **Heading** component.

7. Change the **Text** property of the **Hyperlink** component to `Go to Admin`.

8. Go to the **Events** tab of the **Hyperlink** component, click on + **New Event**, and then select **Quick Start: 'click'**.

9. The previous action will take you to the Action Chain. Drag and drop the **Navigate** action just below the **Start** action. Modify the **ID** property of the **Navigate** action to `navigateToAdminFlow`.

10. Select **Navigate**, click on the **Target** dropdown, and then select **shell**.

11. Click on the **Action** menu from the properties palette and then click **Go to Code,** as per the following screenshot:

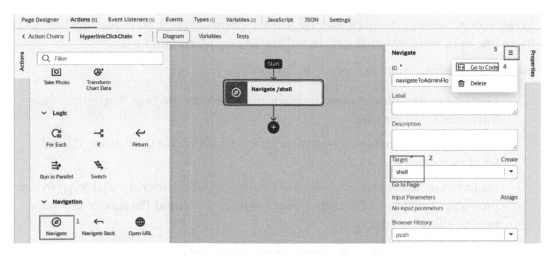

Figure 6.36 – Navigating to another flow

12. The previous action will take you to the JSON file of the page. Now, change the page value to `/shell/admin/admin-start` as per the following screenshot:

| Page Designer | Actions (5) | Event Listeners (5) | Events | Types (1) | Variables (2) | JavaScript | **JSON** | Settings |

```
111        "navigateToAdminFlow": {
112          "module": "vb/action/builtin/navigateToPageAction",
113          "parameters": {
114            "page": "/shell/admin/admin-start"
115          }
116        }
117      }
118    },
```

Flow name   Page name under the flow

Figure 6.37 – Updating the page property

This is how you jump from one flow to another.

> **Tip:**
> Navigation between flows can easily be handled at the shell page level.

The use case is now complete. Run the **main-start** page and then click on the **Go to Admin** hyperlink we added on the page. This action will redirect you to the **admin-start** page of the **admin** flow. Click on the <- **Back** hyperlink, which will take you back to the **main-start** page.

Passing parameters between pages

Whenever you navigate between pages or flows, you may need to pass parameters between pages or flows. Passing parameters between pages or flows is pretty straightforward.

In this section, we will execute a use case where I'll demonstrate how to pass the logged-in username from **main-external-data** to the **main-user-information** page.

The following are the steps to execute the use case:

1. Open **mywebapplication** and the **main-user-information** page. Go to the **Variables** tab of the page.

2. Click **+ Variable** to create a new variable. Enter `userid` as the variable ID and `String` as the type.

3. So, to render this variable as the input variable, select the **userid** variable, go to the properties palette, and then select **Enabled** under the **Input Parameter** section as per the following screenshot:

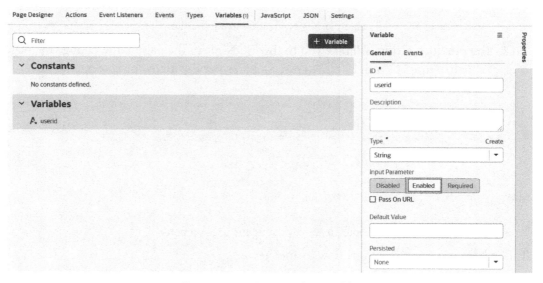

Figure 6.38 – Creating the variable

4. Go to the **Page Designer** tab of the same page and drag and drop the **Hyperlink** component above the first **Heading** component.

5. Change the **Hyperlink Text** property to `[[ $variables.userid ]]`.

6. Go to the **TableFirstSelectedRowChangeChain** Action Chain of the **main-external-data** page, select the **Navigate** action under the success path, and then reselect the **Target** property with `main-user-information` as the value.

    Notice the input parameter, **userid**, under the **Input Parameters** section as per the following screenshot:

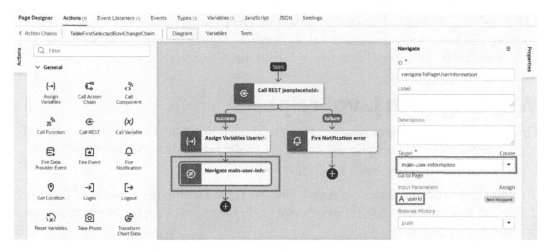

Figure 6.39 – Assigning the value of the input parameter

7. Click on **Assign** right next to **Input Parameters**. Expand **Application | System | user**, drag and drop **username** to **userid** as per the following screenshot, and then click on the **Save** button:

Figure 6.40 – Mapping the variables

This is how you can pass parameters between two pages. We are now ready to test the page.

Preview the **main-external-data** page. Select any row from the table, you will be redirected to the **main-user-information** page, and then you will see the value of the logged-in username at the top of the page.

In this section, we learned how to navigate from one page to another, from one flow to another, and how to pass parameter values from one page to another. Next, we'll look at how to work with JavaScript functions to extend the VB application's functionality.

Working with JavaScript

Oracle VB allows us to write JavaScript to extend the functionality of the web or mobile application as per requirements. You can write **JavaScript (JS)** code at any level (application, flow, page, or shell) of the application.

To define a JS function, the `prototype` function is used within the module. In order to define a JS function, switch to the **JavaScript** tab of the respective application, flow, page, or shell.

The following is the syntax to write a JS function in the application module:

```
AppModule.prototype.functionName = function (param1,param2){
    // write your logic here
    return "xyz";
}
```

The following is the syntax to write the function in the flow module:

```
FlowModule.prototype.functionName = function (param1,param2){
    // write your logic here
    return "xyz";
}
```

The following is the syntax to write a JS function in the page or shell module:

```
PageModule.prototype.functionName = function (param1,param2){
    // write your logic here
    return "xyz";
}
```

In this section, we'll execute a use case that will show calculator functionality using JavaScript.

The following are the high-level steps to achieve the use case:

1. Create a new page to allow numbers to be entered and show the result.

2. Write a JavaScript function to calculate the result depending on the operation (add, subtract, multiply, or divide).

3. Register an event on the buttons to call a JavaScript function.

Creating a new page

The following are the steps to create a new page:

1. Create a web page under the main flow with the page ID `main-calculator`.

2. Drag and drop three **Input Number** and four **Button** components on to the page.

3. In the **main-calculator** page, create three variables with the IDs `number1`, `number2`, and `result` under the **Variables** tab of the **Number** type.

4. Change the properties of all of the UI components as per the following table:

Component Type	Label Hint	Text	Value
Input Number	Number1		{{ $variables.number1 }}
Input Number	Number2		{{ $variables.number2 }}
Input Number	Result (make it ready only)		{{ $variables.result }}
Button		+ Add	
Button		- Subtract	
Button		* Multiply	
Button		/ Divide	

Table 6.2 – Properties of the UI component

The following screenshot shows how the page appears after updating the properties:

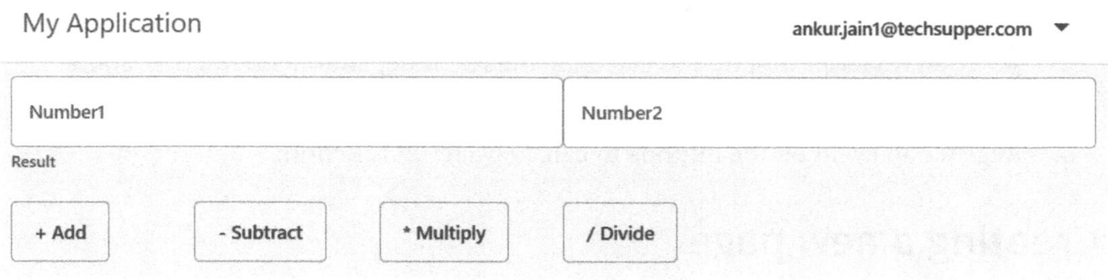

Figure 6.41 – The calculator page

Next, we'll write a JavaScript function to calculate the result of two numbers depending on the button clicked.

Writing a JavaScript function

A JavaScript function will be used to calculate the result of two numbers and return a value depending on the operation.

Open the **main-calculator** page and move to the **JavaScript** tab. Just below the `var PageModule = function PageModule() {};` line, enter the following JavaScript code:

```
PageModule.prototype.calculate = function(number1,number2,op){
    if(op=="add"){
        return number1+number2;
    }
    else if(op=="sub"){
        return number1-number2;
    }
    else if(op=="mul"){
        return number1*number2;
    }
    else if(op=="div"){
        return number1/number2;
    }
}
```

You can make your JavaScript function more complex as per your requirements.

Registering an event on buttons and calling a JS function

We'll register an event on the button component to call a JavaScript function. We will create a single Action Chain for all four buttons.

The following are the steps to register an event and call a JS function:

1. Select the + **Add** button and then move to the **Events** tab from the properties palette.

2. Click on the + **New Event** button and then select **Quick Start: 'ojAction'**.

3. The previous action will create an Action Chain with the name **ButtonActionChain**.

4. Click on the **Variables** tab of the Action Chain and then create a new String variable with the ID operation. Select the **Enabled** property of this variable under the **Input Parameter** section.

5. Go to the **Diagram** tab of the Action Chain and drag and drop **Call Function** (used to call a JavaScript function) from the action just below the **Start** activity.

6. Select the **Call Function** action, go the **Properties** tab of this action, modify the **ID** property to callModuleFunctionCalculate, and then select **calculate** from the **Function Name** dropdown.

7. Once the function is selected, you will observe all the JS parameters under the **Input Parameters** section. Click on **Assign** and perform mapping as per the following table:

Source	Target
$variables.operation	op
$page.variables.number1	number1
$page.variables.number2	number2

Table 6.3 – Mapping the variables

8. Drag and drop the **Assign Variables** action just below **Call Function**. Click on **Assign** from the **Assign Variables** properties. Map $chain.results. callModuleFunctionCalculate to result, and then click on the **Save** button.

9. Go back to the **Page Designer** tab, select the - **Subtract** button, go to the **Events** tab from the property palette, select + **New Event**, and then select + **New Custom Event**.

10. From the opened dialog box, select **ojAction** and then click on the **Select** button. From the next screen, select the existing Action Chain, `ButtonActionChain`, and then click on the **Select Action Chain** button as per the following screenshot:

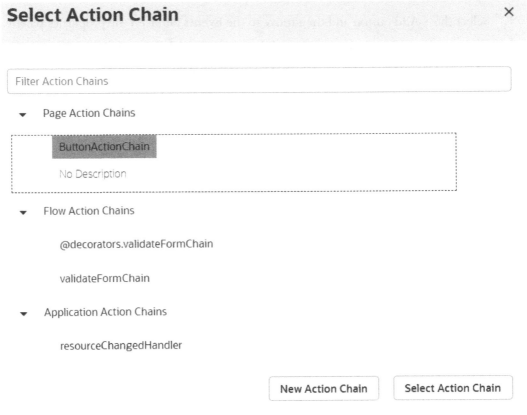

Figure 6.42 – Selecting the Action Chain

11. Repeat the previous *step 9* and *step 10* for the two remaining buttons, * **Multiply** and / **Divide**.

12. Now we need to pass values to the **operation** variable, which we created in *step 4*, on the button Action Chain. When you create the variable under the Action Chain and make it an input parameter, then you will be allowed to set the value of such variables before the event fires. To pass the values of such parameters, perform the following steps.

13. Select the + **Add** button, go to the **Events** tab, and then click on **Assign** right next to the **Input Parameters** section.

14. Assign the hardcoded value as add in the operation variable as per the following screenshot and then click on the **Save** button:

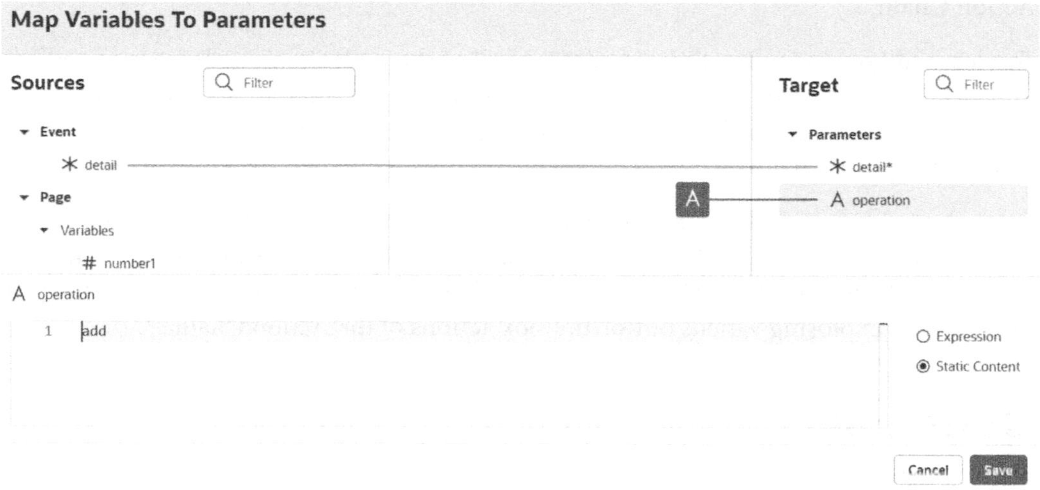

Map Variables To Parameters

Sources		Target	
▾ Event		▾ Parameters	
✳ detail		✳ detail*	
▾ Page		A operation	
▾ Variables			
# number1			

A operation

1   add

○ Expression
⦿ Static Content

Cancel   Save

Figure 6.43 – Assigning a value to the variable

15. Repeat *step 13* and *step 14* for the remaining three buttons and assign operation variable values as sub, mul, and div for the - **Subtract**, * **Multiply**, and / **Division** buttons, respectively.

Once all the steps are complete, we are ready to test the application. Preview the **main-calculator** page and then test the application. The results of the two numbers entered should be visible as per the clicked button.

In this section, we learned how to write a JavaScript function to extend the functionality of the VB application.

Summary

In this chapter, we worked on various real-time use cases that will help you to work with mini projects, and now you will be able to work with Business Objects and Service Connections. You learned how to create a web application, and how to create different pages to read, write, update, and delete data from Business Objects. You learned how to use various out-of-the-box options of the **Table** component to interact with Business Objects without writing a single line of code. You learned how to change the default flow and default page of the flow of a web application.

You learned how to create a new page, create a Service Connection, pull data from external REST APIs using a Service Connection, and populate it on the **Table** component. You learned how to navigate between two pages, two flows, and how to create input variables to pass data from one page to another. You learned how to register an event and implement business logic in the Action Chain using various out-of-the-box actions of the Action Chain.

You learned how to work with JavaScript, as well as the syntax to write JavaScript code at different levels. You saw how to write JavaScript in the page module, and how to call it on the button action. Having learned so much, you have now moved closer to building your own web applications.

In the next chapter, we'll execute another set of real-time use cases that will show another set of VB functionalities, such as how to validate a web form on the client side using JavaScript, the various life cycle methods of the VB, how to load the data prior to the page loading, and exploring various out-of-the-box actions of the Action Chain.

Questions

1. What is SDP?
2. Can we pass multiple parameters between pages?
3. Can we call a Business Object using the Call REST activity?

7

Working with Life Cycle Events, Validations, and UI Logic

In this chapter, we'll work with the life cycle events of our page, which will help you to execute your custom code before or while exiting the page. Life cycle events are very important to understand as they help you to perform cleanup and other important tasks before a user enters or exits a page. For example, you can redirect a user to the login page if a user is trying to access a secured page or you want to abort the user session before the user leaves a secured page. We'll execute an example where you will see how to use a life cycle event to load data before a page loads.

We'll show you how to populate the data from relational Business Objects in two separate tables and how to populate child data based on the selection of a parent row. You will learn how to validate a web form on the client side.

We'll show you how to implement various logic related to UI components, such as hiding/showing UI components, calculating a value based on the value of other fields, enabling a logout feature, and so on. You will also learn how to create dependent lists of values from two different Business Objects.

In this chapter, we will cover the following topics:

- Exploring life cycle events
- Loading data on page load
- Showing the parent-child relationship on a page
- Enabling client-side validation on forms
- Working with various UI logic
- Creating dependent lists of values

After completing this chapter, you will be familiar with the life cycle events of a page, how they work, and how to use them in a VB application. You will be able to use the **ADP** variable to load data from a Business Object and use it to populate a table. You will be able to perform client-side validation on a web form using JavaScript. You will be able to perform various UI logic in a VB application and you will be able to create dependent lists of values.

Technical requirements

To complete this chapter, you need the following:

- A **Visual Builder** instance
- **VB** login credentials
- A Business Object

You can find the full source code used in this chapter here: `https://github.com/PacktPublishing/Effortless-App-Development-with-Oracle-Visual-Builder/tree/main/Chapter07`.

Exploring life cycle events

Each and every page in a VB application goes through a life cycle in which a series of actions or tasks is performed. These actions include the initialization of a page, the initialization of types and variables, the rendering of UI components, allowing a user to save the changes before they exit a page, and the cleanup of the resources after leaving the page. It's really important to understand the life cycle of a page so that you can write your code at the correct life cycle stage.

Similarly, an application and its flows have their own life cycles. An application can contain multiple flows, and a flow can contain multiple pages.

Every stage of the page has associated events that you can use to write your code. For example, you want users to log in before they try to access a secured page, and you want to delete the user's session after they have left that page.

Let's learn about the different life cycle events of a page through the following figure:

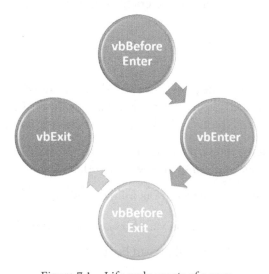

Figure 7.1 – Life cycle events of a page

The following sections will provide explanations of each and every life cycle event of a page.

vbBeforeEnter

This event is triggered before a user tries to navigate from one page to another. Visual Builder will start the navigation to the next page, but it will not crush the state of the previous page.

Let's try to understand how the **vbBeforeEnter** event is helpful for VB applications. Let's suppose a user is trying to access a secured page for which the user doesn't have permission. In that case, you can cancel the navigation and redirect the user to an "unauthorized" page or the login page. You can write your redirect code in the Action Chain associated with the **vbBeforeEnter** event.

With this event, you can fetch data from the following variables scope:

- **$application**: All the application variables can be used in the event Action Chain.
- **$flow**: All the parent flow variables can be used in the event Action Chain.
- **$parameters**: All the input parameters from the URL can be used in the event Action Chain.

vbEnter

This event is triggered after all the page-scope variables are added and initialized with their default values, values from URL parameters, or persisted values. This event is generally used to fetch data from Business Objects or Service Connections for reusability purposes.

For example, you can fetch data from a Business Object or Service Connection on page load and populate various UI components with that data.

With this event, you can fetch data from the following variables:

- **$application**: All the application variables can be used in the event Action Chain.
- **$flow**: All the parent flow variables can be used in the event Action Chain.
- **$parameters**: All the input parameters from the URL can be used in the event Action Chain.

vbBeforeExit

This event is triggered before page exit. Once all the Action Chains associated with the **vbBeforeExit** event are complete, the page instance is destroyed, and future attempts to access the page will throw an exception.

For example, let's suppose that a user has filled in a form and is trying to navigate to another page before saving their form. So, in this event, you can execute an Action Chain and warn the user that their unsaved changes would be lost.

vbExit

This event is triggered when exiting a page. With this event, you can associate the Action Chain that you want to execute after navigating to another page. This event is primarily used to clean up resources.

For example, you can destroy the logged-in user session after a user logs out from an application.

In this section, we learned about various page life cycle events that will help you to execute the necessary code depending on your requirements. In the next section, we'll look at how to use the **vbEnter** event to load data before the page load.

Loading data on page load

In the previous section, we learned about the different life cycle events of a page; now we will execute a **vbEnter** event, which will help to load page data before a page is loaded.

In this section, we will execute a use case that will load data from the **Employee** Business Object before page load and show the data in a table component. The following are the high-level steps to achieve the use case:

1. Create a type and a variable of the **Array Data Provider (ADP)** type.
2. Register the vbEnter event and load the **Employee** Business Object data.
3. Populate the **Employee** Business Object data from the ADP variable in a table.

We'll create a new web application with the name chapter7 under our **VBCSBook** application and develop all the use cases in this web application. Refer to *Chapter 3, Exploring Visual Builder Ingredients*, specifically the *Understanding the application's structure* section, to see how to create a new web application.

ADP is one of the out-of-the-box data types. It keeps a collection of data as an array that is accessible in the page/app.

Let's execute this use case.

Creating a type and an ADP variable

The following are the steps to create a type and an ADP variable:

1. Open the **main-start** page of the **chapter7** web application.

2. Go to the **Types** tab, click on **+ Type**, and select **From Endpoint**.

3. Expand **Business Objects | Employee**, select **GET /Employee/{Employee_Id}**, and click on the **Next** button as per the following screenshot:

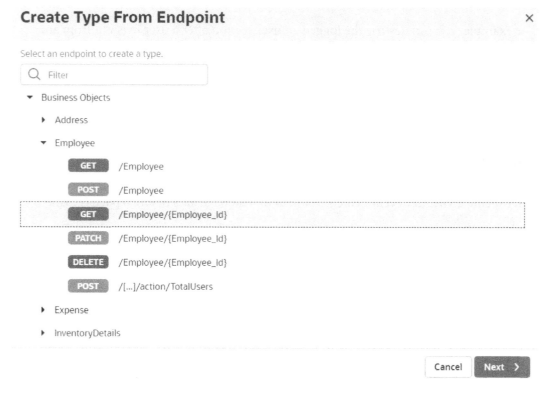

Figure 7.2 – Select the endpoint

4. From the next screen, select **id**, **firstName**, **lastName**, **fullName**, **emailAddress**, **contactNumber**, **age**, **qualification**, and click on the **Finish** button.

5. The previous action will create a type with the ID get_Employee.

6. Switch to the **Variables** tab, click on **+ Variable**, enter EmployeeADP as the variable ID, and set **Type** as Array Data Provider, as per the following screenshot:

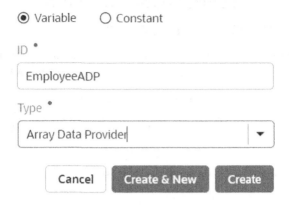

Figure 7.3 – Create a variable

7. Select the **EmployeeADP** ID that we just created, go to the **Properties** palette of the variable, select **get_Employee** from under **Item Type**, and set `id` for **Key Attributes**, as per the following screenshot:

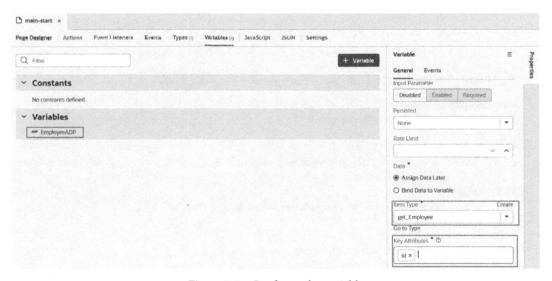

Figure 7.4 – Configure the variable

The previous steps will create a type and a variable.

Registering the vbEnter event and loading the Employee Business Object data

In this section, we'll look at how to use the **vbEnter** event, call the **Employee** Business Object, and assign the Business Object response to the **EmployeeADP** variable.

The following are the steps to register the **vbEnter** event:

1. Select the **main-start** page, go to the **Event Listeners** tab, and click on **+ Event Listener.**

2. From the **Create Event Listener** dialog box, select **vbEnter**, and click the **Next** button:

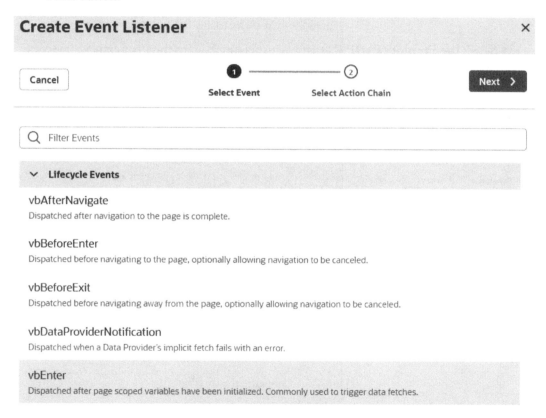

Figure 7.5 – Select the vbEnter event

3. The next screen will allow you to create or select the existing Action Chain in the **Page**, **Flow**, or **Application** scope. Click on **Page Action Chains +** and enter the Action Chain name as `loadEmployeeData` as per the following screenshot. Click on the **Finish** button to complete the dialog box:

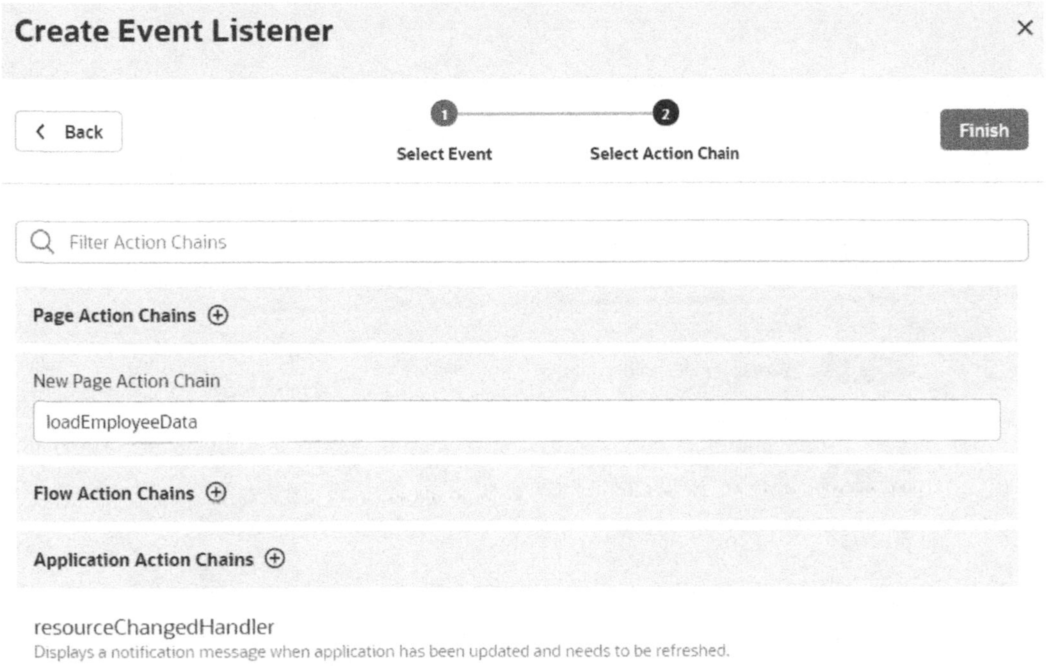

Create Event Listener   ×

‹ Back   ①————————②   Finish
                Select Event   Select Action Chain

Q Filter Action Chains

Page Action Chains ⊕

New Page Action Chain

loadEmployeeData

Flow Action Chains ⊕

Application Action Chains ⊕

resourceChangedHandler
Displays a notification message when application has been updated and needs to be refreshed.

Figure 7.6 – Create the Action Chain

The previous action will create a new Action Chain on the page scope.

4. Hover over **loadEmployeeData** and click on **Go to Action Chain**. This action will take you to the Action Chain to implement the logic.

5. Drag and drop the **Call REST** action just below the **Start** action. Rename the **ID** property of the **Call Endpoint** action as `callRestEndpointEmployee` from the **Properties** palette.

6. Click on **Select** to the right of **Endpoint** for the **Call REST** action from the properties palette.

7. From the **Select Endpoint** dialog box, expand **Business Objects | Employee**, and select the **GET /Employee** endpoint. Click the **Select** button:

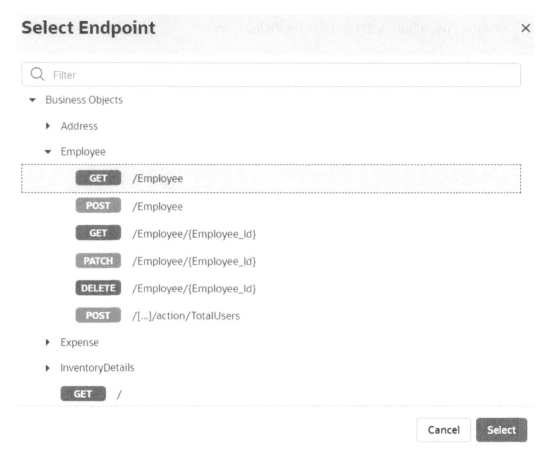

Figure 7.7 – Select the endpoint

8. On the **Success** path, drag and drop the **Assign Variables** action, and change the **ID** property to **assignVariablesEmployeeData**. Click on **Assign** to the right of **Variables** in the **Properties** palette for the **Assign Variables** action.

9. In the **Assign Variables** dialog box, map the source to the target as follows:

    ```
    Action Chain/Results/callRestEndpointEmployee/items to Page/
    EmployeeADP/data
    ```

    The following screenshot shows the source and target mapping:

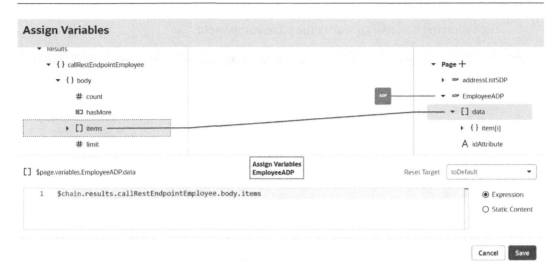

Figure 7.8 – Map the fields

That completes the Action Chain logic.

> **Important Note:**
> You can associate multiple Action Chains with a single event listener.

This Action Chain will be fired before the **main-start** page loads.

Populating the Employee Business Object data

In this section, we'll look at how to use **ADP** variables to populate a table component with data.

The following are the steps to populate data in a table using the ADP variable:

1. Open the **main-start** page, go to the **Page Designer** tab, and drag and drop the **Table** component on the page.

2. Select the **Table** component, go to the **Data** tab in the properties palette, hover on the **Data** property, click on the **Select Variable** icon, and select the **EmployeeADP** variable inside the **Page** scope.

3. In the same **Data** tab, hover over the **Table Columns** property, select the **Edit Columns** icon, and select **id, firstName, lastName, fullName, emailAddress, contactNumber, age**, and **qualification**. As soon as you select the fields, they will be visible in the table along with the data.

The following screenshot shows the table component:

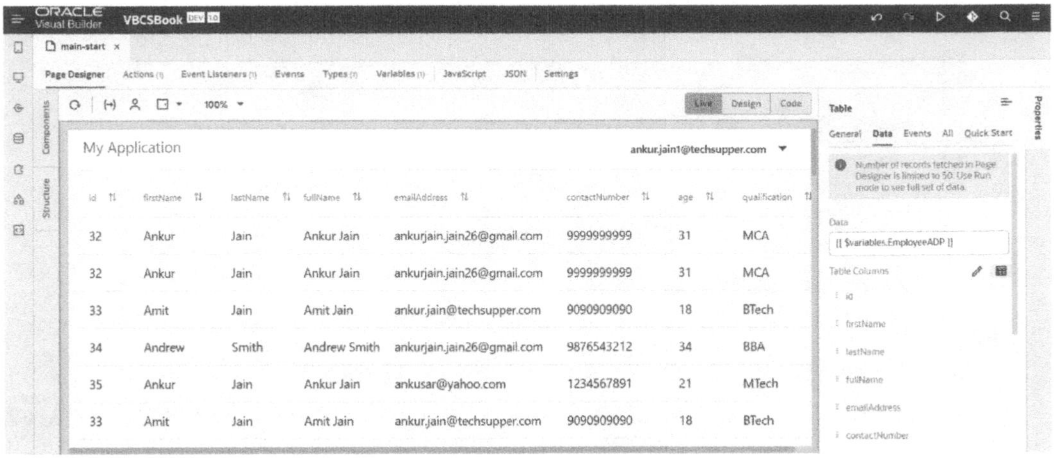

Figure 7.9 – Run the page and see the data

Preview the page and the data will be loaded in the table component through the **vbEnter** event. You can use the **EmployeeADP** variable to populate another component too.

In this section, you learned how to use the **vbEnter** event to load data on page load. Now you can use this event to execute any code that you want before page load. In the next section, we will work with the parent-child relationship.

Showing a parent-child relationship on a page

In this section, we'll look at how to show relational Business Object data in two different tables. In the first table, we'll show the employee data, and in the second table, we'll show the address of the employee selected in the first table.

The following are the high-level steps to execute the use case:

1. Create a table to populate with the employee data from the **Employee** Business Object.

2. Create a table to populate with the address data from the **Address** Business Object.

3. Implement the logic to show the addresses of the selected employee.

We'll use the **main-start** page that we created in the previous section and consider the **Employee** table as the first table.

Creating a table to populate the addresses

The following are the steps to populate the table component with the addresses:

1. Open the **main-start** page and create a new variable with the `fullName` ID of the **String** type, and assign the default value as `' '` using the **Default Value** property.

2. Return to the Page Designer, and drag and drop the **Heading** component just below the first table.

3. Bind the **Text** property of the **Heading** component as `[['Address information of '+ $variables.fullName ]]`.

4. Drag and drop the **Table** component just below the **Heading** component.

5. Select the **Table** component, open the properties palette, go to the **Quick Start** tab, and select the **Add Data** option.

6. From the **Add Data** dialog box, select the **Address** Business Object and select the **Next** button.

7. On the next screen, select **address1**, **address2**, **city**, **state**, **country**, and **zipCode**, and click the **Next** button.

8. Initially, we don't want to populate the addresses in the address table because the addresses data will be populated based on the employee selected from the employees table. So, on the next screen, we have to add a filter criterion that will restrict the table not to populate address data initially.

    Select **filterCriterion** and click on the **Click to add condition** link as shown in the following screenshot:

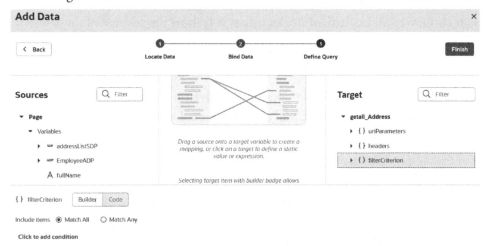

Figure 7.10 – Enable filterCriterion

9. From the **IF** dropdown, select **employeeId**, set the operator as `equals($eq)`, and enter any values that you would never expect in the address table for the employee ID. Enter `-1` for the time being and click on the **Finish** button:

Figure 7.11 – Add condition

Notice that the address table will not be populated due to the filter criterion.

Implementing the logic to show the address of the selected employee

In this section, we will implement the logic that will show the address of the selected employee in the address table.

The following are the steps to implement the logic:

1. Select the employee table, go to the **Events** tab from the properties section, select **+ New Event**, and select **Quick Start: 'first-selected-row'**. This action will create an Action Chain and will take you to that Action Chain.

2. In the Action Chain, drag and drop the **Assign Variables** action and click on **Assign** to the right of **Variables** in the properties palette.

3. From the open **Assign Variables** dialog box, expand **addressListSDP** on the target side, select **filterCriterion**, and click on the **Click to add condition** link. From the **IF** dropdown, select **employeeId**, set operator as `equals($eq)`, and select **$variables.rowKey** from the value dropdown:

Figure 7.12 – Enable the filter criterion

4. As shown in the previous screenshot, the Action Chain has two variables: **rowData** and **rowKey**. The **rowData** variable contains the complete data set of the selected row. So, the expression **$variables.rowData.fullName** will give you the full name of the selected employee.

5. Now we want to assign the **fullName** variable with the full name of the selected employee. So, select the **fullName** variable on the **Target** side and enter the expression as $variables.rowData.fullName as in the following screenshot. Click on the **Save** button to close the dialog box:

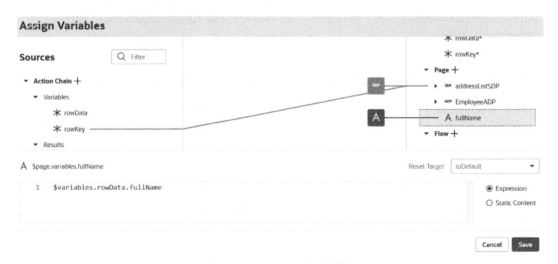

Figure 7.13 – Map the fields

This completes the logic for populating the address of a selected employee.

Import data in the **Address** Business Object, preview the application, then select any one of the rows, and the address table should be populated with the associated employee data, if any.

The following screenshot shows the address of the selected employee:

My Application   ankur.jain1@techsupper.com ▼

id ⇅	firstName ⇅	lastName ⇅	fullName ⇅	emailAddress ⇅	contactNumber ⇅	age ⇅	qualification ⇅
32	Ankur	Jain	Ankur Jain	ankurjain.jain26@gmail.com	9999999999	31	MCA
33	Amit	Jain	Amit Jain	ankur.jain@techsupper.com	9090909090	18	BTech
34	Andrew	Smith	Andrew Smith	ankurjain.jain26@gmail.com	9876543212	34	BBA
35	Ankur	Jain	Ankur Jain	ankusar@yahoo.com	1234567891	21	MTech
36	Gyial	Hasan	Gyial Hasan	gyial@test_test.com	9897654322	54	BBA

Address information of Ankur Jain

Address1 ⇅	Address2 ⇅	City ⇅	State ⇅	Country ⇅	Zip Code ⇅
343/2A	2B	Shahdara	Delhi	India	110032

Figure 7.14 – Run the page and see the result

This is how you can show relational data in two different tables.

In this section, we learned how to show data from two different relational Business Objects using two different tables and show the child data based on the selected parent data. In the next section, we'll look at how to validate web forms on the client side using JavaScript.

Enabling client-side validation on forms

Client-side validation is one of the most important things in each and every web or mobile application; it helps to validate the data on the client side before a request is sent to the server. In this section, we'll look at how to validate a form on the client side using JavaScript.

In this section, we'll create a web form to onboard a new employee and will apply client-side validation before we save the data in a Business Object.

The following are the high-level steps to execute this use case:

1. Create a web form.
2. Create JavaScript to validate the web form.
3. Implement the logic to validate the form and insert data into the Business Object.

We'll look at the preceding steps in detail in the upcoming sections.

Creating a new web form

The following are the steps to create a new web form:

1. Create a new page with the `main-onboard-employee` Page ID under the **chapter7** web application.
2. Create a type using **GET /Employee/{Employee_Id}** from the **Employee** Business Object type. Refer to the *Loading data on page load* section, specifically the *Creating a type and an ADP variable* section, to see how to create a type.
3. Create a variable with the `NewEmployee` ID of type **get_Employee** as in the following screenshot:

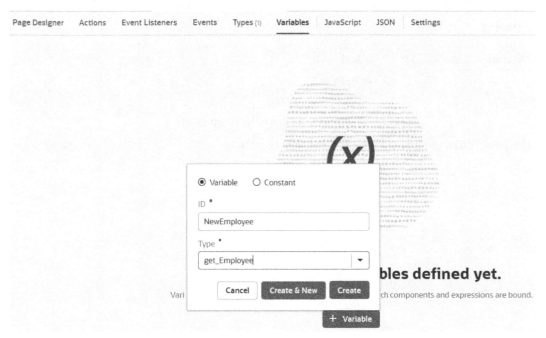

Figure 7.15 – Create a variable

4.   Drag and drop the UI components on the page as per the following table:

Component Type	Label Hint	Text	Required	Value
Input Text	First Name		Enable	{{ $variables.NewEmployee.firstName }}
Input Text	Last Name		Enable	{{ $variables.NewEmployee.lastName }}
Email	Email Address		Enable	{{ $variables.NewEmployee.emailAddress }}
Input Text	Contact Number		Enable	{{ $variables.NewEmployee.contactNumber }}
Input Text	Qualification		Enable	{{ $variables.NewEmployee.qualification }}
Input Number	Age		Enable	{{ $variables.NewEmployee.age }}
Button		+ Add Employee		

Table 7.1 – A table of UI components

The page looks as shown in the following screenshot:

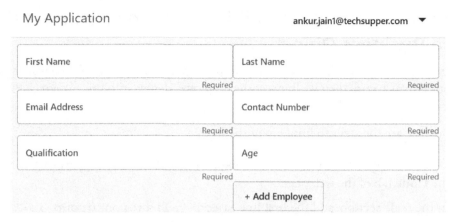

Figure 7.16 – UI of the page

This completes our web page.

Creating JavaScript to validate a form

As a next step, we'll create a JavaScript code that will validate the web form. If the values are entered in the required fields, then only save the data into the Business Object; otherwise, show the validation messages.

The following are the steps to create JavaScript code:

1. Open the **main-onboard-employee** page and move to the **JavaScript** tab.

2. Enter the following code just below the var PageModule = function PageModule() {}; line:

```
PageModule.prototype.validateForm = function(form) {
    var myform = document.getElementById(form);
    if (myform.valid === "valid") {
        return true;
    } else {
        myform.showMessages();
        myform.focusOn("@firstInvalidShown");
        return false;
    }
}
```

The previous JavaScript function will validate all the required fields of the web form. If any one of the fields is blank, the function will return false; otherwise, it will return true.

Implementing logic to validate a form and insert data into a Business Object

In this section, we'll call the previous JavaScript on button click, and if the JavaScript function returns `true`, then we'll insert the employee details into the employee Business Object; otherwise, we'll show the validation messages.

The following are the steps to implement the logic:

1. Open the **Page Designer** tab of the **main-onboard-employee** page, then move to the **Code** tab of the web page.

2. In the code section, add the first line as `<oj-validation-group id="new-employee">` and the last line as `</oj-validation-group>`.

3. Switch back to the **Design** tab, select the **+ Add Employee** button, go to the **Events** tab in the properties pallet, click **+ New Event**, and select `Quick Start:'oj Action'`.

4. On the Action Chain, drag and drop the **If** action (this allows you to check the condition) just below the **Start** action, then change the **ID** property to `ifValidateForm`. In the **Condition** property of the **If** action, set the condition as `{{ $page.functions.validateForm("new-employee") }}`. **new-employee** is the ID of the `<oj-validation-group>` tag.

5. In the **true** path, drag and drop the **Call REST** action, then change the **ID** property to `callRestEndpointAddEmployee`. Click **Select** to the right of **Endpoint**, and select the `POST /Employee` endpoint of the **Employee** Business Object.

6. Select **Assign** to the right of **Parameters** as in the following screenshot:

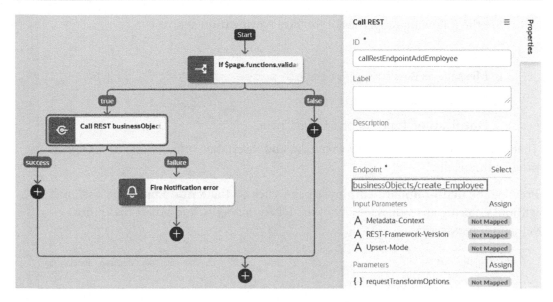

Figure 7.17 – Assign the payload

7. From the **Assign Variables** dialog box, drag and drop **NewEmployee** on **body** as in the following screenshot, and click on the **Save** button:

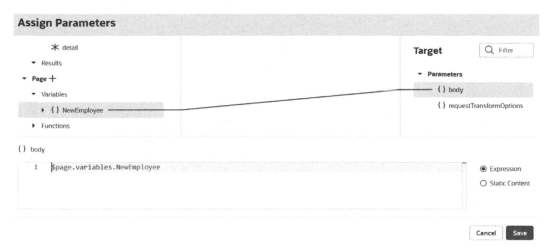

Figure 7.18 – Map the fields

8. Drag and drop the **Fire Notification** (used to display notification messages inline on the browser window) action on the success path.

9. Set the following properties of the **Fire Notification** action:

    a. **Summary** as `Success`

    b. **Message** as `Employee created successfully`

    c. **Display Mode** as `transient`

    d. **Notification Type** as `confirmation`

That's all the logic to validate the web form and insert data into the Business Object programmatically.

Preview the **main-onboard-employee** page, click on the **+ Add Employee** button without entering any values for any of the UI components, and notice the inline validation messages:

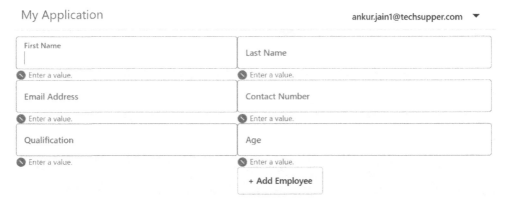

Figure 7.19 – Run the page and view the result

Now, enter values in all the fields and click on the **+ Add Employee** button. The employee details should be saved into the **Employee** Business Object and you will see a confirmation message on the page as shown in the following screenshot:

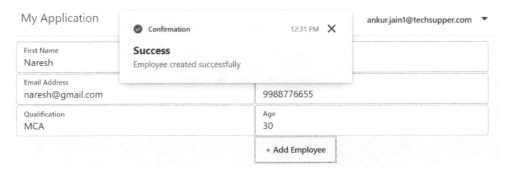

Figure 7.20 – Run the page and view the result

Open the **Employee** Business Object and you should see data there.

In this section, we learned how to validate a web form on the client side using JavaScript and show the inline messages if values are not entered in the required fields. Next, we'll look at how to implement various logic at the UI level.

Working with various UI logic

In this section, we'll see how to implement different logic for UI components, such as logic for hiding/showing UI components, calculating values, enabling a logout feature, and so on.

In this section, we are going to cover the following:

- Hiding/showing UI components
- Calculating fields
- Enabling a logout feature
- Validating input using a regex

Hiding/showing UI components

It's a very frequent requirement to hide or show UI components when some other UI component is interacted with. For example, you might show a form if the user clicks on a button and hide the form when the user clicks on the button again.

The following are the steps to take to hide/show UI components using JavaScript:

1. Create a new web page with the **main-ui-logics** Page ID under the **chapter7** web application.

2. Drag and drop the UI components on the page as per the following table:

Component Type	Label Hint	Text	Id
Button		Advance Search	
Form Layout			advancesearch
Input Text	First Name		
Input Text	Last Name		
Email	Email Address		
Input Text	Contact Number		

Table 7.2 – A table of UI components

Make sure all the **Input Text** components are inside the form layout.

3. Select the **Form Layout** component from the **Structure** palette and set the **Max Columns** property to 2 and set the **ID** property as advancesearch. Go to the **All** tab from the properties palette of the **Form Layout** component, go to the **style** property, and enter display:none. This code will hide the form initially.

4. Go to the **JavaScript** tab of the page and enter the following JavaScript code:

```
PageModule.prototype.showHide = function() {
    var x = document.getElementById(
        "advancesearch").style.display;
    if (x === "none") {
        document.getElementById(
            "advancesearch").style.display = "block";
    } else {
        document.getElementById(
            "advancesearch").style.display = "none";
    }
}
```

5. Return to the **Page Designer** tab, select the **Button** component, and register the **ojAction** event.

6. Go to the Action Chain of the **ojAction** event, then drag and drop the **Call Function** action just below the **Start** action.

7. Select the **showHide** function from the **Function Name** property of the **Call Function** action.

The following screenshot shows the page:

Figure 7.21 – UI of the page

All the configuration is complete now. Just switch to the **live** mode of the page. Initially, the form layout will not be visible. Click on the **Advance Search** button; this will show or hide the form layout.

Calculating fields

Sometimes you need to calculate values based on the input of other fields and show the calculated values in a different field. For example, on a web page, there may be a date field that allows you to enter a date of birth, and based on the date of birth entered, a different UI component may display an age figure in years. In this section, we want to execute this use case. So, let's see how to execute such type of use-case requirement using VB.

The following are the steps to calculate age based on date of birth:

1. Open the **main-ui-logics** page and create a variable with age ID of type **Number**.

2. Drag and drop the **Input Date** component on the **main-ui-logics** page just below the **Form Layout** component. Change the **Label Hint** property of this component to Date of Birth.

3. Drag and drop the **Text** component just below the **Input Date** component. Set the **Value** property as `[['You are age is ' + ($variables.age?$variables.age:'')]]` for the **Text** component.

4. In the text **Value** attribute, we use the **ternary** operator to check if **age** is not blank, then we show the value of **age**; else, we leave it blank with the hardcoded string.

5. Go to the **JavaScript** tab of the **main-ui-logics** page and enter the following JavaScript code to calculate age based on the date of birth:

```javascript
PageModule.prototype.calculateAge = function(dateOfBirth)
{
    var  currentDate = new Date();
    var birthDate = new Date(dateOfBirth);
    var totalAge = currentDate.getFullYear() -
        birthDate.getFullYear();
    var month = currentDate.getMonth() -
        birthDate.getMonth();
    if (month < 0 || (month === 0 && currentDate.
      getDate() < birthDate.getDate())) {
        totalAge--;
    }

    return totalAge;
}
```

6. Return to the **Page Designer** tab, select the **Input Date** component, and register a **value** event from the **Events** tab of the properties palette.

7. Drag and drop the **Call Function** action just below the **Start** action and change the **ID** property to `callModuleCalculateAge`. Select the **calculateAge** function from the **Function Name** dropdown.

8. Click on **Assign** to the right of **Input Parameters** and map **$variables.value** to **dateOfBirth** as in the following screenshot, then click on the **Save** button:

Assign Input Parameters

Sources 🔍 Filter   Target 🔍 Filter

▾ Action Chain +   ▾ **Parameters**
　▾ Variables   　{ } dateOfBirth
　　✳ value
　▾ Results
▾ Page +
　▾ Variables
　　# age

{ } dateOfBirth

```
1  $variables.value
```
　　　　　　　　　　　　　　　　　　　　　　　⦿ Expression
　　　　　　　　　　　　　　　　　　　　　　　○ Static Content

　　　　　　　　　　　　　　　　　　　　1:1

Cancel **Save**

Figure 7.22 – Map the fields

9.　Drag and drop the **Assign Variables** action just below the **Call Function** action. Click on **Assign** to the right of **Variables**, map `$chain.results.callModuleFunctionCalculateAge` to `$page.variables.age`, and click on the **Save** button.

Now the configuration is complete. Go to the **main-ui-logics** page and go to the **live** mode, enter a date of birth, and you should see that an age is shown, as in the following screenshot:

My Application　　　　　　　　　ankur.jain1@techsupper.com ▾

Advance Search

Date of Birth
01/10/1991　　　　　　　　　📅

You are age is 29

Figure 7.23 – Run the page and view the result

The **value** event will be fired as soon as you enter a value in the date of birth field and call the associated Action Chain.

Enabling a logout feature

Whenever you develop any application inside the VB, you will see the logged-in user's name in the top-right corner of every page, along with a **Sign Out** option:

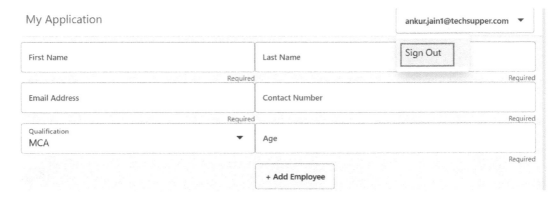

Figure 7.24 – Sign Out button

The sign-out button functionality is not enabled by default. You have to enable it manually. The logged-in username and button are set on the **shell** page of the application.

The following are the steps to enable the logout feature:

1. Open the **shell** page of the **chapter7** application inside **Root Pages**.

2. Go to **Structure** for the page and select the **Menu** component, then go to the **Events** tab and register the **ojAction** event as in the following screenshot:

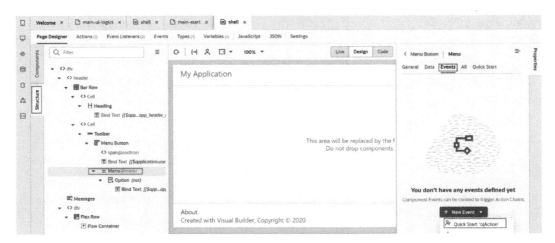

Figure 7.25 – Register event for sign-out button

3. Drag and drop the **If** action just below the **Start** action and set the condition as `[[ $variables.menuId ==='out']]`.

> **Important Note:**
> `out` is the ID of the sign-out menu component; hence, we are checking a condition if a user clicks on the sign-out menu, and only then do we allow users to sign out.

4. Drag and drop the **Logout** action on the **true** path. This action allows you to set the logout URL in the **Logout URL** property.

    The following is the structure of the logout URL:

    `https://<unique_idcs_identifier>.identity.oraclecloud.com/ oauth2/v1/userlogout`

    You have to replace `unique_idcs_identifier` with the **IDCS** identifier of your Oracle Cloud instance.

5. Enter the logout URL in the **Logout URL** property.

That's all about enabling a logout feature in a VB application. Run the application and click on the **Sign Out** button. You will be signed out completely from the VB application.

Validating an input component using a regex

Whenever you develop a web form, you always need to take valid data from users and restrict users from entering enter junk data into the web form. For example, you will want users to enter only alphabet characters in the name fields and use the correct email address format in the email field.

Oracle VB allows us to validate data using the **Validator** property of the input components.

The following are the steps to validate an input text field using a regex:

1. Open the **main-ui-logics** page under the **chapter7** web application.

2. Select the first input text component from the page structure, go to the properties palette, go to the **All** tab, and enter the following JSON in the **Validator** property:

```
[{"type":"regexp", "options":{"pattern":"[a-zA-Z ]*$",
"hint":"Enter a valid value.", "messageDetail": "Only
characters are allowed"}}]
```

Run your page, enter an invalid value in the first name field, and the component should throw an error, as in the following screenshot:

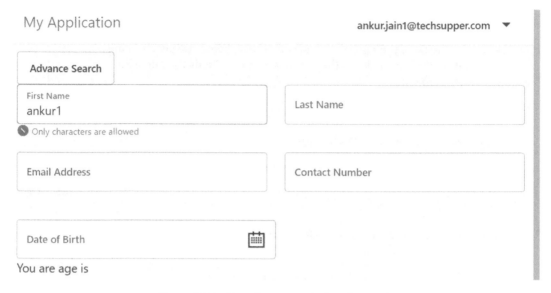

Figure 7.26 – Run the page and view the result

The **Validator** property of the input component accepts the JSON array in the previous format. You can use the same format to validate other components too and provide different regexes in the **pattern** property.

In this section, we learned how to implement logic for UI components, such as logic for hiding or showing UI components, calculating values based on another value, enabling a logout feature, and validating input using the **Validator** property. In the next section, we'll look at how to create dependent Select (Single) components.

Creating dependent Lists Of Values

Dependent **Lists of Values** (**LOVs**) are when two or more LOVs are created, and the values of one LOV depend on the values of the other LOV. For example, the values of a **State** LOV may depend on the values of a **Country** LOV.

In this section, we'll create two LOVs using the **Select (Single)** component. In the first LOV, we'll populate **email address** using the **Employee** Business Object, and in the second LOV, we'll populate **inventory name** from the **InventoryDetails** Business Object.

The following are the steps to create dependent LOVs:

1. Create a new web page with the Page ID `main-dependent-lov` under the **chapter7** web application.

2. Drag and drop the **Select (Single)** component on the new page and modify the **Label Hint** property to `Employee`.

3. Go to the **Quick Start** tab from the properties palette of the **Select (Single)** component and select **Add Options**.

4. From the **Add Options** dialog box, select the **Employee** Business Object, and click on the **Next** button.

5. From the next screen, drag and drop `emailAddress` on **Label** and `id` on **Value**, then enter `Select Employee` for **Placeholder** and click on the **Next** button:

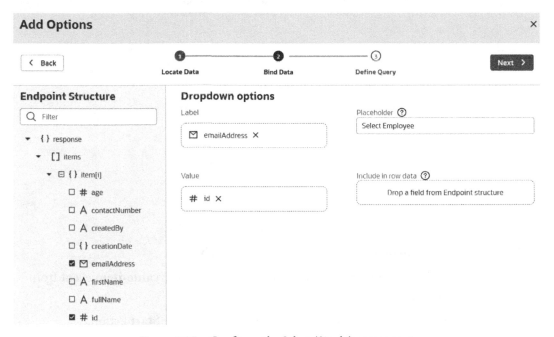

Figure 7.27 – Configure the Select (Single) component

6. Click on the **Finish** button to complete the dialog box.

7. The previous steps will create one LOV and will populate the employee's email address as a label.

8. Drag and drop the **Select (Single)** component again just below the first **Select (Single)** component and modify the **Label Hint** property to `Inventory Details`.

9. Go to the **Quick Start** tab from the property palette of the second **Select (Single)** component and select **Add Options**.

10. From the **Add Options** dialog box, select the **InventoryDetails** Business Object, and click on the **Next** button.

11. From the next screen, drag and drop `name` on **Label** and `id` on **Value**, then enter `Select Inventory Details` for **Placeholder** and click on the **Next** button.

12. From the next screen, select **filterCriterion**, click on **Click to add condition**, select **employeeId** from the **IF** dropdown, select **equals ($eq)** from the **operator** dropdown, and enter `-1` for **value**, as in the following screenshot:

Figure 7.28 – Configure the filter criterion

13. Click on the **Finish** button to complete the dialog box.

14. Select the first **Select (Single)** component and register the **value-item** event from the **Events** tab.

15. Drag and drop the **Assign Variables** action just below the **Start** action.

16. Click on **Assign** to the right of **Variables**.

17. From the **Assign Variables** dialog box, expand **inventoryDetailsListSDP**, select **filterCriterion**, and click on **Click to add condition**.

18. Select **employeeId** from the **IF** dropdown, select **equals ($eq)** from the **operator** dropdown, and enter `$variables.key` for **value**.

19. Click on the **Save** button to finish the dialog box.

The configuration is complete now. Switch the page to **live** mode, select any one of the email addresses from the first LOV, and the corresponding inventory name should be populated in the inventory details LOV if available.

The following screenshot shows the dependent LOVs:

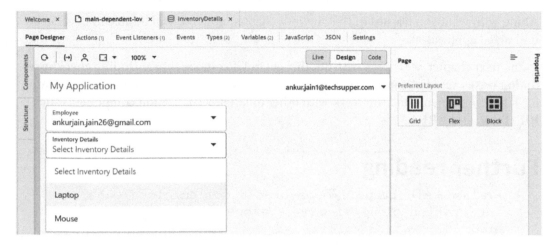

Figure 7.29 – Run the page and view the result

This is how you can create dependent LOVs.

In this section, we learned how to create dependent LOVs using Business Objects. You can use a similar approach to create dependent LOVs from Service Connections.

Summary

In this chapter, we learned about the life cycle events of a page and the significance of each life cycle event in detail with examples. This will help you to implement logic at the correct stage based on your web/mobile application's requirements. You learned how to use one of the out-of-the-box events, **vbEnter**, to load data on page load. We created an ADP variable to load data and used the variable to populate a table.

You learned how to use two related Business Objects to populate data in two tables and populate a child table data based on the row selected in the parent table. With this, you learned how to use **filterCriterion** to filter data on a page. You learned how to use JavaScript to validate web forms on the client side.

You learned how to implement logic in the UI layer, such as for hiding or showing UI components based on interaction with other components, calculating age based on date of birth using JavaScript, and enabling a logout feature for your VB application, and you learned how to validate UI components using the **Validator** property. You also learned how to create dependent LOVs using Business Objects.

Along with what you learned in the previous chapter, now you will be able to develop a mid-sized application.

In the next chapter, we'll work with another set of UI components, including **checkboxes**, **dialog boxes**, and **list components**. We'll implement **sorting**, **searching**, and **pagination** for table components and will work with other different visualization components such as **PIE**, **BAR**, and **AREA**.

Further reading

- Read about ADP: `https://docs.oracle.com/en/cloud/paas/integration-cloud/visual-developer/array-data-provider.html`

- Read about `<oj-validation-group>`: `https://www.oracle.com/webfolder/technetwork/jet/jetCookbook.html?component=validationGroup&demo=formFieldsValidation`

- Read about validators: `https://www.oracle.com/webfolder/technetwork/jet/jetCookbook.html?component=validators&demo=regExpValidator`

Questions

1. Which select component should you use: **Select (One)** or **Select (Single)**?

2. Can we use a `vbEnter` event to load data at the flow or application level?

3. What is the difference between **Service Data Provider** (**SDP**) and **Array Data Provider** (**ADP**)?

Section 3: Building Web and Mobile Apps Using Various VB Components

This section covers a lot of examples of various use cases related to real-life case studies. This will enable you to jump into your real-life projects and work independently. We will explore various UI components along with their different features, such as sorting, searching, pagination, and so on. We have covered how to extend Oracle and non-Oracle applications with the help of VB, which is the main intent of the platform. We will start creating mobile applications and build them for different mobile devices running on Android and iOS.

This section comprises the following chapters:

- *Chapter 8, Exploring Other Visual Components and Their Advanced Functionalities*
- *Chapter 9, Extending Oracle and Non-Oracle SaaS Applications*
- *Chapter 10, Working with Business Processes*
- *Chapter 11, Building a Mobile Application with Live Examples*

8

Exploring Other Visual Components and Their Advanced Functionalities

In this chapter, we'll work with another set of visual components that will allow you to develop your visual application more interactively. We'll play with a table that will allow us to modify the records inline. We'll work with other sets of **Oracle JET (JET)** components, such as lists, checkboxes, and dialogs. We'll also explore the advanced functionalities of the table component, such as sorting and resizing columns, searching the data, and how to enable pagination.

We'll look at how to use the dialog component to get consent from the user before an employee record is deleted. We'll work with the checkbox component and populate it with static and dynamic data. We'll then work with the list component to view the data in a different view.

Along with this, we'll work with different visualization components, such as pie, area, and bar charts, to visualize the data in a different form.

In this chapter, we will cover the following topics:

- Developing an editable table
- Enabling sorting, column resizing, searching, and pagination in a table
- Working with dialogs
- Working with checkboxes
- Working with List View
- Working with visualization components

After completing this chapter, you will be able to work with different Oracle JET components and their advanced functionalities, such as sorting, searching, pagination, and so on. You will be able to work with dialog boxes for different types of requirements. You will be able to use checkboxes. You will also be able to visualize your data using different charts such as pie, bar, and so on.

Technical requirements

To complete this chapter, you should have the following:

- A **Visual Builder** instance
- **VB** login credentials
- A Business Object
- A Service Connection

We will develop a new web application with the name **chapter8** under the **VBCSBook** application, and will execute all the use cases under the chapter8 web application.

You can find the full source code used in this chapter here: `https://github.com/PacktPublishing/Effortless-App-Development-with-Oracle-Visual-Builder/tree/main/Chapter08`.

Developing an editable table

An **editable table** is a table that allows you to update records inline. This is a very common requirement in every web application that allows users to update records inline. So, in this section, we'll develop a page with a table that allows us to update the records inline.

We'll use the following steps to achieve this (developing an editable table) use case:

1. Populate the table from the Business Object using the ADP variable.

2. Register events on the table.

3. Implement the logic to support inline editing in a table.

4. Add a button to save all modified records.

We'll look at the aforementioned steps in the following sections.

Populating the table from the Business Object using the ADP variable

ADP type variables are basically used whenever you want to implement functionality such as search, update, sort, and so on. So, we'll create a table based on the ADP variable. Refer to the *Loading data on page load* section in *Chapter 7, Working with Life Cycle Events, Validations, and UI Logic*, to create a table based on the ADP variable. Create the exact same table with the same structure under the **chapter8** web application and use the **main-start** page. We'll skip this step to reduce the redundancy of the content and will move on to the next step.

Registering events on the table

You should have completed the first step and have a table populated with the **Employee** Business Object. In this section, we'll register two out-of-the-box table events, namely, ojBeforeRowEdit and ojBeforeRowEditEnd. The ojBeforeRowEdit event is triggered before the table enters into edit mode, and the ojBeforeRowEditEnd event is triggered before the table exits edit mode.

The following are the steps to implement the events:

1. Create a new variable with the CurrentEditRow ID of the get_Employee object type on the **main-start** page. The variable will hold the information of the row that will enter edit mode.

2. Go to the **Page Designer** tab, select the table, and move to the **Events** tab. Then, select **+ New Event | Quick Start: 'ojBeforeRowEdit'**, as shown in the following screenshot:

Figure 8.1 – Configuring the table event

3. The previous action will take you to the **TableBeforeRowEditChain** Action Chain. Drag and drop the **Assign Variables** action just below the **Start** action.

4. Click **Assign** right next to **Variables** from the **Properties** palette of **Assign Variables**.

5. From the opened **Assign Variables** dialog box, drag and drop `$variables.rowData` to `CurrentEditRow`, and then click on the **Save** button, as shown in the following screenshot:

Figure 8.2 – CurrentEditRow data mapping

6. Return to the **Page Designer** section of the page and register the **ojBeforeRowEditEnd** event on the table as we did in *step 2*.

7. *Step 6* will create another Action Chain with the name `TableBeforeRowEditEndChain`. In this Action Chain, drag and drop the **Fire Data Provider Event** (used to dispatch an event on a data provider) action just below the **Start** action.

8. Select the **EmployeeADP** variable from the **Event Target** property. Then, select the **Mutate** option under the **Type** property and click **Assign** right next to **Parameters**, as shown in the following screenshot:

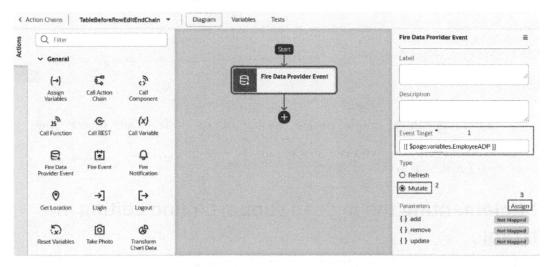

Figure 8.3 – Configuring the Fire Data Provider Event component

9. From the opened dialog box, map $page.variables.CurrentEditRow to update.data, and then click on the **Save** button, as in the following screenshot:

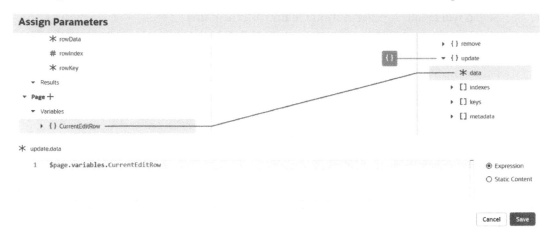

Figure 8.4 – Updating the data mapping

This will update the **EmployeeADP** variable with the updated data after the row is edited.

Let's see the next step in the next section.

Implementing the logic to support inline editing in a table

In this section, we'll implement the logic that will allow a user to inline edit in a table. The following are the steps to implement the logic:

1. Select the table, move to the **All** tab from the **Properties** palette of the table, then select **rowEdit** from the **edit-mode** property.

2. Drag and drop the **Input Text** component on the **firstName**, **lastName**, and **contactNumber** columns.

3. Drag and drop the **Email** component on the **emailAddress** column.

4. Then, drag and drop the **Input Number** component on the **age** column.

5. Also, drag and drop the **Select (Single)** component on the **qualification** column.

> **Important Note:**
> When you drag and drop UI components on the table columns, a separate column template is created for every column. You can go to the **Code** view of the page to see.

6. Select the dropped components one by one from the page **Structure** palette and uncheck the **Readonly** property, except for **Select (Single)**.

> **Tip:**
> Refer to the *Creating and modifying Business Objects* section in *Chapter 4, Creating and Managing Business Objects*, to create a new Business Object.

In order to populate the **Select (Single)** component, a new Business Object is created with the name **Qualification**, which will hold the qualifications. We created only a single field with the name Qualification and added qualifications (MBA, MCA, BBA, BCA, and BTech) as in the following screenshot:

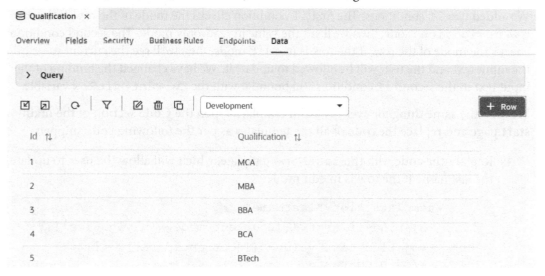

Figure 8.5 – Data in the Sales Business Object

7. Then, select the **Select (Single)** component from the page structure. Move to the **Quick Start** tab from the **Properties** palette and select the **Add Options** option.

8. From the opened **Add Options** dialog box, select the **Qualification** Business Object and select the **Next** button.

9. On the next screen, drag and drop **qualification** on both the **Label** and **Value** attributes. Enter Select Qualification for **Placeholder** and click the **Next** button.

10. Click the **Finish** button to complete the dialog box.

11. Go to the **Code** view of the page and modify the `firstName` template as per the following code:

```
<template slot="firstName">
    <oj-bind-if test="[[$current.mode=='navigation']]">
     <oj-bind-text value="[[$current.data]]">
     </oj-bind-text>
    </oj-bind-if>
    <oj-bind-if test="[[$current.mode=='edit']]">
     <oj-input-text value="{{$variables.
         CurrentEditRow.firstName }}"></oj-input-text>
    </oj-bind-if>
</template>
```

Let's try to understand the preceding code.

We added two `if` conditions. The first `if` condition checks the mode of the row. If the row is in `navigation` mode, then we'll see the value in read-only mode. The second condition checks the mode of the row; if the row is in `edit` mode, then we'll see the current value in the input text and the user will be allowed to update it. We have changed the binding of the input text in the second `if` condition and bound it with the `CurrentEditRow` variable.

We'll do the same thing for every column template. Open the **Code** section of the **main-start** page and replace the code of all the templates as per the following code snippets:

- Replace the code with the `lastName` template, which will allow the user to update the last name if the row is in edit mode:

```
<template slot="lastName">
 <oj-bind-if test="[[$current.mode=='navigation']]">
  <oj-bind-text value="[[$current.data]]"> ]]">
  </oj-bind-text>
 </oj-bind-if>
 <oj-bind-if test="[[$current.mode=='edit']]">
  <oj-input-text value="{{ $variables.CurrentEditRow.
      lastName }}"></oj-input-text>
 </oj-bind-if>
</template>
```

- Replace the code with the `emailAddress` template, which will allow the user to update the email address if the row is in edit mode:

```
<template slot="emailAddress">
    <oj-bind-if test="[[$current.mode=='navigation']]">
     <oj-bind-text value="[[$current.data]]"> ]]">
     </oj-bind-text>
    </oj-bind-if>
    <oj-bind-if test="[[$current.mode=='edit']]">
    <oj-input-text virtual-keyboard="email"
        validators='[{"type":"regexp", "options":
        {"pattern":"([a-zA-Z0-9_\\-\\.]+)@([a-zA-Z0-
        9_\\-\\.]+)\\.([a-zA-Z]{2,5})", "hint":"Enter an
        email address.", "messageDetail": "Value must
        be of the form xxx@xxx.xx"}}]' value="{{
        $variables.CurrentEditRow.emailAddress }}">
    </oj-input-text>
    </oj-bind-if>
    </template>
```

- Replace the code with the `contactNumber` template, which will allow the user to update the contact number if the row is in edit mode:

```
<template slot="contactNumber">
    <oj-bind-if test="[[$current.mode=='navigation']]">
     <oj-bind-text value="[[$current.data]]"> ]]">
     </oj-bind-text>
    </oj-bind-if>
    <oj-bind-if test="[[$current.mode=='edit']]">
    <oj-input-text value="{{ $variables.CurrentEditRow.
        contactNumber }}"></oj-input-text>
    </oj-bind-if>
    </template>
```

- Replace the code with the `qualification` template, which will allow the user to update the qualification if the row is in edit mode:

```
<template slot="qualification">
    <oj-bind-if test="[[$current.mode=='navigation']]">
     <oj-bind-text value="[[$current.data]]"> ]]">
     </oj-bind-text>
```

```
    </oj-bind-if>
    <oj-bind-if test="[[$current.mode=='edit']]">
    <oj-select-single data="[[$page.variables.
        qualificationListSDP]]" item-text="qualification"
        placeholder="Select Qualification" value="{{
        $variables.CurrentEditRow.qualification }}">
    </oj-select-single>
    </oj-bind-if>
    </template>
```

- Replace the code with the age template, which will allow the user to update the age if the row is in edit mode:

```
<template slot="age">
    <oj-bind-if test="[[$current.mode=='navigation']]">
      <oj-bind-text value="[[$current.data]]"> ]]">
      </oj-bind-text>
    </oj-bind-if>
    <oj-bind-if test="[[$current.mode=='edit']]">
      <oj-input-number value="{{ $variables.
          CurrentEditRow.age }}" style="text-align:
          right;">
      </oj-input-number>
    </oj-bind-if>
</template>
```

After making all the changes, you will be able to update all the fields (first name, last name, email address, qualification, contact, and age) as per the configuration. Now the logic is completed to enable the inline editing in a table.

Adding a button to save all modified records

In this section, we'll look at how to save the modified records with a button click. The following are the steps to save the records:

1. Drag and drop the **Button** component above the table component and change the **Text** property to **Save**.

2. Register the **ojAction** event on the button component. In **ButtonActionChain**, drag and drop the **For Each** action (which allows you to loop over the array) just below the **Start** action. Modify the **ID** property as `forEachEmployeeADP`.

3. Then, select **Assign** to the right of **Parameters** of the **For Each** action. From the opened **Assign Parameters** dialog box, drag and drop $page.variables. EmployeeADP.data on **items** and click on the **Save** button:

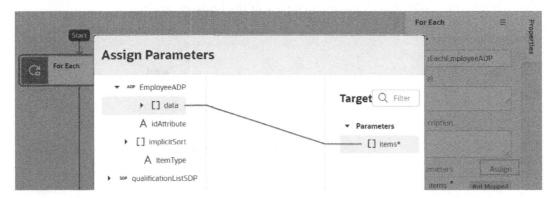

Figure 8.6 – For Each data mapping

4. Drag and drop the **Call REST** action inside the **For Each** action. Modify the **ID** property to callRestEndpointUpdateEmployee as in the following screenshot:

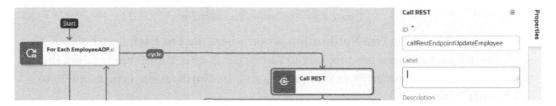

Figure 8.7 – Dragging and dropping the Call REST endpoint action inside the For Each action

5. Click **Select** right next to **Endpoint**. From the opened **Select Endpoint** dialog box, select the PATH /Employee/{Employee_Id} endpoint under the **Employee** Business Object and click on the **Select** button.

6. Select the **Call REST** action and click on **Assign** next to **Input Parameters**. Drag and drop the page/variables/EmployeeADP/data/items[0]/id parameter on uriParams/Employee_Id.

   You need to pass the ID of the current employee in the loop, so change the source expression to $page.variables.EmployeeADP.data[$current.index]. id. Click on the **Save** button to complete the mapping.

   > **Important Note:**
   > $current.index will provide the current element inside the loop.

7. Click on **Assign** to the right of **Parameters**. From the opened **Assign Parameters** dialog box, configure the target **body** expression to `$page.variables.EmployeeADP.data[$current.index]` and click on the **Save** button. The following screenshot shows the mapping of the **body** parameter:

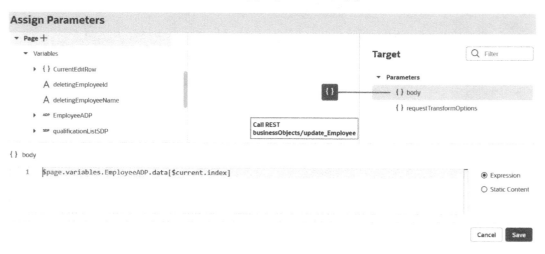

Figure 8.8 – The body data mapping

8. Drag and drop the **Fire Notification** action where the **For Each** loop finishes. Configure the **Summary** property to `Records have been modified`, the **Display Mode** property to `transient`, and the **Notification Type** property to `confirmation`.

The configuration is completed now. Preview the page and you should see that all the employee records are populated on the table in read mode.

In order to enable edit mode, double-click on the row, modify the records, click outside of the table to make the change take effect, and click on the **Save** button to save the modified records.

The following screenshot shows the table in editable mode:

My Application								ankur.jain1@techsupper.com ▼

Save

id ⇅	firstName ⇅	lastName ⇅	fullName ⇅	emailAddress ⇅	contactNumber ⇅	qualification ⇅	age ⇅
32	Ankur The row is in edit mode	Jain	Ankur Jain	ankurjain.jain26@gmail.com	9999999999	MBA ▼	31
33	Amit	Gupta	Amit Gupta	ankur.jain@techsupper.com	9090909090	BTech	18
34	Andrew	Smith	Andrew Smith	ankurjain.jain26@gmail.com	9876543212	BBA	34
35	Ankur	Jain	Ankur Jain	ankusar@yahoo.com	1234567891	MTech	21
36	Gyial	Hasan	Gyial Hasan	gyial@test_test.com	9897654322	BBA	54
37	Naresh	Kumar	Naresh Kumar	naresh@gmail.com	9988776655	MCA	30

Figure 8.9 – Table in edit mode

This is how you can make the table editable.

> **Tip:**
> You can implement some business logic that will only send rows (which were updates) back to the DB instead of looping over all the rows.
>
> Here is a VB cookbook example: `https://vbcookbook.oracle.com/?page=shell&shell=batch-editable-table&batch-editable-table=batch-editable-table-start&batch-editable-table-start=recipe`.

In this section, we learned how to make an editable table that allows users to update records inline. Along with this, we learned how to populate **Select (Single)** from a different Business Object in the same table. In the next section, we will look at how to enable sorting, column resizing, searching, and pagination in a table.

Enabling sorting, column resizing, searching, and pagination in a table

In this section, we'll work with advanced functionalities of table components. We'll look at how to enable/disable sorting, along with column resizing. We'll also filter data from a table, along with data search and paginating the data.

Enabling/disabling sorting on the table

Sorting allows you to arrange the data into ascending or descending order to view the data in sorted order. You can enable or disable sorting on every column of a table. By default, sorting is enabled on all the columns of a table.

The following screenshot shows the up and down arrows on all the columns, which allow you to sort the data:

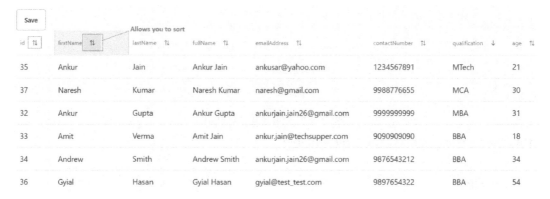

Figure 8.10 – Sorting on the table

The sorting is controlled by the **sortable** property of the column. If the value of this property is *enabled*, then the sorting is on, and if the value of this property is *disabled*, then the sorting is off.

The following are the steps to **disable** the sorting of a column:

1. Select the table, open the **Properties** palette, and move to the **Data** tab.

2. Under the **Table Columns** property, hover over any of the columns (hover over the **id** column for the time being) whose sorting property you want to disable and click on the **Column Detail** icon as shown in the following screenshot:

Figure 8.11 – Column Detail icon

3. Go to the **Columns, Sortable** property and select the **Disabled** value from the option list. Now, locate the **id** column of the table and notice that the up and down arrows are not visible, as shown in the following screenshot:

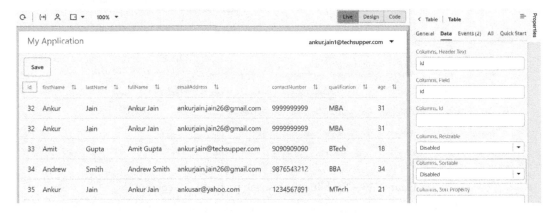

Figure 8.12 – Disabling sorting

Similarly, select the **Enabled** or **Auto** value to enable sorting.

Using these simple steps, sorting can be enabled or disabled on any column.

Enabling/disabling column resizing

Resizing allows you to increase or decrease the width of a column. Sometimes increasing the width is required to view large-sized data properly. Unlike sorting, the resizing property is disabled by default on the columns.

The resizing of a column is controlled by the **resizable** property of a column. If the value of this property is *enabled*, then you can resize the column, and if the value of this property is *disabled*, then you cannot resize the column.

The following are the steps to update the **resize** property of a column:

1. Select the table, open the **Properties** palette, and move to the **Data** tab.

2. Under the **Table Columns** property, hover over any one of the columns (hover over the **id** column for the time being) whose resizable property you want to enable and click on the column details icon.

3. Go to the **Columns, Resizable** property and select the **Enabled** value from the option list, as in the following screenshot:

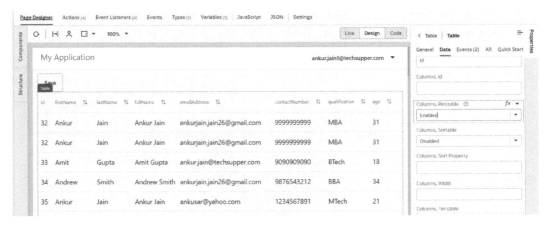

Figure 8.13 – Enabling the resizing property of a column

Switch to the **Live** mode of the page, hover over the **id** column, and now you will be able to resize the column width. Similarly, you can enable the resizable property for other columns too. In order to disable it, select the **Disabled** value from the **Columns, Resizable** property.

Filtering data from a table

Filtration (searching) is the mechanism to find data from a large set of collections, and it plays an important role when you have a very large set of data. In this section, we are going to create a table using the **Employee** Business Object, and a search form that will allow filtering the data based on first name, last name, email address, or qualification.

After completing this section, the page will look like as in the following screenshot:

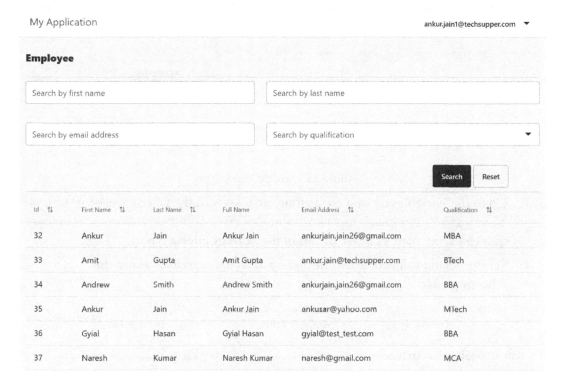

Figure 8.14 – Page UI

We need to follow these steps to execute the use case:

1. Design a new page to perform the search.

2. Implement **filterCriterion** to filter the data.

We'll look at both of the preceding steps in detail in the next sections.

Designing a new page to perform the search

The following are the steps to create a new page that will have a search form and a table from which data will be filtered based on different criteria, such as first name, last name, and so on:

1. Create a new page with the `main-search-page` page ID under the `chapter8` application.

2. Create a custom type with the `SearchCriteria` ID and set **Type** as **Object**. Add three **String** type variables with the `attribute`, `op`, and `value` IDs under the `SearchCriteria` variable, as in the following screenshot:

Figure 8.15 – SearchCriteria type

3. Go to the **Variables** tab and create four variables with the `firstNameCriteria`, `lastNameCriteria`, `emailAddressCriteria`, and `qualificationCritieria` IDs of the **SearchCriteria** type.

4. Set the default values of **attribute** and **op** of all four variables as per the following table:

Variable	Default Value	Description
firstNameCriteria.attribute	firstName	It is the field name in the **Employee** business object.
firstNameCriteria.op	$co	It is the sign of the **contains** operator.
lastNameCriteria.attribute	lastName	It is the field name in the **Employee** business object.
lastNameCriteria.op	$co	It is the sign of the **contains** operator.
emailAddressCriteria.attribute	emailAddress	It is the field name in the **Employee** business object.
emailAddressCriteria.op	$eq	It is the sign of the **equals** operator.
qualificationCriteria.attribute	qualification	It is the field name in the **Employee** business object.
qualificationCriteria.op	$eq	It is the sign of the **equals** operator.

Table 8.1 – Configuring the variables

5. Go back to the page designer, drop the **Heading** component, change the **Text** property to Employee, and set **Level** to H6.

6. Drag and drop the **Horizontal Rule** component just below the **Heading** component.

7. Drag and drop the **Form Layout** component just below the **Horizontal Rule** component and set the **Max Columns** property to 2.

8. Drag and drop the components under **Form Layout** and configure the properties as per the following table:

Component Type	Placeholder	Value
Input Text	Search by first name	{{ $variables.firstNameCriteria.value }}
Input Text	Search by last name	{{ $variables.lastNameCriteria.value }}
Email	Search by email address	{{ $variables.emailAddressCriteria.value }}
Select (Single)	Search by qualification	{{ $variables.qualificationCritieria.value }}

Table 8.2 – Table of UI components

9. Configure the **Select (Single)** component with the Qualification Business Object to populate it with all the qualifications. Refer to the *Implementing the logic to support inline editing in a table* section to populate this **Select (Single)** component.

10. Drag and drop the two **Button** components to the right corner of the page. Change the **Text** property of the button components to Search and Reset, respectively. Change the **Chroming** property to Solid of the **Search** button.

11. Drag and drop the **Horizontal Rule** component at the end of the page.

12. Drag and drop the **Table** component just below the **Horizontal Rule** component. Configure this table with the **Employee** Business Object using the **Quick Start** option.

This completes the page UI.

Implementing filterCriterion to filter the data

In this section, we'll configure the **filterCriterion** property of the **Service Data Provider (SDP)** to filter the data based on the search criteria.

Before we implement the logic, let's work on the **Reset** button functionality, which will allow resetting the values of the search form to the default state. The following are the steps to enable the reset functionality:

1. Click on the **Reset** button and register the **ojAction** event.

2. In **ButtonActionChain**, drag and drop the **Reset Variables** (used to reset the values of variables to their default state) action just below the **Start** action.

3. From the **Variables to Reset** property, set the four variables, namely, `$page.variables.firstNameCriteria.value`, `$page.variables.lastNameCriteria.value`, `$page.variables.emailAddressCriteria.value`, and `$page.variables.qualificationCritieria.value`, to reset their values.

That's about all there is to reset the variables values to their default state.

Let's implement the logic to filter out the data. The following are the steps to implement the logic:

1. Click on the **Search** button and register the **ojAction** event.

2. In **ButtonActionChain1**, drag and drop the **Assign Variables** action just below the **Start** action. Using this **Assign Variables** action, we'll check the value of all four variables (created in the previous section). If the value is blank, then assign `' '`, else assign the value of it.

3. Click **Assign** right next to **Variables**, and from the opened **Assign Variables** dialog box, assign the source expression, `$page.variables.firstNameCriteria.value?$page.variables.firstNameCriteria.value:' '`, to the target, `$page.variables.firstNameCriteria.value`. Repeat this step for the rest of the other three variables. Click on the **Save** button to close the dialog box.

    The following screenshot shows the source-to-target mapping:

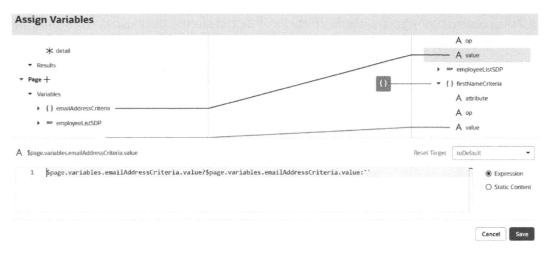

Figure 8.16 – Data mapping of criteria variables

4. Drag and drop the **Assign Variables** action just below the first **Assign Variables** action. Click **Assign** right next to **Variables**.

5. From the opened **Assign Variables** dialog box, drag and drop the variables, namely, `$page.variables.firstNameCriteria`, `$page.variables. lastNameCriteria`, `$page.variables.qualificationCritieria`, and `$page.variables.emailAddressCriteria`, from the source to the `$page.variables.employeeListSDP/filterCriterion/criteria` target. Click on the **Save** button to close the dialog box.

The following screenshot shows the source-to-target mapping:

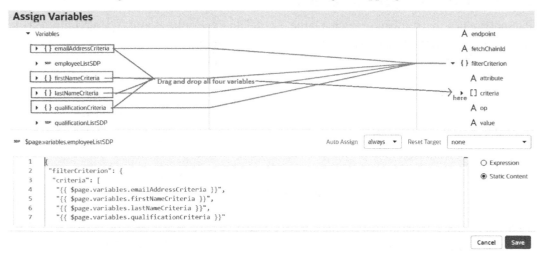

Figure 8.17 – Data mapping of the filter criterion

All the required configuration is completed and it's time to test the page. Preview this page and filter the data based on the defined search form.

The following screenshot shows filtered data based on qualification:

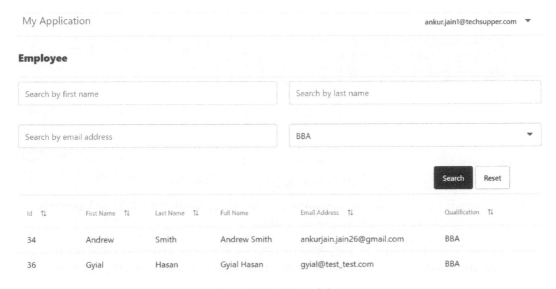

Figure 8.18 – Filtered data

Test the page with other search input parameters. Click on the **Reset** button to reset the value of the input text to its default values.

Implementing pagination

Pagination is a mechanism to fetch a large set of data in chunks as and when required. This is always a common requirement for implementing pagination; when there is a large set of data, show it in a `collection` component such as a table or list, load a small set of data initially, and get the other set of data into chunks when required. The modern approach to implementing pagination is to load data whenever required using the **scrolling** option. In this section, we'll look at how to implement pagination in a table using the scrolling option.

> **Important Note:**
> Whenever you implement pagination, make sure the REST API from where you fetch the data supports pagination too.

To implement pagination, we have imported a new Business Object with the name `Countries` using the **Data Manager**. Refer to the *Importing a Business Object* section in *Chapter 4, Creating and Managing Business Objects*, to know how to import Business Objects.

> **Tip:**
>
> You can download the Excel sheet (`https://github.com/PacktPublishing/Effortless-App-Development-with-Oracle-Visual-Builder/blob/main/Chapter08/Countries.xls`) and import it using the Data Manager to create a new **Countries** Business Object.

The following are the important properties that you should know about when implementing pagination:

- **scroll-policy**: This property specifies how data will be fetched as the user scrolls down the table. The permitted values are `auto`, `loadAll`, and `loadMoreOnScroll`. The default value is `loadMoreOnScroll`.

- **scroll-policy.fetch-size**: This property controls the number of records in each block. The default value is `25`.

- **scroll-policy-options.max-count**: This property controls the total number of records to be fetched. The default value is `500`.

- **style:height**: This is the **CSS** property that specifies the height of the table.

The following are the steps to implement pagination in a table:

1. Create a new page with the `main-paginate-data` ID under the `chapter8` web application.

2. Drag and drop a **Table** component on the page and configure it with a **Countries** Business Object using the **Add Data** option under the **Quick Start** tab. Also, include the `country`, `region`, `population`, `gDP`, `deathrate`, `birthrate`, and `literacy` fields while configuring the **Add Data** wizard.

3. If you want to show the sequence number in a table, drag and drop the **Input Number** component as the first column in the table. Select the table, go to the **Data** tab, and change the new column name to `S. No`.

4. Set the **S. No** column as `Readonly`. From the **Data** tab of this column property, set the **Value** expression as `{{ $current.index+1 }}`. `$current.index` will provide the index number of the rows, which starts from `0`, so we add `1` to start **S. No** from `1`.

5. Run the page and see that all the records will be fetched in a block of 25 (because of the default size of the `scroll-policy.fetch-size` property). The Business Object REST APIs will be called multiple times to fetch all the records (depending on the `scroll-policy-options.max-count` property value).

6. Select the table, open the **Properties** palette, move to the **All** tab, search for the **Style** property, and set the value as `height:500px`. This will set the height of the table and will allow you to load the records when you scroll down the table. Run the page and see the vertical scroll bar on the table. Initially, 25 records will be fetched from the Business Object, and when you scroll down the table, another request will be sent to the Business Object to fetch 25 more records, and so on.

7. You can set the `scroll-policy.fetch-size` property to fetch more records initially and the `scroll-policy-options.max-count` property to fetch the total number of records. In order to set the value to these two properties, search the `scroll-policy-options` property, hover over it, and go to the sub-properties of it.

The following screenshot shows a table in which pagination is implemented. Scroll down using the vertical scroll bar and notice that the records should be fetched. Sometimes it may take seconds to fetch another set of records depending on the network and data. You can go to the browser **network** tab to monitor REST API calls:

My Application							ankur.jain1@techsupper.com ▼
S. No ↑↓	Country ↑↓	Region ↑↓	Population ↑↓	GDP ↑↓	Deathrate ↑↓	Birthrate ↑↓	Literacy ↑↓
1	Afghanistan	ASIA (EX. NEAR EAST)	31056997	700	20.34	46.6	36
2	Albania	EASTERN EUROPE	3581655	4500	5.22	15.11	86.5
3	Algeria	NORTHERN AFRICA	32930091	6000	4.61	17.14	70
4	American Samoa	OCEANIA	57794	8000	3.27	22.46	97
5	Andorra	WESTERN EUROPE	71201	19000	6.25	8.71	100
6	Angola	SUB-SAHARAN AFRICA	12127071	1900	24.2	45.11	42
7	Anguilla	LATIN AMER. & CARIB	13477	8600	5.34	14.17	95
8	Antigua & Barbuda	LATIN AMER. & CARIB	69108	11000	5.37	16.93	89
9	Argentina	LATIN AMER. & CARIB	39921833	11200	7.55	16.73	97.1

Figure 8.19 – A table with pagination

If you are populating the table from external REST APIs, make sure the REST APIs support two pagination parameters such as **limit** and **offset**. For non BO/Oracle Cloud Apps REST services, you should create a transform option as part of the REST service definition in VB. This will help VB by providing it with the data about how to perform pagination and searches.

In this section, we learned about the various capabilities of table components, such as how to enable/disable sorting on columns, allow columns to be resized, enable filter criteria to search the data from the SDP, and paginate the table data. In the next section, we'll look at how to use the dialog component.

Working with dialogs

The **Dialog** component is one of the out-of-the-box components that is used to open a pop-up window. A dialog can be used to provide information, take consent from a user before performing some action, and so on.

In this section, we'll execute a use case wherein we'll create a table with **delete** functionality. When a user tries to delete an employee record, a dialog box will be opened to take consent. If they agree to delete the user, only then will that user be deleted.

For this use case, we'll use the **main-start** page of the **chapter8** web application.

The following are the steps to complete the use case:

1.   Use the dialog component.
2.   Open and close the dialog on an action.
3.   Implement the logic to delete a user.

In the next section, we'll look at the preceding steps in detail.

Using the dialog component

In this section, we'll use the dialog component, which will be opened when a user tries to delete a user. We'll use these steps to implement the dialog component:

1.   Open the **main-start** page and create two variables with the deletingEmployeeName and deletingEmployeeId IDs, of the String and Number types, respectively. These variables will hold the full name and ID of the employee that needs to be deleted.

2.   Drag and drop the **Dialog** component just below the table. The dialog component will not be visible on the page. You can view it either in the page structure or in the **Code** view. Alternatively, you can show the dialog in the visual editor by switching its **Initial Visibility** attribute in the **Properties** palette.

3.   Go to the **Code** view of the page, find the **dialog** component, and replace the existing code of dialog with the following code. The changed content is marked in bold:

```
<oj-dialog style="display:none" dialog-title="[['Delete
    User ('+ $variables.deletingEmployeeName+')' ]]" id="
    delete-user-dialog">

  <div slot="body">

    <div class="oj-flex">Are you sure you want to delete
    user?</div>

  </div>
```

```
<div slot="footer">
    <oj-button>Delete</oj-button>
    <oj-button>No</oj-button>
</div>
</oj-dialog>
```

The changes are self-explanatory. The dialog box is ready as per the requirement.

Opening and closing the dialog on an action

In this section, we'll see how to open and close the dialog component. The following are the steps to open and close the dialog:

1. Open the designer of the **main-start** page and create a new column in a table. Drag and drop the **Icon** component to after the last column of the table and change the column name to `Action`.

2. Select the **Icon** component from under the column of the table, go to the **Properties** palette, and click on the **Icon** property under the **General** tab. This action will open the **Icon Gallery** dialog box. Search the **Delete Trash Can** icon and select it. That will change the icon of the component. The following screenshot shows the column along with the delete trash can icon:

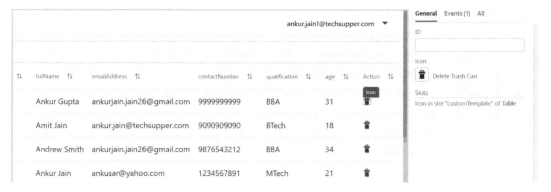

Figure 8.20 – Delete trash can icon

3. Register the **click** event on the **Icon** component. Under the Action Chain of this event, drag and drop the **Assign Variables** action just below the **Start** action.

4. Then, map the `$page.variables.EmployeeADP.data [$variables.current.index].fullName` variable to `$page.variables.deletingEmployeeName`. Also, map the `$variables.key` variable to `$page.variables.deletingEmployeeId`.

5. Then, we drag and drop the **Call Component** (a declarative way to call a method on JET components) action. From the **Properties** palette of the **Call Component** action, select the ID of the **delete-user-dialog** dialog from the **Component** property. Select or enter the **open** value from the **Method Name** dropdown, as shown in the following screenshot:

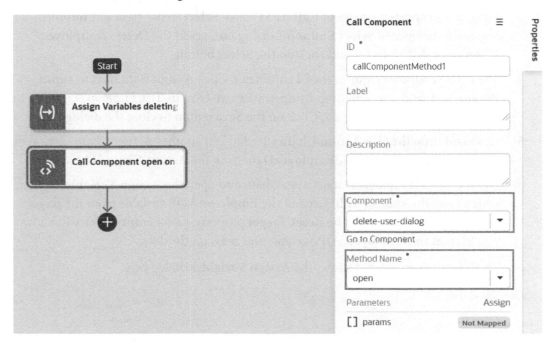

Figure 8.21 – Configuration of the Call Component action

The previous action will open the dialog component based on the dialog ID (**delete-user-dialog**).

6. Return to the page designer, go to the page structure, select the **No** button under the **dialog** component, and register the **ojAction** event. Now, repeat *step 5* to close the dialog box. Instead of the **open** value, select or enter **close** from the **Method Name** property.

After completing this section, you will be able to open and close the dialog component using the delete icon and the **No** button.

Implementing the logic to delete a user

In this section, we'll implement the logic on the **Delete** button of the dialog that will delete the employee from the **Employee** Business Object, refresh the table, and close the dialog.

The following are the steps to implement the logic:

1. Register the **ojAction** event on the **Delete** button, which is under the **dialog** component.

2. Drag and drop the **Call REST** action just below the **Start** action.

3. From the **Properties** palette of **Call REST**, click **Select** to the right of **Endpoint**, and from the opened **Select Endpoint** dialog box, select the **Delete /Employee/ {Employee_Id}** endpoint and click on the **Select** button.

4. The delete endpoint requires the **id** parameter. Click **Assign** right next to **Input Parameters**, and drag and drop `$page.variables.deletingEmployeeId` to `uriParams.Employee_Id`. Click on the **Save** button to close the dialog.

5. Drag and drop the **Call Action Chain** (used to call another Action Chain) action on the **success** path. Select **loadEmployeeData** from the **Action Chain ID** property.

6. Open the **loadEmployeeData** Action Chain and open the **Assign Variables** action, which is on the **success** path. Expand the **EmployeeADP** variable from the target tree and select **data**. From the **Reset Target** property, select **empty**. This will allow you to reset the **EmployeeADP** variable and reassign the data.

The following screenshot shows the **Assign Variables** dialog box:

Figure 8.22 – Configuring the empty value

7. Return back to the delete button Action Chain and drag and drop the **Fire Data Provider Event** action just below the **Call Action Chain** action. From the **Properties** palette of this action, select the **EmployeeADP** variable from the **Event Target** property and select **Refresh** from the **Type** property.

8. Drag and drop the **Call Component** action just below the **Fire Data Provider Event** action, select **delete-user-dialog** from the **Component** property, and select or enter **close** from the **Method Name** property. This will close the dialog once the employee is deleted.

Now all the configuration is completed. Preview the **main-start** page, click the delete icon, and select the **Delete** button from the opened dialog box. The delete action will delete the employee from the **Employee** Business Object, close the dialog, and refresh the table.

The following screenshot shows the dialog to delete the user:

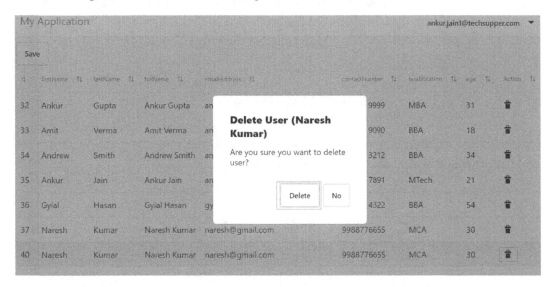

Figure 8.23 – Dialog component

If you select the **No** button from the dialog, the dialog box will simply be closed.

In this section, we learned how to use the dialog component to take consent from the user to delete an employee, and we learned how to use the **Call Component** action of the Action Chain. In the next section, we'll look at how to use the checkbox component.

Working with checkboxes

The **Checkbox Set** component is a useful component that allows us to select multiple options at a time and process the data based on the selected checkbox. **Checkbox Set** is an out-of-the-box component that allows you to create checkboxes and can be populated with static or dynamic data. Let's play with the Checkbox Set component.

Creating a checkbox with static data

In this section, we will use the Checkbox Set component and populate it with **static** data. The following are the steps to create checkboxes using static data:

1. Create a new page with the `main-checkbox` page ID under the `chapter8` web application.

2. On the **main-checkbox** page, drag and drop the **Heading** component and set the **Text** property to `Static Checkboxes`.

3. Drag and drop the **Checkbox Set** component just below the **Heading** component. Once you drop the **Checkbox Set** component, a single checkbox with the label **Option1** will be created by default. Set the **Label Hint** property to `My favorite colors`.

4. Select the **Checkbox Set** component, go to the **Quick Start** tab from the **Properties** palette, and select **Create Static List of Options**.

5. In the opened **Create Static List of Options** dialog box, add four entries by clicking on the + **Option** button. Set **Label** and **Value** as `Red`, `Green`, `Yellow`, and `Orange`, and then click on the **Finish** button.

The following screenshot shows the Checkbox Set component:

Figure 8.24 – Static checkboxes

This is how you can create checkboxes using static data. As shown in the previous screenshot, the checkboxes appear before the label.

> **Important Note:**
> You can set multiple values in the class attribute separated by spaces.

The following are a few properties that you can set on the Checkbox Set component in order to render it differently:

- Set the **class** property value to `oj-checkboxset-input-end` in order to set the label before the checkboxes.

- Set the **class** property value to `oj-choice-direction-row` in order to show the checkboxes in a single row.

Now, let's see how to populate checkboxes with dynamic data.

Creating a checkbox with dynamic data

In this section, we'll show you how to populate checkboxes using dynamic data. We'll use the **Employee** Business Object to render the checkboxes dynamically.

The following are the steps to create checkboxes with dynamic data:

1. Drag and drop the **Heading** component just below the first **Checkbox Set** component and set the **Text** property to `Dynamic Checkboxes`.

2. Drag and drop the **Checkbox Set** component just below the **Heading** component and change the **Label Hint** property to `Employees Email Address`.

3. Select the **Checkbox Set** component, go to the **Quick Start** tab from the **Properties** palette, and select **Add Options**.

4. Select the **Employee** Business Object from the opened **Add Options** dialog box and click on the **Next** button.

5. On the next screen, select **emailAddress** for the **Label** attribute and **id** for the **Value** attribute. Click on the **Next | Finish** buttons to complete the dialog box.

   You will see that the checkboxes will be created dynamically as per the following screenshot:

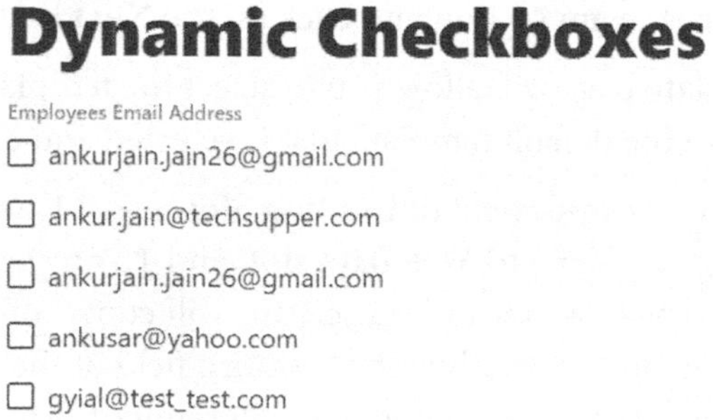

Dynamic Checkboxes

Employees Email Address

☐ ankurjain.jain26@gmail.com

☐ ankur.jain@techsupper.com

☐ ankurjain.jain26@gmail.com

☐ ankusar@yahoo.com

☐ gyial@test_test.com

Figure 8.25 – Dynamic checkboxes

This is how you can create checkboxes with static or dynamic data.

In this section, we learned how to use the Checkbox Set component and populate it with static or dynamic data. We also learned about different properties that can be used to render checkboxes differently. In the next section, we'll work with another useful collection component, that is, **List View**.

Working with List View

List View is an out-of-the-box component that allows you to display items as a list or grid. This is a collection component like a table that is used to bind the array data provider to populate a collection of data.

In this section, we'll execute a use case where the data will be fetched from one of the external REST APIs and show the data in the List View component.

In order to execute this use case, a Service Connection is created using the REST endpoint (`https://reqres.in/api/users/`).

> **Important Note:**
> Refer to the *Creating a Service Connection from an endpoint* section in *Chapter 5, Creating and Managing Service Connections*, to know how to create Service Connections.

The following are the steps to use the List View component and populate it with external REST API data:

1. Create a new page with the `main-list` page ID under the `chapter8` web application.

2. Drag and drop the **List View** component on the page. Move to the **Quick Start** tab from the **Properties** palette of **List View** and select the **Add Data** option.

3. From the opened **Add Data** dialog box, select the `GET /users/` Service Connection under the **api** section and click on the **Next** button.

4. The **Select Template** page will allow you to select the template for the List View component. Leave the default template that is selected and click on the **Next** button.

5. Drag and drop the `avatar` field to **Leading Slot**, `email` to **Overline slot**, id to **Default slot**, `first_name` to **Metadata slot**, and `last_name` to **Trailing Slot**. Change the data type of avatar to `Image` (this will convert the `avatar` field to an `Image` component automatically). The `avatar` field of the REST API is pointing to the image URL, so the `Image` component will render the image automatically from the URL. Click on the **Next** and **Finish** buttons to complete the dialog box.

This completes the **List View** component. The following screenshot shows the list view and the populated REST API data:

Figure 8.26 – The List View component

This is how you can use the List View component to populate data from the REST API.

Showing data in the Card Layout view

The List View component allows you to show the data in the **Card Layout** view too. To populate the data into the Card Layout view, you just need to change the **Styling** property to **Card Layout**.

The following are the steps to populate data into the Card Layout view:

1. Create another page with the `main-list-card-layout` page ID under the `chapter8` web application.

2. Follow *step 2* to *step 4* from the previous section. While configuring the **Add Data** dialog box, select another template from the **Select Template** page.

3. Select **avatar**, **first_name**, and **last_name** from the **Bind Data** page. Change the data type of **avatar** to **Image**. Click the **Next | Finish** buttons to complete the wizard.

4. When the List View component is rendered, it will show the label of the selected fields by default. Go to the **Code** view and remove all the `<oj-label>` tags to remove the labels.

5. In the **Code** section, you will see the `<img>` tag too. This is because of the data type of `avatar`, which we changed while configuring the **List View** component. Replace the `<img>` tag with the following line of code (replace `img` with the `avatar` component):

```
<oj-avatar class="oj-flex-item oj-sm-flex-initial"
src="[[ $current.data.avatar ]]" size="xxl"></oj-avatar>
```

6. Select the **List View** component, and then select the **Card Layout** checkbox under the **Styling** property to show the list view in Card Layout view.

The following screenshot shows the list view in Card Layout view:

Figure 8.27 – Card Layout view of the List View

This is how you use the List View component and render it in a different view. You can certainly register events on the List View component for further processing.

In this section, we have learned how to use the List View component, populate it from the external REST API, and show the data in a different view to make it look and feel better. In the next section, we'll be working with different visualization components, such as bar, area, and pie charts.

Working with visualization components

Visual components allow you to visualize data in the form of charts that represent the data in a more sophisticated way and allow us to develop a dashboard for leaders using different charts such as pie, bar, bubble, and so on. For example, in order to represent sales data year-wise, we can create a bar chart to represent the sales data. So, instead of creating a table or list, it can be better to represent the data in the form of different charts.

In this section, we'll work with different charts to visualize data in different forms.

Creating a bar chart

Bar charts are used to compare different sets of data. They are basically used to show the number, frequency, and other measures.

The bar chart is an out-of-the-box component in VB that allows us to represent data in the form of a bar.

In order to create a bar chart, a new Business Object with the name `Sales` is created and a few records have been inserted into that. The following screenshot shows the **Sales** Business Object with data:

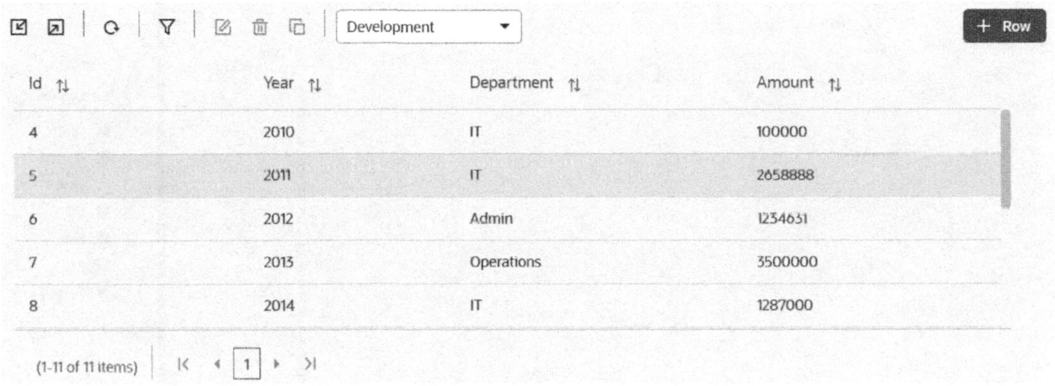

Id ↑↓	Year ↑↓	Department ↑↓	Amount ↑↓
4	2010	IT	100000
5	2011	IT	2658888
6	2012	Admin	1234631
7	2013	Operations	3500000
8	2014	IT	1287000

(1-11 of 11 items)

Figure 8.28 – Sales Business Object

> **Tip:**
> You can download the `.csv` file (`https://github.com/PacktPublishing/Effortless-App-Development-with-Oracle-Visual-Builder/blob/main/Chapter08/Sales.csv`) and import it using the Data Manager to create a new **Sales** Business Object.

The following are the steps to create a bar chart:

1. Create a new page with the `main-charts` page ID under the `chapter8` web application.

2. Drag and drop **BAR Chart** onto the page. Go to the **Quick Start** tab from the **Properties** palette and select the **Add Data** option.

3. From the opened **Add Data** dialog box, select the **Sales** Business Object, and then click on the **Next** button.

4. From the next screen, select or drag and drop the **amount** field on the **Values (Y Axis)** field; select or drag and drop the **year** field on the **Categories (X Axis)** field; select or drag and drop the **department** field on the **Colors (Series)** field. Then, select the **Next | Finish** buttons to complete the dialog box.

   Once the configuration is completed, the bar chart will be rendered on the page as in the following screenshot:

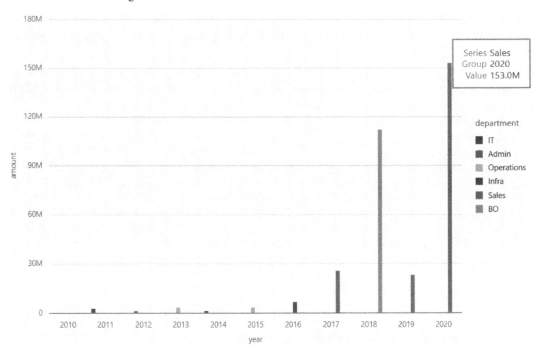

Figure 8.29 – Bar chart

Hover over the bars to view the exact **Series**, **Group**, and **Values** values, as seen in the previous screenshot.

Go to the **Properties** palette of the bar chart and use it with different properties. You can change the orientation of the chart from vertical to horizontal using the **orientation** property. Use the **Animation** and **Style** properties to change the view of the chart. Change the *x* and *y* axes titles using the **X Axis**, **Title** and **Y Axis**, **Title** properties, respectively. Similarly, you can explore other properties too from the **Properties** palette.

Creating a pie chart

Pie charts are basically used to show the percentage or proportion of data. Each slice of the pie chart represents the percentage or proportion of the data.

The pie chart is an out-of-the-box component in VB that allows us to represent data in the form of slices.

The following are the steps to create a pie chart:

1. On the same page, **main-charts**, drag and drop **PIE Chart** right next to the bar chart. Go to the **Quick Start** tab from the **Properties** palette and select the **Add Data** option.

2. From the opened **Add Data** dialog box, select the **Sales** Business Object and click on the **Next** button.

3. From the next screen, select or drag and drop the **amount** field on the **Slice Values** field; select or drag and drop the **year** field on the **Slice Colors** field. Then, select the **Next | Finish** buttons to complete the dialog box.

Once the configuration is completed, the pie chart will be rendered on the page as in the following screenshot:

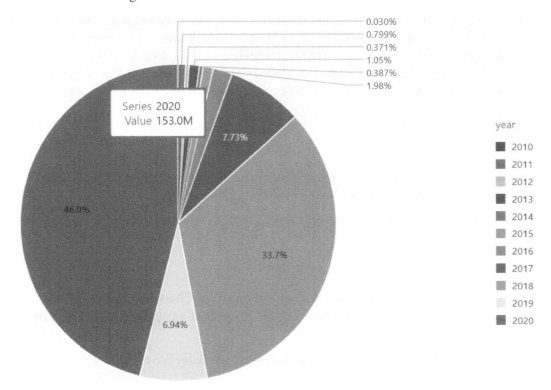

Figure 8.30 – Pie chart

You can view the pie chart in 3D too, just by enabling the **3D** property under the **Style** property. Use the **Legend, Title** property to change the legend title to make it more meaningful. You can change the legend position using the **Legend, Position** property.

Creating an area chart

Similar to the bar and pie charts, area charts can be created using the **Area Chart** component. To use **Area Chart**, we'll use the **Sales** Business Object to display the sales year-wise. A new page is created with the `main-area-chart` page ID.

The following are the steps to create an area chart:

1. Drag and drop the area chart onto the **main-area-chart** page. Go to the **Quick Start** tab from the **Properties** palette and select the **Add Data** option.

2. From the **Add Data** dialog box, select the **Sales** Business Object and click on the **Next** button.

3. From the next screen, select or drag and drop the **amount** field on the **Values (Y Axis)** field; select or drag and drop the **year** field on the **Categories (X Axis)** field; select or drag and drop the **department** field on the **Colors (Series)** field. Then, select the **Next | Finish** buttons to complete the dialog box.

The following screenshot shows the area chart:

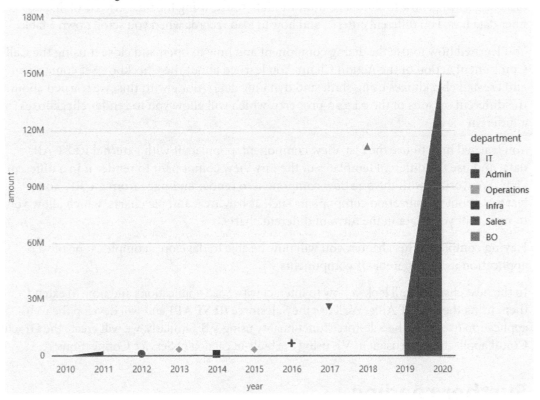

Figure 8.31 – Area chart

Select the area chart, go to the **Properties** palette, and use the different properties to view the chart in a different view.

In this section, you learned about visualization components and created bar, pie, and area charts to visualize the data in different forms.

Summary

In this chapter, we learned about new visual components such as Dialog, Checkbox Set, and List View, and different visual components such as bar, pie, and area charts. You learned how to create a table to update the records inline and save the modified records into a Business Object. You learned about the advanced functionalities of table components, such as enabling/disabling sorting, how to allow a column width to resize, using the filter criteria of SDP to filter data based on different criteria, and how to load records when you scroll down a table.

You learned how to use the dialog component and how to open and close it using the Call Component action of the Action Chain. You learned about the Checkbox Set component and created checkboxes using static and dynamic data. Along with this, we learned about the different options of the `class` property, which will allow you to render checkboxes in a different view.

You learned how to use the List View component, populate it with external REST API data, and use the different templates of the List View component to render it in a different view. We worked with the `avatar` component to render an image from a URL. You learned about visualization components such as bar, area, and pie charts, which allow you to represent your data in the form of different charts.

Having completed this chapter, you will now be able to develop a complex type of web application using different UI components.

In the next chapter, we'll look at how to interact with **SaaS** applications and how to extend them using their REST APIs. We'll use the **Salesforce REST API** and will develop the web application to extend the Salesforce functionality using VB. Similarly, we will create the **Oracle Cloud** application extension in VB using the built-in catalog of Service Connections.

Further reading

- Refer to the Oracle documentation to know more about the Fire Data Provider Event action: `https://docs.oracle.com/cd/E83857_01/paas/app-builder-cloud/visual-builder-developer/fire-data-provider-event-action.html`

- Refer to the Oracle documentation to enable pagination for your external APIs: `https://docs.oracle.com/en/cloud/paas/app-builder-cloud/visual-builder-developer/edit-service-connection.html#GUID-20253ACD-E2BE-408F-9523-C21C21B827AD`

- Refer to the Oracle Cookbook to explore visualization components: `https://www.oracle.com/webfolder/technetwork/jet/jetCookbook.html?component=home&demo=rootVisualizations_childChart`

- Another way to add **filterCriterion** to filter the data: `https://blogs.oracle.com/shay/filtering-data-in-visual-builder-lists-and-tables-revisited`

Questions

1. Do we need to double-click on a row to make it editable? Also, is there any other approach to do this?
2. What is `filterCriterion`?
3. Is `filterCriterion` available in the array data provider?

9
Extending Oracle and Non-Oracle SaaS Applications

Extending **Software as a Service (SaaS)** applications such as **Oracle Cloud, HCM**, and **Salesforce** is one of the most common requirements across any organization. You can develop custom screens using VB to extend the SaaS application's functionality and interact with their day-to-day activities directly from the VB application without logging in to the SaaS application.

In this chapter, we will develop custom VB screens and show how to extend Oracle and non-Oracle SaaS applications. We are going to use Salesforce as a non-Oracle SaaS application and develop a few custom screens in VB to communicate with the Salesforce application. We'll list and create new accounts and opportunities from the VB application that will be created in the Salesforce application.

Similarly, we'll create another set of custom screens that will allow us to interact with the Oracle Cloud application. In these custom screens, we'll interact with the REST API accounts to show all the customers and allow them to update records. We will also create another set of screens from where you can nominate customers for their feedback and which will store all the nominated customers in the VB application.

We'll create a multilingual application that will allow end users to view the application in their language of choice.

In this chapter, we will cover the following topics:

- Extending a Salesforce application
- Extending an Oracle Cloud application
- Creating a multilingual application

After completing this chapter, you will be able to extend Oracle and non-Oracle SaaS applications using the VB and you will also be able to develop a multilingual application.

Technical requirements

To complete this chapter, you will require the following:

- A **Visual Builder** instance
- **VB** login credentials
- A Salesforce instance
- An Oracle Cloud instance

You can find the full source code used in this chapter here: `https://github.com/ PacktPublishing/Effortless-App-Development-with-Oracle-Visual- Builder/tree/main/Chapter09`.

Extending a Salesforce application

In this section, we'll extend a Salesforce application's functionality using the VB. In order to extend a Salesforce application, a new web application with the name `salesforceext_chapter9` is created under the **VBCSBook** application. While creating this application, select **Tabbed** as the navigation style and add two navigation items with the names `Opportunity` and `Account` as per the following screenshot:

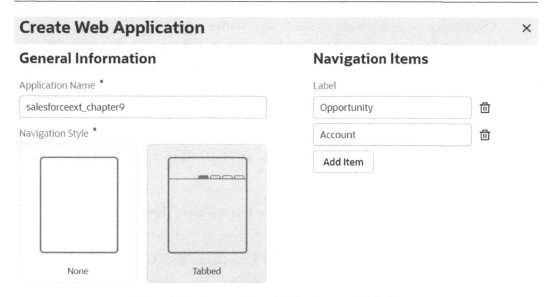

Figure 9.1 – A new web application to extend Salesforce

The **salesforceext_chapter9** application will be created with two flows with the names **Opportunity** and **Account**. We'll manage (list and create) Salesforce opportunities under the **Opportunity** flow and accounts under the **Account** flow.

Pre-requisites for extending the Salesforce app

In order to extend the Salesforce application, the following are required:

- The Salesforce developer instance. You can use `https://developer.salesforce.com/signup` to create a free Salesforce account and `https://login.salesforce.com` to log in.

- We'll use the **Salesforce REST API** using the **OAuth2.0** protocol, so it is necessary to create a connected app in Salesforce that will provide the consumer key (client ID) and consumer secret (client secret). The client ID and client secret will be used to generate the access token, which will be used to call other Salesforce REST APIs.

> **Tip:**
> You can use the documents (available at `https://help.salesforce.com/articleView?id=connected_app_create_basics.htm&type=5` and `https://help.salesforce.com/articleView?id=connected_app_create_api_integration.htm&type=5`), one by one, to create the connected app.

- A Salesforce username and password, along with a client ID and client secret, will be used to generate the access token. The password that needs to be supplied is a combination of **password + security token**. Therefore, you need to obtain a security token from Salesforce.

> Tip:
> Follow the document at this URL in order to obtain the security token: `https://help.salesforce.com/articleView?id=user_security_token.htm&type=5`.

We'll use the following Salesforce REST APIs for this use case. These APIs will be used for the following purposes:

- To query the **Opportunity**, **Opportunity Line Items**, and **Account** data: **GET** (`https://ap15.salesforce.com/services/data/v50.0/query`)

- To create a new opportunity: **POST** (`https://ap15.salesforce.com/services/data/v50.0/sobjects/Opportunity`)

- To create a new account: **POST** (`https://ap15.salesforce.com/services/data/v50.0/sobjects/Account`)

In the next section, we'll create a Service Connection with the Salesforce APIs.

Creating a Service Connection

We need to create a Service Connection using the Salesforce REST APIs. To do this, perform the following steps:

1. Open the **VBCSBook** application, open the **Services** tab from the application navigator, and click on the + button and **Service Connection** to create a new Service Connection. Then, select **Define by Endpoint** from the opened dialog box.

2. Enter the API URL, `https://ap15.salesforce.com/services/data/v50.0/query`, and then click on the **Next** button.

3. Go to the **Server** tab and select **OAuth 2.0 Resource Owner** from the **Authentication** dropdown. Supply the Salesforce username and password under the **Username** section, and **Client ID** and **Secret** under the **Client ID** section.

4. Enter the **Token URL** as `https://login.salesforce.com/services/oauth2/token`.

5. Select the **Dynamic, the service does not support CORS** option from the **Connection Type** dropdown.

6. Switch to the **Request** tab, go to the **Parameters** tab, and then add a new dynamic query parameter with the name q and check the **Required** checkbox to make it required.

7. Switch to the **Test** tab, go the **URL Parameters** tab, enter the query, `select id,name,stagename,amount,closedate,probability,iswon from opportunity`, in the **q** parameter, and then click on the **Send Request** button. Click on the **Save as Example Response** button to save the response as a sample.

8. Then, click on the **Create** button to create the Service Connection successfully.

As part of this use case, we'll create two separate screens to create accounts and opportunities that will be created in Salesforce directly, so we need to add the following two **POST** endpoints to the same Salesforce server:

- `/sobjects/Opportunity`
- `/sobjects/Account`

> **Important Note:**
> Refer to *Chapter 5, Creating and Managing Service Connections*, under the *Adding more endpoints to the Service Connection* section, to learn how to add Service Connections to the same server.

To add `/sobjects/Opportunity` and `/sobjects/Account` to the Service Connection, copy and paste the following request and response **JSON** body in the **Request** and **Response** tabs:

- The following JSON request will be used to create a new opportunity, `/sobjects/Opportunity`:

```json
{
    "AccountId": "0012v00003AZLNJAA5",
    "IsPrivate": false,
    "Name": "postman",
    "Description": null,
    "StageName": "Prospecting",
    "Amount": 9300.0,
    "CloseDate": "2021-12-30"
}
```

- The following JSON request will be used to create a new account,
  `/sobjects/Account`:

```json
{
    "Name":"Google India",
}
```

The following JSON response will be captured when a new account and opportunity is created in Salesforce. Copy and paste it in the response for both endpoints:

```json
{
    "id": "0062v00001R0hMgAAJ",
    "success": true,
    "errors": []
}
```

Now, the required endpoints are added to the Service Connection. Let's create a few common types and variables at the `salesforceext_chapter9` application level.

Click on the **salesforceext_chapter9** web application and create the following type:

Create a custom type with an `Account` ID of the object type and add four fields, `Id`, `Name`, `Industry`, and `Type`, of the `String` type.

Create the following variables:

- Create a variable with the ID `Accounts` of the `ADP` type. Select `Account` as the item type, and `Id` as the key attribute.

- Create a variable with the ID `OpportunityQuery` of the `String` type and then enter `select Id,Name,Stagename,Amount,Closedate,Probability,Iswon from opportunity` as the default string. This variable holds the query to obtain the opportunity data.

- Create a variable with the ID `OpportunityLineItemQuery` of the `String` type and enter `select Id,Name,TotalPrice,UnitPrice,ProductCode from OpportunityLineItem where OpportunityId=` as the default string. This variable holds the query to get the **Opportunity Line Item** (OLI) data based on the `Opportunity` ID.

- Create a variable with the name `AccountQuery` of the `String` type and enter `select Id,Name,Type,Industry from Account` as the default string. This variable holds the query to get the `Account` data.

In the next section, we'll create a page that will be used to fetch accounts and to create a new account in Salesforce.

Listing and creating accounts

In this section, we'll get a list of accounts from Salesforce and populate them in a table. Also, we'll create a form to add a new account. These are the steps to achieve this:

1. Click on the **salesforceext_chapter9** web application, go to the **Event Listeners** tab, and then register the **vbEnter** event. Then, add a new Action Chain with the name `loadData` and click on the **Finish** button.

> **Important Note:**
> Refer to *Chapter 7, Working with Life Cycle Events, Validations, and UI Logic*, under the *Registering the vbEnter event and loading Employee Business Object data* section, to learn how to register a **vbEnter** event.

2. Go to the **loadData** Action Chain, drag and drop the **Call REST** action just below the **Start** action, and select the **GET/query** endpoint of the Salesforce Service Connection.

3. Click **Assign** on the right of **Input Parameters**, drag and drop `application.variables.AccountQuery` on `uriParams.q`, and then click on the **Save** button from the opened dialog box.

4. Drag and drop the **Assign Variables** action under the success path, and then click on **Assign** next to **Variables**. Drag and drop `chain.results.callRestEndpoint1.body.records` on `application.variables.Accounts.data`, and then set the **Reset Target** property as `empty`.

   The **loadData** Action Chain will fetch all the accounts from Salesforce and assign them to the **Accounts** ADP variable.

5. Open the **account-start** page, drag and drop a **Table** component, go to the **Data** tab from the **Properties** palette, and select `application.variables.Accounts` from the **Data** property.

6. Add the fields `Id`, `Name`, `Industry`, and `Type` from the **Table Columns** property.

7. Set the **Style** property of the table to `height:300px`.

Now, the table will be populated with all the accounts that are in Salesforce. Next, we'll add a form on the same page that will allow you to add a new account:

1. Under the **accounts-start** page, create a type using the **From Endpoint** option, select POST /sobjects/Account, and then select **Name** under **Request**, as per the following screenshot:

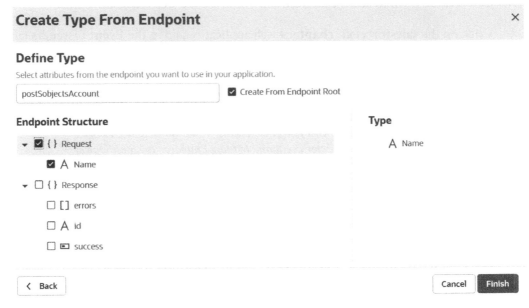

Figure 9.2 – Creating a type

2. Create a variable with the ID NewAccount of the **postSobjectsAccount** type.

3. Drag and drop the **Heading** component just below the table and change the **Text** property to Add Accounts.

4. Drag and drop the **Form Layout** component just below the **Heading** component and change the **Max Columns** property to 2.

5. Drag and drop the **Input Text** and **Button** components inside the form layout.

6. Change the **Label Hint** field to Account Name, and select variables. NewAccount.Name as the value of the **Input Text** property.

7. Change the **Text** property of the button to + Add Account and register the **ojAction** event on the button.

8. In the button's Action Chain, drag and drop the **Call REST** action just below the **Start** action. Select POST /sobjects/Account, which is used to create a new account.

9. Assign page.variables.NewAccount to the body.

10. Drag and drop the **Call Action Chain** under the success path and select loadData from the **Action Chain ID** property. This action will call the account query again from Salesforce and refresh the table.

The configuration is now complete. Run the application and then switch to the **Account** tab. All the accounts should be populated in the table. Add a new account under the **Add Accounts** section. As soon as you add a new account, the account will be created in Salesforce and will be visible in the table too.

The following screenshot shows the accounts data. A new account, **Oracle United State**, has been added, which is reflected in the table:

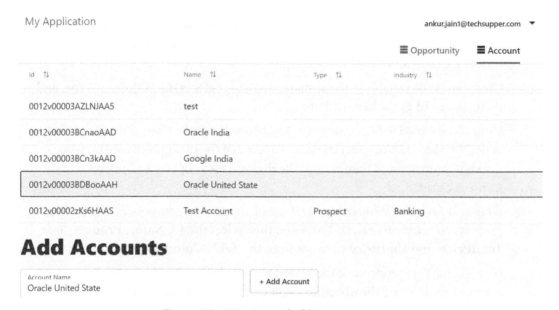

Figure 9.3 – Viewing and adding new accounts

Let's now move on and work with the opportunity flow.

Listing opportunities

In this section, we'll work with the opportunity flow, and look at how to list and create new opportunities in Salesforce. We'll also show the opportunity line items in a dialog when a particular opportunity is selected from the table.

The following are the steps to complete the opportunity flow:

1. Open the **opportunity-start** page, drag and drop the **Table** component on to the page, move to the **Quick Start** tab, and then select the **Add Data** option.

2. Select the **GET/query** endpoint of Salesforce and then click the **Next** button. From the next screen, select **Id**, **Name**, **StageName**, **Probability**, **IsWon**, **Amount**, and **CloseDate**. Select **Id** as the primary key and then click the **Next** button.

3. Drag and drop `application.variables.OpportunityQuery` on to `uriParameters.q` and then click the **Finish** button.

4. Set the **style** property of the table to `height:300px`.

All the Salesforce opportunities will be listed in a table after completing the previous steps. Next, we'll show **Opportunity Line Items** in a dialog, when an opportunity is selected from a table:

1. Create an object `Type` with the ID `OLI` and then create `Id`, `Name`, and `ProductCode` fields of the `String` type. We also create `TotalPrice` and `UnitPrice` fields of the `Number` type.

2. Create an ADP variable with the name `OLIADP`, select **OLI** as the item type, and then choose **Id** as the key attribute.

3. Drag and drop a **Dialog** component just below the table, change the ID of the dialog to `oli-dialog`. Set `width:900px;` of the dialog component using the **style** property and then change the **dialog-title** property to `Opportunity Line Items`.

4. Drag and drop the **Table** component inside the **Dialog** component. Set the **Data** property to `variables.OLIADP` and then select the **Id**, **Name**, **ProductCode**, **TotalPrice**, and **UnitPrice** columns from the **Table Columns** properties.

5. Change the **Text** property of the button to `Ok`, which is inside the **Dialog** component. Register the **ojAction** event on that button and configure the Action Chain to close the dialog box.

> **Important Note:**
> Refer to *Chapter 8, Exploring Other Visual Components and Their Advanced Functionalities,* under the *Opening and closing the dialog on an action* section, to learn how to close the dialog.

6. Return to the **Page Designer** tab of the **opportunity-start** page. Register the **first-selected-row** event on the opportunity table.

7. Inside Action Chain of the table event, drag and drop the **Call REST** action and then select the **Get/query** endpoint of Salesforce.

8. Configure the **q** parameter with the expression `$application.variables.` `OpportunityLineItemQuery+"'"+ $variables.rowKey+"'".` This expression will append the opportunity ID of the selected row with the **Opportunity Line Item** query. Make sure that the **Expression** checkbox is selected from the opened dialog box.

9. Drag and drop the **Assign Variables** action under the success path. Map the `chain.results.callRestEndpoint1.body.records` source to the target, `page.variables.OLIADP.data`. Update the **Reset Target** property to `empty`.

10. Drag and drop **Call Component** to below **Assign Variables**. Select **oli-dialog** from the **Component** property and then select or enter **open** from the **Method Name** property.

Now, when you click on any of the opportunities from the table, a dialog will be opened that will show all **Opportunity Line Items** of the selected opportunity as per the following screenshot:

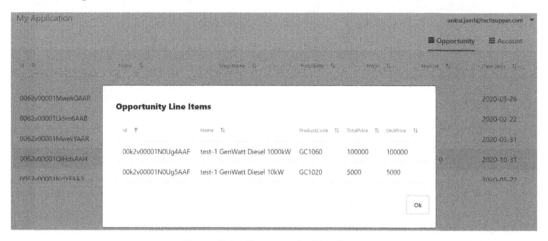

Figure 9.4 – Opportunity Line Items

Next, we'll create a form on the same **opportunity-start** page that will allow us to create new opportunities.

Creating opportunities

In this section, we'll create a form that will be used to create new opportunities and that will be created in Salesforce directly. The following are the steps to achieve this:

1. Open the **opportunity-start** page and create a new **Type** using the **From Endpoint** option. Select the `POST /sobjects/Opportunity` endpoint from the opened **Create Type From Endpoint** dialog box, and then click on the **Next** button.

2. From the next screen, select the checkbox to the right of the **Request** node, which will select all the fields under the **Request** node, and then click on the **Finish** button. This action will create a type with the ID `postSobjectsOpportunity`.

3. Create a new variable with the ID `NewOpportunity` and then select `postSobjectsOpportunity` as the type.

4. Return to the **Page Designer** tab, drag and drop the **Heading** component just below the table, and change the **Text** property to `Add Opportunities`.

5. Drag and drop the **Form Layout** component just below the **Heading** component and change the **Max Columns** property to 2.

6. Configure the UI components inside **Form Layout** as per the following table:

Component Type	Label Hint	Value	Data	Item Text
Input Text	Opportunity Name	{{ $variables.NewOpportunity.Name }}		
Select (Single)	Stage	{{ $variables.NewOpportunity.StageName }}		
Input Number	Amount	{{ $variables.NewOpportunity.Amount }}		
Radio Button Set	Type of opportunity	{{ $variables.NewOpportunity.IsPrivate }}		
Select (Single)	Account		[[$application.variables. Accounts]]	Name
Input Date	Close Date	{{ $variables.NewOpportunity.CloseDate }}		
Text Area	Description	{{ $variables.NewOpportunity.Description }}		

Table 9.1 – List of UI components

7. In order to configure the **Stage Select** (**Single**) component, a new Business Object is created with the name Stage, along with a single column with the name Stage Name. Three rows are added with the values Prospecting, Qualification, and Need Analysis in the Stage Business Object. These values are as per the Salesforce stage data. We bind **Stage Select** (**Single**) to **Stage** Business Object in order to populate stage values. While configuring this, select the **stageName** field in both **Label** and **Value**.

8. Configure **Radio Button Set** with the static values. Use **Create Static List of Options** under the **Quick Start** tab to create a static list. Enter Public and Private for **Label**, and false and true for **Value**, respectively, as per the following screenshot:

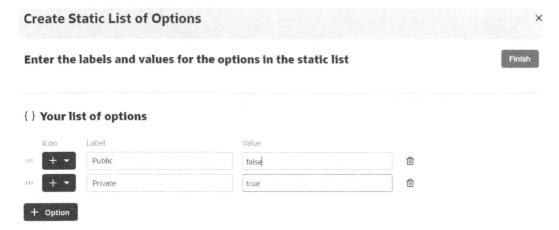

Figure 9.5 – Configuring the radio button set component for the opportunity type

We also need to set the class property of the Radio Button Set component to oj-choice-direction-row.

9. Register the value-item event on Account **Select** (**Single**). In the Action Chain of this event, drag and drop the **Assign Variables** action, and then map the variables.data.Id source to the page.variables.NewOpportunity. AccountId target. This action will map the selected account ID to the AccountId variable during runtime.

10. Return to the **Page Designer** tab, drag and drop the **Button** component on to the page after **Form Layout**, and change the **Text** property to + Add Opportunity.

11. Register the **ojAction** event on the + **Add Opportunity** button. In this Action Chain of the event, drag and drop the **Call REST** action just below the **Start** action, and then choose the POST /sobjects/Opportunity endpoint. Assign page. variables.NewOpportunity to the body.

12. Drag and drop the **Fire Data Provider Event** action under the success path. Select `page.variables.getQueryListSDP` from the **Event Target** property, and then select `Refresh` from the **Type** property.

Now the configuration is complete. Run the page and create a new opportunity using the **Add Opportunity** form. As soon as a new opportunity is added, it will be created in Salesforce and reflected in the table, too, as per the following screenshot:

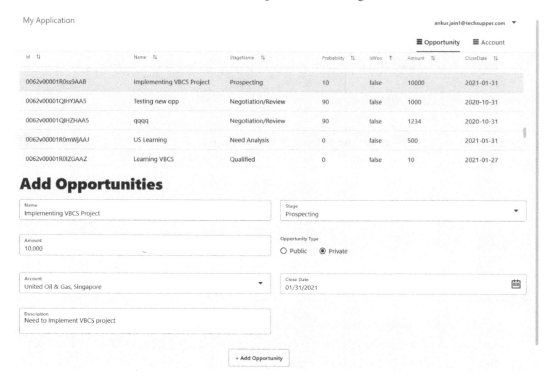

Figure 9.6 – Listing and adding new opportunities

That's everything regarding extending the Salesforce application using the VB. In this complete use case, we extended two Salesforce opportunities and accounts objects, and similarly, more functionalities can be added. The advantage of this extension is to provide access to the VB application in order to view and create new opportunities and accounts directly without providing access to the Salesforce system. In the next section, we'll look at how to extend the Oracle Cloud SaaS application using the VB.

Extending an Oracle Cloud application

Extending Oracle Cloud applications using VB is a common requirement. VB provides a built-in catalog that allows us to interact with the Oracle Cloud application directly with the help of their REST APIs.

In this section, we'll create a feedback nomination application from where Oracle Cloud application customers can be nominated for their feedback. We'll show all the customers (accounts) from the Oracle Cloud application and allow these to be modified as well.

> **Important Note:**
> In order to execute this use case, the Oracle Cloud application backend must be added. If it has not been added already, please do so. Refer to *Chapter 5, Creating and Managing Service Connections*, under the *Managing Backends in the Visual Applications* section, to learn how to add a backend.

A new web application with the name `oraclecloudext_chapter9` is created under the **VBCSBook** application. While creating this application, select **Tabbed** as the navigation style and add two navigation items with the names `Customers` and `Nomination`.

Let's move on and build the Oracle Cloud SaaS extension.

Adding an accounts REST endpoint

We will use the **accounts** services of the Oracle Cloud CRM application, so we need to add the accounts REST endpoints to the already added **crmRestApi** Service Connection.

> **Important Note:**
> Refer to *Chapter 5, Creating and Managing Service Connections*, under the *Creating Service Connections with Oracle Cloud Applications* section, to learn how the **crmRestApi** Service Connection was added.

Add the accounts REST endpoint to the **crmRestApi** Service Connection.

> **Important Note:**
> While adding these endpoints, if you see any warning such as **The following definitions, which are referenced by the selected endpoints, could not be fetched: "standardLookupsLOV, languagesLOV". Lookups for some fields might not be available**, simply ignore this and go ahead and add the endpoints.

Add the /accounts and /accounts/{account_id} endpoints as per the following screenshot:

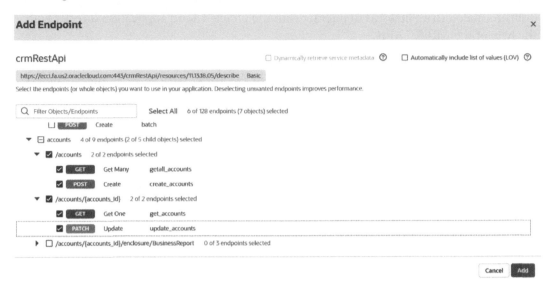

Figure 9.7 – Adding accounts endpoints

Once the relevant accounts endpoints are added to the Service Connection, you will be able to get and update the accounts in Oracle Cloud application from the VB application. In the next section, we'll use these endpoints to list and update the account details.

Listing and updating the accounts

In this section, we will fetch all the accounts from the Oracle Cloud application and display them in the table. Along with this, we will allow the information pertaining to existing accounts to be updated too. All the updates, which will be executed from the VB screen, will be updated directly in the Oracle Cloud application.

The following are the steps to list and update the accounts:

1. Open the **customers-start** page under the **oraclecloudext_chapter9** web application.

2. On the **customers-start** page, drag and drop the **Table** component.

3. Go to the **Quick Start** tab of the **Table** property and select the **Add Data** option.

4. From the opened **Add Data** dialog box, select **accounts** under the **crmRestApi** Service Connection and then click on the **Next** button.

5. From the next screen, select the **CEOName**, **CEOTitle**, **Country**, **EmailAddress**, and **URL** fields. Change the **URL** type to `Hyperlink` and then click on the **Next** button.

6. Click on the **Finish** button to complete the dialog box. As soon as the dialog is complete, the accounts will be populated in a table.

7. Click on **Hyperlink** under the **URL** column of the table, copy the value, which is under the **Text** property, and paste it in the **URL** property under the **Data** tab. Modify the **Text** property to `{{ $current.row.URL? 'Visit Site':'' }}`.

   The following screenshot shows all the accounts fetched from the Oracle Cloud application in real time:

My Application				ankur.jain1@techsupper.com ▼
			☰ Customers	☰ Nomination
Update Customer				
Chief Executive Name	Chief Executive Title	Count...	Email	URL
Ratan	Vice President	AE	ratan@tata.com	Visit Site
Rathor	Senior VP	US	rathor@cp.com	Visit Site
		IN		
		IN		
		IN		
		US		
		AE		
		US		

Figure 9.8 – List of customers

As per the previous screenshot, the information is not updated for a few accounts in the Oracle Cloud application. So, let's add the functionality that will allow us to update the account details.

8. Select the **Table** component, move to the **Quick Starts** tab from the table's **Properties** palette, and then select the **Add Edit Page** option.

9. From the opened **Add Edit Page** dialog box, select **accounts** under the **crmRestApi** Service Connection and then click on the **Next** button.

10. From the next page, select **accounts** under the **crmRestApi** Service Connection and then click on the **Next** button.

11. From the next page, select the **CEOName**, **CEOTitle**, **EmailAddress**, and **URL** fields. Change the **EmailAddress** type to `Email`, and the **URL** type to `URL`. Update **Button label** to `Update Customer`, **Page Title** to `Edit Customer`, and then click on the **Finish** button.

The previous configuration will add an **Update Customer** button to the top of the table. Run the application, select any of the accounts, and then click the **Update Customer** button. You will be redirected to the new page with the pre-populated information pertaining to the account, if available.

The following screenshot shows the **Edit Customer** page:

My Application   ankur.jain1@techsupper.com   ▼

                                                    ≣ Customers   ≣ Nomination

Edit Customer

Chief Executive Name
Amresh

Chief Executive Title
Senior Director

Email
amresh@testing.com

URL
https://www.testing.com

Cancel   Save

Figure 9.9 – Updating the customer

Update the account information and then click on the **Save** button. Once you click on the **Save** button, the information will be updated in the Oracle Cloud application and will be visible in the customer's table.

Adding nomination functionality

As the next step, we'll add the customer **nomination** functionality. In this functionality, we'll create a page that will allow us to nominate the customers, another page that will show all the nominated customers, and from the same page, the nominations can be withdrawn.

A new Business Object with the name `Nomination` is created to store all the nominated customers with three fields, with the names `cEOName` of the `String` type, `emailAddress` of the `Email` type, and `nominated` of the `Boolean` type.

Select the **Nominated** field under the **Fields** tab of the **Nomination** Business Object, select the **Set to default if value not provided** option under the **Value Calculation** property, and then select the **true** value. This will update the **Nomination** field with the value `true` if not provided while adding a new row.

The following screenshot shows the **Nomination** Business Object:

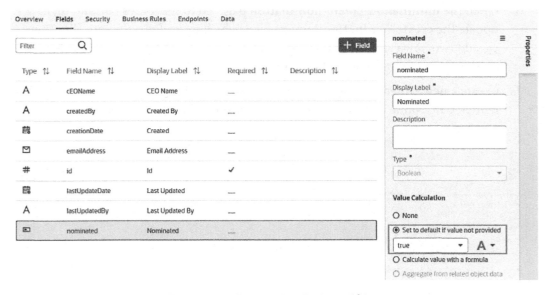

Figure 9.10 – Nomination Business Object

The following are the steps to add the nomination functionality:

1. Open the **nomination-start** page and drag and drop the **Table** component on to the page.

2. Bind this table with the **Nomination** Business Object using the **Add Data** option. Select the **cEOName**, **emailAddress**, and **nominated** fields from the **Add Data** dialog box.

The nominated customers will be populated on the table if they exist. Initially, the table will be blank as no nominated customer exists in the Business Object. By way of a next step, we'll create a page that will allow us to nominate a customer.

3. Select the table component on the **nomination-start** page, go to the **Quick Start** tab from the table's **Properties** palette, and then select the **Add Create Page** option.

4. From the opened **Add Create Page** dialog box, select the **Nomination** Business Object and then click on the **Next** button.

5. From the next screen, select **cEOName**, change **Button label** to Nominate Customer and **Page Title** to Nominate Customer, and then click on the **Finish** button.

   Once you click on the **Finish** button, a new page will be created with the ID nomination-create-nomination and with a single **Input Text** field.

6. Open the **nomination-create-nomination** page, go to the **Types** tab, and then update the **createNominationRequest** type, which is created automatically. Then, we add two new variables to this type, with the ID emailAddress of the **String** type, and nominated of the **Boolean** type.

7. Create a new **Object** type with the ID Accounts and then add two String fields named **CEOName** and **EmailAddress**, as per the following screenshot:

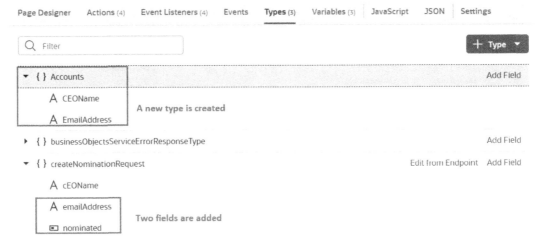

Figure 9.11 – Creating a type

8. Go to the **Variables** tab and create a new **Array Data Provider** variable with the ID `AccountsADP`. Select **Accounts** as the item type and `EmailAddress` as the **Key Attributes** field of the **AccountsADP** variable property.

9. Go the **JavaScript** tab and add the following **JavaScript**:

```
PageModule.prototype.getCustomersToNominate =
function(customersData,nominatedCustomers){
    var customersToNominate = [];
    var find = false;
      for (var i=0;i<customersData.length;i++){
          if(customersData[i].EmailAddress!=null){
          find = false;
          for (var j=0;j<nominatedCustomers.length;j++){
          if(customersData[i].
              EmailAddress==nominatedCustomers[j].
              emailAddress){
            find = true;
            break;
          }
        }
        if(!find){
            customersToNominate.push(customersData[i]);
        }
      }
    }

    return customersToNominate;
  }
```

The JavaScript function accepts two input parameters. The first input parameter, `customersData`, will accept all the customers fetched from the Oracle Cloud application. The second input parameter, `nominatedCustomers`, will accept all the customers who are already nominated and stored in the Nomination Business Object. The JavaScript function will return all the customers who are not nominated by comparing the email addresses from both the input parameters.

10. Go to the **Event Listeners** tab, click the **+ Event Listener** button, register the **vbEnter** event, and create a new Action Chain with the name `loadData` at the page level.

11. Go to the **loadData** Action Chain and drag and drop the **Run in Parallel** (used to execute multiple actions in parallel) action just below the **Start** action.

12. Drag and drop the **Call REST** action two times under **Run in Parallel** as per the following screenshot:

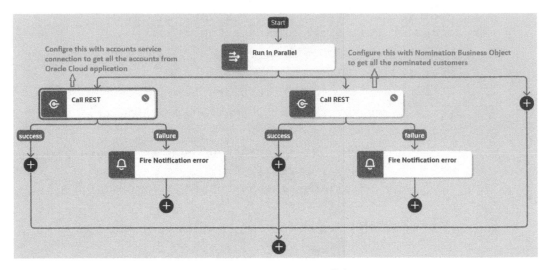

Figure 9.12 – Run in Parallel

13. Configure the first **Call REST** action to call the GET /accounts REST endpoint to get all the accounts from the Oracle Cloud application, and then configure the second **Call REST** action to call the GET /Nomination Business Object to obtain all the nominated customers.

14. Drag and drop **Call Function** when the **Run in Parallel** action completes.

15. Select **getCustomersToNominate** from the **Function Name** dropdown, and then configure **Input Parameters** from the source, chain.results. callRestGetallAccounts.body.items, to the target, customersData, and from the source, chain.results.callRestGetallNomination. body.items, to the target, nominatedCustomers.

16. Then, select **Array** from the **Return Type** dropdown. The following screenshot shows the **Call Function** action:

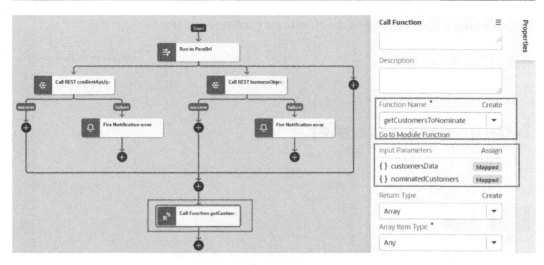

Figure 9.13 – Configuring the call module function action

17. Drag and drop the **Assign Variables** action just below the **Call Function** action. Select **Assign** right next to **Variables** and assign the source, callFunctionGetCustomersToNominate, to the target, page.variables. AccountsADP.data, and then update the **Reset Target** property to empty.

18. Go back to the **Page Designer** tab on the **nomination-create-nomination** page, delete the **Input Text** component, and then drag and drop the **Select (Single)** component.

19. Then, change **Label Hint** to Customers. Move to the **Data** tab from the **Properties** palette of the **Select (Single)** component, configure the **Data** property with variables.AccountsADP, and then set the **Item Text** property to CEOName.

20. Register the **value-item** event on the **Select (Single)** component. In the Action Chain of the **value-item** event, drag and drop the **Assign Variables** action just below the **Start** action.

21. Click on **Assign** right next to **Variables** and map the source, variables.data. CEOName, to the target, page.variables.nomination.cEOName. Also, map the source, variables.data.EmailAddress, to the target, page. variables.nomination.emailAddress.

Now, the configuration is complete and all nominated customers can be viewed. To nominate the customers, run the application and move to the **Nomination** tab. Initially, the table will be blank. Click on the **Nominate Customer** button to nominate the customer. In the **Select (Single)** component, you will see all the customer names. Select the customer name to nominate and then click on the **Save** button.

The following screenshot shows the **Nominate Customer** page:

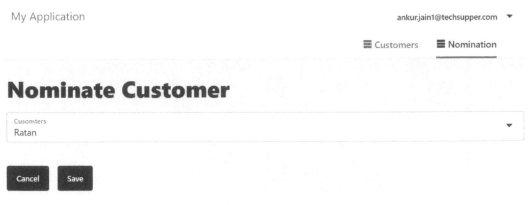

Figure 9.14 – Nominating a customer

Once you click on the **Save** button, the information will be saved to the **Nomination** Business Object. You will be returned to the previous page and can view the nominated customer as per the following screenshot:

Figure 9.15 – List of nominations

When you click again on the **Nominate Customer** button, you will not see **Ratan** in the **Customer** dropdown, as **Ratan** has already been nominated.

Withdrawing nominations

Now, once a customer has been nominated, we may need to withdraw the nomination. The following are the steps to show how to withdraw nomination functionality:

1. Open the **nomination-start** page, open the **Page Designer** tab of the page, and drag and drop the **Switch** component to the **Nominated** column.

2. Select the **Switch** component, go to the **Data** tab from the **Properties** palette, and select **current.data** from the **Value** property.

3. Register the **value** event on the **Switch** component. In the Action Chain of the **value** event, drag and drop the **Call REST** action just below the **Start** action.

4. Click **Select** right next to **Endpoint**, select PATCH /Nomination/{Nomination_ id} from the opened **Select Endpoint** dialog box, and then click on the **Select** button.

5. Select **Assign** right next to **Input Parameters** and then map the source, variables.key, to the target, uriParams.Nomination_Id.

6. Select **Assign** right next to **Parameters**, and assign { "nominated" : $variables.value} to **body** as per following screenshot, and then click on the **Save** button:

Figure 9.16 – Set the nominated field

The withdraw nomination functionality is complete. Run the application and switch to the **Nomination** tab. In the nominated customer table, click on the toggle button to withdraw the nomination. Once clicked, the **Nomination** Business Object will be updated.

The following screenshot shows a list of nominated customers along with the `Switch` component, which will allow you to withdraw the nomination and nominate the customer again:

Figure 9.17 – Withdrawing the nomination

That is everything regarding extending the Oracle Cloud SaaS application using the VB. You can add more functionality to the VB application and interact with the Oracle Cloud application directly.

In this section, we learned how to use the built-in Oracle Cloud application catalog to extend the Oracle Cloud SaaS application. We covered how to fetch data from the Oracle Cloud application in real time and how to update the data in the Oracle Cloud application directly. We extended the functionality and created another custom screen to nominate the customers. All the nominations are stored in the VB local database. In the next section, we'll look at how to create a **multilingual application**.

Creating a multilingual application

Oracle VB allows us to build an application that can be rendered in different languages, called a **multilingual application**. A multilingual application enables an end user to view the application in their language of choice. In this section, we'll demonstrate how to create a multilingual application in VB.

In order to make a multilingual application, we need to convert strings into other languages and upload them in translation bundles, which is a JSON file containing keys and values.

We'll use the **customers-start** page of the **oraclecloudext_chapter9** application to render it in two different languages, **English** and **French**.

The following sections demonstrate how to develop multilingual applications in VB.

Configuring an application to set the selected language locale

The following are the steps to set the locale of the selected language:

1. Go to **Source View** from the application navigator and open the `app-flow.json` file under the **oraclecloudext_chapter9** application.

2. Enter the following line of code after `"security": {}` in the `app-flow.json` file. The modified (bold) content is given as follows (*don't forget to put a comma (,)*):

```
"localization": {
    "locale": "{{ window.localStorage.getItem('current.
        locale') || navigator.language }}"
}
```

The previous code will set the `locale` property to a locale value when we switch the application to render in a different language. By default, the `locale` browser will be set.

The following screenshot shows the **localization** property updated in the `app-flow.json` file:

Figure 9.18 – Setting the localization property

3. Open the `index.html` file as shown in the preceding screenshot, and paste the following code before the `<oj-vb-content config="[[vbApplication]]"></oj-vb-content>` line:

```
<script>
var html = document.documentElement;
var locale = localStorage.getItem('current.locale');
if (locale) {
html.lang = locale;
```

```
    }
    </script>
```

4. Go back to the **oraclecloudext_chapter9** application and open the **customers-start**
    page. Move to the **JavaScript** tab and enter the following lines of JavaScript code:

```
PageModule.prototype.settingLocale =
function(currentLocale){
    if (currentLocale)  {
        window.localStorage.setItem('current.locale',
            currentLocale);
    }
};
```

The previous JavaScript code will set the `current.locale` property to the selected locale.

Generating translatable strings

Translatable strings are used to store data in different languages. The following are the
steps to generate translatable strings:

1. Go to the **customers-start** page, select the table, go to the **Data** tab from the **Properties**
    palette, hover on the **CEOName** column, and then select the **Column Detail** icon.

2. Click the **Make String Translatable** icon from the **Columns, Header Text** property.
    When you click on the **Make String Translatable** icon, this opens the inline
    popup. This popup allows you to change the **Text** and **Key** values. The **Key** value is
    generated automatically (a random string) for each and every text. Update **Key** to
    ceo_name to make it more meaningful, as per the following screenshot:

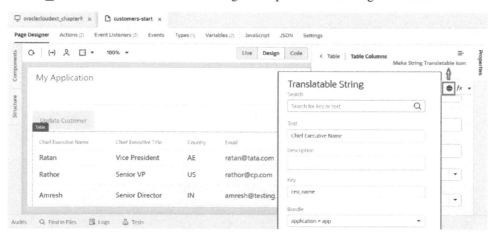

Figure 9.19 – Creating translatable strings

3. Click on the **Save** button after updating **Key**. Notice that **Columns, Header Text** will be changed by an expression that specifies the key.

4. Repeat *step 1* and *step 2* for the rest of the columns (**Chief Executive Title**, **Country**, **Email**, and **URL**) and change the **Key** values to `ceo_title`, `country`, `email`, and `url`, respectively.

Now, translatable strings have been generated for the table columns.

Downloading and uploading the bundle

In this section, we'll download the resource bundle, create separate files to support different languages, bundle them, and upload the bundle again to the VB application. The following are the steps to download and upload the bundle:

1. Open the `app-strings.json` file under the `Resources/strings/apps/nls` folder of the **oraclecloudext_chapter9** application. Initially, it contains only a single key-value definition. This will be updated automatically when we upload the bundle to support different languages.

2. Open the `apps-strings.json` file under the `root` folder and view all the translatable strings, which we created in the previous section, as per the following screenshot:

Figure 9.20 – Translatable strings

3. From the application menu in the top-right corner of the page, click on **Settings**.

4. Go to the **Translations** tab and click on **ARB** (**Application Resource Bundle**) under the **Download All String** section. This action will download a `.zip` file named `VBCSBook-strings-all-arb.zip`.

5. Extract the `.zip` file. The unzipped folder will contain different folders for each and every application.

6. Open the `oraclecloudext_chapter9_app` folder under the unzipped folder and you will see that there is a single file named `app-strings.arb`. This file will contain all the translatable strings.

7. Make a copy of this file in the same folder and rename it `app-strings-fr-FR.arb` (**fr-FR** represents the language of translation and the country as French (France)).

8. Open the `app-strings-fr-FR.arb` file. For all the translatable strings, replace the key value with the *French* translation. The following file shows the translatable strings (marked in bold); the email and URL are the same in both English and French:

```
    "ceo_name" : "Nom du directeur général",
     "@ceo_name" : {
        "description" : "",
        "source_text" : "Chief Executive Name"
     },
     "ceo_title" : "Titre de directeur général",
     "@ceo_title" : {
        "description" : "",
        "source_text" : "Chief Executive Title"
     },
     "country" : "Pays",
     "@country" : {
        "description" : "",
        "source_text" : "Country"
     },
     "email" : "Email",
     "@email" : {
        "description" : "",
        "source_text" : "Email"
     },
```

```
"url" : "URL",
"@url" : {
    "description" : "",
    "source_text" : "URL"
}
```

9. Save the file and zip the `oraclecloudext_chapter9_app` folder. Make sure that the zipped folder contains both the ARB files.

10. Return to the VB application and, from the **Translation** page under the **Settings** application, upload the `oraclecloudext_chapter9_app.zip` folder from the **Upload Updated Bundle** section.

11. Once the bundle file is uploaded successfully, you will receive a confirmation message and the bundle will be added under the `nls` folder as per the following screenshot:

Figure 9.21 – Uploading the bundle

12. Open the `app-strings.json` file under the `fr-FR` folder, which will show all the translatable strings.

13. Open the parent `app-strings.json` file under the `nls` folder and you will see two key-value definitions as per the following screenshot:

```
1  {
2    "root" : true,
3    "fr-FR" : true
4  }
```

Figure 9.22 – The app-strings.json file

The updated bundle has been uploaded successfully.

Adding a language switcher

In this section, we'll add a **language switcher** in the form of a radio button, which will allow the application to be rendered in the required language.

The following are the steps to make a language switcher:

1. Open the **customers-start** page, and drag and drop the **Radio Button Set** component above the **Update Customer** button.

2. Open the **Properties** palette of the **Radio Button Set** component, change the **Label Hint** property to `Language Switcher`, and then change the **Styling** property to `Row`.

3. Go to the **Quick Start** tab and click the **Create Static List of Options** button. From the opened dialog box, add two entries as per the following screenshot, and then click on the **Finish** button:

Figure 9.23 – Configuring the Radio Button Set component

4. Register the **value** event on the **Radio Button Set** component.

5. In the Action Chain of the **value** event, drag and drop the **Call Function** action. Select the **settingLocale** method under the **Function Name** property and map the source, `variables.value`, to the target, `currentLocale`.

6. Drag and drop the **Open URL** (used to open any URL) action just below the **Call Function** action. Enter `index.html` under the **URL** property. This will load the application after changing the language.

> **Important Note:**
> `index.html` is the file that maintains all the UI-related code. You can see this page in **Source View** under the application navigator.

All the configuration required is complete. Run the application and see that the application is rendered in **English** by default. Select the **French** radio button and you will see that the table columns are rendered in French:

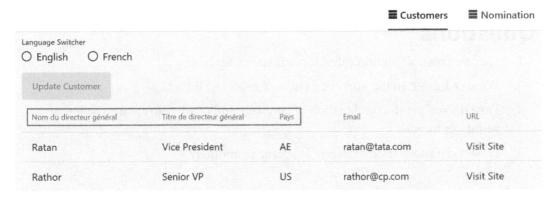

Figure 9.24 – Application in the French language

Click on the **English** radio button and you will see the table columns rendered in English.

This is how multilingual applications are created and allow users to view the application in their language of choice. In this section, we learned how to create a multilingual application to render the application in a different language.

Summary

In this chapter, we learned how to extend Oracle and non-Oracle SaaS applications. We extended the Salesforce application using the REST APIs. We created an application where we saw how to get all the opportunities from Salesforce in a table and created a new opportunity using the custom form. We created another set of screens to populate all the accounts and allow a user to create new accounts, too.

We learned how to extend the Oracle Cloud application using the inbuilt catalog. We created a set of custom screens in VB to list all the accounts and allow modification of them in real time. We extended the functionality and created another set of custom screens to nominate the customers and store them locally.

We learned how to create a multilingual application to render the application in a different language. We created an application to render the application in both English and French.

In the next chapter, we'll look at how to create a connection with Processes, add business processes to a VB application, and enable a user to take actions (approve/reject) directly from the VB screen.

Questions

1. Can we create a Salesforce developer instance for free?
2. What is `fr-FR` in the `app-strings-fr-FR.arb` file?
3. How do you get the combination of language and country to create a different resources bundle?
4. How is data converted from one language to another?

10
Working with Business Processes

Business processes that are created and deployed in **Process Cloud** can be initiated from VB, and pending tasks can be managed from the VB application directly. The benefit of integrating Processes with VB is to provide a unified application where end users can initiate, view, review, approve, and reject all the tasks aligned under the respective user without logging into the Process workspace.

In this chapter, we'll look at how to add Process backend that will be used to consume the Process task in the VB application. Once the backend is added, we'll create a VB application where users can initiate processes.

We'll create another set of screens in the same VB application that will allow managing tasks and provide an option to approve or reject a task directly from the VB application. Users can view the complete dataset they have initiated.

We'll look at how to configure the process server under the VB application, which will be used to configure a different target server when you switch the VB application from one stage to another.

In this chapter, we will cover the following topics:

- Adding the Process backend
- Registering business processes
- Initiating a process from the VB application
- Managing process tasks
- Configuring a connection to a process server

After completing this chapter, you will be able to consume business processes in the VB application and allow a user to take action on pending tasks.

Technical requirements

To complete this chapter, you should have the following:

- A **Visual Builder** instance
- **VB** login credentials
- A OIC instance
- A deployed process in process server

You can find the full source code used in this chapter here: `https://github.com/PacktPublishing/Effortless-App-Development-with-Oracle-Visual-Builder/tree/main/Chapter10`.

Adding the Process backend

In order to work with a business process in VB, a Process backend must be added under the tenant settings of the Visual Builder instance. Refer to *Chapter 5, Creating and Managing Service Connections*, under the *Adding a new backend* section, to know how to add a backend server.

> **Important Note:**
> If a Visual Builder instance is part of an **Oracle Integration Cloud** (OIC) instance, then the Process backend will exist by default and you won't need to add it manually.

If the Visual Builder instance is not part of OIC, then the Process backend needs to be added manually to point to the Process instance. When you add the backend, under the **Tenant** settings you will only see **None, Propagate Current User Identity**, and **Oracle Cloud Account** options under the **Authentication** drop-down list. You can override these settings at the application level to view more **Authentication** options such as **Basic, OAuth 2.0 Client Credentials**, and so on.

The following screenshot shows the **Edit Server** dialog to override the **Tenant** settings at the application level:

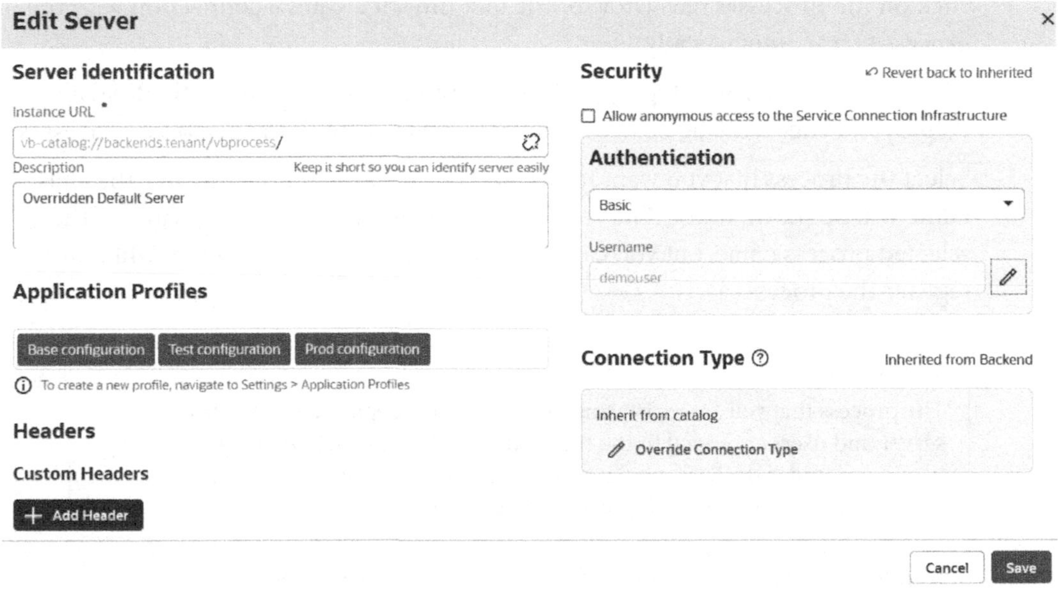

Figure 10.1 – Edit Server dialog box

In this section, we learned how to add a Process backend in a Visual Builder instance and how to override the settings. In the next section, we'll look at how to add business processes to the VB application.

Registering the business processes

Once a business process is created in Process instance, you can register the business processes in the Visual Builder application and manage the processes in web or mobile applications.

A **business process** is developed in Process instance, which will be used to raise a **Travel Reimbursement** request. A level-one approval is added in the process to approve and reject the request.

Download the application using the following URL, import it into the Process instance, and activate it:

```
https://github.com/PacktPublishing/Effortless-App-Development-
with-Oracle-Visual-Builder/blob/main/Chapter10/VBCSBookPCSApp.
exp
```

The following are the steps to register business processes in the VB application:

1. Open the **VBCSBook** application and go to the **Processes** navigator. When you click on the **Processes** navigator for the first time, it creates a connection with the process server automatically.

2. Click on the **+ Register Deployed Process** button, which will open the **Register Deployed Process** dialog box. The dialog box will show all the deployed processes.

3. Select the process that you want to register. Once you select the process, the alias name will be shown in the **Alias** textbox. The alias name will be the same as the selected process name, but you can change it if required. Click on the **Add** button to register the process.

> **Important Note:**
> The process that you are registering, make sure it is deployed on the Process server and users are added to the roles. Also, make sure **Default Target Server** is selected under the Base configuration application profile. For development purposes, continue to use **Player Target Server**.

The following screenshot shows the process registration process:

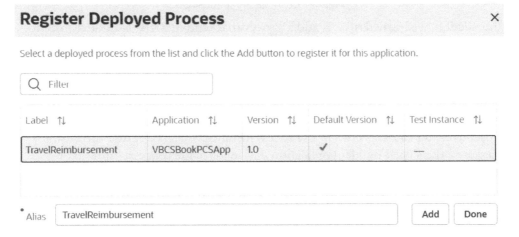

Figure 10.2 – Register Deployed Process dialog box

4. Click on the **Done** button to close the dialog box. Once a process is registered, it will be visible in the **Processes** navigator.

5. Click on the process name that is registered. Go to the **Code Snippets** tab and see the various actions. You can use **HTML** and **JSON** code in the VB application to interact with registered processes.

The following screenshot shows the HTML code of the registered process:

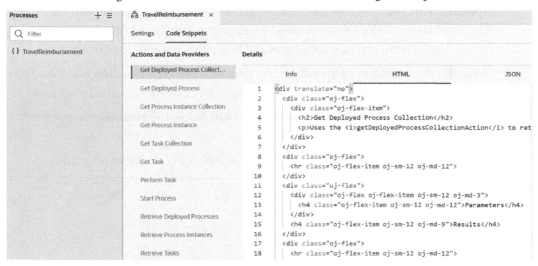

Figure 10.3 – Process HTML code

As you can see, the **Info** tab will provide information about the metadata of the selected action such as **Retrieve Deployed Processes**, **Retrieve Process Instances**, and so on.

In order to execute all the use cases in this chapter, a new web application is created with the Page ID chapter10 using the **Tabbed** style pattern, and two tabs are created with the names Initiate Process and Manage Processes.

> **Important Note:**
> In order to develop the use case in this chapter, we are using a Visual Builder instance that is part of an OIC instance as the Process instance is part of it.
> It is recommended to use VB, which is part of OIC, if you want to work with business processes in VB.

In this section, we learned how to register a deployed process in a VB application, and we saw the HTML code generated after registering the process. In the next section, we'll look at how to initiate the registered process.

Initiating the process from the VB application

In this section, we'll create a form in the VB application that will allow us to initiate the registered **TravelReimbursement** process.

The following are the steps to initiate the process from VB:

1. Open the **initiate-process-start** page under the **chapter10** web application.

2. Open the **Variables** tab and create five variables of the `String` type with the ID `firstName`, `lastName`, `travelReason`, `travelStartDate`, and `travelEndDate`, and one variable of the `Number` type with the ID `amount`.

3. Go to the **Page Designer** tab of the page, drag and drop the **Heading** component on the page, and change the **Text** property to `Raise Travel Reimbursement`.

4. Drag and drop the **Form Layout** component just below the **Heading** component, and change the **Max Columns** property to 2.

5. Configure the UI component under **Form Layout** as per the following table:

Component Type	Label Hint	Value
Input Text	First Name	{{ $variables.firstName }}
Input Text	Last Name	{{ $variables.lastName }}
Input Text	Travel Reason	{{ $variables.travelReason }}
Input Number	Amount	{{ $variables.amount }}
Input Date	Travel Start Date	{{ $variables.travelStartDate }}
Input Date	Travel End Date	{{ $variables.travelEndDate }}

Table 10.1 – List of UI components

6. Drag and drop the **Button** component after the **Form Layout** component, and change the **Text** property to Submit.

7. Select the **Submit** button and register the **ojAction** event.

8. In this Action Chain of the button event, drag and drop the **Start Process** (used to initiate the deployed process) action just below the **Start** action. Update the ID property to startTravelProcess.

9. Click **Select** right next to **Process Interface** from the **Start Process** property palette. From the opened **Select Process Interface** dialog box, expand the **Process Aliases | TravelReimbursement** option and select **Submit Request**. Click on the **Select** button as per the following screenshot:

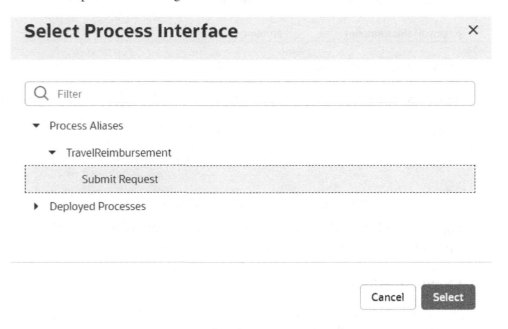

Figure 10.4 – Select the Process REST endpoint

10. The selected process requires the input parameters. Click **Assign** right next to **Input Parameters**. From the **Assign Input Parameters** dialog box, map the source to target as per the following table, and click on the **Save** button after the mapping is completed:

Source	Target
page.variables.firstName	firstName
page.variables.lastName	lastName
page.variables.travelReason	travelReason
page.variables.amount	amount
page.variables.travelStartDate	travelStartDate
page.variables.travelEndDate	travelEndDate
application.user.email	emailAddress (This will map the email address of logged in user)

Table 10.2 – Mapping of Process REST endpoint

11. Drag and drop **Fire Notification** under the success path, configure the **Summary** property to [["You are request has been initiated with process id " + $chain.results. startTravelProcess.content.id]], and set **Notification Type** as confirmation.

Now, we have completed the configuration to initiate the task. Run the application, fill in the form, and click on the **Submit** button to initiate the process.

The following screenshot shows the process ID after it is initiated:

Figure 10.5 – Travel reimbursement request

You can open the Process workspace and should see the task visible with process ID **2292**. This is how the process can be initiated from the VB application.

In this section, we learned how to initiate processes from the VB application using the **Start Process** action of the Action Chain. In the next section, we'll look at how to manage process tasks from the VB application.

Managing process tasks

When a process has commenced, a task is generated and then the approver needs to take some action on this like **review**, **approve**, or **reject** for taking the task forward. So we'll add an action dropdown by which user will be able to take an action on the tasks pending in his/her bucket. We'll create a page by which the users can manage all the pending tasks and approve or reject the tasks directly from the VB application without going to the Process workspace

The following are the steps to manage process tasks from the VB application:

1. Open the **manage-processes-start** page, drag and drop the **Table** component on the page, set the **style** property to height:200px;.

2. Click the **Table | Quick Stat | Add Data** options.

3. From the opened **Add Data** dialog box, select **task** under the **Process Objects** section as per the following screenshot, and click on the **Next** button:

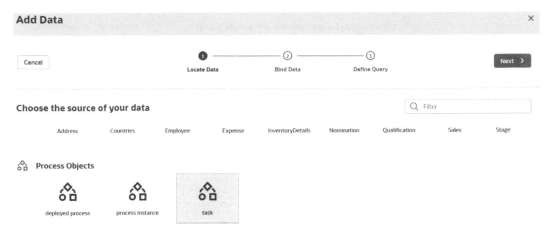

Figure 10.6 – Select the task

4. From the next screen, select **label**, **creationUser**, **creationDate**, **priority**, and click on the **Next** button. Click on the **Finish** button to complete the dialog box.

5. Select a table, go to the **Data** tab, and change the table columns' names to `Application Name`, `Initiated By`, `Initiated Date`, and `Priority` to make it more logical.

   Run the application, move to the **Manage Processes** tab, and you will see that all the tasks are populated in a table. The following screenshot shows all the process tasks:

		☰ Initiate Process	☰ **Manage Processes**
Application Name ↑↓	Initiated By ↑↓	Initiated Date ↑↓	Priority ↑↓
VBCSBookPCSApp	Ankur Jain	2021-01-17T10:25:31.000Z	3
VBCSBookPCSApp	Ankur Jain	2021-01-17T11:01:25.000Z	3

Figure 10.7 – Tasks are populated in a table

6. Return to the VB designer, go back to the **Page Designer** tab of the **manage-processes-start** page, select the table, go to the **Quick Start** tab, and click the **Add Task Actions** option.

7. From the opened **Add Task Actions** box, select the **Finish** button. This action will add a drop-down list along with a **Submit** button. The drop-down list will show all the task actions, such as **SUBMIT**, **APPROVE**, **REJECT**, and so on.

Run the application again, move to the **Manage Processes** tab, and select any one of the tasks from the table. Select any one of the actions from the **Choose an Action** drop-down list and click on the **Submit** button.

The following screenshot shows all the actions that can be taken on the selected task:

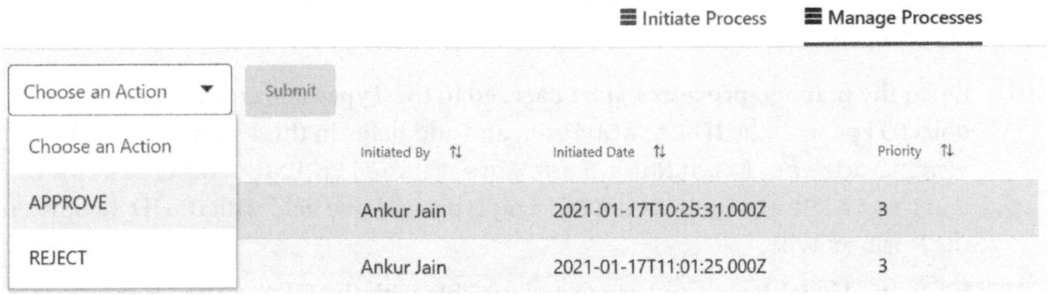

Figure 10.8 – Actions on the task

Once the task is approved, either it will be completed or will go for the next action. If it is completed, the tasks will be removed from the table as the table only populates pending tasks.

That's all about managing process tasks from the VB application.

In this section, we learned how to populate a table with all the process tasks and added the **Choose an Action** dropdown, which will allow the user to act on a task directly from the VB application. In the next section, we'll look at how to extract the data object and show it in a table.

Extracting the data object

In the previous section, we saw how to populate the processes tasks in a table and allow users to take necessary action on the task if required. In this section, we'll implement functionality that will fetch the data object (information entered by user while submitting the process) that was submitted while raising the Travel Reimbursement request.

In order to get the data object, the Process REST API will be used. The data object `/ic/api/process/v1/processes/{processId}/dataobjects` REST endpoint will be used to extract the data object for a process instance.

Create a Service Connection using the Process GET REST API to get the data object, `https://<OIC_URL>/ic/api/process/v1/processes/{processId}/dataobjects`. Replace `OIC_URL` with the actual hostname of OIC and use **Basic Authentication** to authenticate the REST API.

> **Important Note:**
> Refer to *Chapter 5, Creating and Managing Service Connections*, under the *Creating a Service Connection from an endpoint* section, to learn how to create a Service Connection using the REST endpoint.

Once the Service Connection is created, follow these steps to show the data object of the selected process task:

1. Open the **manage-processes-start** page, go to the **Types** tab, create a custom object **Type** with the ID DataObject, and add fields in this type with the IDs emailAddress, firstName, lastName, travelEndDate, travelReason, and travelStartDate of the String type, and one field with the ID amount of the Number type.

2. Go to the **Variables** tab and create one variable with the ID DataObjectADP of the Array Data Provider type. Set DataObject as **Item Type**, and emailAddress as the key attribute.

3. Return to the **Page Designer** tab, drag and drop the **Heading** component just below the table, and change the **Label Hint** property to Data Object.

4. Drag and drop the **Table** component just below the **Heading** component. Bind the **Data** property with the DataObjectADP variable. Select all the columns from the **Table Columns** property.

5. Go to the **JavaScript** tab of the **manage-processes-start** page and enter the following code:

```javascript
PageModule.prototype.convertToJson = function(data){
    var jsonArray = [];
    jsonArray = JSON.parse(data)
    return jsonArray;
}
```

The Process REST API provides the data object as a JSON string. So the JavaScript code will convert the JSON string into a JSON object and will return it as an array.

6. Select the first table from the page, go to the **Events** tab, and register the **first-selected-row** event.

7. In the Action Chain of this event, drag and drop the **Call REST** action just below the **Start** action and change the **ID** property to `callRestEndpointDataObject`. Select the Process **GET** endpoint as per the following screenshot:

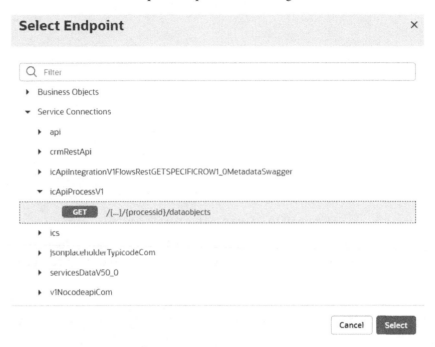

Figure 10.9 – Select the data object REST endpoint

8. Assign the source `variables.rowData.processInstance.id` to the target `uriParams.processid` as the input parameter of the selected REST endpoint.

9. Drag and drop **Call Function** under the success path, select the `convertToJson` function from the **Function Name** property, and update the `ID` property to `callFunctionConvertToJson`. Select the **Assign** property right next to **Input Parameters** and map the source `chain.results.callRestEndpointDataObject.body.dataVariableFlatTree[0].value` to `data`, and click on the **Save** button. Select `Array` from the **Return Type** property of the **Call Function** action.

10. Drag and drop **Assign Variables** action below the **Call Function** action, click **Assign** right next to **Variables**, and map the source `chain.results.callModuleFunction1` to the target `page.variables.DataObjectADP.data`. Update the **Reset Target** property to `empty`.

That's all about extracting the data object of a process task.

Now, we run the application, move to the **Manage Processes** tab, select any one of the tasks from the table, and see the data object populated in another table that was inserted while raising the Travel Reimbursement request:

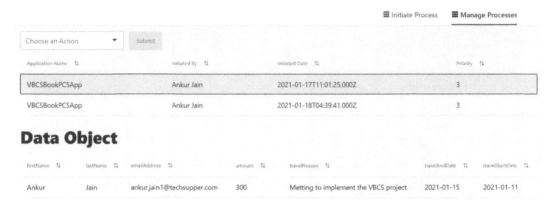

Figure 10.10 – Data object of the selected task

In this section, we learned how to fetch the data object corresponding to a process task and display it in a table. In the next section, we'll look at how to configure a process server connection.

Configuring a connection to a process server

When you create a VB application that uses the business process, VB sets up a default process server configuration. The following are the steps to view all the default process servers and to configure the process server:

1. Click the **Services** tab from the application navigator, and go to the **Backends** tab.

2. Then, click on **Process Applications** and go to the **Servers** tab. You'll see a **Process Server**, which in development mode and is configured to point to a test environment of the Oracle Process Cloud Service instance as per the following screenshot:

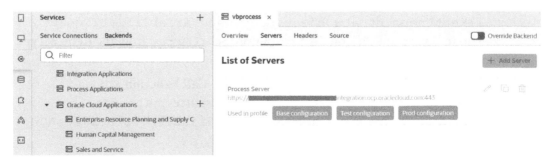

Figure 10.11 – Default process server

When you register any process under the **Processes** tab or you use a Process Quick Start, the Tenant settings will be overridden and one more **Player Target Server** will be visible under the Process Applications backend as shown in the following screenshot:

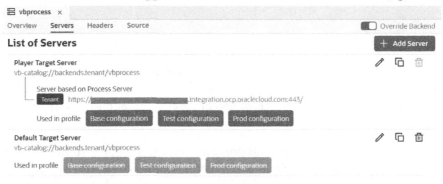

Figure 10.12 – Player Target Server

3. The target server is set up under **Application Profiles**. Click on the action from top right corner, click the **Settings** menu from the top right corner, and move to the **Application Profiles** tab and see that **Player Target Server** is set up for all the configured application profiles by default as per the following screenshot:

Figure 10.13 – Application profiles

4. In order to change the target server, click any one of the profiles from **Application Profiles** and change **Process Applications** to `Default Target Server`. This configuration is required when you publish the VB application.

    The following screenshot shows that the target server is changed to `Default Target Server` for the **Prod Configuration** application profile, which is the default profile for the publish application:

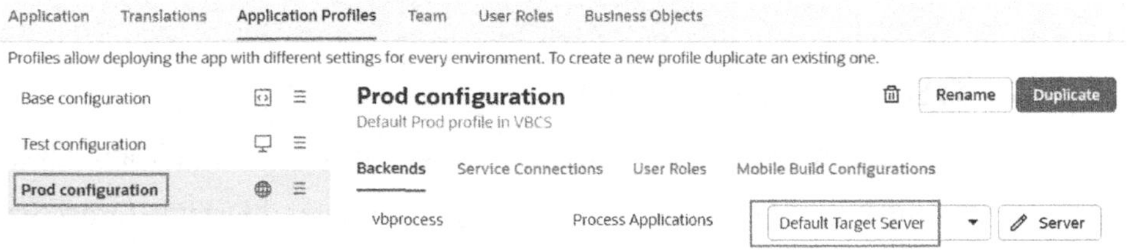

Figure 10.14 – Update the process server

This is how you can configure the process server in the VB application.

In this section, we learned how to configure the process server in the VB application and change the target servers.

Summary

In this chapter, you learned how to work with business processes in the VB application. You learned how to add and override the Process backend in Visual Builder. You also learned how to register the deployed business process in VB and see the HTML code of the registered process.

You learned how to initiate the business process from the VB application. We created a form in the VB application that allows you to enter a reimbursement request and submit the request. This initiates the Travel Reimbursement process and shows the generated process ID.

We also developed a page in the VB application to manage all the process tasks and populate them in a table. We added the action dropdown, which allows taking actions (APPROVE/REJECT) directly from the VB application without logging in to the Process workspace. We also added another functionality that retrieves the data object of the submitted task and populates it in a table. You learned how to configure the connection to a process server.

In the next chapter, we'll develop a mobile application in VB and add the various functionalities to the mobile application. We'll develop different pages and use different UI components. We'll show how to develop a **Progressive Web App** (**PWA**) and will also show how to compile an application to support different platforms.

Further reading

- Learn about Oracle Processes: https://www.oracle.com/in/cloud/integration/process-cloud-service/
- View all the Process REST APIs: https://docs.oracle.com/en/cloud/paas/integration-cloud/rest-api/index.html

Questions

1. Is it recommended to override the default settings of the Process Application Backend?
2. What is the difference between the Player Target Server and Default Target Server?

11
Building a Mobile Application with Live Examples

In the last few chapters, we have built a lot of web applications using various **JET** components and used Business Objects and Service Connections extensively to interact with the data.

As **Visual Builder** allows us to develop mobile applications, in this chapter, we'll build a mobile application and compile it for various mobile devices. We'll look at how to create a mobile application using a real-world example.

We'll develop a doctor's appointment mobile application, by means of which we can view a list of available doctors, view a doctor's full details, and book an appointment with a selected doctor. We'll provide a swipe option to view the doctor's details and to book an appointment, and we'll create a separate page to view the earlier appointments.

We'll look at different setting options of the mobile application that will allow a mobile application to render in both **Portrait** and **Landscape** modes. We'll demonstrate how to expose the mobile application as a **Progress Web App** (**PWA**) and run it on computers and mobile devices. We'll learn how to define a build configuration for **Android** and **iOS** devices and run it on both devices, separately, as a native application.

In this chapter, we will cover the following topics:

- Developing a mobile application
- Developing a doctor's appointment mobile application
- Configuring mobile application settings
- Enabling PWA support from mobile applications
- Defining a build configuration for different devices

After completing this chapter, you will be able to develop full-fledged mobile applications, expose them as PWA apps and run them on different devices. You will be able to build configurations for Android and iOS devices.

Technical requirements

To complete this chapter, you will require the following:

- A **VB** instance
- **VB** login credentials
- A `Keystore` file
- A provisioning profile
- Android and iOS devices

You can find the full source code used in this chapter here: `https://github.com/PacktPublishing/Effortless-App-Development-with-Oracle-Visual-Builder/tree/main/Chapter11`.

Developing a mobile application

A mobile application can be created in the same way as we create a new web application. Although mobile applications are independent, they can access all data sources, including Business Objects and Service Connections that are created under the VB application.

The following are the steps to create a new mobile application:

1. Open the VB application and go to the **Mobile Applications** navigator.

2. Click on the **+ Mobile Application** button to create a new mobile application.

3. From the opened **Create Mobile Application** dialog box, enter chapter11 in the **Application Name** field.

4. You can select from any one of the **Navigation Style** patterns to create a new mobile application. Select **Horizontal** as the **Navigation Style** pattern. Create two navigations with the names My Appointment and Book Appointment, and then click on the **Next** button as per the following screenshot:

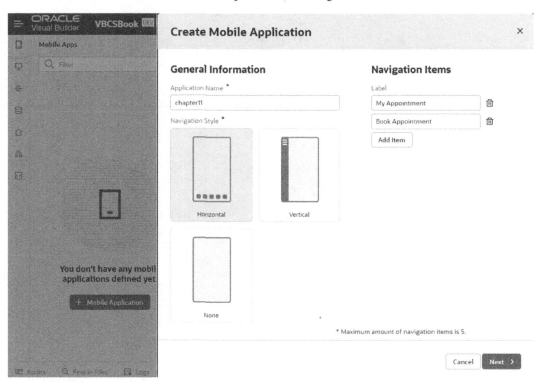

Figure 11.1 – Creating a mobile application

5. The following screen allows you to select a page template for each navigation item. Select the **List** template for both the navigation items and then click on the **Create** button.

Once the mobile application has been created, an application structure will be created similar to the web application as per the following screenshot:

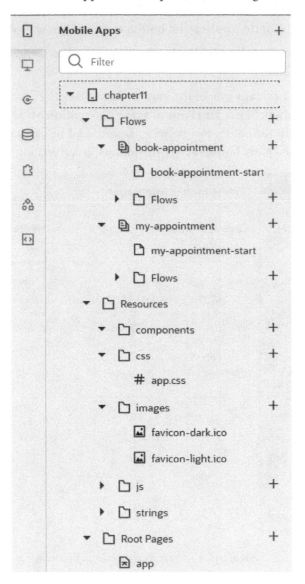

Figure 11.2 – Mobile application structure

This is how the mobile application is created. In this section, we learned how to create a new mobile application and what the mobile structure looks like. In the next section, we'll look at how to develop a doctor's appointment application.

Developing a doctor's appointment mobile application

In this section, we'll develop a doctor's appointment mobile application that can be used to view all booked appointments as well as book a new appointment from a list of doctors.

In order to complete this use case, two Business Objects are created with the names `Appointment` and `Doctors`. The `Doctors` Business Object contains the doctor's details.

You can download the Excel sheet (from `https://github.com/PacktPublishing/Effortless-App-Development-with-Oracle-Visual-Builder/blob/main/Chapter11/Doctors%20and%20Appointment%20Business%20Objects%20file.xlsx`) and import it using the **Data Manager**.

> **Important Note:**
> Refer to *Chapter 4*, *Creating and Managing Business Objects*, under the *Importing a Business Object* section, to know how to import Business Objects.

In the next section, we'll see how to book an appointment.

Booking an appointment

In this section, we'll show a list of doctors from the `Doctors` Business Objects and create a new form to book an appointment with a doctor.

The following are the steps to complete this use case:

1. Open the **book-appointment-start** page, select the page title, and change the **Page Title** property to `Available Doctors`.

2. Select the **List View** component, navigate to the **Quick Start** tab, and select the **Add Data** option.

3. From the opened **Add Data** dialog box, select the `Doctors` Business Object and then click on the **Next** button.

4. From the next screen, leave the default template selected and then click on the **Next** button.

5. From the next screen, drop **doctorName** on the **Leading** slot, **rating** on the **Overline** slot, **address** on the **Metadata** slot, and **expertise** on the **Default** slot, and then click on the **Next** button.

6. From the next screen, click on the **Finish** button to complete the wizard.

7. Go to the **Code** tab of the page and replace the `<oj-bind-text value="[[ $current.data.rating ]]"></oj-bind-text>` code with the following code:

```
<oj-rating-gauge value="[[ $current.data.rating ]]"
  class="oj-sm-flex-initial" selected-state.
  color="green" readonly>
</oj-rating-gauge>
```

8. The preceding code will show the doctor's rating in the `rating gauge` component. Run the application and click on the **Book Appointment** tab to view a list of doctors as per the following screenshot:

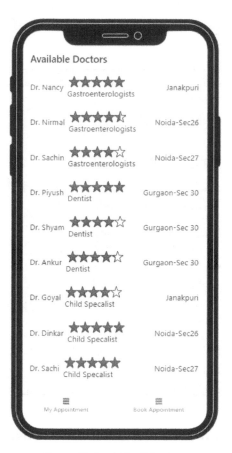

Figure 11.3 – List of doctors

As a next step, we'll provide two options. One is to view the doctor's details, and the other is to book the appointment. We'll use the right swipe feature to provide these two options.

9. Open the **Types** tab of the book-appointment-start page, click Edit from Endpoint right next to the getallDoctorsResponse variable, and then add the about, degree, and doctorEmail variables from the opened dialog box.

10. Go back to the **Page Designer** tab, select the **List View** component, go to the **General** tab from the **Properties** palette, and then click on + **Custom Swipe Tile** to add the swipe option. Add two tiles with the names View and Appointment as per the following screenshot:

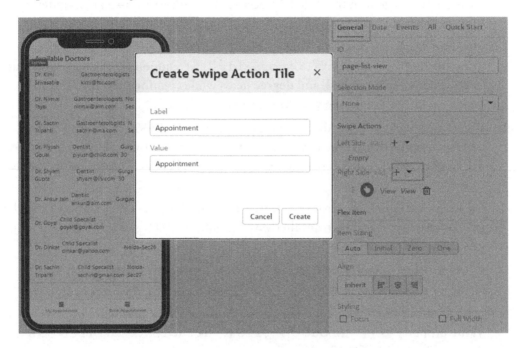

Figure 11.4 – Enabling the swipe option

11. Switch the application to **Live** mode, right swipe any one of the doctor's records, and you will see two options as per the following screenshot:

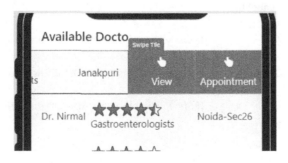

Figure 11.5 – Swipe options

We have successfully displayed the list of doctors. Now, we can start creating a new form to book an appointment with a doctor.

Configuring the View swipe option

In the following steps, a new page will be created that will show the information pertaining to a doctor when a user taps on the **View swipe** option:

1. Create a new page with the Page ID `book-appointment-details` under the **book-appointment** flow and select the **Summary** template while creating this page.

2. Open the **book-appointment** flow, go to the **Types** tab, and create a new type using the `GET /Doctors/{Doctors_id}` REST endpoint. Select the **id**, **about**, **doctorName**, **doctorEmail**, and **degree** fields while creating this type. This will create a type with the name `get_Doctors`.

3. Create another type using the `POST /Appointment` REST endpoint. Select **id**, **address**, **appointmentDateTime**, **appointmentNote**, **doctorEmail**, **doctorName**, and **expertise** fields while creating this type. This will create a type with the name, `create_Appointment`.

4. Go to the **Variables** tab, create a new variable with the ID `DoctorDetails` of the **get_Doctors** type, and then another variable with the ID `NewAppointment` of the **create_Appointment** type.

5. Open the **book-appointment-details** page, open the **Page Designer** tab, and change the **Page Title** property to `Doctor Details`.

6. Drag and drop the **Text** component inside **Summary Placeholder**. Update the **Value** property to `[[ "About "+ $flow.variables.DoctorDetails. doctorName ]]` of the **Text** component.

7. Drag and drop the UI components as per the following table:

Component Type	Label Hint	Value	Read Only
Text Area		{{ $flow.variables.DoctorDetails.about }}	true
Input Text	Degree	{{ $flow.variables.DoctorDetails.degree }}	true
Input Text	Email Address	{{ $flow.variables.DoctorDetails.doctorEmail }}	true

Table 11.1 – UI components for the book-appointment-details page

The configuration is complete and the detailed information pertaining to a doctor can be viewed.

Configuring the Appointment swipe option

In this section, we'll configure the Appointment swipe option that will be used to take an appointment from a doctor. The following are the steps to configure the Appointment swipe option:

1. Create a new page with the Page ID book-appointment-dr under **book-appointment** flow and select the **Form** template while creating the page.

2. The **book-appointment-dr** page appears as per the following screenshot:

Figure 11.6 – Default page

3. Open the **Page Designer** tab of the page and modify the **Page Title** property to Dr. Appointment.

4. Configure the UI component as per the following table under **Form Layout**:

Component Type	Label Hint	Value	Read Only
Input Text	Dr. Name	{{ $flow.variables.NewAppointment.doctorName }}	true
Input Text	Dr. Expertise	{{ $flow.variables.NewAppointment.expertise }}	true
Input Text	Dr. Email Address	{{ $flow.variables.NewAppointment.doctorEmail }}	true
Input Date Time	Appointment Date Time	{{ $flow.variables.NewAppointment.appointmentDateTime }}	
Text Area	Appointment Note	{{ $flow.variables.NewAppointment.appointmentNote }}	

Table 11.2 – List of UI components for the book-appointment-dr page

5. Drag and drop the **Button** component at the end of the form. Select the **Submit** button, change the **Text** property to Book Appointment, and the **Chroming** property to Call To Action. Go to the **Events** tab and register the **ojAction** event.

6. Drag and drop the **Call REST** action just below the **Start** action. Select the POST / Appointment REST endpoint using the **Select** action right next to **Endpoint**.

7. Click **Assign** right next to **Parameters** and map the source, flow.variables. NewAppointment, to the target, body, from the **Assign Parameters** dialog box, and then click on the **Save** button.

8. Drag and drop the **Fire Notification** action under the success path. Set the **Summary** property to [["You are appointment with "+ $flow. variables.NewAppointment.doctorName + " has been booked"]], and set the notification type to confirmation.

9. Drag and drop the **Navigate Back** action just below the **Fire Notification** action.

This completes the configuration of the page for making an appointment with a doctor.

Configuring the swipe events

Next, we will configure the events of the swipe options. When you create the swipe option, it creates an Action Chain with the name `performSwipeOperationChain`. Open the **Action** tab from the **book-appointment-start** page and observe the **performSwipeOperationChain** Action Chain as per the following screenshot:

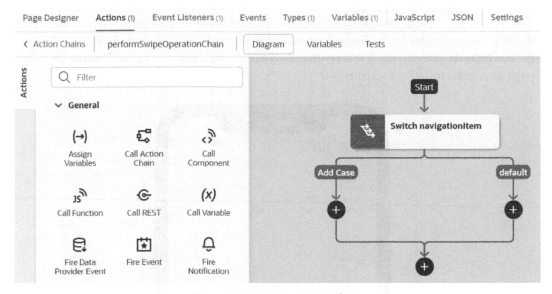

Figure 11.7 – Swipe Action Chain

These are the steps to configure this **performSwipeOperationChain** Action Chain, which will allow you to move to the designated page when you select any of the swipe options:

1. Drag and drop the **Assign Variables** action just below **Add Case**. When you drop the action, it will allow you to edit the **Case Value** value. Enter the **Case Value** value as `View` (this is the value of the **View** swipe option) and click on the **Create** button.

2. Click on **Assign** right next to **Variables** of the **Assign Variables** action, and map the source, `variables.rowData`, to the target, `flow.variables.DoctorDetails`.

3. Drag and drop the **Navigate** action just below the **Assign Variables** action and configure the **Target** property to `book-appointment-details`.

4. Drag and drop the **Assign Variables** action just below the other **Add Case** option. When you drop the action, it will allow you to edit the **Case Value** value. Enter `Appointment` as the **Case Value** value (this is the value of the **Appointment** swipe option) and then click on the **Create** button.

5. Click on **Assign** right next to **Variables** of the **Assign Variables** action and then map the source, `variables.rowData`, to the target, `flow.variables.NewAppointment`.

6. Drag and drop the **Navigate** action just below the **Assign Variables** action and configure the **Target** property to `book-appointment-dr`.

That is everything regarding configuring the Action Chain for the swipe option. Now, run the application, move to the **Book Appointment** navigation, right swipe any one of the doctor records, and tap the **View** option. This action will take you to the **Doctor Details** page as per the following screenshot:

Figure 11.8 – Doctor Details page

Go back to the doctor list page, right swipe any one of the doctor records, and tap on the **Appointment** option. This action will take you to the book appointment page. Enter the appointment details and then click on the **Book Appointment** button.

Once you click on this button, the record will be saved to the **Appointment** Business Object and you will be redirected to the previous page. The following screenshot shows the book appointment page:

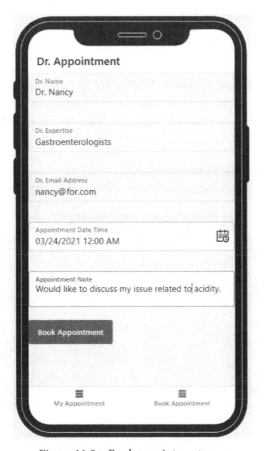

Figure 11.9 – Book appointment page

Now, all the configuration is complete in terms of listing the doctor's details, viewing the doctor's details, and booking an appointment with a doctor. Next, we'll configure the **My Appointments** option to list the appointments.

Listing the appointments

In this section, we'll configure the **My Appointments** flow, which will show all the appointments. The following are the steps for configuring this flow:

1. Open the **Page Designer** tab of the **my-appointment-start** page and update the **Page Title** property value to My Appointments.

2. Select the **List View** component on the page, go to the **Quick Start** tab, and then select the **Add Data** option.

3. From the opened **Add Data** dialog box, select the **Appointment** Business Object, and then click the **Next** button.

4. From the next screen, leave the default template selected and then click on the **Next** button.

5. From the next screen, drop **doctorName** on the **Leading** slot, **expertise** on the **Overline** slot, **appointmentDateTime** on the **Metadata** slot, and **address** on the **Default** slot. Click on the **Next** button, followed by the **Finish** button, to complete the dialog box.

The configuration for the **My Appointments** flow has been completed. Run the application again and view all the booked appointments as per the following screenshot:

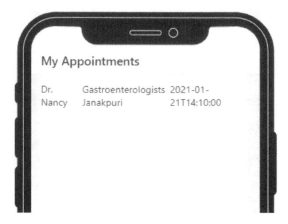

Figure 11.10 – The My Appointments page

As you can see, the doctor's appointment mobile application is now ready. You can add more functionalities to the same application as per your requirements.

In this section, we learned how to create a real-time mobile application where we added different pages and wired them together to develop a full-fledged mobile application. We added the swipe feature to add more options for the doctor's record. In the next section, we'll look at various general settings for the mobile application.

Configuring mobile application settings

Once your application is developed, you can review the mobile application settings and modify them as per your organization's requirements.

Click on the mobile application name's **chapter11 | Settings | General** tabs. The following screenshot shows the mobile application settings:

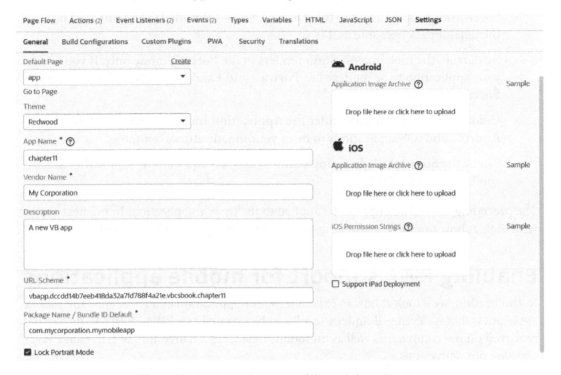

Figure 11.11 – General settings of the mobile application

The following are the settings that can be modified for the mobile applications:

- Select the default page from the **Default Page** dropdown. By default, this is **app**, but if you have another page, you can select the other page and this will be rendered as the default page when you open the application.

- Select the mobile application theme from the available themes using the **Theme** dropdown.

- The **App Name** field displays the application name. By default, the value of this field is the name of the mobile application. You can modify it if required. The application name will be displayed when the app is installed on the mobile device.

- Enter the name of the vendor who developed the application in the **Vendor Name** field.

- Then, enter the description of the application in the **Description** field.

- Enter the unique URL scheme in the **URL Scheme** field or leave the default URL scheme as it is.

- Specify the package name in the **Package Name / Bundle ID Default** field or leave the default package name as it is.

- By default, the mobile application renders in the **Portrait** mode only. If you want your application to be rendered in **Portrait** and **Landscape** mode, deselect the **Lock Portrait Mode** checkbox.

- Upload the custom images under the **Application Image Archive** label for the Android and iOS applications to meet your organization's branding.

- Check the **Support iPad Deployment** checkbox if you want to deploy the mobile application on an **iPad**.

The preceding general settings can be applied to the mobile application. In the next section, we'll look at how to expose a mobile application as a **Progress Web App** (**PWA**) app.

Enabling PWA support for mobile applications

In this section, we'll look at how to expose a mobile application as a PWA app. The mobile application that is developed under the VB can be exposed as a PWA. A PWA app can be rendered on the computer as well as on mobile devices as a native app. But, in fact, PWA apps are not native apps.

An important difference between PWA and native app is that when the developer publishes an update to the app, PWA apps will automatically fetch the update to the device. However, native apps will require the end user to download the new version of the app and install it. The PWA app exposed from the VB has the following features:

- It allows us to install the application from a browser and add it to the home screen.

- You can add the PWA app to the mobile device's home page and it works as a native app.

- The PWA app can work offline as well.

- No URL is displayed when you run the PWA app.

The following are the steps to enable PWA support:

1. Click on the mobile application name and then navigate to the **Settings** tab, followed by the **PWA** tab.

2. Click the **Enable Progressive Web App (PWA)** toggle button.

3. Once you enable the PWA option, you will see a few other setting options, including **Manifest Settings**, **Resources**, and **Advance File Caching**, as per the following screenshot:

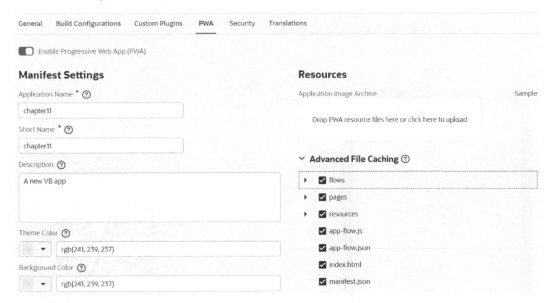

Figure 11.12 – Enabling the PWA option

As you can see, the **Manifest Settings** option allows you to change the application name, short name, description, theme color, and the background color. You can review these settings and update them if required.

The **Resources** options allows you to upload the custom splash screen and icon. By default, the splash screen and icon provided by **Oracle** are used.

You can download a sample (using the **Sample** link as per *Figure 11.12*) of the resources bundle with the various types (and sizes) of images needed. This can help you create a parallel set of resources to replace the default Oracle resources.

The **Advanced File Caching** option allows you to enable the cache for different resources. By default, all the resources are cached when you run the PWA application for the first time on your device. You can change the cache settings from this section.

4. Once the PWA option is enabled, run the application and you will see the **Build my App** option on the right-hand side of the page. This option will build your application and switch the application from **Development** to **Stage**.

5.   When you click on the **Build my App** option, the **Stage Application** dialog box will be opened. Select the **Populate Stage with Development data** (copy the development database data to the stage database) option and then click on the **Stage** button. Once the application has been successfully built, a QR code will be generated as per the following screenshot:

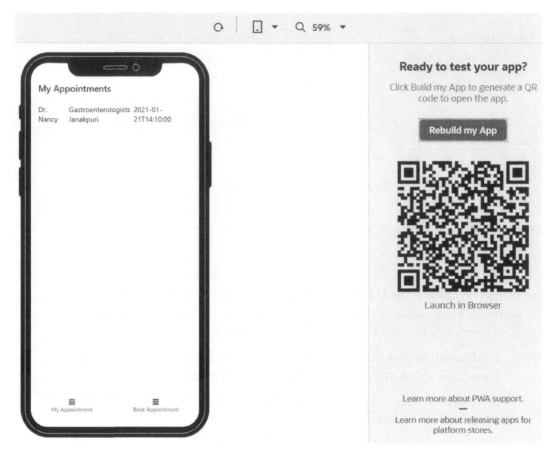

Figure 11.13 – QR code for the PWA application

6. For Android devices, scan the QR code and open it in the **Chrome** browser. The browser will prompt the **Add to Home Screen** option. Click on the **Add** button. Once the application has been added, you can view it on the device's home screen and run the application directly from the device's home screen. The following screenshot shows the **Add to Home Screen** option:

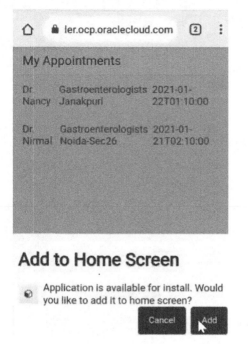

Figure 11.14 – Add to Home Screen option on an Android device

7. For iOS devices, scan the QR code and open it in the **Safari** browser. Click on the **Share** icon and choose the **Add to Home Screen** option as per the following screenshot:

Figure 11.15 – Add to Home Screen option on an iOS device

8. For computer devices, click on the **Launch in Browser** option just below the QR code. Once it is open in the browser, the browser prompts you the **Add to Home Screen** option. Click on the **Add** button to install it on your computer device.

This is how the mobile application can be exposed as a PWA app. While exposing the mobile application as a PWA app, you have to bear a few things in mind, as explained in the following section.

A few restrictions regarding the PWA app

Here are a few restrictions that we need to be mindful of while using the PWA app:

1. Only mobile applications can be exposed as PWA apps as of now.

2. Only Chrome and Safari browsers are supported for Android and iOS devices, respectively.

3. For iOS devices, a share icon is used to add the PWA app to the home screen.

4. For iOS devices, the service worker cache is limited to **50 Mib** per partition.

5. For iOS devices, deep links are not supported. When you click on the deep link, it will open the link in a separate browser window.

> **Important Note:**
> These limitations will be solved in the future release of Oracle VB.

That is everything regarding exposing the mobile application as a PWA app. In this section, we learned how to expose a mobile application as a PWA app, and how to install the application on Android, iOS, and computer devices. In the next section, we'll look at how to build a configuration for Android and iOS devices.

Defining a build configuration for different devices

The mobile applications developed in **Visual Builder** can run on Android and iOS devices as a native app. In order to run a mobile application on different devices, separate build configurations are required for Android and iOS.

In this section, we'll look at how to build a configuration for both Android and iOS devices.

Build configuration for Android

You can define one or more build configurations for Android devices. In order to define a build for Android, you need to have the Keystore file along with its credentials. The Keystore file can be generated via **Java Keytool** or **Android Studio**.

> **Important Note:**
> Refer to the https://developer.android.com/studio/
> publish/app-signing#generate-key link to generate the
> Keystore file from Android Studio.

The following are the build configuration steps for Android:

1. Click on the mobile application name, chapter11, and navigate to the **Settings** | **Build Configurations** tabs.

2. Click on the **+ Configuration** button and choose the **Android** option as per the following screenshot:

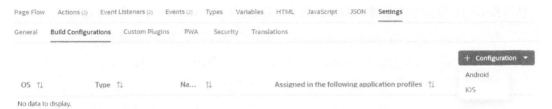

Figure 11.16 – Build Configurations screen

3. From the opened **Android Build Configuration** dialog box, configure the options as per the following table, and then click on the **Save Configuration** button:

Option	Description
Configuration Name	Enter the build configuration name as **AndroidBuild1**
Build Type	Select the build type. If you are making a build for testing choose **Debug**, and if the build is for production release, then choose **Release**. Select Release for this build.
Application Profile	Select the application profile from the available list. Let the default one for this build.
App ID	Enter the unique application id. Let the default one for this build.
Version Name	Enter the version name. Let the default one for this build.
Version Code	Enter the integer number in the field.
Keystore	Upload the Keystore file for signing the application.
Keystore Password	Enter the Keystore password.
Key Alias	Enter the Keystore alias name.
Key Password	Enter the Key password

Table 11.3 – Configure options for an Android build

The following screenshot shows the configuration for an Android build:

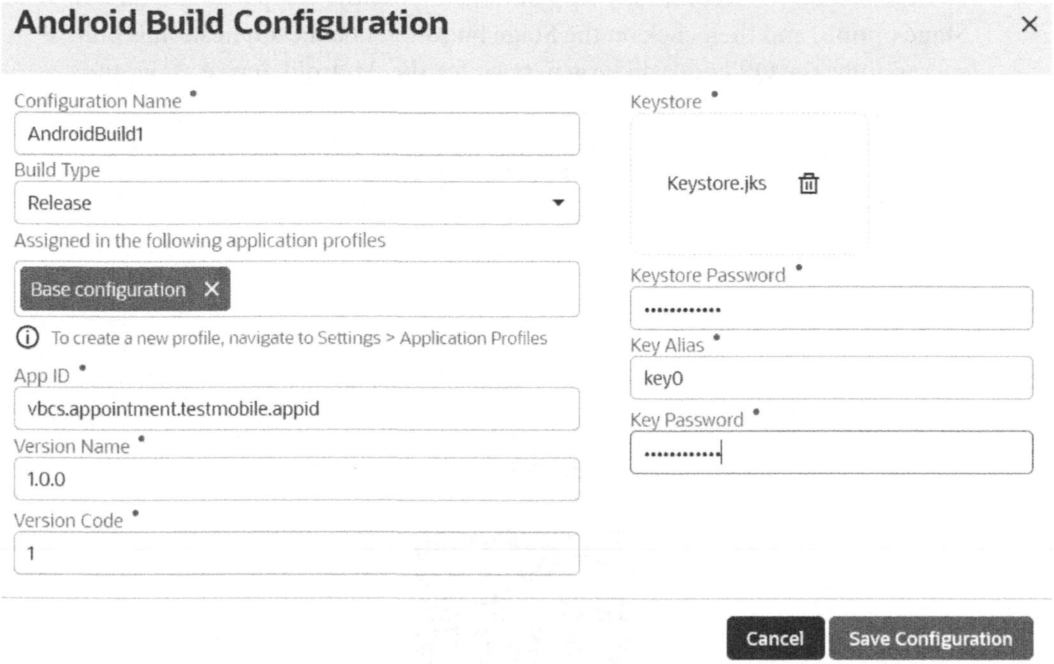

Android Build Configuration   ✕

Configuration Name *

AndroidBuild1

Build Type

Release   ▼

Assigned in the following application profiles

[Base configuration ✕]

ⓘ To create a new profile, navigate to Settings > Application Profiles

App ID *

vbcs.appointment.testmobile.appid

Version Name *

1.0.0

Version Code *

1

Keystore *

Keystore.jks 🗑

Keystore Password *

•••••••••••

Key Alias *

key0

Key Password *

•••••••••••

[Cancel] [Save Configuration]

Figure 11.17 – Build configuration for an Android device

4. Once the build is configured, it will be visible in the **Build Configuration** table as one row. After this build configuration is complete, you can view, edit, and delete the build using the action menu right next to the build name.

5. Run the application again, and this time you will see two tabs, **Native App** and **PWA**. Click on the **Rebuild my App** button, choose the **Keep existing data in Stage** option, and then click on the **Stage** button. Once the application is built successfully, the QR code will be generated for the Android device as per the following screenshot:

Figure 11.18 – QR code to install an app on an Android device

6. Open the **bar code scanner** app or camera from your Android device and scan the QR code. Once the QR code is scanned, open it in the browser, which will allow you to install the .apk file. Install the application and open it as you would any other mobile application on your device.

We have completed the build configuration for Android.

Build configuration for iOS

Similar to the Android build, you can define one or more builds for iOS devices as well. In order to define a build configuration for iOS, you require the **provisioning profile**. The provisioning profile can only be created if you have membership of the **iOS developer program** or the **iOS developer enterprise program**. A provisioning profile contains development certificates, unique device identifiers, and an application ID.

The following are the steps to define a build configuration for iOS:

1. Click on the mobile application name, **chapter11**, and navigate to the **Settings | Build Configurations** tabs.

2. Click on the **+ Configuration** button and then choose **iOS**.

3. From the opened **iOS Build Configuration** dialog box, configure the options as per the following table and then click on the **Save Configuration** button:

Option	Description
Configuration Name	Enter the build configuration name as **iOSBuild1**
Build Type	Select the build type. If you are making a build for testing choose **Debug**, and if the build is for production release, then choose **Release**. Select Debug for this build.
Bundle Id	Enter or accept the default value generated for the Bundle Id. It should be unique for each application installed on an iOS device.
Application Profile	Select the application profile from the available list. Let the default one for this build.
Bundle Version Name	Enter or accept the default bundle version name.
Bundle Version	Enter or accept the default bundle version.
Certificate	Drag or upload the certificate associated with the provisioning profile. It must be in the **P12** format.
Certificate Password	Enter the certificate password that was provided to secure the provisioning profile certificate when it was exported from the Keychain access app.
Provisioning Profile	Upload the provisioning profile.
Signing Identity	Enter the entire Common Name (CN) of the certificate. For example: **iPhone Distribution: TechSupper (Y1TDVM1P2K)**

Table 11.4 – Configuration options for iOS build

The following screenshot shows the configuration for the **iOS** build:

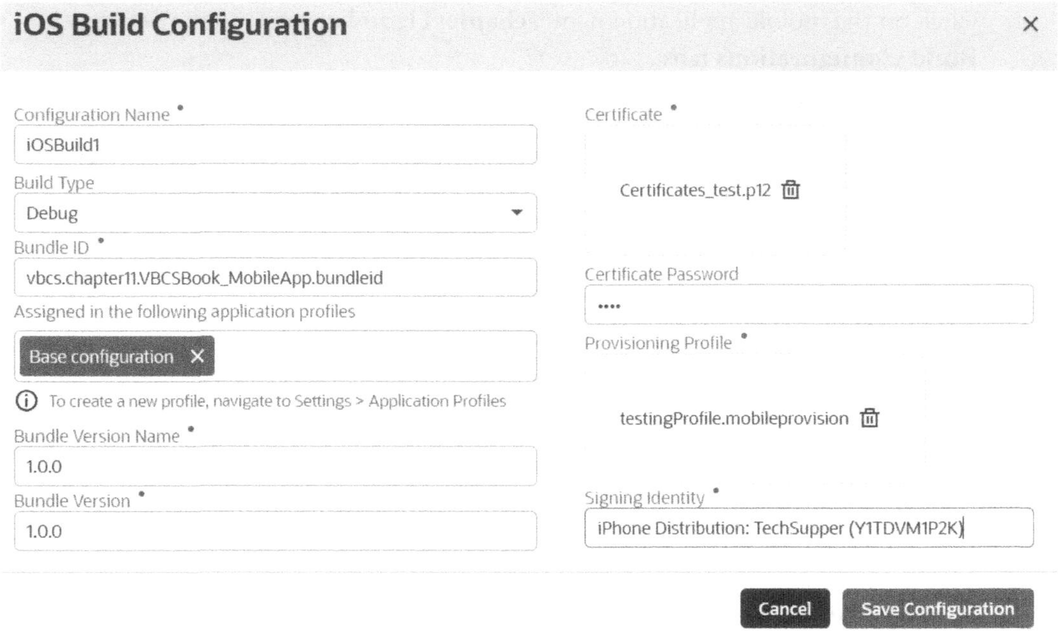

iOS Build Configuration   ×

Configuration Name *   Certificate *
iOSBuild1

Build Type   Certificates_test.p12 🗑
Debug   ▼

Bundle ID *   Certificate Password
vbcs.chapter11.VBCSBook_MobileApp.bundleid   ••••

Assigned in the following application profiles

Base configuration ✕   Provisioning Profile *

ⓘ To create a new profile, navigate to Settings > Application Profiles

Bundle Version Name *   testingProfile.mobileprovision 🗑
1.0.0

Bundle Version *   Signing Identity *
1.0.0   iPhone Distribution: TechSupper (Y1TDVM1P2K)

                                             Cancel   Save Configuration

Figure 11.19 – Building a configuration for an iOS device

Once the build is configured, it will be visible in the **Build Configuration** table as an another row. Run the application and click on the **Rebuild my App** button. A new QR code will be generated for the iOS device as well. Scan the QR code from your iOS device and install it on the device.

There is an option to leverage **Cordova** plugins to allow the app to further interact with advanced device features. The mobile app is actually a hybrid app that leverages Cordova as a way to package the app as a native app.

In this section, we learned how to define a build configuration for Android and iOS devices and generate the QR code to install the application on Android and iOS devices.

Summary

In this chapter, you learned how to create a mobile application using a real-world example. We looked at different templates to create different pages. We developed a doctor's appointment mobile application, by means of which you can view a list of available doctors, view a doctor's full details, and book an appointment with a doctor at your preferred time. You learned how to enable the swipe feature to enable various options.

You looked at various options that allow you to change the settings of a mobile application. Now, you will be able to upload custom images for Android and iOS devices. You learned how to enable a mobile application to render in both portrait and landscape mode. You learned how to expose a mobile application as a PWA app and run it on the computer and mobile devices as a native application.

You learned how to define the build for Android and iOS devices and the pre-requisites for defining the build. You saw how the QR code can be generated for Android and iOS devices once you run the application.

In the next chapter, we'll work with different aspects of security related to web and mobile applications that will allow you to secure applications. We'll cover how to allow anonymous access for web and mobile applications, Business Objects, and Service Connections. We'll see how to create user roles in the applications to secure the pages and UI components and we'll enable user role-based and data security in the application.

Further reading

- PWA applications: `https://en.wikipedia.org/wiki/Progressive_web_application`.

- How to enroll for the iOS developer membership program: `https://developer.apple.com/support/app-account/`.

- An Oracle blog with tips for Android and iOS builds: `https://blogs.oracle.com/vbcs/visual-builder-mobile-app-native-build-configuration-tips`.

Questions

1. Can we also make a build configuration for **Windows** mobile devices?

2. Why is the `Keystore` file required to build a configuration for Android devices?

Section 4: Security, Recommendations, Best Practices, and Troubleshooting

Data and application security is one of the topmost priorities in the world of computing. VB allows us to secure both data and applications from unauthorized users. We'll talk about how to create different users and roles and restrict data and pages to prevent access from unauthorized users.

Along with this, we will talk about the best practices and recommendations to start your web or mobile applications that will enhance the performance of the application. This will take you on to another chapter where we will explain various ways to troubleshoot and debug the application. You will also learn how to use **Visual Builder Studio (VB Studio)** to manage the life cycle of application code.

This section comprises the following chapters:

- *Chapter 12, Securing VB Applications*
- *Chapter 13, Understanding and Managing Various Stages of a VB App*
- *Chapter 14, Best Practices and Recommendations for VB Applications*
- *Chapter 15, Troubleshooting and Debugging VB Applications*
- *Chapter 16, Managing VB Apps Using Visual Builder Studio*

12
Securing VB Applications

In previous chapters, we developed various web and mobile applications. We used Business Objects, Service Connections, and various UI components to build visual applications.

In this chapter, we'll look at how to enable security for the web and mobile applications to prevent unauthorized access to the application. Security plays a vital role in the software world, especially when you publish your software over the internet. In this chapter, we'll look at different security aspects to secure the web and mobile applications.

In this chapter, we'll understand the inbuilt **authentication roles** and **user roles** and how these roles are assigned to users when they log in to the applications. We'll look at how to enable anonymous access on different **Visual Builder** (**VB**) components, such as web and mobile apps, Business Objects, and Service Connections, so that users can access the applications without login credentials.

We will look at how to create and manage custom user roles to secure the different VB components. We'll enable role-based and data security to develop secure and robust web and mobile applications and prevent access to the applications and data from unauthorized users.

We'll understand the different authentication and connection types, which will help us to choose the correct values when we create or modify the Service Connections. We'll also describe how to enable basic authentication for mobile applications.

In this chapter, we will cover the following topics:

- Understanding authentication roles and user roles
- Enabling anonymous access
- Creating and managing user roles
- Enabling role-based security
- Enabling data security
- Understanding Service Connection authentication and connection types
- Configuring basic authentication for a mobile app

After completing this chapter, you will be able to secure your applications from unauthorized users. You will know how to enable role-based and data security in VB applications. You will also learn about various authentication and connection type options when creating and updating Service Connections.

Technical requirements

To complete this chapter, you should have the following:

- A **VB** instance
- **VB** login credentials

You can find the full source code used in this chapter here: `https://github.com/PacktPublishing/Effortless-App-Development-with-Oracle-Visual-Builder/tree/main/Chapter12`.

Understanding authentication roles and user roles

Authentication is the mechanism that allows us to manage access to different pages and data in an application. VB itself creates two default authentication roles, namely, **anonymous user** and **authenticated user**:

- **Anonymous user**: This authentication role is assigned to all users who access the anonymous-enabled application.

- **Authenticated user**: This authentication role is assigned to all users who log in to the application. All the users in this role can manage all the components and Business Objects unless access is disabled for this role. All developers have this role by default.

In addition to these two roles, you can create custom roles in VB and assign authenticated users to fine-tune access to the application resources such as pages, data, and so on.

You can enable either authentication access, anonymous access, or both to the application. By default, the user is assigned as either an anonymous user or authentication user, or both depending on the access of the application. If the application requires authentication, all users are granted the authentication user role when they log in. If anonymous access is enabled, users that log in to the application are granted both roles, and users who don't log in are granted the anonymous user role only.

User roles are used to secure access to Business Objects and the data inside Business Objects. Users cannot be created from the visual application; users or groups will be created from the **Oracle Identity Console** and it is the responsibility of the **IDCS administrator** to create users or groups in IDCS. You, as a VB developer, can create the user roles inside the VB application and assign users or groups to the user roles. The user roles created in the VB application are stored in a `user-roles.json` file.

In this section, we learned about authentication and user roles and which role is assigned to the logged-in user. In the next section, we'll look at how to enable anonymous access for web and mobile applications, Business Objects, and Service Connections.

Enabling anonymous access

In this section, you will learn how to enable anonymous access in the VB application so that users can view the application without login credentials. Anonymous access allows users to access the application without login credentials. By default, all applications are secured and require logging in using the **Oracle Cloud** account credentials. When you enable anonymous access on the web or mobile applications, that doesn't mean users will also be able to retrieve data from Business Objects or Service Connections. You have to explicitly enable anonymous access on the Business Objects and Service Connections.

The security and authentication settings that you modify are only applicable for stage and publish applications. If the application has already been staged or published, the settings are unaffected. You have to create a new version, apply the settings, and stage or publish it to effect the changes.

> **Important Note:**
>
> The service administrator must disable the **Allow only secure applications to be created** option under the **Tenant** settings to allow the anonymous access to the application.

The following figure describes the different options to provide anonymous access to the application and data sources:

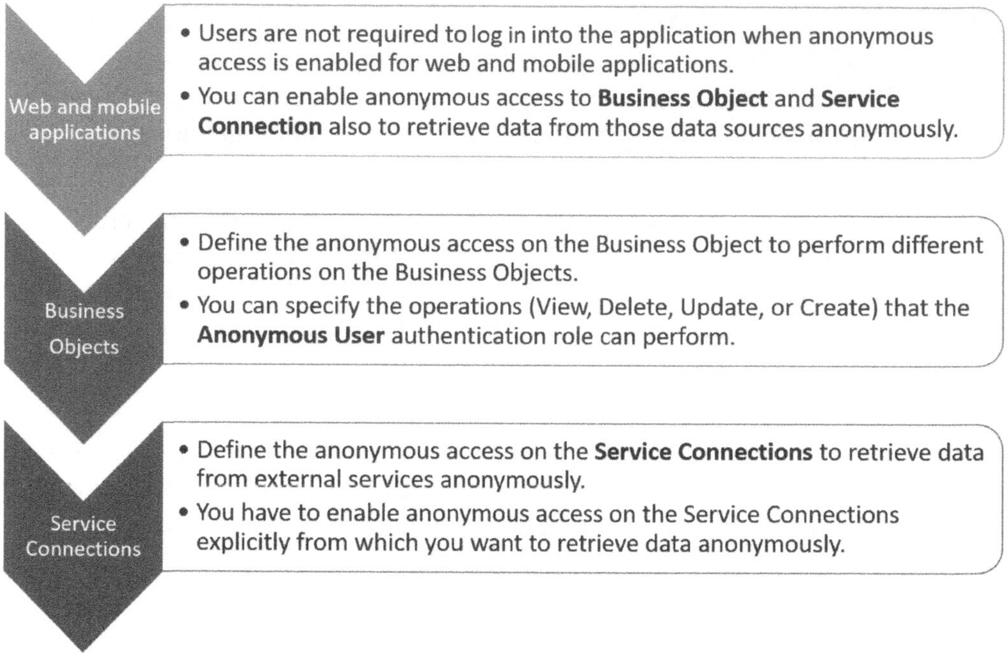

- Users are not required to log in into the application when anonymous access is enabled for web and mobile applications.
- You can enable anonymous access to **Business Object** and **Service Connection** also to retrieve data from those data sources anonymously.

Web and mobile applications

- Define the anonymous access on the Business Object to perform different operations on the Business Objects.
- You can specify the operations (View, Delete, Update, or Create) that the **Anonymous User** authentication role can perform.

Business Objects

- Define the anonymous access on the **Service Connections** to retrieve data from external services anonymously.
- You have to enable anonymous access on the Service Connections explicitly from which you want to retrieve data anonymously.

Service Connections

Figure 12.1 – Different components to provide anonymous access

You have to enable anonymous access for all the different levels in order to view the data anonymously too. If you enable anonymous access for just the web or mobile applications and the page is intended to display the data from Business Objects or Service Connections too, then the user will not be able to view the data.

In the next section, you will see how to enable anonymous access for web or mobile applications.

Anonymous access for web or mobile applications

The following are the steps to enable anonymous access for the web or mobile applications:

1. Click on the web or mobile application from the application navigator.

2. Go to the **Settings** tab, and then the **Security** tab.

3. Select the **Allow anonymous access** checkbox, shown in the following screenshot:

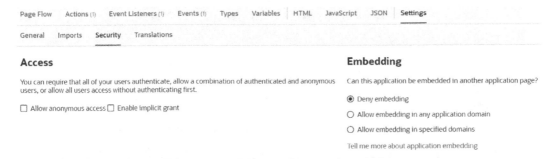

Figure 12.2 – Enabling anonymous access for the web application

Once anonymous access is enabled, users will be able to access the web or mobile applications without logging in.

Anonymous access for Business Objects

The following are the steps to enable anonymous access for Business Objects:

1. Click on any of the Business Objects from the Business Objects navigators.

2. Go to the **Security** tab and enable role-based security if is not enabled already.

3. Select the operations (**View**, **Create**, **Update**, or **Delete**) that you want to enable for the **Anonymous User** authentication role, as in the following screenshot:

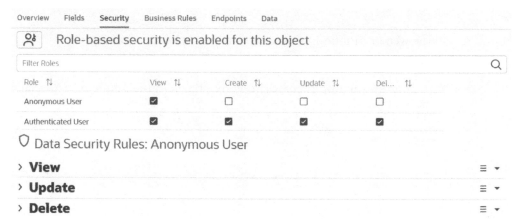

Figure 12.3 – Enabling anonymous access for Business Objects

As shown in the previous screenshot, only the **View** operation is allowed for anonymous access. Once the **View** operation is enabled for anonymous access, users will be able to access the Business Object data via web or mobile applications without login credentials.

You can also enable anonymous access to the **describe endpoint** for Business Objects.

In order to enable anonymous access for the describe endpoint, take the following steps:

1. Select **Settings** from the top-right menu and navigate to the **Business Objects** tab.

2. Expand the **Security** section and select the **Allow anonymous access to Business Objects describe endpoint** checkbox, as shown in the following screenshot:

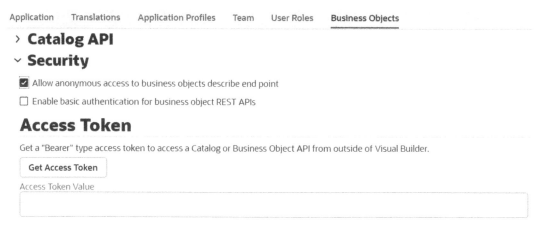

Figure 12.4 – Enabling anonymous access for the describe endpoint

If anonymous access is enabled for the describe endpoint, you have to include the `auth` word in the describe endpoint, as follows: `https://vbinstance-cloudinstance.builder.ocp.oraclecloud.com/ic/builder/rt/application/1.0/resources/auth/data/describe?metadataMode=minimal`.

As can be seen in *Figure 12.4*, we can expand the **Catalog API** section to view the describe endpoints under the **Metadata** section. The describe endpoints are different for each phase of the application.

In the next section, we'll look at anonymous access for Service Connections.

Anonymous access for Service Connections

The following are the steps to enable anonymous access for Service Connections:

1. Click on any of the Service Connections from **Services** under the application navigator.

2. Go to the **Servers** tab and click on the pencil icon from the list of servers.

3. Select the **Allow anonymous access to the Service Connection Infrastructure** checkbox to enable anonymous access, as shown in this screenshot:

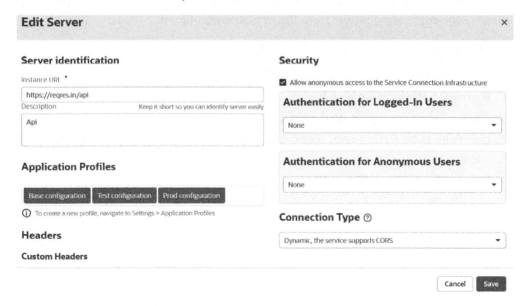

Figure 12.5 – Enabling anonymous access for a Service Connection

4. Once this checkbox is selected, you will see another **Authentication for Anonymous Users** dropdown. Choose any of the options from the available list or let the default option be selected.

In this section, we learned how to enable anonymous access for web and mobile applications, Business Objects, and Service Connections, which will allow users to access the applications without login credentials. In the next section, we'll look at how to create and manage custom user roles.

Creating and managing user roles

Apart from authentication and anonymous roles, VB allows the creation of custom user roles too. User roles are used to secure the data of Business Objects, as well as to secure pages and the UI components of a page.

An example of this is securing the **Employee** Business Object in a way that admin users can perform all the operations, but regular users can only view the data. Similarly, we want to hide the **Create Employee** button for regular users.

When you create a user role, you assign users and groups that are created in IDCS to the user roles. The user roles that are created are the same across all the application profiles; however, the users and groups may differ. While you assign the users and groups to a user role, select the application profile from the available dropdown.

The following are the steps to create a user role:

1. Open the **VBCSBook** application, click on **Settings** from the top-right menu, and then go to the **User Roles** tab.

2. Click on the **+ Create Role** button. From the opened **Create Role** dialog box, enter the name as `EmployeeRole` and click on the **Create** button, as in the following screenshot:

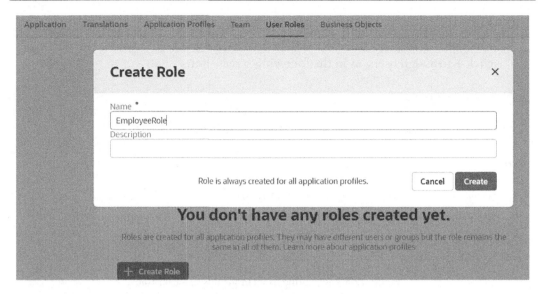

Figure 12.6 – Creating a user role

3. Once a role is created, it will be visible in the **User Roles** tab. Create one more role with the name `AdminRole`.

    The following screenshot shows the **Users Roles** tab with two roles:

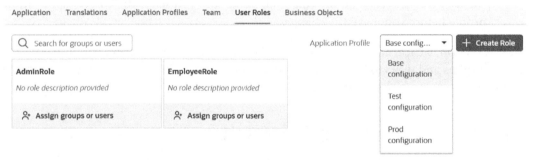

Figure 12.7 – The User Roles tab

In the previous screenshot, you see the **Application Profile** dropdown, which populates all the application profiles created in the VB application.

4. Select the suitable application profile for which you want to assign users or groups. Select the **Test configuration** application profile for the time being as this is the default application profile for stage applications.

5. In order to assign groups or users to a user role, click on the **Assign groups or users** link. The **Change Assignments** dialog box will open, which will show all the groups created in IDCS.

6. Click on the + sign corresponding to each group you want to assign. To assign individual users, type the username in the **Users** input box to search the user, and click + to assign users, as in the following screenshot:

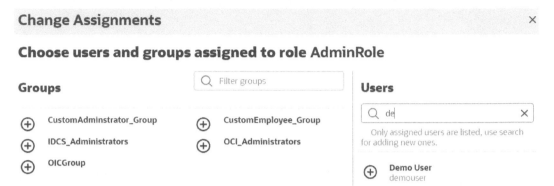

Figure 12.8 – Assigning users or groups to a user role

For the time being, assign the **CustomAdminstator_Group** group to **AdminRole** and the **CustomEmployee_Group** group to **EmployeeRole**. Both groups are assigned different users in IDCS.

7. In order to update the group or role assignment for a particular user role, hover over the user role and click on the edit icon. Make sure you select the correct application profile before you make the changes.

In this section, we learned how to create user roles in the VB application and how to assign groups and users to the user roles. In the next section, we'll look at how to enable role-based security in the application.

Enabling role-based security

Role-based security allows securing the entire flow, page, or certain components on a page, for example, hiding a button component from a page for a certain user role or restricting access for the entire page for a certain user role. Role-based security makes the application secure and prevents access to the application flow, page, or components from unauthorized users.

In order to secure UI components on a page, use the following expression:

```
<oj-bind-if test="[[ $application.user.roles.user_role_name]]"
> </oj-bind-if>
```

In the preceding code, replace user_role_name with the user role name that is created in the **User Roles** tab, as follows:

```
<oj-bind-if test="[[ $application.user.roles.AdminRole ]]" >
</oj-bind-if>
```

We'll use the oraclecloudext_chapter9 web application to apply the security. Here are the steps to show the **Update Customer** button only if the logged-in user role falls under AdminRole:

1. Open the **customers-start** page and go to the **Code** view of the page.

2. Enclose the **div** section within the **<oj-bind-if>** component, as shown in the following screenshot:

```
<div class="oj-flex">
  <oj-radioset label-hint="Language Switcher" class="oj-flex-item oj-sm-12 oj-md-6 oj-choice-direction-row" on-value-changed="[[$lis
    <oj-option value="en-US">English</oj-option>
    <oj-option value="fr-FR">French</oj-option>
  </oj-radioset>
</div>
<oj-bind-if test="[[ $application.user.roles.AdminRole ]]">
<div class="oj-flex">
  <oj-toolbar id="oj-toolbar-for-oj-table--1362109087-1" chroming="solid" class="oj-flex-item oj-sm-12 oj-md-12">
    <oj-button disabled="[[ $page.variables.oj_table_1362109087_1SelectedId === '' ]]" on-oj-action="[[$page.listeners.editAccountsB
  </oj-toolbar>
</div>
</oj-bind-if>
```

Figure 12.9 – Securing the UI component

Update Customer button will be rendered for users who belong to AdminRole.

3. In order to test the role-based security, VB allows us to switch the role using the **Who Am I** option, which can be used to preview the application in different user roles. Go to the **Design** view of the page, select the **Who Am I** option, select the **EmployeeRole** checkbox from the **Who Am I?** dialog box, and click the **Select Roles** button, as shown in the following screenshot:

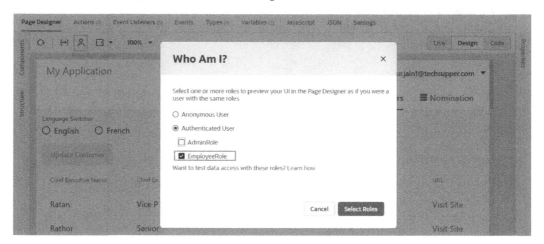

Figure 12.10 – Who Am I option

4. Once you click on the **Select Roles** button, the **Update Customer** button will not be visible on the page. Click on the **Who Am I** option again and select **AdminRole**. This time, the **Update Customer** button will be visible.

In order to restrict the complete page or flow, the following **JSON** code snippet needs to be added to the JSON file of a page or flow:

```
,
  "security": {
    "access": {
      "requiresAuthentication": true,
      "roles": ["user_role_name"]
    }
  }
```

The preceding JSON code takes an array of roles for which you only want to provide access on the flow or page.

The following are the steps to secure the **customers-edit-accounts** page and allow access to `AdminRole` only:

1. Open the **JSON** tab of the **customers-edit-accounts** page.

2. Add the preceding JSON code and replace `user_role_name` with the actual user role name. Replace it with `AdminRole` for this demonstration, as in the following screenshot:

Page Designer	Actions (3)	Event Listeners (3)	Events	Types (2)	Variables (4)	JavaScript	JSON

```
297          "oj-button": {
298            "path": "ojs/ojbutton"
299          }
300        }
301
302      },   Don't forget to put comma
303        "security": {
304        "access": {
305          "requiresAuthentication": true,
306          "roles": ["AdminRole"]
307        }
308      }
309    }
```

Figure 12.11 – Securing the page

Don't forget to add a comma, as highlighted in the preceding screenshot.

3. Go to the **Page Designer** tab of the page and select **EmployeeRole** from the **Who Am I** dialog box. The page will not be accessible and you will get the **403 forbidden** error on the page. Open the **Who Am I** dialog box again and select **AdminRole**. This time, you will be able to see the complete page.

This is how role-based security works in the VB application.

In this section, we learned how to enable role-based security and secure a part of the page and the complete page as well. In the next section, we'll look at how to enable data security.

Enabling data security

Role-based security is not enough to develop a completely secure application because the role-based security is applied at the client side and it's very easy for anyone to change the role name in the browser console and view the restricted UI. So, along with role-based security, data security is also important. **Data security** restricts what a user can fetch from the backend APIs.

If data security is applied with role-based security, and if someone spoofs the role from the browser console, then the REST call will return an empty dataset. Data security is applied on the server side so that it is always secure.

For the custom Business Objects created inside VB, security can be applied at the Business Object level, but field-level security is not possible. For external REST APIs, no additional security can be applied in the VB application. You have to rely on external API security to secure the data fetched from external REST calls.

For demonstration purposes, we'll use the **Nomination** Business Object and secure it. We'll allow viewing all the nomination records for users who are in `AdminRole`; however, the `EmployeeRole` users can view only those records that have been created or updated by themselves.

The following are the steps to apply security on the **Nomination** Business Object:

1. Open the **Nomination** Business Object and navigate to the **Security** tab.

2. Click on the role-based security option if it is not enabled already, as shown in the following screenshot:

Overview   Fields   **Security**   Business Rules   Endpoints   Data

Role-based security is disabled for this object

Click to enable role-based security

When role-based security is disabled, all users who have access to this application can perform any action on the object.

Tell me more about securing my business objects.

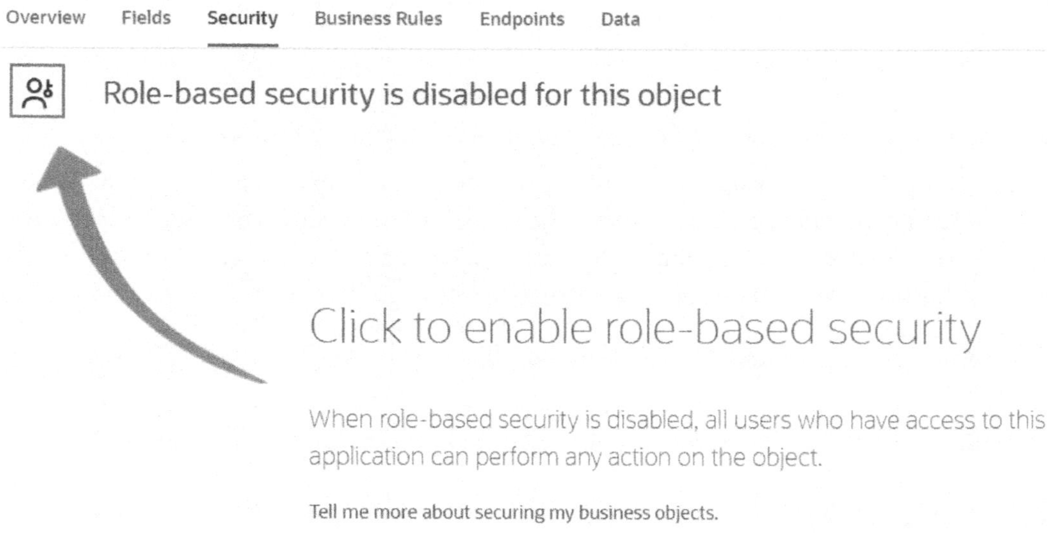

Figure 12.12 – Enabling role-based security for a Business Object

3. Uncheck all the checkboxes corresponding to the **Authenticated User** role.

4. Select the **EmployeeRole** role, click the action menu on the right side of the **View** operation, and select **Allow if user created the row**, as in the following screenshot:

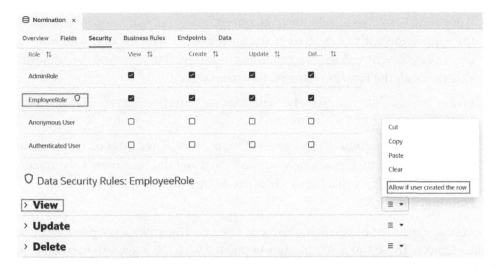

Figure 12.13 – Securing the Business Object operations

This configuration allows `EmployeeRole` users to view only those records created and updated by themselves. You can expand the **View** operation and see the actual generated query. Do the same for the **Update** and **Delete** operations too.

You can allow `EmployeeRole` users to only view records but restrict their ability to create/update/delete records by deselecting the checkbox corresponding to the user role.

5. Since the security is enforced for the staged and published application, we can stage the application. Click on the **Stage** option from the top-right menu, select the **Populate Stage with Development Data** option, and click on the **Stage** button.

6. Go to the **Visual Builder (VB)** home page of your application, click the **Stage** option, and select **oraclecloudext_chapter9**, as in the following screenshot:

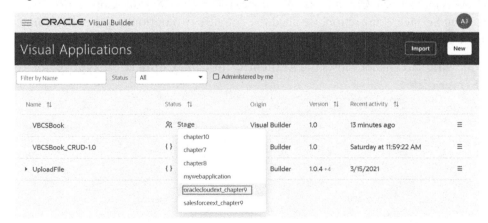

Figure 12.14 – Accessing the stage application

7. After you click on **oraclecloudext_chapter9**, a new tab will be opened and the application will be rendered. If you are logged in with the user who is in `CustomAdminstrator_Group`, which is assigned to `AdminRole`, you will be able to see all the records on the **Nomination** screen.

8. Log in using a different user who is in `CustomEmployee_Group` that is assigned to the `EmployeeRole` user role.

9. Go to the **Nomination** tab and you will see only those records created or updated by the logged-in user. Add a new nomination using the **Nominate Customer** button and you'll see that the newly added nomination is visible on the **Nomination** page.

The access is controlled by two fields, namely, `createdBy` and `lastUpdatedBy`, in the Business Object. These two fields are auto-populated with the logged-in username once a new record is inserted or updated.

This is how you enforce security at the data level in a custom Business Object.

In this section, we learned how to enable data security at the Business Object level and how to disable and enable access to different operations of the Business Object. In the next section, we'll understand the authentication and connection type options of the Service Connection.

Understanding Service Connection authentication and connection type

In the previous few chapters, we created a Service Connection to interact with external REST APIs and Oracle Cloud APIs. When we create a new Service Connection or modify an existing Service Connection, we need to configure two options, **authentication** and **connection type**, to handle the authentication of the external REST APIs.

The following screenshot shows the **Authentication** and **Connection Type** options on the **Edit Server** dialog:

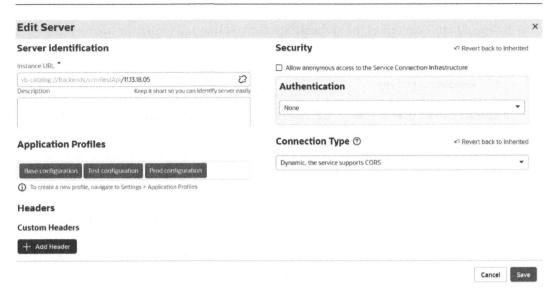

Figure 12.15 – Authentication and Connection Type options

As you can see, both the dropdowns have different values and we need to choose them as per the **REST API's authentication mechanism**. The authentication mechanism is divided into two categories, namely, **identity propagation** and **fixed credentials**. In the next sections, we'll look at both categories in detail.

Identity propagation

In this authentication mechanism, when a user logs in to the web or mobile application, the logged-in user identity is passed to the external REST API call to authenticate the REST calls. In this mechanism, the **JWT** token is passed to the external APIs.

In order for the identity propagation authentication mechanism to work, the external API should understand that the IDCS identity token has been passed by VB and the user subject has been extracted from the token. The token usually contains the user identity and sometimes the scope, which identifies the resources that the user is authorized to access.

The following table describes the authentication types that fall under the identity propagation mechanism:

Authentication Type	Description
Propagate Current User Identity	This is used to pass the user identity to the external API calls and works in the following two ways: 1. If a user logs into the native mobile application using application-level Basic authentication, the logged-in user identity will be passed to the REST calls. 2. If a user logs into the web application, and **Enable implicit** grant checkbox is selected from the application security settings, then the authentication token is passed to the REST calls.
Oracle Cloud Account	This is usually used when you call the Oracle Cloud Application services or any services hosted in the same IDCS where your VB is hosted such as Integration Cloud.
OAuth2.0 User Assertion	This is used to call any REST API which can be represented as a Resource app in Oracle IDCS.

Table 12.1 – Identity propagation authentication types

In the next section, we'll look at the fixed credentials category.

Fixed credentials

In this authentication mechanism, the fixed credentials are passed to the external API calls to authenticate the APIs. The following table describes the authentication types that fall under the fixed credentials mechanism:

Authentication Type	Description
None	This is used for the REST calls where authentication is not required.
Basic	This is used when a fixed username and password are required to authenticate the REST calls. When you choose the Basic authentication type, the **VB authentication proxy** is used automatically irrespective of the value is selected from the **Connection Type** drop-down. It is not recommended for the production use.
Client Credentials OAuth 2.0	This is used when the REST calls support the OAuth 2.0 client credentials policy. The client id, client secret, scope (optional), and token URL are required to use this policy.
Resource Owner OAuth 2.0	This is used when the REST call supports the OAuth 2.0 resource owner policy. The client id, client secret, username, password, scope (optional), and token URL are required to use this policy.
Oracle Cloud Infrastructure API Signature 1.0	This is used when there is a requirement to call the Oracle Cloud Infrastructure (OCI) REST APIs. For this policy select the **Always use proxy, irrespective of CORS support** from the **Connection Type** drop-down. In order to use this policy following things are required: 1. An API Key which comprises of the **Tenancy OCID**, the **User OCID** and the **fingerprint** of a valid public key uploaded to OCI. 2. A private key in **PEM** format corresponding to the public key.

Table 12.2 – Fixed credentials authentication types

That is all for the authentication types to call the external REST APIs.

When the REST APIs configured in a Service Connection are called, the requests are routed either directly or through a **VB proxy**. The route (direct or VB proxy) of the REST API call depends on the values of the authentication and connection type dropdowns. The CORS setting on external REST services could also be needed if the calls are going through the VB Proxy. The remote server will need to white list the VB server as a trusted source so that it can access the services.

The application will have a performance benefit if the REST API's requests are served directly. In the case of a direct call, the external REST API's servers must add the application domain in its **Cross-Origin Resource Sharing (CORS) allow list**. The following are the authentication types used for a direct call:

- Oracle Cloud account

- Propagate current user identity

- **OAuth 2.0** (all types)

- None

The VB proxy is the server-side component of VB. If the requests are served via the VB proxy, the application will have a performance implication as the request goes via another extra network layer. But a request that goes via the VB proxy is always secure as the credentials are never exposed at the client side.

In this case, the external REST API's server doesn't need to add the application domain to its CORS allow list. All the authentication types can be used with the VB proxy. In the case of basic authentication, the REST API calls are always served via the VB proxy.

The following are possible values in the connection type dropdown:

- **Dynamic, the service supports CORS**: This is used when REST APIs support the CORS policy. If the REST API authentication supports direct calls, then REST API calls will be served directly.

- **Dynamic, the service does not support CORS**: This is used when REST APIs don't support CORS. In this case, requests are served via the VB proxy.

> **Important Note:**
> A mobile app that uses basic or **OCI Infrastructure API Signature 1.0** authentication is always routed directly as mobile apps are exempted from the CORS policy.

- **Always use proxy, irrespective of CORS support**: All REST calls are served using the VB proxy when this authentication type is selected.

> **Important Note:**
> Any HTTP request configured in a Service Connection is served via the VB proxy irrespective of the connection type selected.

The following table describes different permutations and combinations when using authentication and connection type together:

Application Type	Authentication	Connection Type	REST API calls happen via
Any type	Any type	Always use proxy	VB proxy
VB development environment/Web app/PWA	Any type	Dynamic - Service doesn't support CORS	VB Proxy
Any type, including Native mobile app	All except Basic authentication and OCI Infrastructure API Signature 1.0	Dynamic - Service doesn't support CORS	Direct
Any type, including Native mobile app	Basic authentication or OCI Infrastructure API Signature 1.0	Dynamic - Service doesn't support CORS	VB Proxy

Table 12.3 – Results when different combinations are used

In this section, we learned about different authentication and connection types that are used when creating or modifying Service Connections. We understood how REST calls are served via a direct or VB proxy. In the next section, we'll look at how to configure a mobile application to use the basic authentication mechanism.

Configuring basic authentication for a mobile app

By default, mobile applications developed in VB are secured using the **Oracle Cloud authentication** mechanism, where users need to pass **Oracle Identity Cloud** credentials to log in to the mobile apps.

However, VB provides an option to configure the mobile application to use basic authentication too. In order to configure basic authentication, use the following steps:

1. Go to the **Settings** tab of the mobile application and switch to the **Security** tab. Select the **Basic** option for **Authentication Mechanism** as in the following screenshot:

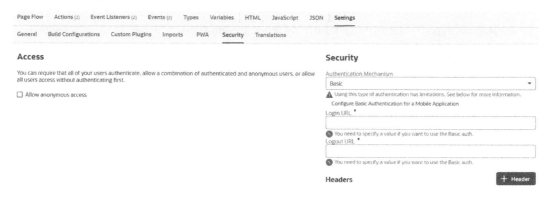

Figure 12.16 – Enabling the Basic authentication option for the mobile app

2. To configure the **Basic** authentication, you need to supply custom **Login URL** and **Logout URL** values, as shown in the previous screenshot. These two URLs can be of a third-party server or an Oracle Cloud service URL that supports basic authentication. Additionally, you can supply any HTTP header. Create the HTTP header using the **+ Header** button.

3. After you configure the basic authentication and run the application, the mobile application will render a login page where you need to supply the username and password. Once the username and password are passed, the user credentials will be converted into the basic authentication header and the login URL will be invoked to supply the basic authentication header. Upon successful login, the user will land on the mobile application.

In the next section, you will find out about a few restrictions when you enable basic authentication for mobile applications.

A few restrictions when using basic authentication for a mobile app

You need to deal with a few restrictions when you use basic authentication in the mobile application, as follows:

- Custom user roles cannot be used to secure the flows, pages, UI components, and Business Objects.

- The built-in variable, **user**, cannot be used to get the logged-in user details such as first name, last name, email address, and so on.

- The mobile application can't use the VB proxy to serve the REST calls. The REST API calls will always be served directly.

- Only the **Dynamic, the service supports CORS** connection type can be used in the Service Connection.

- Only the **Propagate Current User Identity** and **None** authentication policies can be used in the Service Connection.

> **Important Note:**
> Basic authentication is not supported for mobile apps exposed as a PWA.

In this section, we learned how to configure the mobile application for using basic authentication instead of Oracle Cloud authentication.

Summary

In this chapter, you learned about various aspects of security that will help to develop a secure and robust application in VB. We described inbuilt authentication roles and user roles and how they are assigned to the user when they log in to the application. You learned about the anonymous role of the VB application and how to enable anonymous access for web and mobile apps, Business Objects, and Service Connections. You also learned how to enable anonymous access for the Business Object describe endpoint.

You learned about creating and managing the custom user roles and assigning users and groups to them. You learned how to secure UI components and render them as per the logged-in user role. You learned about the Who Am I options, which allow testing the application with different roles without actually deploying the application. Along with role-based security, you learned how to secure Business Object data and secure it using custom user roles.

You explored different authentication and connection types that we use when creating or modifying the Service Connections. You learned about different types of authentication, such as identity propagation and fixed credentials. You learned how VB calls the REST endpoint using two ways, either directly or via the VB proxy. You learned how to enable basic authentication for the mobile application and what the restrictions are when you use basic authentication for mobile apps.

In the next chapter, we will learn how to create different versions of the application, migrate applications from one instance to another, what the various phases of a VB application are, and how to manage the complete life cycle of a VB application starting from development to stage and stage to publish. We'll look at how to onboard team members in the VB application to work together.

Further reading

- Learn how to use the Oracle Cloud Signature API Signature 1.0 authentication policy: `https://blogs.oracle.com/vbcs/using-oci-api-signature-authentication-from-visual-builder`

- Refer to this YouTube video to learn how to integrate **OKTA** with **Oracle IDCS**: `https://www.youtube.com/watch?v=O-EO5GsWmaY`

- Refer to this YouTube video to learn how to create users and groups in Oracle IDCS: `https://www.youtube.com/watch?v=IEnz6EbmYB4`

Questions

1. Can we integrate a third-party identity provider such as OKTA or **Microsoft AD**?

2. Can we enable anonymous access for the web and mobile applications?

3. How do we create users and groups in Oracle IDCS?

13

Understanding and Managing Various Stages of a VB App

So far, we have developed various web and mobile applications including **Business Objects** and **Service Connections**. In this chapter, we will talk about various aspects in regards to managing the **Visual Builder** (**VB**) application and various statuses of the VB application. We'll look at how to create different versions of the VB application and how to clone the VB application.

We'll also learn how to promote a VB application from one VB instance to another and what we'll need to reconfigure after the application is promoted. We'll describe and show how to stage and publish the visual application.

We'll learn how to add team members to an application to enable other developers to work independently on applications.

In this chapter, we will cover the following topics:

- Managing the VB application
- Versioning of the VB application
- Cloning the VB application
- Promoting the VB application
- Staging and publishing the VB application
- Adding team members to the application

After completing this chapter, you will be able to manage the VB application, create different versions of the application, and promote the application from one instance to another. You will also be able to stage and publish the VB application.

Technical requirements

To complete this chapter, you should have the following:

- A **VB** instance
- **VB** login credentials

Managing the VB application

The VB home page allows us to manage the VB application. The VB home screen shows all the applications that are created by you or in which you have been added as a team member. Each application is displayed as a single row including all the versions of the application.

Every application has different options using which we can perform various tasks. Click on the action menu icon right next to the application to view all the available options, as in the following screenshot:

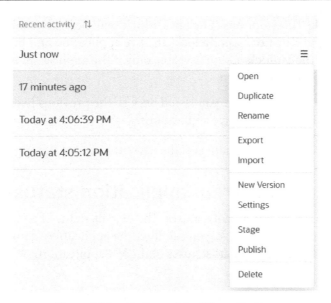

Figure 13.1 – Options of the VB application

As you can see, these are all the options from the menu:

- **Open**: This option opens the application to make changes.
- **Duplicate**: This option allows you to create a copy of the application.
- **Rename**: This option allows you to rename the application.
- **Export**: This option allows you to export the application as an archive file.
- **Import**: This option allows you to upload an archive file to update the application.
- **New Version**: This option allows you to create a new version of the application.
- **Settings**: This option opens the settings page of the application. Each version of the application has different settings.
- **Stage**: This option allows you to stage the application.
- **Publish**: This option allows you to publish the application.
- **Delete**: This option allows you to delete the application. Please note that you cannot recover the application once deleted.

- **Lock/Unlock**: These options (**Lock** or **Unlock**) will be visible only if the application is in live mode. The **Lock** option locks the live application and prevents users from accessing it. The **Unlock** option is visible only if the application is locked and allows you to unlock the application.

- **Rollback**: This option allows you to roll back to the previous live version. This option is available only for live applications.

A few options are displayed depending on the current status of the application.

Glancing at the different application statuses

Every VB app goes through different statuses. The default status of an application is **Development**. From the home page, you can filter the application status-wise. The following table describes the various statuses of the VB application:

Status	Description
Development	This is the default status of the application. For each version you create, the default status will be Development.
Stage	This status is displayed when you stage the application. The tile contains a link to the application that opens the application's stage URL in a browser.
Live	This status is displayed when you publish the application. The tile contains a link to the application that opens the application's live URL in a browser.
Live Locked	This status is displayed when you lock the published application.
Obsolete	This status is displayed when you publish the new version of the application.

Table 13.1 – Different statuses of the application

That's all for the different statuses of the VB application.

In this section, we discussed various options of the application along with their description. We also learned about the different statuses of the application. In the next section, we'll talk about the versioning of the VB application.

Versioning of the VB application

VB allows us to create different versions of an application to enable parallel development. When a new version is created, a separate copy is created of the same application with the same artifacts and a separate database schema.

We can stage and publish any version of the VB application. You can stage multiple versions of the same application but only a single version can be published at a time. If multiple versions of the same application are staged, they will all have a separate URI to identify the version; however, all the versions will have the same URI once published.

Once the application is published, you cannot do any modifications to the live application. So, if you want to make any changes or fix any issues, you have to create a new version of the VB application.

We can use these steps to create a new version of the application:

1. Open the Visual Builder home page and click on the action menu to the right of any of the applications for which you want to create a new version.

2. Click on the **New Version** option from the action menu, as shown in the following screenshot:

Figure 13.2 – New Version option of the VB application

3. In the opened **New Application Version** dialog box, enter the unique version of the application in the **New Version** field or leave the suggested version as it is. Then, enter a description (optional), and then click on the **Create** button, as shown in the following screenshot:

Figure 13.3 – New Application Version dialog box

Every time you create a new version of an application, it will always be in **Development** status. All the versions of the same application will be displayed in a hierarchical tree.

In this section, we learned how to create a new version of the application. In the next section, we'll look at how to clone the VB application.

Cloning the VB application

VB allows us to create a fresh copy of the VB application as an independent application that will have all the resources and the database schema. But the copy of the VB application will have a different name, application ID, and URI.

We can follow these steps to clone a VB application:

1. Open the Visual Builder home page and click on the action menu to the right of any of the applications for which you want to create a new version.

2. Click on the **Duplicate** option from the action menu.

3. From the opened **Duplicate Application** dialog box, enter the details for **Application Name**, **Application ID**, and **Description** (optional), and then click on the **Duplicate** button, as shown in the following screenshot:

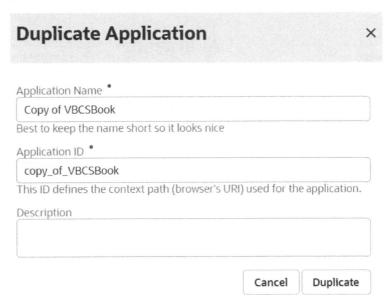

Figure 13.4 – Duplicate Application dialog box

When you create a copy of an application, it will be treated as a separate application.

In this section, we learned how to create a copy of the VB application. In the next section, we'll look at how to promote the VB application from one instance to another.

Promoting the VB application

Promoting means to migrate the VB application from one instance to another. Promotion of the VB application is straightforward; you simply need to export the VB application from the source instance and import it in the target instance. When you export the application, an archive file is exported containing all the resources, such as web and mobile applications, Business Objects, and Service Connections. VB removes the external REST endpoint credentials from the Service Connection during export. When you import it onto the target instance, you have to reconfigure the Service Connection credentials.

The following diagram depicts the promoting process:

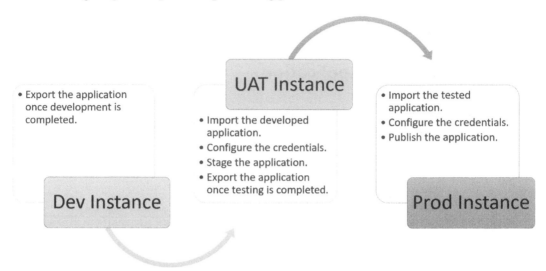

Figure 13.5 – Promoting process

In the previous diagram, we considered three VB instances, namely, development (**Dev**), **UAT**, and production (**Prod**). On the development instance, the developers do the development, and once the development is over, the application will be exported. The exported application will be imported on the UAT instance, the Service Connection credentials will be configured if required, and the application will be staged.

On the **UAT** instance, the testing team can perform the testing, and once testing is over, the application will be exported from the **UAT** instance. The exported application from the **UAT** instance will be imported on the production instance, the Service Connection credentials will be configured, if required, and the application will be published.

Exporting the application

The exported application contains all the resources as an archive file. The VB application you export can be used to create a new copy of the application by importing it into the same instance, or it can be imported to a new instance.

When you export the application, you will be prompted to export the application with or without data that is in the Business Objects. If the **Contains Application Setup Data** option is selected on the **Overview** page of the Business Object, then the data will always be part of the exported application of those Business Objects, even if you choose the **Export without Data** option.

We can execute the following steps to export the application:

1. Open the Visual Builder home page and click on the action menu to the right of any of the applications that you want to export.
2. Click on the **Export** option from the action menu.
3. From the opened **Export Application** dialog box, choose either the **Export with Data** or **Export without Data** option, as shown in the following screenshot:

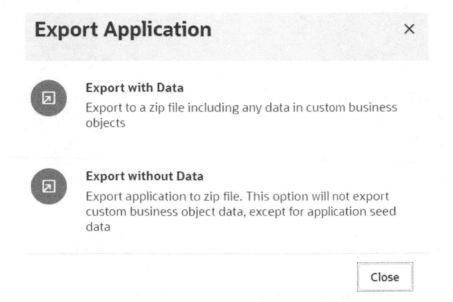

Figure 13.6 – Export Application dialog box

4. Choose the **Export with Data** option for this demonstration. Once the application is exported, a .zip file will be saved on your local drive. Open the .zip file and see the various folders inside the unzipped folder.

In the next section, you will look at how to import the VB application.

Importing the application

You can import an application that has previously been exported from the VB instance to create the new application. Use the **Import** button in the top-right corner of the Visual Builder home page.

You can also replace an existing application using the **Import** option that is available in the action menu to the right of the application. When you click on the **Import** option, the **Import Resources** dialog box will be opened, as in the following screenshot:

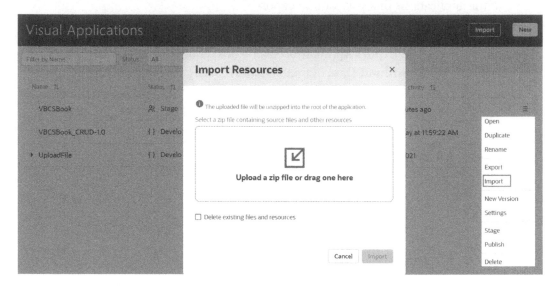

Figure 13.7 – Import option and the Import Resources dialog box

Upload the .zip file from the opened dialog option. If you choose the **Delete existing files and resources** checkbox, all the existing files will be deleted from the existing application.

We can use these steps to import the application to create a new copy of the application:

1. Open the VB instance where you want to import the application and go to the Visual Builder home page.

2. Click on the **Import** button in the top-right corner, as shown in the following screenshot:

Figure 13.8 – Import option

3. From the opened **Import** dialog box, click on the **Application from File** option and select the archived file. The details for **Application Name** and **Application ID** will be filled in automatically based on the archive filename.

4. Modify it with the correct application name and application ID as per your source instance (if the VB instance is different from the one where you are importing the application), and then click on the **Import** button, as shown in the following screenshot:

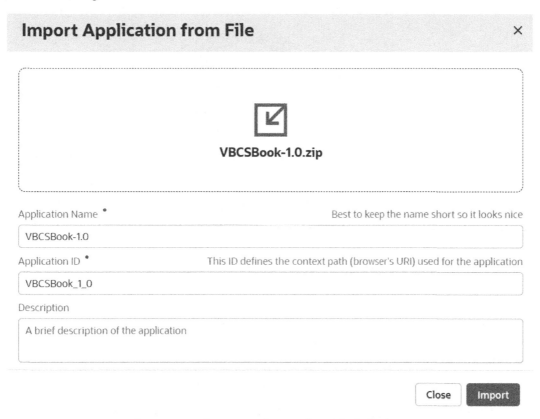

Figure 13.9 – Import Application from File dialog box

5. Once the application is imported successfully, open **Service Connections** and update the credentials if required to run the application successfully.

> **Important Note:**
> The source instance from which you export the application must be the same or an earlier version of the instance where you want to import the application.

In this section, we learned about the process of promoting a VB application and how to export and import the application on the target instance. In the next section, we'll look at different phases of the VB application.

Staging and publishing the VB application

The VB application goes through three different phases to complete the life cycle of a web or mobile application. The following diagram shows the three different phases of a VB application:

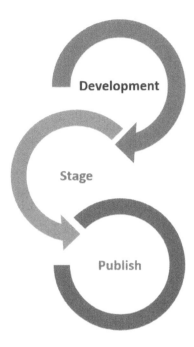

Figure 13.10 – Different phases of an application

As you can see, these are the three phases of an application:

- **Development** is the initial phase of the application and is used by developers to develop the application.

- **Stage** is the second phase of the application. The application is switched into this phase when application development is completed and ready for testing.

- **Publish** is the final phase of the application. The application is switched into this phase when the application functionality is ready to go live.

Every phase of the VB application has a different database schema.

> **Important Note:**
> When you stage a VB application containing a mobile application, at least one mobile application build configuration must exist, else the stage of the visual application will fail.

When the application is switched to the **Stage** or **Publish** phases, the application resources are deployed on the **VB runtime engine** that serves the requests.

The application must be in the **Stage** phase to be published. When an application is published, the **Stage** version becomes the live version. After the application is published, you cannot modify the application, so it's important to review all the application settings (such as credentials, environment-specific values, and so on) before you publish it. If you want to make any changes to the published application, you have to create a new version, modify the application, switch to stage, and then publish it.

We'll learn about staging and publishing the VB application in the following sections.

Staging the VB application

Once the application development is completed, you need to provide the application URL to the stakeholders, who will validate the functionality of the application. So, you have to switch the phase of application from Development to Stage, and once the application is staged, a unique URL will be generated, which you can distribute to various types of users to test the functionality as per their role. For each version of the application, the stage URL will be unique.

When you stage the application, the following process takes place on your behalf:

- The complete application structure is copied to a directory on the VB server.

- Every time you stage the application, the staging database structure is updated with the development database.

- A unique URL is exposed to access the web application and to download the mobile application. The stage URL is different for each version.

When staging the application, you need to choose from one of the available options depending on the stage iteration. These options are used to manage the Business Object data. The following table describes the different options with descriptions of when you stage the application:

Iteration#	Option: Description
1st	1. **Stage application with a clean database:** No Business Object data will be copied from Development to Stage database. 2. **Populate Stage with Development data:** All Business Object data will be copied from Development to Stage database.
2nd, 3rd, and so on	1. **Keep existing data in Stage:** No Business Object data will be copied from Development to Stage database. 2. **Stage application with a clean database:** All the existing Business Object data will be deleted from Stage database. 3. **Replace Stage data with Development data:** All Business Object data will be replaced from Development to Stage database.

Table 13.2 – Different options during stage

We can follow these steps to stage the application:

1. Open the Visual Builder home page and click on the action menu to the right of any of the applications that you want to stage.

2. Click on the **Stage** option from the action menu. If you are staging the application for the first time, you need to choose either the **Stage application with a clean database** or **Populate Stage with Development data** option, as shown in the following screenshot:

Figure 13.11 – Stage Application dialog box

3. Refer to *Table 13.2* to understand the options and choose any of the options to manage your Business Object data. Choose **Populate Stage with Development data** for this demonstration and click on the **Stage** button.

4. After the application is staged, if you update your application to make some enhancements or bug fixes, you have to stage the application again to make the change effective. For the subsequent stage of the application, follow the same stage application procedure, and choose either the **Keep existing data in Stage** option, the **Stage application with a clean database** option, or the **Replace Stage data with Development data** option, as shown in the following screenshot:

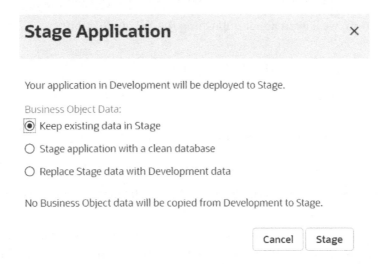

Figure 13.12 – Stage Application dialog box on the subsequent iteration

5. Choose any of the available options to manage the Business Object data and click on the **Stage** button.

6. Once your application is staged successfully, you can distribute the stage application URL to the stakeholders for testing. To get the URL, click on the **Stage** option under the **Status** column, and click on any of the web applications to get the URL, as shown in the following screenshot:

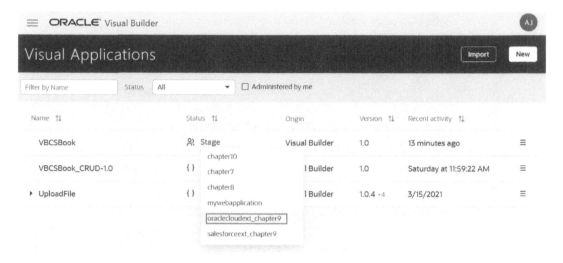

Figure 13.13 – Stage option of the application

Once you click on any of the web applications listed on your screen, you will be redirected to a different tab. Copy the URL and distribute it wherever you want.

In the next section, we'll learn about publishing the VB application.

Publishing the VB application

Once the changes and testing are completed, you can publish the application and make it available for end users.

When you publish the application, the following process takes place on your behalf:

- The directory containing the staged application becomes live.
- Every time you publish the application, the live database structure is updated with the stage database.
- A unique URL is exposed to access the live web application and to download the mobile application. For the subsequent publishing of the application, the URL remains the same irrespective of the version.

Similar to staging, you need to choose any of the available options to manage the Business Object data when publishing the application. The following table describes the different options with descriptions when you publish the application:

Iteration#	Option: Description
1st	1. **Include data from Stage:** All the Business Object data in Live database will be replaced by Stage database. 2. **Publish application with a clean database:** No Business Object data will be copied from Stage to Live database.
2nd, 3rd, and so on	1. **Keep existing data in live:** No Business Object data will be copied from Stage to Live database. 2. **Replace Live with Stage data:** All the Business Object data in Live database will be replaced by Stage database. 3. **Publish application with a clean database:** The existing data will be removed from Live database and no Business Object data will be copied from Stage to Live database.

Table 13.3 – Different options during publishing

These are the steps we can use to publish the application:

1. Open the Visual Builder home page and click on the action menu to the right of any of the applications that you want to publish.

2. Click on the **Publish** option from the action menu. If you are publishing the application for the first time, you need to choose either the **Include data from Stage** option or the **Publish application with a clean database** option, as shown in the following screenshot:

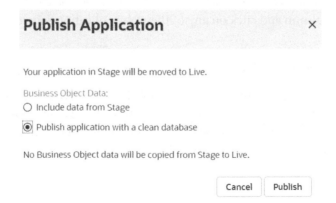

Figure 13.14 – Publish Application dialog box

3. If you update the application, then you have to re-publish the application to make the change effective. But in order to make the changes, you have to version the application, stage it, and only then you will see the **Publish** option. The previously published version will be locked. In the subsequent iteration, choose either the **Keep existing data in Live** option, the **Replace Live with Stage data** option, or the **Publish application with a clean database** option, as shown in the following screenshot:

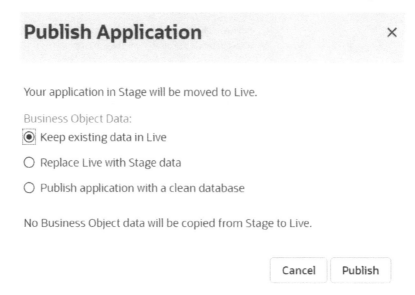

Figure 13.15 – Publish Application dialog box on the subsequent iteration

4. Select any one of the options as per *Table 13.3*. Click on the **Publish** button to publish the application.

5. Once your application is published successfully, you can distribute the published application URL to the end users. To get the URL, click on the **Live** option under the **Status** column and click on any of the web applications on your screen to get the URL.

That is all for staging and publishing the VB application.

In this section, we learned about staging and publishing the VB application. We saw how to stage and publish the application and various options that you need to select when switching the application phases. In the next section, we'll demonstrate how to add team members to the application.

Adding team members to the application

If you want your team members to collaborate on your VB application, then you can add them as team members in the application. The team members you want to add to the VB application must be part of **Oracle IDCS**.

We can use these steps to add team members to the application:

1. Open any of the VB applications in which you want to add team members.

2. Go to the menu in the top-right corner and click on the **Settings** option.

3. Go to the **Team** tab. The **Members** section already displays added team members, and the **History** section displays the history of the last update of the application along with the email address of the team member who made the changes.

4. Under the **Members** section, select or search the name of the team member you want to add and click on the **Add** button, as in the following screenshot:

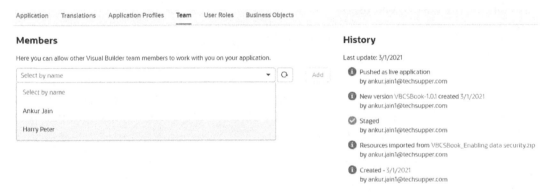

Figure 13.16 – Adding team members

Once the team member is added, their name will be displayed under the **Members** section and the newly added team member can collaborate in the application.

> **Important Note:**
> In order to add team members, the user should be added to the VB **Application Roles** instance from Oracle IDCS.

In this section, you learned how to add team members to the application to collaborate on the development activities.

Summary

In this chapter, you learned how to manage the VB application and explored various options and the different statuses of the VB application. You learned about the versioning of the application and how to create various versions of the application. Along with versioning, you learned how to create a clone of the application.

You also learned about promoting the VB application and explored the complete process to promote the application from one instance to another. You learned how to export the application as an archive file and import it to another instance. We explored different phases of the VB application and how an application can be switched from one phase to another.

You learned about the staging of the VB application, various options while you stage the application, how to stage the application, and distributing the URL to validate the functionality. We learned about publishing the application, various options you need to deal with while publishing the application, how to publish the application, and then distributing the URL to end users.

You also learned how to add team members to the VB application to contribute to the development activities.

In the next chapter, we will talk about various best practices to develop an application that will enhance the performance of the application. We'll describe various best practices and recommendations when creating Business Objects and Service Connections that will reduce development and migration efforts too.

Questions

1. Can we modify the variable values in the published application?

2. Can we insert or modify the data in a Business Object once the application is published?

3. Is it mandatory for the user to be part of Oracle IDCS to add them as a team member?

14
Best Practices and Recommendations for VB Applications

In this chapter, we'll talk about various best practices and recommendations to develop VB applications. Best practices help to improve the developer's productivity and increase the application's performance. If you follow the best practices and recommendations, it will help you to develop bug-free applications and reduce the efforts and maintenance costs associated with the application.

I have categorized the best practices and recommendations into three different categories. The first category is related to the UI components and the applications. While you develop the web or mobile application, you should observe best practices in order to increase the performance of the application.

The second category is related to Business Objects. We'll describe the best practices and recommendations as regards using Business Objects to enhance the performance of your application. The third category is related to Service Connections. We'll describe various options that you should follow while using the Service Connections that will help you to increase the performance of applications. You should follow all the best practices described in this chapter to develop a robust application.

In this chapter, we will cover the following topics:

- Best practices and recommendations for enhancing an app's performance
- Best practices for using Business Objects
- Best practices for using Service Connections

After completing this chapter, you will be able to develop a robust application that can load faster.

Technical requirements

To complete this chapter, you will require the following:

- A **Visual Builder** instance
- **VB** login credentials

Best practices and recommendations for enhancing an app's performance

While developing any software in any technology, it is really important to follow best practices in order to deliver robust software. Regardless of the complexity of software, our aim should be to deliver the world's best software. Best practices increase productivity and enhance the performance of the application, which helps to increase adoption of the software.

We should always follow best practices, listed as follows, while developing the VB application. This will help you to rectify issues after delivering the applications:

- Reusability of the Action Chain
- Environment-specific values
- Using the Run in parallel action
- Caching the Select (Single) data
- Regular restaging and republication
- Using application profiles
- Optimizing the application
- Avoiding deprecated components
- Meaningful names of actions and variables

In this section, we'll focus on the aforementioned best practices that you need to follow right from the outset.

Reusability of the Action Chain

As we described in *Chapter 3, Various Visual Builder Ingredients*, under the *Understanding variables, and their types, and their scopes* section, there are different scopes that can be used to create variables, types, and Action Chains.

Action Chain can be created at any level, such as applications, flows, and pages. The Action Chain that is created at the application level can be used in any flows and pages. You can call the Action Chain using the **Call Action Chain** action of the Action Chain or you can refer to the Action Chain while registering the new event.

The following screenshot shows the **Select Action Chain** dialog box, which shows all the Action Chains defined inside the different scopes:

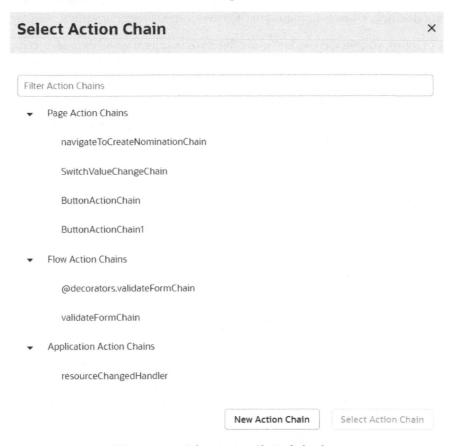

Figure 14.1 – Select Action Chain dialog box

While registering the custom event, you can select the already defined action and reuse the Action Chain instead of creating a new one. Leveraging the reusability of the Action Chain will reduce the efforts and maintainability of the duplicate code. Let me describe it with the help of a live example where the reusability of Action Chains can help.

Let's suppose you register a **vbEnter** event and associate an Action Chain to load the data from the data sources and display the data on any UI component. At some point in time, you will want to fetch the fresh data from the same data source, so instead of creating a new Action Chain or calling the data source again, you can call the same Action Chain at any UI action.

Environment-specific values

While you develop applications, you may need to use values that can vary from environment to environment or change from time to time. There are two options where you can maintain the environment-specific values. One is to create variables, and another is to create Business Objects to maintain the environment-specific values.

As a best practice, you should use Business Objects to maintain environment-specific values, as Business Objects can be changed at any point in time without changing the code even if the application is live. If you maintain the values in the variables and you publish the application, then you will not be able to modify the variables once the application is published.

Let me provide you with a few examples where you may need to maintain the environment-specific values:

- Example 1: When you are using any deep link to redirect users to a different site or to a different application when clicking any link and that deep link varies from one environment.

- Example 2: Unique IDs on which basis you want to fetch the data from backend APIs and these IDs can vary from one environment.

In the next section, we'll look at the running in parallel concept.

Using the Run in parallel action

Sometimes, you need to execute different sets of codes to run independently and wait for their responses to combine the result. **Run in parallel** is one of the actions of the Action Chain that will help you to run the multiple sets of code in parallel. As a result, this action will help to increase the performance of the applications as the multiple actions are executed in parallel without waiting for another one. Wherever you have a requirement to execute multiple codes in parallel, use this action in the Action Chain.

Let me help you with an example where this action can increase the performance of the application.

Suppose you have a few **Select (Single)** UI components on the page that you want to populate with the data of different external REST APIs. Instead of calling all REST APIs in sequential order, we'll call all the REST APIs in parallel and hold the data in the **Array Data Providers** (**ADPs**) to populate the Select (Single) component.

Caching the Select (Single) data

There are instances where you need to use the Select (Single) component and load it with the data, which doesn't change very often. You can use the **Add Data** option in order to populate the component, which takes care of calling and fetching the data from REST APIs.

This option is straightforward and easy to use, but it may have a few performance implications during runtime. When the **Add Data** option is used, a **Service Data Provider** (**SDP**) is created automatically that gets populated with the REST API data. During runtime, every time you click the **Select (Single)** component to choose any value, it makes a call to the REST API to fetch the data. This approach decreases the performance of the page as it calls the REST API multiple times. So instead of fetching the data every time, we can fetch it once, and use it to populate the components.

We can use the following steps to populate the **Select (Single)** component, which will provide us with a number of performance benefits:

1. Create an ADP variable at the scope of an application or flow.
2. Register the **vbEnter** event and call the REST API.
3. Assign the REST response to an ADP variable.
4. Use the ADP variable to populate the **Select (Single)** component.

Let's look at the next practice regarding restaging and republication.

Regular restaging and republication

Oracle recommends to restage and republish applications when the new version of Visual Builder is released. This ensures that the application uses the latest bug and security fixes in the VB. As an administrator of the **Oracle Cloud Console**, you may receive notifications reminding you to use this practice.

Using application profiles

It's always recommended to use application profiles to specify the different application configurations for different environments and deployments; for example, creating different application profiles, one for each life cycle stage (Development, Stage, and Publish) to specify the Service Connection to the different REST server instances.

Refer to *Chapter 5, Creating and Managing Service Connections*, under the *Creating the application profiles* section, to learn more about the application profile and how to create it.

Optimizing the application

While changing the phase of the application from Development to Stage, the VB applies a few parameters to tune the performance of the application automatically. When you hit the staged application for the first time in the browser, the VB resources are cached in the browser and then, for subsequent calls, they will be fetched from the disk cache instead of hitting the VB server again. As a result, the performance of the application will be enhanced because resources are fetched from the cache.

The following screenshot shows the result of the **Network** tab of the browser console when the staged application is loaded the first time:

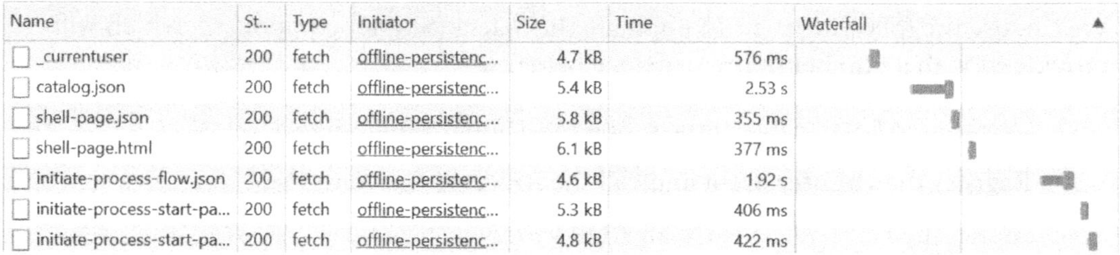

Name	St...	Type	Initiator	Size	Time	Waterfall	▲
☐ _currentuser	200	fetch	offline-persistenc...	4.7 kB	576 ms		
☐ catalog.json	200	fetch	offline-persistenc...	5.4 kB	2.53 s		
☐ shell-page.json	200	fetch	offline-persistenc...	5.8 kB	355 ms		
☐ shell-page.html	200	fetch	offline-persistenc...	6.1 kB	377 ms		
☐ initiate-process-flow.json	200	fetch	offline-persistenc...	4.6 kB	1.92 s		
☐ initiate-process-start-pa...	200	fetch	offline-persistenc...	5.3 kB	406 ms		
☐ initiate-process-start-pa...	200	fetch	offline-persistenc...	4.8 kB	422 ms		

Figure 14.2 – Network tab when the application is rendered for the first time

The following screenshot shows the result of the **Network** tab when the application is loaded a second time:

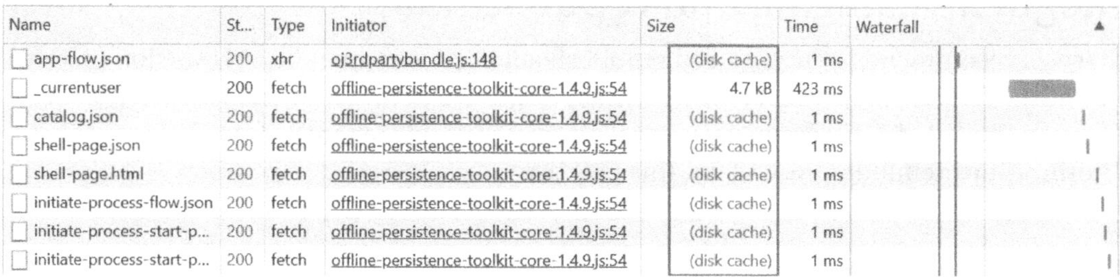

Name	St...	Type	Initiator	Size	Time	Waterfall	▲
☐ app-flow.json	200	xhr	oj3rdpartybundle.js:148	(disk cache)	1 ms		
☐ _currentuser	200	fetch	offline-persistence-toolkit-core-1.4.9.js:54	4.7 kB	423 ms		
☐ catalog.json	200	fetch	offline-persistence-toolkit-core-1.4.9.js:54	(disk cache)	1 ms		
☐ shell-page.json	200	fetch	offline-persistence-toolkit-core-1.4.9.js:54	(disk cache)	1 ms		
☐ shell-page.html	200	fetch	offline-persistence-toolkit-core-1.4.9.js:54	(disk cache)	1 ms		
☐ initiate-process-flow.json	200	fetch	offline-persistence-toolkit-core-1.4.9.js:54	(disk cache)	1 ms		
☐ initiate-process-start-p...	200	fetch	offline-persistence-toolkit-core-1.4.9.js:54	(disk cache)	1 ms		
☐ initiate-process-start-p...	200	fetch	offline-persistence-toolkit-core-1.4.9.js:54	(disk cache)	1 ms		

Figure 14.3 – Network tab when the application is rendered a second time

Compare both the preceding results (*Figure 14.2* and *Figure 14.3*) and notice the **Time** column to see how quickly the resources are loaded the second time. This is because the resources are fetched from the disk cache. The same tuning will be applied when you publish the application.

Apart from this, Visual Builder offers quite a number of **NPM** packages that you can use to audit, optimize, build, and deploy the applications using **Grunt**. There are a lot of tasks that you can use to optimize your web and mobile application code.

Oracle recommends using the vb_package grunt task which contains the vb_optimize task. Refer to the following document to know more about it: https://docs.oracle. com/en/cloud/paas/visual-builder/visualbuilder-building- applications/audit-build-and-deploy-visual-applications-using- grunt.html#GUID-45E08FDC-4D3F-437A-AB1E-F06E398C9730.

Avoiding deprecated components

The **Oracle JET** components are used to develop user interfaces in the VB. From time to time, Oracle releases new JET components with new features and functionalities. Oracle recommends using new components instead of old components as Oracle marks them as deprecated.

The old components will continue to work in the old application, but it is recommended to use new components in the new applications. For every deprecated component, there is a newer version available in the **Component** palette. For example, **Select (One)** is one of the deprecated components, and its replacement is **Select (Single)**.

To learn more about the deprecated components, go to the **Components** pane from the **Navigator** application. The deprecated components are marked with a **warning triangle** as per the following screenshot:

Figure 14.4 – Deprecated component

In the **Components** palette, you will see both deprecated and new versions of the component.

Meaningful names of actions and variables

As such, there are no written rules that you should follow when providing a name for variables and actions. However, it is always beneficial to provide a meaningful name to variables and actions as it helps us and other developers to guess the purpose of the variables. You can follow your own naming conventions throughout the application. In order to identify different types of artifacts, you can provide them with suffixes; for example, _v for variables, _t for types, and _a for Action Chain.

It is recommended to provide meaningful names different artifacts as this helps to debug the code quickly and find things easily in the browser console.

That is everything regarding best practices and recommendations that you should follow while developing web and mobile applications. Apart from these, you can use your past experience to follow other best practices you employed previously in other projects.

In this section, you learned various best practices and recommendations to use various components that will help you to increase the performance of the application as well as increase the productivity of developers. In the next section, we'll look at best practices when using Business Objects.

Best practices for using Business Objects

Business objects are a part of the VB that allow us to maintain transactional data and offer various inbuilt features. If you use out-of-the-box features of the Business Objects, it will help you to develop the application faster and the performance of the application will also be enhanced. Business objects provide a built-in feature to cache the data on the client side. Caching features help to increase the performance of the application.

Business objects are used to maintain the transactional data of the application. All the communication between Business Objects and applications happens via the REST APIs, which are exposed automatically by Business Objects. It's really important to know the best practices for using Business Objects so as to increase the performance of the application.

These are the best practices and recommendations you need to follow while using Business Objects:

- Using the Contains Application Setup Data option
- Data validation and calculation
- Enabling security
- Enabling data caching

In the following sections, we'll discuss each of the aforementioned best practices.

Using the Contains Application Setup Data option

When you create a new Business Object, you will see an option, **Contains Application Setup Data**, on the **Overview** tab of the Business Object. This option is useful for those Business Objects that contain the foundational data of your application and you want this data in each phase of the application.

If this option is enabled for Business Objects, then the data of Business Objects will always be part of your archive file when you export the application or switch the phase (from Development to Stage to Publish) of the application, irrespective of the option you select during the exporting or switching phase.

So, if you have Business Objects where you have the foundational data for your application, such as **Country** and **State**, then enable this option. As a benefit, you don't need to import or insert the foundational data manually in those Business Objects.

The following screenshot shows that the **Contains Application Setup Data** option is enabled for the **Country** Business Object:

Figure 14.5 – Contains Application Setup Data option

This looks like a small option, but it's very helpful.

Data validation and calculation

While creating a new field in a Business Object, you will see various options to enable the data validation or to make a value calculation as per the following screenshot:

Figure 14.6 – Data validation and value calculation

As you can see, you can use various validations for the fields, for example, setting the minimum and maximum length of values and enabling the **Calculate value with a formula** option to make some value calculations.

As a best practice, using out-of-the-box functionality to execute data validation on a field level may reduce development time. Also, if someone uses the Business Object REST APIs directly to insert/update the data, then data will be validated prior to insertion or being updated. As a result, the data will always be valid and you won't need to sanitize the data. Along with the validation, use the **Value Calculation** section to make the calculative fields. For example, you can insert the default value in the field, if a value is not supplied.

Enabling security

Data security is one of the primary concerns when you develop web or mobile applications. VB allows out-of-the-box features, by means of which you can secure the data residing in the Business Objects. We can create different roles as per your application requirements and allow users to access the data that they are authorized to access. Refer to the *Enable data security* section from *Chapter 12, Securing the VB Applications*, to know how to enable data security.

Enabling data caching

Data caching allows you to cache the data on the client side and helps you to increase the performance of the application. The data caching feature on a Business Object is supported from the **Visual Builder 20.10** version onward. There are few considerations that you need to keep in mind before you enable data caching on the Business Object:

- Don't cache the data that changes very frequently, such as inventory details.

- Don't cache sensitive data because the data is cached on the browser's disk cache and it's easy for anyone to get access to this data, such as passwords and credit card details.

- Set the max age property for how long you want to cache the data and when you want to pull fresh data after a period of time.

The following screenshot shows the caching options of a Business Object:

Figure 14.7 – Resource Cache Control

As you can see, these are the are best practices and recommendations that you should follow when using Business Objects in the VB to enhance performance of the applications:

- **Sensitive**: This option is used for the Business Object that contains sensitive data and you never want to cache this data, such as a password and credit card details. This is the default option that disables caching from the Business Object.

- **Public Shared**: If this option is enabled, the data can be cached by the browser. We enable this option for data that does not change very often, such as a list of countries. When you select this option, you are required to set the **Max age(seconds)** option to set the time span for how long you want to cache the data. Following the specified amount of time, the data will be refreshed from the server to the browser's cache.

- **Private**: We can use this option if the data is user-specific, such as the information pertaining to a user, and you don't want to cache this data in the public cache, just in the browser's cache of the user. When you select this option, you are required to set the **Max age(seconds)** option to set the time span for how long you want to cache the data. Following the specified amount of time, the data will be refreshed from the server to the browser's cache.

- **Custom**: This option provides full control over defining your own caching strategy. You will be allowed to set different options (**no-cache**, **public**, **private**, **no-store**, **must-revalidate**, and **max-age**) to define the cache setting.

> **Important Note:**
> The cache settings are effective only for Stage and Publish applications.

In this section, you learned about best practices and recommendations regarding Business Objects such as the **Contains Application Setup Data** option, using the inbuilt data validation of Business Object fields, security, and data caching. In the next section, we will learn about best practices and recommendations regarding the use of Service Connections.

Best practices for using Service Connections

Service connections play a vital role in the VB, enabling external **REST** APIs and **Oracle Cloud Application** APIs to be called using the inbuilt catalog. We must use the **security connection** in a very smart manner in order to reduce the efforts and to increase performance of the applications.

Service connections are used to call any REST APIs to interact with external systems. In the earlier chapters, we created the Service Connections to call external REST APIs, **SaaS REST APIs**, in order to interact with different systems. Since the Service Connections make the calls to an external system, this may slow down the performance of your application if not used in the correct manner.

Here are a few best practices and recommendations that you should follow while using Service Connections:

- Adding multiple endpoints to the same server
- Using the fine-tuned REST APIs
- Caching the data
- Getting the data in chunks
- Using the inbuilt catalog

In the following sections, we'll explain the aforementioned best practices and recommendations for using Service Connections.

Adding multiple endpoints to the same server

When you create a new Service Connection to call any REST API, a new entry is added under the **Service Connections** tab of the **Services** navigator. Visual Builder provides a way to organize multiple endpoints under the same Service Connection if you want to call any other REST APIs that are hosted on the same REST server (for example, `https://restserver.com/posts` and `https://restserver.com/users`).

If you want to call the preceding two endpoints, we can create a Service Connection with any one of the endpoints first and then add another endpoint to the same Service Connection. A single Service Connection can have multiple endpoints hosted on the same server.

> **Important Note:**
> Refer to *Chapter 5, Creating and Managing Service Connections*, under the *Adding more endpoints to the Service Connections* section, to know how to add endpoints to the existing server.

This feature makes your application management easier and also enhances the performance of the application.

The following screenshot shows the multiple endpoints that are added to the same server:

Filter Endpoints
+ Endpoint
/query
GET Get Many getQuery getQuery
/sobjects/Opportunity
POST Create postSobjectsOpportunity postSobjectsOpportunity
/sobjects/Account
POST Create postSobjectsAccount postSobjectsAccount

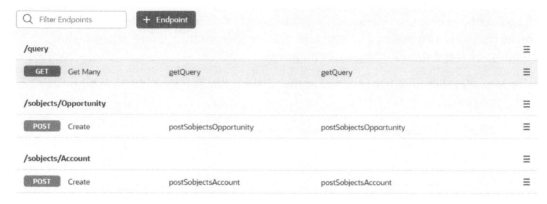

Figure 14.8 – Multiple endpoints added to the same server

This is the best practice for managing multiple endpoints hosted on the same server.

Using the fine-tuned REST APIs

REST calls contribute a lot to the slowing down of applications. Therefore, it is always recommended to use the fine-tuned REST API to interact with the external systems, otherwise the performance of the application will be impaired. We can use the browser network debugger to know how much time the REST API is taking as per the following screenshot:

Name St... Type Initiator Size Time Waterfall
opportunity-flow.json 2... fetch third-party-libs.js:... 4.8 kB 306 ms
opportunity-start-pag... 2... fetch third-party-libs.js:... 6.2 kB 319 ms
opportunity-start-pag... 2... fetch third-party-libs.js:... 5.5 kB 328 ms
query?q=select%20Id... 2... fetch third-party-libs.js:... 7.6 kB 701 ms

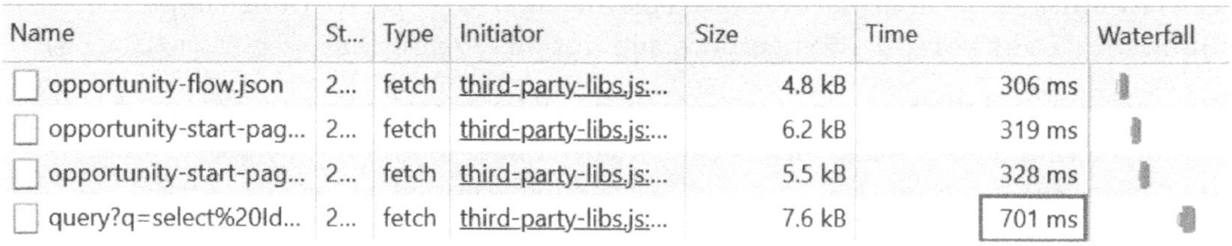

Figure 14.9 – REST API time in the Network tab

As you can see, observe the **Time** column to know how much time each REST API is taking. The time represents the complete time that the REST API took to complete the whole transaction.

Using the optimized REST APIs will help to enhance performance of the application and increase its adoption.

Caching the data

When the data is not changing frequently, we can use the Business Objects caching section for some considerations. As a benefit, the network call will be reduced and the performance of the application will be enhanced.

Getting the data in chunks

Fetching thousands of records in a single REST call may degrade the performance of the application. If you have a requirement to fetch thousands of records and display them on the page, the recommended approach is to get a small amount of data initially and display it on the screen. We can run the REST API in the background, store the data in the variables, and then display the data when the user needs to view it.

Another good example may be if you want to show a lot of information relating to a user, such as primary information, contact details, and salary details. In this instance, we can use the **tabbed view** and hide the data between tabs. This will only fetch the primary information initially and render it on the screen, and when a user clicks on another tab, it sends another hit to the REST API, fetches the data, and displays it on the screen.

The following screenshot shows the tabbed view of the Salesforce information:

Id ↑↓	Name ↑↓	StageName ↑↓	Probability ↑↓	IsWon ↑↓	Amount ↑↓	CloseDate ↑↓
0062v00001NrJAMAAA3	My Learning Opp	Prospecting	10	false	100	2020-05-22
0062v00001OCVITAAA5	My Batch Opportunity	Prospecting	10	false	100	2020-05-26
0062v00001NVJgNAAX	Sahu Training Opportunity	Prospecting	10	false	400	2020-06-30
0062v00001NrIdhAAF	fdfdf	Qualification	10	false	222	2020-05-22
0062v00001R0mV7AAJ	VBCS Learning Opp	Prospecting	10	false	100	2021-01-31

Figure 14.10 – Tabbed view of the application

This approach will enhance performance of the application.

Using the inbuilt catalog

If you have a requirement to integrate the SaaS application with the VB application, use the inbuilt **Oracle Cloud Application** catalog instead of using the **Define by Endpoint** option, because the VB application is designed to work closely with Oracle Cloud Application and it understands very well how the Oracle Cloud application API works.

Especially if you want to fetch the limited fields (`InvoiceNumber`, `InvoiceDate`, `ParyNumber`, and `PartyName`) from the SaaS, the REST calls can only fetch the fields in which you are interested by adding the **fields** parameter to the REST call. As a benefit, the performance of the application will be enhanced by fetching just a small number of fields.

For each REST call you make, some additional metadata information is also fetched from SaaS, such as links. If you don't require it, you can avoid this by adding `onlyData=true` to the **Request** parameter of the REST API.

The following screenshot shows the **Request** parameter of one of the Oracle Cloud Application APIs that you can use to fetch limited data:

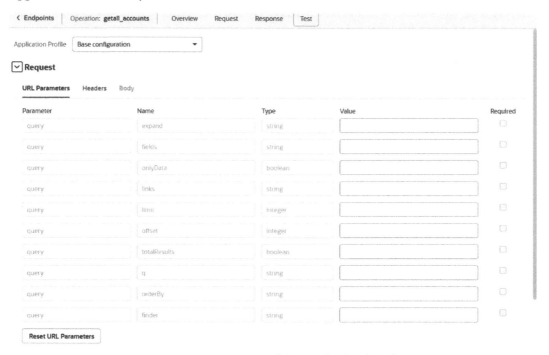

Figure 14.11 – Request parameters of the Oracle Cloud Application API

As you can see, you can set the value of the **onlyData** field to `true` to get just the values and avoid the links in response. Similarly, you can use the **fields** parameter to fetch just the limited fields.

You don't need to create the **Request** parameters explicitly; these are added by default when you add any endpoint from the Oracle Cloud Application catalog. You just need to pass the values in the parameters while you configure the Service Connection in the application.

Summary

In this chapter, you learned various best practices and recommendations for developing web and mobile applications, Business Objects, and Service Connections. You learned what the recommendation is when it comes to using Action Chains, and how you should maintain the values' environment-specific data. You also learned how the **Run in parallel** action will help to enhance performance and about caching the data for the **Select (Single)** component. You learned about the benefits of using application profiles, how the application can be optimized, why deprecated components should not be used, and using meaningful names to make debugging easier.

You learned about various best practices and recommendations for using Business Objects. You learned how a small option, the **Contains Application Setup Data** option of the Business Object, can help when you migrate the application, and you learned about out-of-the-box data validation and calculation on the field's level, as well as the benefits of enabling security. Most importantly, you learned various options for enabling data caching on Business Objects.

You learned about Service Connection best practices that will help to reduce your efforts during application migration and how application performance can be enhanced. You learned the benefits of using the same servers to add multiple endpoints, and how the fine-tuned REST API will enhance performance of the application. You learned about caching the data, getting data in chunks, and using the inbuilt catalog to integrate Oracle Cloud applications.

In the next chapter, we'll talk about various ways of troubleshooting and debugging runtime issues. We'll describe what methods there are for logging error messages so that you can identify any issue at an early stage and rectify it. You will also learn how to handle exceptions and show friendly messages to users in the event of any errors.

Further reading

- What's new in Visual Builder: `https://docs.oracle.com/en/cloud/paas/app-builder-cloud/abcsw/index.html`

- How to optimize code: `https://docs.oracle.com/en/cloud/paas/app-builder-cloud/visual-builder-developer/optimize-your-build-and-audit-your-code-using-grunt.html`

- How to migrate old components with new components: `https://blogs.oracle.com/groundside/visual-builder-migrating-sample-components-to-the-latest-versions`

Questions

1. Do we require extra configuration to tune the application?

15

Troubleshooting and Debugging VB Applications

In this chapter, we'll talk about various ways to troubleshoot and debug the VB application. So far, we have developed a lot of web and mobile applications and tested the happy flow (where the application is tested without seeing any design and runtime issues). *But what if there is an issue in the applications during runtime? How will you debug and troubleshoot the application and fix the issues early?* If you don't know what the issue is and you don't know how to debug it, then it's very difficult to fix it. So, it's very important to know the ways to troubleshoot and debug the application to know the exact issues.

We'll describe how to debug the VB application end to end to find out the issues that occur during development and runtime. As all the data communication happens via REST APIs, it's very important to explore various ways to debug REST APIs and check how they are behaving during runtime.

We'll show how to log messages at different levels such as **JavaScript** and **Action Chain** to make the debugging easier.

Every developer has to deal with errors and exceptions and when an exception occurs in an application, system generated messages are raised that cannot be understood by end users. So, it very important for the developers to suppress the system-generated messages and show user friendly messages to the users. We'll show how to show user friendly message to the users in case of any exceptions occur in the application.

In this chapter, we will cover the following topics:

- Learning about the tools for debugging applications
- Tracking REST calls
- Logging the data to debug issues
- Debugging the application code
- Exception handling

After completing this chapter, you will understand various ways to debug and troubleshoot the VB application to find design and runtime issues quickly and fix them. Also, you will see how to handle exceptions and how to log messages at the different component levels.

Technical requirements

To complete this chapter, you should have the following:

- A **VB** instance
- **VB** login credentials

Learning about the tools for debugging applications

In the software development life cycle, every developer has to deal with different types of known and unknown issues. Developers deliver the application for the end users but sometimes it does not work as expected due to various issues, such as data issues, server issues, network issues, and so on. But it's the developer's responsibility to find out the root cause of the issues and fix it. This is where debugging comes into play.

Visual Builder follows the multi-tier architecture to develop web and mobile applications, so developers might need to debug the applications at each layer to find out the root cause. Since VB is a UI tool, developers have to be dependent on the browser development tools to debug the applications. All browsers (**Chrome, Firefox**, and so on) offer development tools to debug applications. You can simply open the browser development tools using the *F12* key. The following is a screenshot of the **Google Chrome** browser that shows the development tools:

Figure 15.1 – Chrome's browser development tools

Similarly, all other browsers have the same kind of development tools.

> **Important Note:**
> Throughout this chapter, we'll use the **Chrome** browser's development tools to debug the applications.

As you can see from the preceding screenshot, the following are the different consoles available in the browser development tools that will make your life easy to debug applications:

- **Network**: This console allows you to see the traffic between the client and server. You can inspect the properties of an individual's resources such as a complete request including the request parameters, body, content size, and so on, and similarly the complete response, including the response, headers, and so on.

- **Console**: This allows you to see the overall flow of the application. You can track the messages flowing from one page to another, including error messages, notifications, data, and so on.

- **Elements**: This console helps the UI designer to fix UI-related issues such as repositioning UI elements, color changes, alignment of components, and so on.

Similarly, there are other tools available, as shown in *Figure 15.1*, which will help you to debug the application end to end. Developers have to completely rely on those development tools to debug the application.

The VB application runs on a **Verbose** mode of output that provides the complete details on what's happening in the application.

Another layer that you may need to debug is the **Business Objects**. In order to debug the Business Objects, you can use the inbuilt logging mechanisms of **Oracle VB**.

These tools will help you to troubleshoot and debug development and runtime issues.

In this section, you have learned about various tools to troubleshoot and debug the VB application, which will help you to solve issues quickly. In the next section, we'll describe how to track REST calls.

Tracking REST calls

In this section, we'll describe how to track REST calls. Since the data communication in Visual Builder applications happens via REST APIs, it's very important to track the REST calls. When you call any Business Objects or any external REST APIs, a request is made to the server to push or pull data depending on the REST call. Sometimes you may need to track the REST calls end to end to debug the REST API issues.

For example, if the VB application calls any external REST API to push data into the external application but somehow all the records could not be updated successfully in the external application, as a developer, it's your duty to debug the VB application to check where the problem is located.

In order to debug such issues in VB, open the browser development console, move to the **Network** tab, and replicate the issue. Click on the REST API name that you want to track and view the complete REST API details from request to response.

The following screenshot shows the REST call that is made to post the opportunity in Salesforce:

Figure 15.2 – Tracking a REST call

In the previous screenshot, you can see the following sections:

- **Request URL**: This section displays the complete URL that was used to invoke the REST API.

- **Response Headers**: This section displays all the response headers received from the REST server.

- **Request Headers**: This section shows all the headers sent in the request.

- **Request Payload**: This section captures the complete request that is sent to the REST server.

You'll need to switch to the **Response** tab to see what responses you have received from the REST API.

How do we know the actual error if any of the REST APIs fail? Such errors can be seen in the **Network** tab if the REST API has failed. The following screenshot shows a failed REST API call:

Figure 15.3 – Tracking errors in the REST call

The failed API will be marked in red on your screen, and you can look to the **Status Code** section to find out the reason for the error. You can move to the **Response** tab to find out about the actual error if the API throws the failure reason.

If you go to the **Console** tab of the developer tools, you can see the REST API error there too.

The **Network** tab will also display the time taken by each REST API to serve the request. The following screenshot shows the **Network** tab of the browser developer console:

Figure 15.4 – Tracking response time in the REST call

As you can see, the **Time** column displays the complete time taken by each API to complete the request and the **Status** column displays the HTTP status code of the REST API response.

If you want to persist the errors, create a Business Object and insert all relevant error details to debug it offline.

In this section, we learned how to track the REST API calls end to end using the browser development console, how to see the request being sent, and the response received from REST. In the next section, we'll look at various ways to log the error messages that will make debugging easier.

Logging the data to debug issues

In this section, we'll describe various ways to log data to debug development and runtime issues. When you develop applications, logging the data at relevant places is very important. It will help you to debug issues very easily. But make sure you don't log sensitive information such as bank details, credit card details, passwords, and so on due to security reasons.

We'll use logging for different layers to debug issues, such as the following:

- JavaScript
- Action Chains
- Business Objects

In the subsequent sections, we'll see each of the aforementioned loggings in detail.

JavaScript logging

JavaScript is used to write custom logic or to filter out the data. In past chapters, we created some JavaScript code to build custom logic. If you want to debug issues during development and runtime, you can use the following one-line code in JavaScript to log the hardcoded string along with variables:

```
console.log("Hardcoded string "+ variable_name)
```

`console.log()` is an inbuilt JavaScript function that is used to print any kind of messages and variables.

The following screenshot shows the `console.log()` function added in the JavaScript code:

```
define([], function() {
  'use strict';

  var PageModule = function PageModule() {};

  PageModule.prototype.validateForm    = function(form) {
    console.log("Logging from the JavaScript "+form);
    var myformtracker = document.getElementById(form);
    if (myformtracker.valid === "valid") {
      return true;
    } else {
      myformtracker.showMessages();
      myformtracker.focusOn("@firstInvalidShown");
      return false;
    }
  }

  return PageModule;
});
```

Figure 15.5 – The JavaScript console.log() function

All the messages printed by the `console.log()` function can be seen in the browser development console as in the following screenshot:

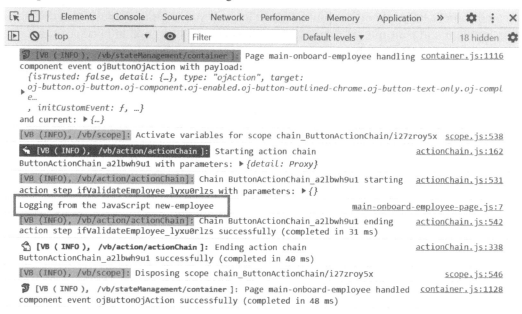

Figure 15.6 – JavaScript log message in the console

The JavaScript logging will help to debug JavaScript-related issues.

In the next section, we'll look at how to log messages at the Action Chain level.

Action Chain logging

In this section, we'll look at how to log messages in Action Chains. Action chains are used to build logic that executes in response to events such as a button click, value change, and so on. In Action Chains, there is no inbuilt logging action as such that can be used to print messages in the browser development console. However, there is an inbuilt **Fire Notification** action that can help you to debug development-related issues. This action shows an inline notification on the page.

For example, if you want to know the values being passed to the Action Chain, you can use the Fire Notification action to see the data inline on the page.

As shown in the following screenshot, three **Fire Notification** actions are added at different steps. The first **Fire Notification** action is added to view the first name that is being passed to the Action Chain. The second **Fire Notification** action is added to show the confirmation message if the REST API sends the success response and the third one is added to show an error message in the case of REST API failure:

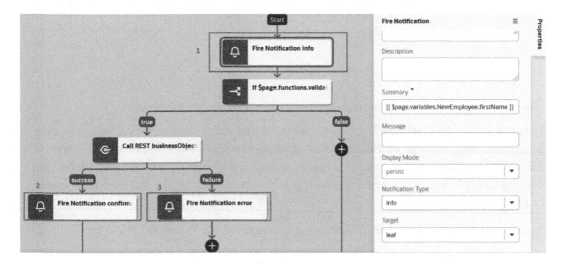

Figure 15.7 – Logging in an Action Chain

The following screenshot shows the value of the **First Name** field being passed to the Action Chain when the **+ Add Employee** button is clicked:

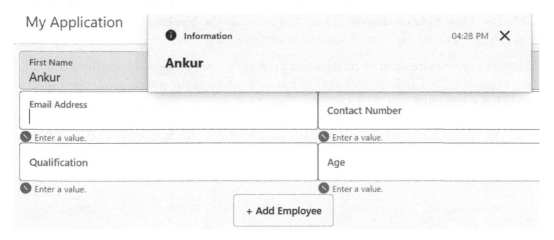

Figure 15.8 – Transient message on the web form

The complete information of the **Fire Notification** action is also printed in the browser console, as shown in the following screenshot:

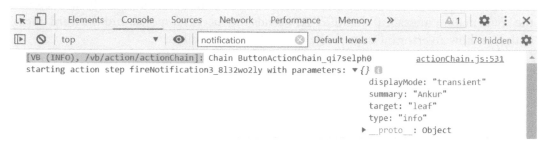

Figure 15.9 – Tracking Fire Notification in the browser console

When you use the **Call REST** action to call the REST APIs, it creates two branches, one for **success** and another for **failure**. In the **failure** branch, VB automatically adds the **Fire Notification** action to print the error messages. Refer to *Figure 15.7* and notice the **Fire Notification** action labeled **3**, which is added automatically by VB under the **failure** branch.

In the next section, we'll look at how to log messages at the Business Object level.

Business Object logging

In this section, we'll look at how to log messages at the Business Object level. The data communication between Business Objects and the UI layer happens using the REST APIs, so the debugging can happen via the browser development console in the case of REST APIs. But if you have created the business rules inside the Business Objects, then these logs can't be tracked from the development console.

The business rules logs can be tracked using the log viewer available inside the VB developer console. Click on the **Logs** links at the bottom of the screen, as shown in the following screenshot:

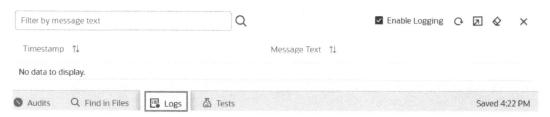

Figure 15.10 – Tracking Business Object logs

By default, the logging is not enabled. Click on the **Enable Logging** checkbox to enable it. This will only be enabled for a single session. If you re-log in to VB, you have to re-enable logging. All the business rules-related logs will be printed in the logs table.

Let's take an example of how to log messages in business rules. Say you have created a **Before Insert Object Trigger** rule in which you want to execute the custom code. In the **Custom Code** editor, you can use the `println` function to log any message. The following screenshot shows the usage of the `println` function:

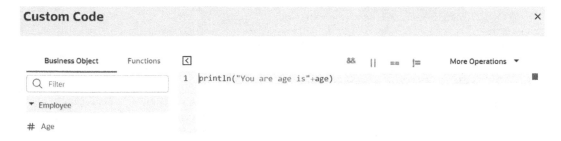

Figure 15.11 – Usage of the println function in custom code

Similarly, the `println` function can be used in the **custom groovy code** to log any message.

In addition to this custom logging, the **Trigger start** and **Trigger end** actions are always logged in the logs. This is how the logs can be added to the Business Objects.

In this section, you learned about various ways to log messages at various levels to debug issues. The logging mechanism will help you in troubleshooting the application. In the next section, we'll look at how to debug the application code.

Debugging the application code

In this section, we'll look at how to debug the application code step by step to identify the issues raised during development and runtime. VB uses **Verbose** mode, which captures the complete details of what's happening inside the application. Verbose mode shows additional information as to what an application is doing. The developer only has to rely on the browser development tools to track the end-to-end flow.

When you run the application, the complete flow of the application is captured in the browser console, including the REST calls, variables assignment, Action Chain flow, events, and so on. Everything is logged in the sequence from the starting of the application until the page loading successfully.

The following screenshot shows the browser developer console that shows all the actions that are captured when the **+ Add** button is clicked:

Figure 15.12 – End-to-end tracking using the browser console

Notice the highlighted sections between the **starting** Action Chain and the **ending** Action Chain. All the actions are captured along with the data. Also, notice that the **callModuleFunctionCalculate** action is executed and has called the JavaScript function named **calculate** with three parameters, **1**, **3**, and **add**. Similarly, other actions are captured in the console too.

In the case of any error at any point in time, it will be captured in the console too. The following screenshot shows an error highlighted along with the reason:

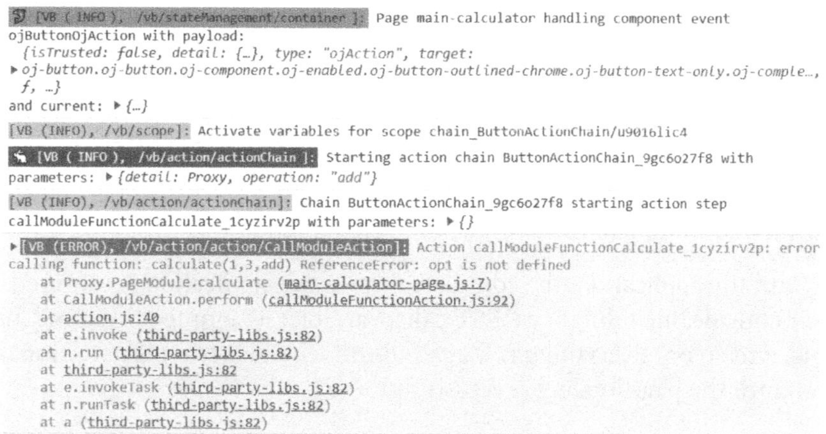

Figure 15.13 – Tracking errors in the console

As you can see, the error indicates that the error occurred while calling the `calculate` function because the `op1` variable is not defined. After seeing this error, you will know the exact issue and can fix it easily.

The browser developer console provides a feature to search the actions with a name and allows you to filter the messages via the logging level. The following screenshot shows the different logging levels to filter messages:

Figure 15.14 – Filtering messages in the browser console

When your application moves to the production stage, you might want to reduce the logging to show only critical information. You can control the level of logging that VB generates in the console in the application settings. To know more about this, refer to this blog: `https://blogs.oracle.com/vbcs/controlling-browsers-console-log-level-in-visual-builder`.

This is how you can debug the application code end to end. You can view what value is assigned to what variables, which JavaScript function is called along with the parameter values, what value is returned back from the function, and much more. The browser development console is one of the most powerful tools that will help you in troubleshooting and fixing the code.

Sometimes you may need to raise an Oracle service request in the case of any application-related issues. In order to debug the issues, Oracle can ask to replicate the issue, download the **HAR** file (a HAR file, or **HTTP Archive** file, tracks the information between the client and server) from the browser development tool, and upload it on the service request.

In this section, we learned how to track the flow of the application step by step, how to see which method is called, along with the parameter values, and how to search the action using the name. These debugging techniques will certainly help you to find out the root cause of the issues. In the next section, we'll look at how to handle exceptions and show a friendly message to users in the case of any errors.

Exception handling

In this section, we'll look at how to handle exceptions in the VB application when any issue is raised and provide a meaningful message to users. When you develop an application and deliver it to the end users to use it, they may face different kinds of issues, such as data issues, network issues, REST API issues, and so on.

When an issue is raised when using the application, a system-generated message is thrown, which an end user cannot understand. So, it's the developer's responsibility to suppress the system-generated message and show user-friendly messages to users.

In the subsequent sections, we'll describe how to handle exceptions at different levels.

Handling REST API exceptions

In this section, we'll look at how to handle exceptions related to REST APIs. In VB, we use REST APIs extensively for data communication, so it's very important to handle exceptions in the case of any issues. In order to call REST APIs, we use the **Call REST** action of the Action Chain.

When you drag and drop this action on an Action Chain, two branches are created automatically by VB, one for success and another for failure. The failure path executes when any issue or exceptions is raised while calling the REST API and it pops up an inline notification message on the page, as shown in the following screenshot:

Id ⇅	Name ⇅	StageName ⇅	Probability ⇅	IsWon ⇅	Amount ⇅	CloseDate ⇅
0062v00001R1P5XAAV	New Debug	Prospecting	10	false	100	2021-02-18
0062v00001NrJAMAA3	My Learning Opp	Prospecting	10	false	100	2020-05-22
0062v00001OCVITAA5	My Batch Opportunity	Prospecting	10	false	100	2020-05-26
0062v00001NVJgNAAX	Sahu Training Opportunity	Prospecting	10	false	400	2020-06-30
0062v00001NrIdhAAF	fdfdf	Qualification	10	false	222	2020-05-22

Figure 15.15 – REST API system-generated message

This error message is fired because the **Fire Notification** action is configured inside the **failure** path, as shown in the following screenshot:

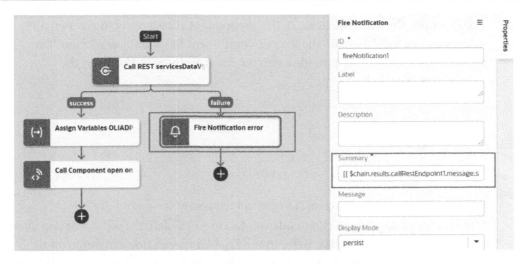

Figure 15.16 – Fire Notification used to display an error message

Instead of showing the system-generated message, which is configured in the **Summary** attribute, we specify a custom user-friendly message so that the user can understand it. In order to review the error messages, open the browser development console to view the complete error details or persist the error messages in the Business Objects to analyze issues further.

Also, testing the REST service calls from outside VB (for example, using POSTMAN or similar tools) will help determine if the issue is in the REST service itself, or in the way that VB interact with it.

This is how you can handle the exceptions raised when calling REST APIs.

In the next section, we'll look at how to handle data-level issues.

Handling data-level issues

In this section, we'll describe how to handle data-level issues. When an application is created to capture data from a user and send it to the external system, or to save in the Business Objects, it's important to take valid data only to minimize the data-level issues. In order to minimize data-level issues, we should allow users to enter valid records only in the web forms.

There are various ways that you can prevent your users from entering invalid records, as follows:

- **Client-side validation**: When you create a web form to take input from users to push into the external systems or Business Objects, it is always recommended to put the client-side validation on the web form using JavaScript and use specific UI components to build a web form that has the inbuilt validations.

For example, the use of the `Email` JET component allows users to enter email addresses in a valid format. The `Email` component has inbuilt validation that will restrict users to only provide a correct email address, as shown in the following screenshot:

Figure 15.17 – Email component

Use JavaScript to perform client-side validation to validate the web form and allow users to only enter valid data. Refer to the *Enabling client-side validation on the forms* section of *Chapter 7, Working with Life Cycle Events, Validations, and UI Logic,* to see how to perform client-side validation. By doing so, you will ensure that only valid data will be sent to the external application or Business Objects.

- **Business Object validation**: Along with the client-side validation, you can put field-level validation on Business Objects. This will ensure that if someone hits the Business Object APIs directly, the APIs will throw an error if passed data that is not valid as per the validations.

- **Usage of the If action**: The **If** action allows you to put different conditions. The conditions you put in If evaluate to either true or false. So, before you execute any business logic, such as calling any external APIs, you can use the If action to add conditions. Accordingly, you can configure true and false branches to execute the custom logic as per your application requirements.

Use all these preceding methods to validate the data before you actually call the REST APIs. This will ensure that data will always be valid and will minimize data-level issues.

This is how data-level issues can be handled in VB.

In this section, we learned how to handle exceptions in VB and show friendly messages to the end users in case of any error. We also learned how to handle data-level issues and ways to handle them.

Summary

In this chapter, you learned about various ways to troubleshoot and debug techniques to handle the issues raised in the VB application. You learned about browser development tools and consoles that will help you to troubleshoot and debug the development and runtime issues. By knowing how to use all these tools, you will be able to easily debug your application and fix your issues easily.

We explained how to track REST API calls end to end, including what request was sent, the request body sent to the REST API, the response received, and how much time a REST API is taking to respond. We also described how to know about an error raised while calling the REST API.

You learned about various ways to log data that will help you to debug issues step by step. We explained at what level logs can be enabled, including the JavaScript call, Action Chains, and Business Objects. Since the VB application is built on multi-layer architecture, you may need to log the message at the relevant places to make your debugging life easier. We explained how to debug the application code step by step, how to track variables, activities, what values are assigned to which variables, and so on. You also learned how to filter messages based on the name and logging level along with screenshots.

You also learned how to handle exceptions raised in the application code, suppress system-generated messages, and show friendly messages to end users. We explained how to handle the REST API exceptions raised when calling the REST APIs in the Action Chain and how to handle data-level issues.

In the next chapter, you will learn how to manage the VB application using **Visual Builder Studio** (**VB Studio**). We'll explain VB Studio and the tools offered by it. We'll demonstrate how to provision VB Studio and how to access it. You will learn how to create projects in VB Studio, how to connect VB with VB Studio, and how to connect the VB application with the VB Studio Git repository. You will learn how to manage the version control of the VB application using the VB Studio Git repositories, including code check-in, pulling updates, modifying the code file using the Git interface, and importing applications from VB Studio Git repositories.

Further reading

- Refer to this blog post to learn more about debugging and troubleshooting techniques in VB: `https://blogs.oracle.com/vbcs/debugging-and-troubleshooting-visual-builder-logic`

- Refer to this blog post to learn how to abort long-running processes: `https://blogs.oracle.com/vbcs/restabort`

- Refer to this blog post to learn how to download an **HTTP Archive (HAR)** format file: `https://support.zendesk.com/hc/en-us/articles/204410413-Generating-a-HAR-file-for-troubleshooting`

Questions

1. Do we need specific tools in VB to troubleshoot and debug VB applications?

2. Is it safe to store exceptions in the Business Objects?

3. In the case of any issues, if Oracle requested the log information, how can you send logs to them?

16

Managing VB Apps Using Visual Builder Studio

In this chapter, we will demonstrate how to manage the VB code lifecycle using **Git** repositories. In order to manage code in Git, we'll use **Oracle Visual Builder Studio** (**VB Studio**), formerly known as **Developer Cloud Service** (**DevCS**), which is a foundation service in Oracle Cloud that you can use to manage the **Agile** development process and automate the **DevOps** lifecycle.

In this chapter, we'll describe Oracle VB Studio, the benefits it offers, and the various capabilities of VB Studio. We'll demonstrate how to provision Oracle VB Studio using the **Oracle Cloud Infrastructure** (**OCI**) dashboard, which will help you manage the DevOps of your VB code. We'll demonstrate how to create a project in VB Studio to create empty Git repositories to manage a VB application.

We'll demonstrate how to connect the VB console with VB Studio, which will help you to connect to Git repositories, and once a VB Studio instance is connected, we'll show how to connect to a specific Git repository with a specific branch. You will learn how to manage VB application code using the VB Studio Git repositories.

In this chapter, we will cover the following topics:

- Understanding Visual Builder Studio
- Provisioning Visual Builder Studio
- Creating a project in VB Studio
- Connecting VB to VB Studio and a Git repository
- Managing VB apps using Git repositories

After completing this chapter, you will be able to use VB Studio and manage the VB application code lifecycle. You will also be able to pull and push code using the VB designer.

Technical requirements

To complete this chapter, you should have the following:

- A **Visual Builder** instance
- **VB** login credentials
- **OCI** login credentials
- A **Visual Builder Studio** instance

Understanding VB Studio

Oracle VB Studio is one of the Oracle Cloud offerings that is used to automate the DevOps cycle and it's available to every Oracle Cloud customer. VB Studio is a free service for every Oracle Cloud customer and there is no extra cost to use it.

VB Studio is a robust application development platform that helps different teams to plan and manage their work efficiently through the application development lifecycle, including designing, building, testing, and deployment. VB Studio is used to automate **CI/CD** processes, which are explained as follows:

- **Continuous Integration** (**CI**): This is a process in which developers continuously pull/push and merge code changes into the master branch and manage conflicts. CI governs the automated testing that runs on recently committed code, which ensures the code in the master branch is always stable.

- **Continuous Delivery** (**CD**): This is a process in which the code is deployed automatically on different configured environments, which reduces the team effort. This automated process reduces the deployment issues that occur during deployment time and minimizes the effort required as well.

The following diagram depicts different phases of the **DevOps** process:

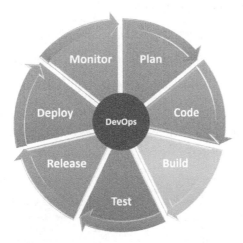

Figure 16.1 – DevOps process

As you can see, the DevOps process starts from the planning phase and ends with monitoring applications. VB Studio allows managing the complete **DevOps** process. The following is a short description of each and every phase of the DevOps process:

- **Plan**: This is the initial phase where you start planning and gathering requirements to build apps. Along with planning, you can document the requirements and design your solution.

- **Code**: Once your planning is completed, you can start developing the application.

- **Build**: Once development is over, you build the application to run it on various platforms.

- **Test**: Various stakeholders will start validating the functionality of the application.

- **Release**: Once testing is completed, you can release the code for production deployment.

- **Deploy**: The code will be deployed automatically on the production environment through the automated scripts.

- **Monitor**: Once the application is live, the operations team will monitor the application for any bugs and issues, and a ticket will be raised. VB Studio has inbuilt functionality to raise and manage issues.

In addition to that, Oracle VB Studio can be used by a variety of users, which are given as follows, to develop and manage applications:

- Oracle Cloud app developers who want to extend applications

- Developers who want to develop web and mobile applications

- Different programmers who want to modify application source code directly

VB Studio provides various tools, such as **GIT, CI, CD, Rich Designer**, and **Boards and Issue Tracking**, that are used for the DevOps process. The following diagram shows the various tools offered by VB Studio:

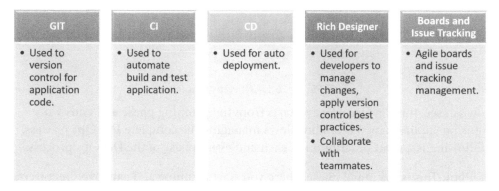

GIT	CI	CD	Rich Designer	Boards and Issue Tracking
• Used to version control for application code.	• Used to automate build and test application.	• Used for auto deployment.	• Used for developers to manage changes, apply version control best practices. • Collaborate with teammates.	• Agile boards and issue tracking management.

Figure 16.2 – Various VB Studio tools

As you can see, using all these tools you can completely automate the DevOps process using VB Studio. It enables developers to deploy their application on the target instance of an **Oracle Cloud Application** or OCI.

VB Studio offers a designer tool that can be used to develop web and mobile applications without using the **Visual Builder** console.

The recent versions of Visual Builder Studio further enhance the integration of the VB development process into the VB Studio. This includes the new Workspace area in VBS which allows you to directly work on your code using the visual editor from inside VBS. This editor offers even deeper git integration options, including the ability to visually resolve conflicts in code merges.

In addition, VBS now includes build-job steps that can automate the packaging and deployment of VB apps onto VB environments. This further helps streamlining the CI/CD process of VB apps.

Refer to this blog to know these features and their benefits for VB developers: `https://blogs.oracle.com/vbcs/the-new-visual-builder-studio-introduction-for-visual-builder-developers`.

In this section, you learned about VB Studio, the purpose of using it, and various inbuilt tools offered by VB Studio. In the next section, we'll look at how to create and access VB Studio.

Provisioning VB Studio

In this section, we'll look at how to provision VB Studio. In order to use VB Studio, you have to provision a VB Studio instance as you provision other instances such as OIC, VB, and so on. You can only provision one VB Studio instance per Oracle Cloud account.

In order to provision a VB Studio instance, you should have the admin privileges to create resources in Oracle Cloud. The following are the steps to provision a VB Studio instance:

1. Log into the Oracle Cloud dashboard using a unique cloud account name and enter the credentials on the login page. Upon successful login, you will land on the **Oracle Cloud Infrastructure (OCI)** dashboard.

2. From the dashboard, click on the hamburger menu in the top-left corner of the screen. Expand **Platform Services** and click on the **Developer** option, as shown in the following screenshot:

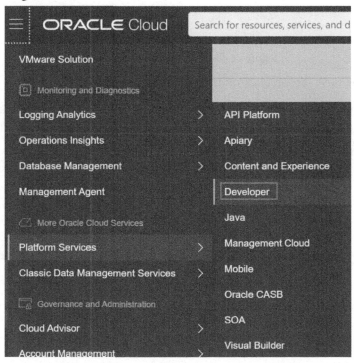

Figure 16.3 – The Developer option on the OCI page

This action will take you to the VB Studio page.

3. Then, click on the **Create Instance** button. Once you click on the button, it will take you to the **Create Instance** form. Enter vbs for **Instance Name** and click on the **Next** button as per the following screenshot:

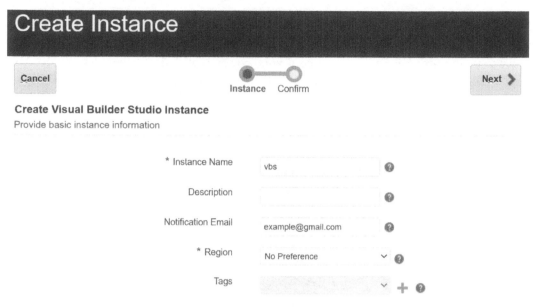

Figure 16.4 – Create a VB Studio instance

4. From the next screen, click on the **Create Instance** button.

Once you click on the **Create Instance** button, VB Studio will start provisioning and may take few minutes to provision. Once the instance is created, it will be visible on the VB Studio page as per the following screenshot:

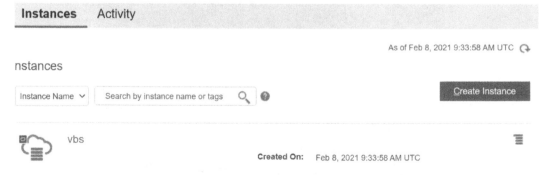

Figure 16.5 – VB Studio instance

Now the VB Studio instance has been provisioned successfully. In the next section, we'll look at how to access the VB Studio instance.

Accessing the Visual Builder Studio instance

In order to access the VB Studio instance, go to the **Visual Builder Studio** page, click on the action menu right next to the instance name, and click on the **Access Service Instance** option as shown in the following screenshot:

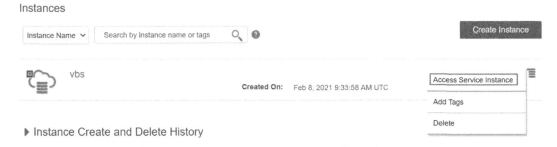

Figure 16.6 – Access the VB Studio instance

The previous action will open the VB Studio page. The following screenshot shows the VB Studio **Organization** page:

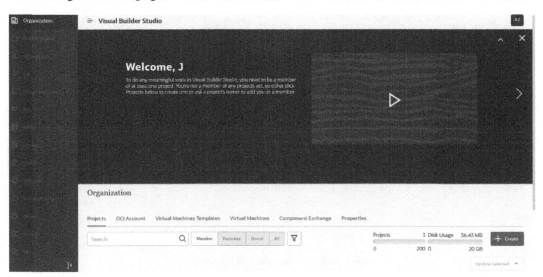

Figure 16.7 – VB Studio page

You can bookmark this page for direct login.

This is how you create and access the VB Studio instance. In order for other developers to access the VB Studio instance, make sure they are added in the Oracle IDCS and have the **DEVELOPER_USER** role of the VB Studio instance.

> **Tip:**
> Refer to the *Creating users and assigning roles* section of *Chapter 2, Provisioning and Understanding the Visual Builder Instance*, to know how to create a user and assign roles.

In this section, you learned how to create a VB Studio instance and how to access it. In the next section, we'll look at how to create a project in VB Studio.

Creating a project in VB Studio

In this section, we'll create a VB Studio project with a default Git repository. VB Studio allows you to create a VB application too. A project in VB Studio is a collection of various resources required to complete the lifecycle of an application.

The following are the steps to create a project in VB Studio:

1. Log into VB Studio. Then, from the **Organization** page, click on the **+ Create** button as per the following screenshot:

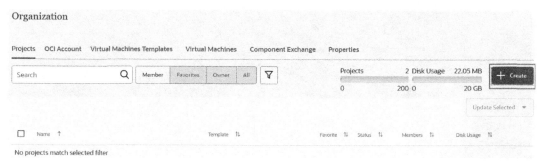

Figure 16.8 – Create the VB Studio project

2. From the opened **New Project** dialog box, enter the details as per the following table, and click on the **Next** button:

Field	Value
Name	Enter the name of the project as **VBCSBook_vbs**
Description	Enter the project description optionally. Enter **This is used to manage VBCS book project**.
Security	**Private:** This option allows access to the project owner and teammates you invite to collborate. **Shared:** Anyone in the organization can access the project. Select **Private** for this project.
Language	Select your preferred language for the email notification for the project. Select English for this project.

Table 16.1 – Values to configure a project

3.   The next page allows you to select the project template. Select **Initial Repository** as per the following screenshot and click on the **Next** button:

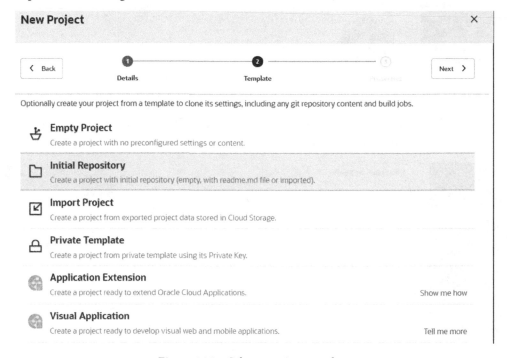

Figure 16.9 – Select a project template

4.   From the next screen, select the **Initialize repository with README file** option under the **Project Properties Initial Repository** section, select **Confluence** from the **Wiki Markup** dropdown, and click the **Finish** button.

The project creation process takes a few minutes as a lot of resources are created for a single project, such as a Git repository, **Wiki**, **Maven**, and so on. Once the project is provisioned successfully, you will be redirected to the **Project Home** page.

The following screenshot shows the **Project Home** page:

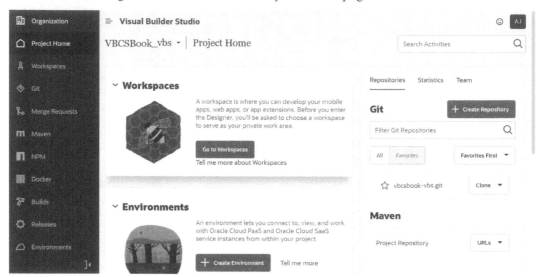

Figure 16.10 – VB Studio Project Home page

5. When a project is created, a Git repository will be created by default with a master branch. Go to the **Git** navigation tab, click on the **Clone** dropdown, and see the Git URL as per the following screenshot:

Figure 16.11 – Git repository

The Git URL can be used to check in and manage code for any type of application. The HTTPS Git URL will be used to check in the VB code in the next section. Copy the HTTPS URL and keep it handy in the notepad. That's how you can create projects in VB Studio.

In this section, you learned how to create a new project using VB Studio based on the **Initial Repository** template. In the next section, we'll look at how to connect the VB application with the VB Studio project and connect to the Git repository.

Connecting VB to VB Studio and a Git repository

In this section, we'll look at how to connect VB to VB Studio to manage the VB code in the Git repository. Once VB is connected to VB Studio, you will be able to manage your VB app code using the Git repository.

The following are the steps to connect the VB app to the VB Studio project:

1. Open any one of the VB applications from the Visual Builder console. For this demonstration, open the **VBCSBook** application.

2. Click on the **Git** icon in the top-right corner of the page, and click the **Configure Visual Builder Studio Credentials** option as shown in the following screenshot:

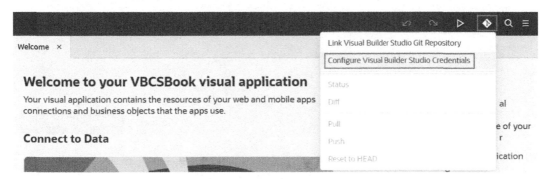

Figure 16.12 – Configure VB Studio credentials

3. The previous action will open the **Configure Visual Builder Studio Credentials** dialog box. Click on the **Add Credentials** button from the opened dialog box.

4. The previous action will open another dialog box. Configure the details as per the following table and click on the **Save Credentials** button:

Field	Value
URL	Enter the VB Studio URL. It will be the same URL which you used to login into the VB Studio
Username	Enter the Username
Password	Enter the password

Table 16.2 – Values to configure the VB Studio instance

The following screenshot shows the information used to configure the VB Studio credentials:

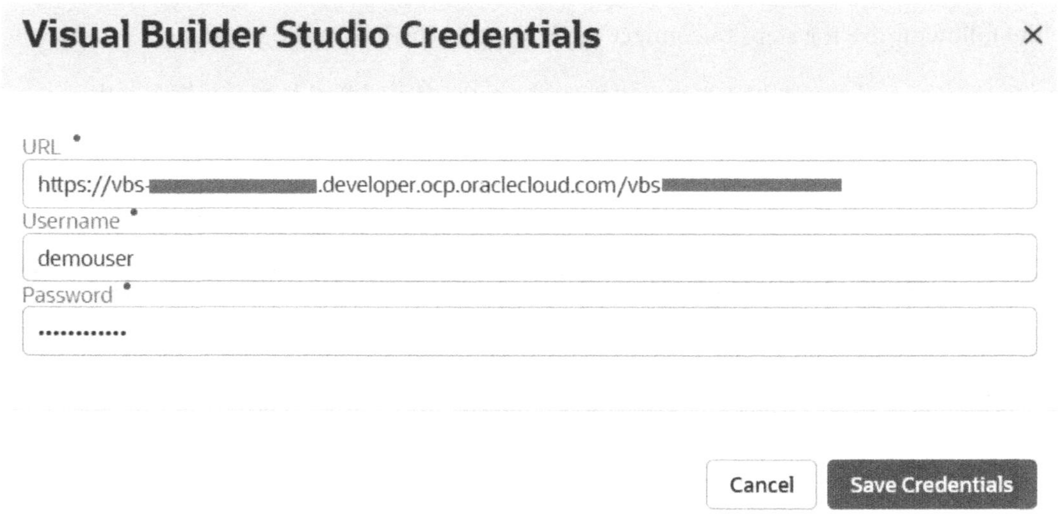

Figure 16.13 – Configure the VB Studio credentials

5. Once the credentials are added, you will be returned back to the previous dialog box and shown the VB Studio details. Click on the **Close** button to close the dialog box.

Now VB has been connected to VB Studio successfully. A single VB instance can be connected to multiple VB Studio instances. Follow the preceding steps (*step 1* to *step 4*) to connect to another VB Studio instance.

In the next section, we'll look at how to link the VB application to the VB Studio Git repository.

Connecting to the Git repository

As the next step, we'll see how to connect to the VB Studio project Git repository that we created in the *Creating a project in VB Studio* section. Before you connect to the Git repository, make sure Visual Builder is connected to VB Studio as per the last section.

The following are the steps to connect the VB app to the Git repository:

1. Open the **VBCSBook** application, click on the **Git** icon in the top-right corner of the page, and click on the **Link Visual Builder Studio Git Repository** option.

2. The previous action will open the **Linked Visual Builder Studio Git Status** dialog box. Click on the **Add Link** button.

3. The previous action will open another dialog box. Enter the details as per the following table and click on the **Save Configuration** button:

Field	Value
URL with Credentials	Select the VB Studio instance from the drop down.
Project Selection	All VB Studio project will be populated automatically which exist in the selected VB Studio instance. Select the **VBCSBook_vbs** for this demonstration.
Repository Selection	Select the existing Git repository. Select the **vbcsbook-vbs.git.**
Branch Selection	Select the **master** branch.

Table 16.3 – Values to configure VB Studio Git repository

The following screenshot shows the information used to link the VB Studio Git repository:

Figure 16.14 – Link with VB Studio Git repository

You will be returned back to the previous dialog box. Click on the **Close** button to close the dialog box.

The **VBCSBook** application has been connected to the Git repository and now you will be able to manage your application code using the Git repository.

In this section, you learned how to connect VB with the VB Studio instance and how to connect the VB application with the Git repository. In the next section, we'll look at how to push and pull application code from Git repositories.

Managing VB apps using Git repositories

In this section, we'll look at how to push and pull code from Git repositories. The Git repositories that we created will be used to manage the version control of your VB application.

VB Studio provides a rich interface to manage an application in Git repositories, which can be used to push, pull, create a new branch, modify code files, and so on.

In the subsequent sections, we'll look at how to manage applications using VB Studio Git repositories.

Pushing code from VB

In this section, we'll look at how to push code from the VB console to VB Studio Git repositories.

The following are the steps to push the application code from the VB console to the VB Studio Git repositories:

1. Open the **VBCSBook** application from the VB console, click on the **Git** icon in the top-right corner of the page, and click on the **Push** option as per the following screenshot:

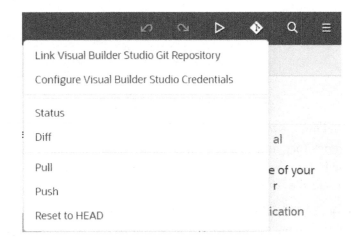

Figure 16.15 – Pushing a VB app to Git

As you can see, the **Diff**, **Pull**, **Push**, and **Reset to HEAD** options will be enabled only if the VB application is connected to the Git repositories. Following is a short description of each of the Git options:

a. **Diff** options show changes between commits, commit, and the working branch.

b. The **Pull** option is used to pull changes from Git if there are any.

c. **Push** is used to push changes into Git if there are any.

d. **Reset to Head** is like the rollback command. It is used to move the current branch backward by two commits.

2. The previous action will open the **Push Content to Git Repository** dialog box with a pre-populated Git repository and branch name, which will already be configured. Enter the details in the **Commit Message** section and click on the **Push to Git** button.

The following screenshot shows the dialog box to push the code into the Git repo:

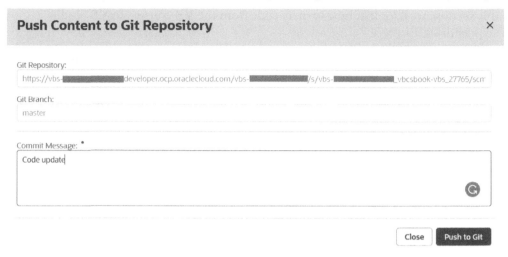

Figure 16.16 – Commit code to Git

3. Once you click on the **Push to Git** button, the code will be pushed into the VB Studio Git repository, and you will see a confirmation message as well. Simply click on the **Close** button to close the dialog box. The VB application has been pushed successfully into the Git repository.

    Now, go back to VB Studio and move to the **Git** navigation. View the complete application code in the Git repository as per the following screenshot:

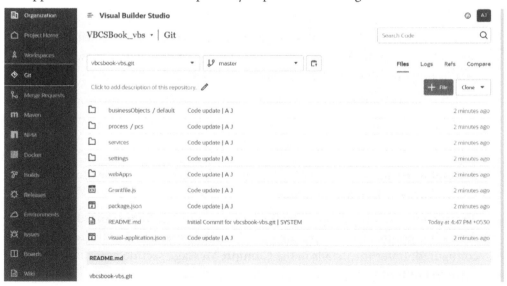

Figure 16.17 – VB Studio Git

Now even if you delete the local copy of the VB application from Visual Builder, the application code will remain there in the Git repository and other developers can import the code directly from the Git repository in VB.

In the next section, we'll look at how to modify the code files directly from VB Studio.

Modifying the code files

We know that VB Studio provides a rich interface that can be used to modify the application code directly. In order to modify the code from VB Studio, we need to perform the following steps:

1. Open VB Studio, go to the **Git** navigation, and open any one of the files that you need to modify. For this demonstration, open the main-start-page.html file under **mywebapplication** as shown in the following screenshot:

Figure 16.18 – Updating the file

2. Click on the **pencil** icon to edit the file, which will open the file in edit mode.

3. Modify the page as per your requirement. For this demonstration, update the **h1** heading text from **Employee Details** to Employees Information.

4. Click on the **Commit** button to commit the change.

5. From the opened dialog box, provide the details for **Commit Summary** and **Details**, and click on the **Commit** button.

6. Once the changes are committed, you will be returned back to the page file.

You can compare the previous and old files in order to check what has been changed in the file. Go to the **Compare** tab and see what content has been changed as per the following screenshot:

Figure 16.19 – Comparing the changes

You can go to the **Logs** tab and see all the updated files date-wise.

In the next section, we'll look at how to pull the updated code in from a VB Studio Git repository to VB.

Pulling Git updates using the VB console

Whenever you update code files directly from a VB Studio Git repository, you may need to pull the updates to your local copy, which resides in VB, to refresh the VB local copy. So, in this section, we'll look at how to pull updates using the VB console.

The following are the steps to pull updates from the VB Studio Git to VB using the VB console:

1. Open the **VBCSBook** application from the VB console, click on the **Git** icon from the top-right corner of the page, and click the **Pull** option.

2. The previous action will open the **Update Application From Git** dialog box. Click on the **Update from Git** button.

3. Once you click on the **Update from Git** button, the VB local copy will be refreshed, and you'll see what code files have been updated as per the following screenshot:

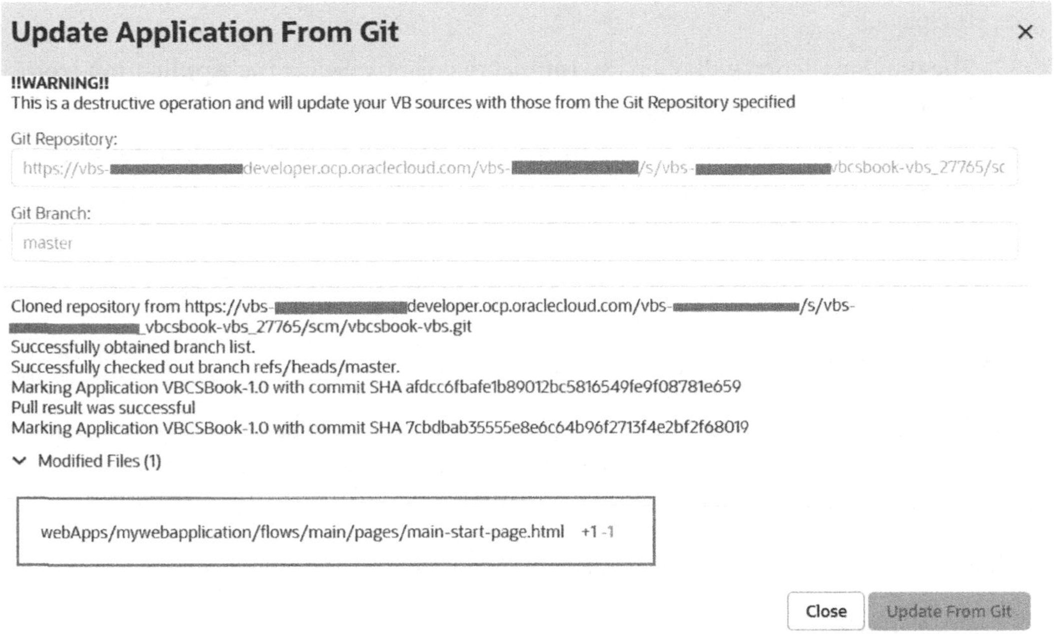

Update Application From Git   ×

!!WARNING!!
This is a destructive operation and will update your VB sources with those from the Git Repository specified

Git Repository:

https://vbs-██████████developer.ocp.oraclecloud.com/vbs-███████████/s/vbs-█████████vbcsbook-vbs_27765/sc

Git Branch:

master

Cloned repository from https://vbs-█████████developer.ocp.oraclecloud.com/vbs-███████████/s/vbs-
██████████vbcsbook-vbs_27765/scm/vbcsbook-vbs.git
Successfully obtained branch list.
Successfully checked out branch refs/heads/master.
Marking Application VBCSBook-1.0 with commit SHA afdcc6fbafe1b89012bc5816549fe9f08781e659
Pull result was successful
Marking Application VBCSBook-1.0 with commit SHA 7cbdbab35555e8e6c64b96f2713f4e2bf2f68019

∨ Modified Files (1)

webApps/mywebapplication/flows/main/pages/main-start-page.html   +1 -1

Close   Update From Git

Figure 16.20 – Pulling changes from Git

4. Click on the **Close** button to close the dialog box.

Now you should see that your local copy is refreshed with the VB Studio Git code. This is how you can pull the changes from VB Studio Git to the VB.

In the next section, we'll look at how to import the application from the VB Studio Git repositories into VB.

Importing the application from VB Studio Git

Sometimes, you may need to import a complete application from VB Studio to VB if your local copy has been deleted or other developers want to work on the application. So, in this section, you will learn how to import the application from VB Studio to VB.

The following are the steps to import an application from VB Studio Git to VB:

1. Go to the VB home page, and click on the **Import** button in the top-right corner of the page.

2. The previous action will open the **Import** dialog box. Select the **Application from Visual Builder Studio** option.

3. The previous action will open another **Import Application from Visual Builder Studio Git** dialog box. Configure the details as per the following table and click on the **Import** button:

Field	Value
URL with Credentials	Select the VB Studio instance from the drop down.
Project Selection	All VB Studio project will be populated automatically which exist in the selected VB Studio instance. Select **VBCSBook_vbs** for this demonstration.
Repository Selection	Select the existing Git repository. Select **vbcsbook-vbs.git**.
Branch Selection	Select the **master** branch.
Application Name	Enter any application name. Enter **VBCSBook_Git**.
Application Id	Application ID will be populated automatically based on the application name.
Description	Enter the description optionally.

Table 16.4 – Values to import the application

The following screenshot shows the information to be entered to import the application from VB Studio Git:

Import Application from Visual Builder Studio Git   ✕

Add Credentials

* URL with Credentials   `https://vbs-████████7.developer.ocp.oraclecloud.com/vbs-████████`   ▾

* Project Selection   VBCSBook_vbs   ▾

* Repository Selection   vbcsbook-vbs.git   ▾

* Branch Selection   master   ▾

* Application Name   VBCSBook_Git

Best to keep the name short so it looks nice

* Application ID   VBCSBook_Git

This ID defines the context path (browser's URI) used for the application

Description   A brief description of the application

Cancel   **Import**

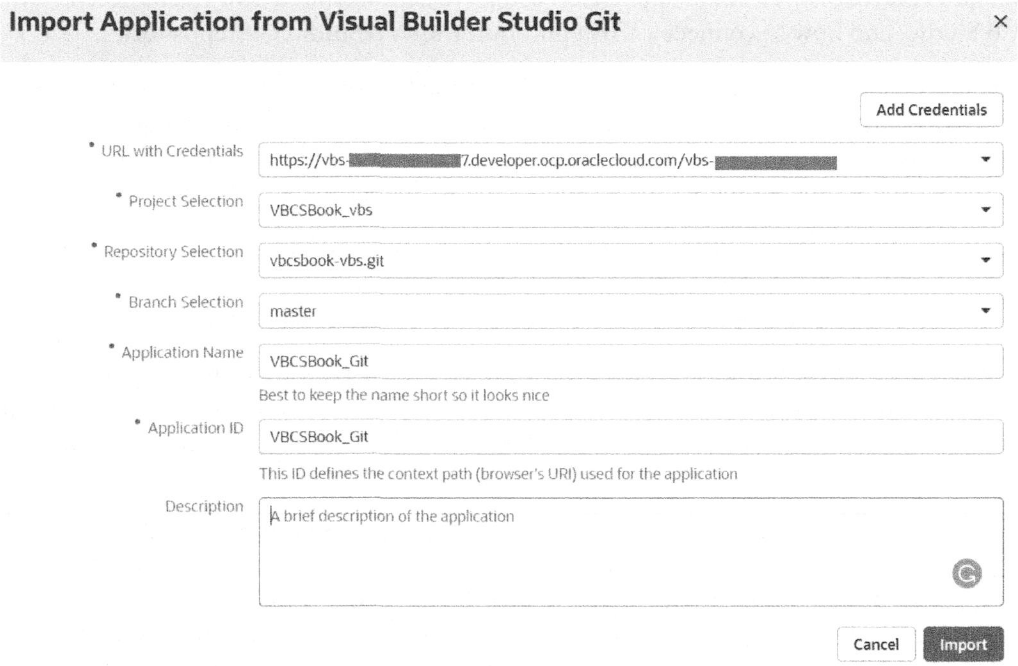

Figure 16.21 – Importing the application from VB Studio Git

Once the application is imported, it will be visible on your VB home page. You can update the application as per your requirement and push the changes to the VB Studio Git.

This is how you manage application code using VB Studio Git repositories.

In this section, you learned how to manage a VB application using Git repositories. You learned how to push code from VB to VB Studio Git, modify code files directly using the Git interface, pull Git changes to VB, and import an application from Git to VB.

Summary

In this chapter, you learned about application code management using Git repositories. We explained about Visual Builder Studio, what it offers, and the audience that can benefit from VB Studio. You learned how to provision a VB Studio instance from an Oracle Cloud account, and how to access it.

You learned about creating a project using VB Studio using the Initial Repository template, which creates an empty Git repository. This Git repository can be used to maintain the version control of any kind of application code. We demonstrated how to connect VB with VB Studio, and how to connect a VB application with VB Studio Git repositories.

You learned about managing a VB application using Git repositories. We demonstrated how to push a VB application from the VB console to a VB Studio Git repository, how to modify code files directly from the Git interface, and how to pull changes from Git to the VB console and import the VB application from VB Studio Git to VB.

I hope you really enjoyed the book, and now you are in the position to build cross-platform applications using VB independently. You learned about various building blocks of VB and developed lots of use cases covering various real-time use cases in a step-by-step approach.

You can apply these use cases in your real-time projects directly and that will save you research time. You learned how to develop mobile applications and compile them to run on different devices. I demonstrated how to use the inbuilt catalog to extend the Oracle Cloud application.

You also learned about various best practices and recommendations that will help you to develop an interactive application and reduce the load time of the application. Make sure to apply all those best practices and recommendations right from scratch to enhance the performance of the application. We also described various techniques to troubleshoot and debug the application to find out design and runtime issues quickly and solve them. I also covered how to use Visual Builder Studio to manage the application code lifecycle.

You can view the **What's new in Oracle Visual Builder** document (`https://docs.oracle.com/en/cloud/paas/app-builder-cloud/abcsw/index.html`) to learn about new features and bugs that are resolved in the upcoming release to gain more knowledge. You can raise your questions and queries in the Oracle Cloud community to get faster responses. You can visit my blog (`https://www.techsupper.com`) and YouTube channel (`https://www.youtube.com/Techsupper`) to gain more knowledge about Oracle products and more on VB.

Further reading

- Refer to the blog to learn about Git: `https://git-scm.com/`
- Refer to the blog to know more about VB Studio: `https://docs.oracle.com/en/cloud/paas/visual-builder/index.html`
- Create a free account using the following link and solve any Oracle-related queries: `https://cloudcustomerconnect.oracle.com/`

Questions

1. Can we connect a VB application with external Git repositories?

2. Do we need to bear any extra cost for Visual Builder Studio?

3. Can we develop a web and mobile application directly from Visual Builder Studio?

4. Can we create different Git branches in VB Studio?

Assessments

Chapter 1, What, Why, and How (WWH) of Visual Builder

Question 1

If someone doesn't know JET, can they use VB?

Answer

It's not required to know JET; you just use the component to develop the UI interface.

Question 2

Can the 5 GB of space in the embedded database be increased on request?

Answer

No, the 5 GB of space can't be increased. Switch the embedded database to point to other Oracle databases, such as Oracle DBaaS or Oracle ATP.

Chapter 2, Provisioning and Understanding the Visual Builder Instance

Question 1

Why is a credit card required during account creation?

Answer

Credit cards are required for verification purposes only. Oracle will deduct only US $1 for verification purposes, which will be reimbursed after some time.

Question 2

Will Oracle charge after the 30-day free subscription period is over?

Answer

No, Oracle will not charge anything unless you elect to upgrade.

Question 3

Does VB come under the free service program?

Answer

No, VB is not a free service. The VB service will be terminated after 30 days of account activation.

Question 4

How can I practice once the VB service is terminated after 30 days?

Answer

You can create a new account with a different email ID but the same credit card and mobile number can be used.

Question 5

Can the embedded database size be increased somehow?

Answer

No, the embedded database size cannot be increased.

Chapter 3, Exploring Visual Builder Ingredients

Question 1

Can we call Business Object REST APIs from outside Visual Builder?

Answer

Yes, the Business Object APIs can be called from outside Visual Builder, such as Postman, SOAP UI, or any other client.

Question 2

Can we add or modify the Business Object REST APIs?

Answer

You can add or modify the Business Object REST APIs if an application has many inter-related Business Objects.

Question 3

What are the various options available to import bulk data into a Business Object?

Answer

You can use a `.csv`, `.xls`, or `.xlsx` file to import bulk data into a Business Object.

Question 4

Are Business Objects and Service Connections reusable components?

Answer

Yes, once a Business Object or Service Connection is created, it can be used in multiple web or mobile applications inside the application.

Question 5

Can we call the SOAP API using a Service Connection?

Answer

No, you can't call the SOAP API via a Service Connection but you can use JavaScript to call SOAP APIs.

Question 6

How can we send email notifications from an Action Chain?

Answer

We can create a service method to send an email that will be exposed as the REST endpoint, and then call that service method from an Action Chain using the Call REST action.

Chapter 4, Creating and Managing Business Objects

Question 1

Can we change the data type of the Business Object field after it is added?

Answer

No, once a field is added, you cannot modify the data type of a field.

Question 2

Can we delete Business Object fields that are created automatically?

Answer

No, you can't delete the seeded fields of a Business Object.

Question 3

Can we change the primary key of a Business Object?

Answer

No, you can't change the primary key.

Question 4

Can we add custom endpoints in a Business Object?

Answer

Yes, you can add custom endpoints using Object Functions.

Question 5

Can we add or delete endpoints?

Answer

Yes, you can add or delete endpoints for those Business Objects that have many inter-related Business Objects. Refer to the documentation to learn about how to add or remove Business Objects: `https://docs.oracle.com/en/cloud/paas/app-builder-cloud/visual-builder-developer/work-endpoints-access-business-objects.html#GUID-4F201BF6-1A18-4887-81D2-000F8876424E`

Question 6

Are Business Objects accessible outside the VB application?

Answer

Yes, using the REST endpoints you can call a Business Object from outside.

Question 7

Once the embedded database is switched to point to a different database, can we revert the changes?

Answer

You'd have to raise an Oracle service request to revert the changes.

Chapter 5, Creating and Managing Service Connections

Question 1

Do we need to modify the backends for Integration Cloud and Process Applications?

Answer

It's not recommended to modify Integration Cloud and Process Application backends if the VB is part of **Oracle Integration Cloud (OIC)**.

Question 2

Can we create a Service Connection with an external REST endpoint that is **OAuth 2.0** enabled?

Answer

Yes. You can create a Service Connection with an external REST endpoint that is **OAuth 2.0** enabled. Select the **OAuth 2.0** policy from the **Authentication** dropdown while creating the connection.

Question 3

How do we connect REST APIs that are behind a firewall?

Answer

You cannot directly connect REST APIs that are behind a firewall using a Service Connection. You need to create the REST Integration in Integration Cloud, consume the REST API that is behind the firewall using **connectivity agent**, and then create a Service Connection using the catalog option. Read more about the connectivity agent at the following link: `https://docs.oracle.com/en/cloud/paas/integration-cloud/integrations-user/managing-agent-groups-and-connectivity-agent.html`.

Question 4

Can single application profiles be used in different servers?

Answer

Yes. Single application profiles can be used in different servers.

Question 5

Is it mandatory to save sample request and response bodies while creating a Service Connection using REST endpoints?

Answer

Yes. It is mandatory to save sample requests and responses to create the sample schema. So, while using a Service Connection in VB, the application can know which fields are exposed in the request and response.

Chapter 6, Building Web Applications Using Real-World Examples

Question 1

What is SDP?

Answer

SDP stands for *Service Data Provider* and represents the data source that fetches the data from REST APIs. It is used to populate a collection type, such as a list and table.

Question 2

Can we pass multiple parameters between pages?

Answer

Yes. Multiple parameters can be passed between pages.

Question 3

Can we call a Business Object using the Call REST activity?

Answer

Since the Business Object exposed the REST endpoint, the Call REST activity can also be used to call Business Objects using their REST APIs.

Chapter 7, Working with Life Cycle Events, Validations, and UI Logic

Question 1

Which select component should you use: **Select (One)** or **Select (Single)**?

Answer

The Select (One) component has been deprecated since **Oracle JET 8.1.0**. It's recommended to use the Select (Single) component as this is the new component introduced in **Oracle JET 9**.

Question 2

Can we use a `vbEnter` event to load data at the flow or application level?

Answer

Yes, a `vbEnter` event can be used at the flow or application level.

Question 3

What is the difference between **Service Data Provider (SDP)** and **Array Data Provider (ADP)**?

Answer

SDPs are created automatically when you associate collection components using the Quick Start menu and are not meant to filter/modify records. However, ADP is used to modify data on the client side for further processing. SDP automatically sets pagination and query parameters while sending the REST requests (for example, for LOV components). In ADP, the developer has full control over what is being sent in the REST call.

Chapter 8, Exploring Other Visual Components and Their Advanced Functionalities

Question 1

Do we need to double-click on a row to make it editable? Also, is there any other approach to do this?

Answer

Double clicking is the default behavior required to edit a row. You can also implement other logic to set the editable property of a row. You can refer `https://blogs.oracle.com/shay/editable-table-with-visual-builder-additional-tips` for more material.

Question 2

What is `filterCriterion`?

Answer

`filterCriterion` is used to filter the records from SDPs. `filterCriterion` accepts the array of a criteria object. The criteria object accepts JSON in the following format:

```
{
  "op": "<operator>",
  "attribute": "<attribute_name_to_filter>",
  "value": "<value_to_filter>"
}
```

Question 3

Is `filterCriterion` available in the Array Data Provider?

Answer

No, `filterCriterion` is not available in the Array Data Provider. We either call the REST endpoint or use JavaScript code to filter the data of Array Data Providers.

Chapter 9, Extending Oracle and Non-Oracle SaaS Applications

Question 1

Can we create a Salesforce developer instance for free?

Answer

Yes. You can create a Salesforce developer instance for free without providing any credit card details.

Question 2

What is `fr-FR` in the `app-strings-fr-FR.arb` file?

Answer

`fr-FR` represents the language and country.

Question 3

How do you get the combination of language and country to create a different resources bundle?

Answer

You can view the combination of language and country online. Refer to the following online documentation to view the country and language code: `https://saimana.com/list-of-country-locale-code/`.

Question 4

How is data converted from one language to another?

Answer

You can use **Google** translator (`https://translate.google.co.in/`) to convert data from one language to another.

Chapter 10, Working with Business Processes

Question 1

Is this recommended to override the default settings of Process Application Backend?

Answer

No, it is not recommended to override the default setting of Process Application Backend, if Processes is part of OIC.

Question 2

What is the difference between Player Target Server and Default Target Server?

Answer

The PCS provides the **Play** functionality, which allows to test processes in the test partition without actually activating processes in live mode. So, the process instances that are kicked off using the Play functionality are fetched using the **Player Target Server** in VB, whereas the processes that are kicked off in live mode are fetched using the **Default Target Server**.

By default, an application profile used the Player Target Server in order to avoid accidentally kicking off a live process.

Chapter 11, Building Mobile Application with Live Examples

Question 1

Can we also make a build configuration for **Windows** mobile devices?

Answer

Oracle recommends using PWA as the distribution approach for Windows mobile devices.

Question 2

Why is the Keystore file required to build a configuration for Android devices?

Answer

The Keystore file is required for signing the mobile application when it builds it.

Chapter 12, Securing the VB Applications

Question 1

Can we integrate a third-party identity provider such as OKTA or **Microsoft AD**?

Answer

Yes, a third-party identity provider can be integrated using the Oracle Identity Console.

Question 2

Can we enable anonymous access for the web and mobile applications?

Answer

Yes, anonymous access can be enabled for the web and mobile applications.

Question 3

How do we create users and groups in Oracle IDCS?

Answer

You must have IDCS admin privileges to create users and groups. You can open the IDCS console and create a user and group using the **Users and Groups** navigation.

Chapter 13, Understanding and Managing Various Stages of a VB App

Question 1

Can we modify the variable values in the published application?

Answer

No, once the application is published, you cannot modify it.

Question 2

Can we insert or modify the data in a Business Object once the application is published?

Answer

Yes, you can insert or modify data in Business Objects even if the application is published.

Question 3

Is it mandatory for the user to be part of Oracle IDCS to add them as a team member?

Answer

Yes, it is mandatory for the user to be part of Oracle IDCS to add them as a team member.

Chapter 14, Best Practices and Recommendations for VB Applications

Question 1

Do we require extra configuration to tune the application?

Answer

When you change the phase of application from Development to Stage, application tuning will happen automatically. However, there are other NPM packages that you can use to optimize the code as well.

Chapter 15, Troubleshooting and Debugging VB Applications

Question 1

Do we need specific tools in VB to troubleshoot and debug VB applications?

Answer

No, there is no VB-specific tool available to troubleshoot and debug the VB application. The developer has to rely on the browser developer tools to debug the application. Oracle may release a specific tool in a future release.

Question 2

Is it safe to store exceptions in the Business Objects?

Answer

Yes, you can store exceptions in the Business Objects. But make sure you purge the data from time to time in order to free up the VB-embedded database space.

Question 3

In the case of any issues, if Oracle requested the log information, how can you send logs to them?

Answer

You can download a HAR file from the browser that tracks all the loggings of the application.

Chapter 16, Managing the VB Apps Using Visual Builder Studio

Question 1

Can we connect a VB application with external Git repositories?

Answer

No, you cannot connect a VB application with external Git repositories.

Question 2

Do we need to bear any extra cost for Visual Builder Studio?

Answer

No, this is a free service offered by Oracle.

Question 3

Can we develop a web and mobile application directly from Visual Builder Studio?

Answer

Yes, you can develop web and mobile applications from Visual Builder Studio.

Question 4

Can we create different Git branches in VB Studio?

Answer

Yes, you can create as many branches as you like in VB Studio Git.

Packt>

Why subscribe?

- Spend less time learning and more time coding with practical eBooks and Videos from over 4,000 industry professionals

- Improve your learning with Skill Plans built especially for you

- Get a free eBook or video every month

- Fully searchable for easy access to vital information

- Copy and paste, print, and bookmark content

Did you know that Packt offers eBook versions of every book published, with PDF and ePub files available? You can upgrade to the eBook version at packt.com and as a print book customer, you are entitled to a discount on the eBook copy. Get in touch with us at customercare@packtpub.com for more details.

At www.packt.com, you can also read a collection of free technical articles, sign up for a range of free newsletters, and receive exclusive discounts and offers on Packt books and eBooks.

Other Books You May Enjoy

If you enjoyed this book, you may be interested in these other books by Packt:

Salesforce for Beginners

Sharif Shaalan

ISBN: 978-1-83898-609-4

- Understand the difference between Salesforce Lightning and Salesforce Classic
- Create and manage leads in Salesforce
- Explore business development with accounts and contacts in Salesforce
- Find out how stages and sales processes help you manage your opportunity pipeline
- Achieve marketing goals using Salesforce campaigns
- Perform business analysis using reports and dashboards
- Gain a high-level overview of the items in the administration section
- Grasp the different aspects needed to build an effective and flexible Salesforce security model

40 Algorithms Every Programmer Should Know

Imran Ahmad

ISBN: 978-1-78980-121-7

- Explore existing data structures and algorithms found in Python libraries
- Implement graph algorithms for fraud detection using network analysis
- Work with machine learning algorithms to cluster similar tweets and process Twitter data in real time
- Predict the weather using supervised learning algorithms
- Use neural networks for object detection
- Create a recommendation engine that suggests relevant movies to subscribers
- Implement foolproof security using symmetric and asymmetric encryption on Google Cloud Platform (GCP)

Packt is searching for authors like you

If you're interested in becoming an author for Packt, please visit `authors.packtpub.com` and apply today. We have worked with thousands of developers and tech professionals, just like you, to help them share their insight with the global tech community. You can make a general application, apply for a specific hot topic that we are recruiting an author for, or submit your own idea.

Leave a review - let other readers know what you think

Please share your thoughts on this book with others by leaving a review on the site that you bought it from. If you purchased the book from Amazon, please leave us an honest review on this book's Amazon page. This is vital so that other potential readers can see and use your unbiased opinion to make purchasing decisions, we can understand what our customers think about our products, and our authors can see your feedback on the title that they have worked with Packt to create. It will only take a few minutes of your time, but is valuable to other potential customers, our authors, and Packt. Thank you!

Index

T

U

V

W

Made in the USA
Monee, IL
25 October 2022